Statistics & Numerical Methods

P. Sudha, M.Sc., M.Phil., B.Ed., MISTE.

R. Deepa, M.Sc., M.Phil., PGDCA., MISTE.

S. Devi, M.Sc., M.Phil., MISTE.

Department of Mathematics
EXCEL GROUP OF INSTITUTIONS
Komarapalayam, Namakkal - 637 303.

For online purchase

www.charulathapublications.com

New No.24, Thambiah Road, West Mambalam, Chennai - 33.

Mobile : 98404 28577

January 2019

Price : **Rs.450/-**

ISBN No. : 978-93-86532-69-5

CHARULATHA PUBLICATIONS

New No.24, Thambiah Road,
West Mambalam, Chennai - 600 033.
Phone : 24745589, 24746546
Email : charulathapublication@yahoo.com
info@charulathapublications.com
www.charulathapublications.com

PREFACE

We have immense pleasure in presenting this first edition of the Text-Book of **Statistics And Numerical Methods** for the students of Second year **B.E/B.Tech** Degree Courses of **Anna University, Chennai**.

Applications of Mathematics is highly important and inevitable in the field of Engineering. It is equally important at this stage to have strong foundation of the subject. In view of this, the subject matter has been explained in a simple language and in clear and concise form. This will surely help the students in understanding the subject in an easier way.

An in-depth explanation of every topic is followed by sufficient solved examples. The exercises given at the end of every topic are designed in such a way that students have to start thinking , reasoning and analysing logically.

Our ultimate aim is to make the subject simple, interesting and overcoming the fear among the students.

As this is our first attempt, we are aware that the book can further be improved. So constructive criticism and suggestions are most welcome for the betterment.

Authors

ACKNOWLEDGEMENT

We express our deep sense of gratitude to our ***Hon.Chairman Prof.Dr.A.K.Natesan*** and our Respected Vice Chairman ***Dr.N.Mathan Karthick***, Excel Group Institutions without whose permission and patronage, this book would not have been a success.

We would like to thank ***Dr.V.K.Shanmuganaathan***, Principal. Excel college of Engineering and ***Dr.E.Palaniswamy***, Principal, Excel College of Engineering and Technology for lending their valuable guidance and continuous support to publish this book. We are also thankful to our colleagues, parents and beloved family members who encouraged us to write this book. Also we express our appreciation and gratefulness to our publisher.

Authors.

SYLLABUS

MA 8452 –STATISTICS AND NUMERICAL METHODS
REGULATION 2017

UNIT - I – TESTING OF HYPOTHESIS

Sampling distribution – Estimation of parameters – Statistical hypothesis – Large sample test based on Normal distribution for single mean and difference of means – Tests based on t, t, Chi-square and F distributions for mean, variances and proportion – Contingency table (test for Independency) – Goodness of fit.

UNIT - II – DESIGN OF EXPERIMENTS

One way and two way classifications – Completely randomized design – Randomized block design – Latin square design - 2^2 factorial design.

UNIT - III – SOLUTION OF EQUATIONS AND EIGENVALUE PROBLEMS

Solution of algebraic and transcendental equations – Fixed point iteration method – Newton Raphson method – Solution of linear system of equations – Gauss elimination method – Pivoting – Gauss Jordan methods – Iterative methods of Gauss Jacobi and Gauss Seidel – Eigenvalues of a matrix inversion by Power method and Gauss Jacobi's method for symmetric power method.

UNIT - IV – INTERPOLATION, NUMERICAL DIFFERENTIATION AND NUMERICAL INTEGRATION

Lagrange's and Newton's divided difference interpolations – Newton's forward and backward difference interpolation – Approximation of derivates using interpolation polynomials – Numerical single and double integrations using Trapezoidal and Simpson's 1/3 rules.

UNIT - V – NUMERICAL SOLUTION OF ORDINARY DIFFERENTIAL EQUATIONS

Single step methods: Taylor's series method – Euler's method – Modified Euler's method – Fourth order Runge-Kutta method for solving first order equations – Multi step methods: Milne's and Adams – Bash forth predictor corrector methods for solving first order equations.

TABLE OF CONTENTS

UNIT - 1

TESTING OF HYPOTHESIS

UNIT - 2

DESIGN OF EXPERIMENTS

UNIT - 3

SOLUTION OF EQUATION AND EIGEN VALUE PROBLEMS

UNIT - 4

INTERPOLATION, NUMERICAL DIFFERENTIATION AND NUMERICAL INTEGRATION

UNIT - 5

NUMERICAL SOLUTION OF ORDINARY DIFFERENTIAL EQUATIONS

UNIT - 1

TESTING OF HYPOTHESIS

1.1 INTRODUCTION

The purpose of hypothesis testing is to determine whether there is enough statistical evidence in favour of certain belief, or hypothesis, about a parameter.

In everyday life, we often have to make decisions based on incomplete information. Hypothesis testing is a kind of statistics inference that involves asking a question, collecting data and then examining what the data tells us about how to precede. In a formal hypothesis test, hypothesis are always statement about the population.

This chapter introduces the basics of hypothesis testing; terminology, the logic of hypothesis testing, test statistics and decision making.

Population

An aggregate of objects under study is called population or universe.

The number of observations in a population is called size of the population and it is denoted by 'N'.

A population contains finite elements then it is called finite population and a population contains infinite number of elements then it is called infinite population.

Sample

A finite subset of individuals in a population is called a sample and the number of individuals in a sample is called sample size and it is denoted by '*n*';

If 'n' is finite then the sample is called finite sample and if '*n*' is infinite then the sample is called infinite sample.

For example,

The students in a college is a population and the students those who are studying Mechanical Engineering in a college is a sample.

Parameters and Statistics

A statistical measure (or) constant obtained from the population is known as a population parameter (or) parameter.

For example,

Population Mean (μ), Population Variance (σ^2), etc, are Parameters.

A statistical measure (or) constant obtained from the sample is known as a sample statistic (or) statistic.

For example, Sample mean ($\bar{x}$), sample variance (s^2), ... are Sample Statistic.

Notation

	Size	Mean	Variance	S.D
Population	N	μ	σ^2	σ
Sample	n	$\bar{x}$	s^2	s

Sampling

The process of selecting a sample from the population is called sampling.

Standard Error: (S.E)

The standard deviation of the sampling distribution of a statistic is known as its standard error.

S.No	Statistic	Standard error
1.	$\bar{x}$	$\frac{\sigma}{\sqrt{n}}$
2.	Difference of two sample means $\bar{x}_1 - \bar{x}_2$	$\sqrt{\frac{\sigma_1^2}{n_1} + \frac{\sigma_2^2}{n_2}}$

Small Samples and Large Samples

When the size of the sample is greater than 30 [ie, n>30], the sample is called large sample.

When the size of the sample is less than 30 [ie, n<30], the sample is called small samples.

Test of Significance

An important aspect of the sampling theory is to study the test of significance which will enable us to decide, on the basis of the results of the sample, whether

(i) The derivation between the observed sample statistic and the hypothetical parameter value (or)

(ii) The derivation between two sample statistics is significant (or) might be attributed due to chance or the fluctuations of the sampling.

Null Hypothesis

For applying the test of significance, we first set up a hypothesis which is a definite statement about the Population Parameter. Usually such a hypothesis is a hypothesis of no difference and it is denoted by H_0.

Alternative Hypothesis

Any hypothesis which is complementary to the null hypothesis H_o is called an alternative hypothesis and it is denoted by H_1.

Critical value (or) Table value

The Value of the test statistic which separates the sample space into rejection region and the acceptance region, is called critical value.

Critical Region

A region corresponding to a test statistic in the sample space which tends to rejection of H_0 is called critical region (or) region of rejection.

The region complementary to the critical region is called the region of acceptance.

Error in Sampling

The main aim of the sampling theory is to draw a valid conclusion about the population parameters on the basis of the sample results. In doing this we may commit the following two types of error.

(i) Type-I error

When H_0 is true, we may reject it P[Reject H_0 when it is true] = α.

'α' is called the size of the type I error, also referred to as producer's risk.

(ii) Type-II error

When H_o is wrong, we may accept it. P [Accept H_o when it is wrong] = β.

'β' is called the size of the type – II error, also referred to as consumer's risk.

	Accept H_0	Reject H_0
H_0 True	Correct decision	Type I error
H_0 False	Type II error	Correct decision

Level of Significance

The Probability 'α' that a random value of the statistic 't' belongs to the critical region is known as the level of significance. In other words, level of significance is the size of the Type – I error. The level of significance usually employed in testing of hypothesis are 5% and 1%.

One Tailed and Two Tailed Tests

A test of any Statistical hypothesis where the alternative hypothesis is one tailed [right tailed or left tailed] is called one tailed test.

For example, in a test for testing the mean of a population in a single tailed we assume that the null hypothesis $H_0 : \mu=\mu_0$ against

$H_1: \mu > \mu_0$ [Right Tailed]

(or) $H_1: \mu < \mu_0$ [Left Tailed]

is called one tailed test.

In a test of statistical hypothesis where the alternative hypothesis is two tailed is called two tailed test.

We assume that $H_0: \mu = \mu_0$

Against $H_1: \mu \neq \mu_0$ [$\mu > \mu_0$ & $\mu < \mu_0$] is called Two tailed Test.

Procedure for Testing of Hypothesis

(i) Setup null and alternative hypothesis.

(ii) Choose the appropriate level of significance. (either 5% or 1% level). This is to be decided before sample is drawn.

(iii) Find the critical value (or) Table Value of Z.

(iv) Compute the test statistic $Z = \dfrac{t - E(t)}{SE(t)}$.

(v) Compare the computed value of Z with the significant value Z_α.

(vi) If $|Z| < Z_\alpha$, we accept H_0

If $|Z| > Z_\alpha$, we reject H_0.

Table for critical values on using normal probability

Critical Values	**Level of Significance**		
	1%	**5%**	**10%**
Two Tailed Test	$\lvert Z_\alpha \rvert = 2.58$	$\lvert Z_\alpha \rvert = 1.96$	$\lvert Z_\alpha \rvert = 1.645$
Right Tailed Test	$Z_\alpha = 2.33$	$Z_\alpha = 1.645$	$Z_\alpha = 1.28$
Left Tailed Test	$Z_\alpha = -2.33$	$Z_\alpha = -1.645$	$Z_\alpha = -1.28$

1.2 TEST OF SIGNIFICANCE FOR LARGE SAMPLE

If the sample size n >30, then the sample is called large sample.

Now we consider the following tests under large sample test based on normal distribution.

(i) Test of significance for single mean.

(ii) Test of significance for difference of means.

(iii) Test of significance for single proportion.

(iv) Test of significance for difference of proportion.

1.2.1 Test of Significance for single mean

Suppose we want to test whether the given sample of size 'n' has been drawn from a population with mean μ (or) to test whether the difference between sample mean and population mean is significant or not.

Working rule:

(i) We set up null hypothesis that there is no difference between μ and $\bar{x}$.

ie, $H_0 : \mu = \bar{x}$

$\therefore \quad H_1 : \mu \neq \bar{x}$ [Two tailed test]

(or) $\mu < \bar{x}$ [left tailed test]

(or) $\mu > \bar{x}$ [Right tailed test]

(ii) Choose the appropriate level of significance.

(iii) Find the critical value.

(iv) Test Statistic $Z = \frac{\bar{x}-\mu}{\sigma/\sqrt{n}}$ [If σ is given]

(or)

$$Z = \frac{\bar{x}-\mu}{s/\sqrt{n}}$$ [If s is given].

(v) Compare the computed value of Z with significant value Z_{α}' write your conclusion.

Note:

1) 95% confidence (or) fiducial limits are $\bar{x} \pm 1.96\frac{\sigma}{\sqrt{n}}$

2) 99% confidence (or) fiducial limits are $\bar{x} \pm 1.96\frac{\sigma}{\sqrt{n}}$

EXAMPLES

(1) A sample of 900 members has a mean 3.4cms. Can it be reasonably regarded as a sample from a large population of mean 3.2 and S.D 2.3 cms?

Solution:

Given Sample size n=900

Sample mean $\bar{x}$=3.4

Population mean μ=3.2

Population S.D σ=2.3 [σ is given]

(i) Null hypothesis H_0: μ= 3.2

Alternative hypothesis H_1: $\mu \neq 3.2$ [Two tailed test].

(ii) Level of significance α =5% =0.05

(iii) Critical value at 5% level is Z_{α}=1.96

(iv) Test Statistic $Z = \dfrac{\bar{x}-\mu}{\sigma/\sqrt{n}}$

$$= \frac{3.4-3.2}{2.3/\sqrt{900}} = 0.261$$

(v) Here $|Z| = 0.261 < Z_\alpha$

$\therefore$ H_0 is accepted.

$\therefore$ The sample is drawn from the population with mean 3.2 and variance 2.3.

(2) The height of the college students in a city are normally distributed with S.D 6 cms. A sample of 100 students has mean height 158 cms. Test the hypothesis that the mean height of the college students in the city is 160 cms. [use 1% level of significance].

Solutions:

Given n=100, $\bar{x}$=158, μ=160, σ=6 [σ is given]

α=1%

(i) H_0: μ=160

H_1: μ≠160 [Two tailed test].

(ii) Level of significance α=1%

(iii) Critical value at α=1% level is Z_α=2.58

(iv) Test statistic $Z = \dfrac{\bar{x}-\mu}{\sigma/\sqrt{n}} = \dfrac{158-150}{6/\sqrt{100}} = -3.3333$

(v) $\therefore$ $|Z| = 3.3333 > Z_\alpha$

$\therefore$ We reject H_0 and accept H_1.

$\therefore$ Difference is significant.

(3) The average marks in Mathematics of a sample of 100 students was 51 with a S.D of 6 marks. Could this have been a random sample from a population with average marks of 50?

Solution:

Given n=100, $\bar{x}$=51, s=6, μ=50 [s is given]

(i) H_0: μ=50

H_1: μ≠50 [Two tailed test]

(ii) Level of significance α=5% = 0.05

(iii) Critical value at α=5% level is $Z_\alpha = 1.96$

(iv) Test statistic $Z = \dfrac{\bar{x}-\mu}{s/\sqrt{n}} = \dfrac{51-50}{6/\sqrt{100}} = 1.6667$

(v) $\therefore |Z| = 1.6667 < Z_\alpha$

$\therefore$ H_0 is accepted.

$\therefore$ A random sample is drawn from a population with average marks of 50.

(4) An insurance agent has claimed that the average age of policy holders who issue through him is less than the average for all agents which is 30.5 years. A random sample of 100 policy holders who had issued through him gave the following age distribution.

Age:	16-20	21-25	26-30	31-35	36-40
No of persons:	12	22	20	30	16

Calculate the Arithmetic mean and S.D of this distribution and use these values to test his claim at 5% level of significance.

Solution:

Age:		Mid point (x)	$d = \dfrac{x-28}{5}$	d^2	f	fd	fd^2
16-20	15.5-20.5	18	–2	4	12	–24	48
21-25	20.5-25.5	23	–1	1	22	–22	22
26-30	25.5-30.5	28	0	0	20	0	0
31-35	30.5-35.5	33	1	1	30	30	30
36-40	35.5-40.5	38	2	4	16	32	64
					100	16	164

Here A=28, h=5, N=Σf=100

W.K.T

$$\bar{x} = A + \frac{h\Sigma fd}{N} = 28 + \frac{5\times 16}{100} = 28.8$$

S.D $\quad s = h\sqrt{\dfrac{\Sigma fd^2}{N} - \left(\dfrac{\Sigma fd}{N}\right)^2}$

$$= 5\sqrt{\frac{164}{100} - \left(\frac{16}{100}\right)^2} = 6.35$$

$\therefore \quad \bar{x} = 28.8, \quad s = 6.35$

Given $\mu = 30.5$, n=100

(i) $H_0: \mu=30.5$

$H_1: \mu<30.5$ [Left Tailed Test].

(ii) Level of significance α=5% = 0.05

(iii) Critical value $Z_\alpha = -1.645$

(iv) Test statistic $Z = \dfrac{\bar{x} - \mu}{s/\sqrt{n}}$

$$= \frac{28.8 - 30.5}{6.35/\sqrt{100}} = -2.677$$

(v) Here $|Z| = 2.677 > Z_\alpha$

$\therefore$ H_0 is rejected and H_1 is accepted. The arrange age of policy holders is less than the average for all agents.

(5) An insurance agent has claimed that the average age of policy holders who insure through him is less than the average for all agents which is 30.5 years. A random sample of 100 policy holders who had insured through him reveal that the mean and S.D are 28.8 years and 6.35 years respectively. Test his claim at 5% level of significance.

Solution:

Given n=100, μ=30.5, s=6.35, $\bar{x}$=28.8, α=5% [s is given]

(i) $H_0: \mu=30.5$

$H_1: \mu<30.5$ [Left Tailed Test].

(ii) Level of significance α=5%

(iii) Critical value at α=5% level is $Z_\alpha = -1.645$.

(iv) Test statistic $Z = \dfrac{\bar{x} - \mu}{s/\sqrt{n}} = \dfrac{28.8 - 30.5}{6.35/\sqrt{100}} = -2.68$

(v) Here $|Z| = 2.68 > Z_\alpha$

$\therefore$ H_0 is rejected and H_1 is accepted.

(6) The mean life time of a sample of 400 fluorescent light tube produced by a company is found to be 1570 hours with a S.D of 150 hours. Test the hypothesis that the mean life time of the bulbs produced by the company is 1600 hours against the alternative hypothesis that it is greater than 1600 hours at 1% level of significance.

Solution:

Given n=400, $\bar{x}$=1570, μ=1600, s=150

(i) H_0: μ = 1600

H_1: μ > 1600 [Right tailed test]

(ii) Level of Significance α=1% = 0.01

(iii) Critical value at α=1% level is Z_α=2.33

(iv) Test statistic $Z = \frac{\bar{x}-\mu}{s/\sqrt{n}} = \frac{1570-1600}{150/\sqrt{400}} = -4$

$\therefore |z| = 4.$

(v) Here $|z| = 4 > z_\alpha = 2.33$

∴ H_0 is rejected and H_1 is accepted.

∴ The life time of the bulbs is greater than 1600 hours.

(7) A survey is proposed to be conducted to know the annual earnings of the old statistics graduates of Delhi university. How large should the sample to taken in order to estimate the mean annual earnings within plus and minus Rs. 1000 at 95% confidence level?. The standard deviation of the annual earnings of the entire population is known to be Rs. 3000.

Solution:

Given σ=3000, α=5% =0.05

$$P\left[\left|\bar{x}-\mu\right| < 1000\right] = 0.95 \qquad \rightarrow (1)$$

From normal probability tables,

$$P\left[|Z| \le 1.96\right] = 0.95$$

$$\Rightarrow \quad P\left[\left|\frac{\bar{x}-\mu}{\sigma/\sqrt{n}}\right| \le 1.96\right] = 0.95$$

$$\Rightarrow \quad P\left[\left|\bar{x}-\mu\right| \le 1.96 \times \frac{\sigma}{\sqrt{n}}\right] = 0.95 \qquad \rightarrow (2)$$

From (1) and (2)

$$1.96\frac{\sigma}{\sqrt{n}} = 1000 \qquad \Rightarrow \qquad 1.96 \times \frac{3000}{\sqrt{n}} = 1000$$

$$\Rightarrow \quad \sqrt{n} = \frac{1.96 \times 3000}{1000} = 5.88$$

$$\Rightarrow \quad n = (5.88)^2 = 34.56 = 35$$

(8) The mean weight obtained from a random sample of size 100 is 64 gms. The S.D of the weight distribution of the population is 3gms. Test the statement that the mean weight of the population is 67gms at 5% level of significance. Also setup 99% confidence limits of the mean weight of the population.

Solution:

Given n=100, μ=67, $\bar{x}$=64, σ=3.

(i) H_0: μ=67

H_1: $\mu \neq 67$ [Two Tailed Test].

(ii) Level of significance α=5%

(iii) Critical value at α=5% level is Z_α=1.96

(iv) Test statistic $Z = \dfrac{\bar{x}-\mu}{\sigma/\sqrt{n}} = \dfrac{64-67}{3/\sqrt{100}} = -10$

(v) Here |Z|= 10> Z_α

$\therefore$ H_0 is rejected and H_1 is accepted.

The sample is not drawn from the population.

(vi) The 99% confidence limits are $\bar{x} \pm 2.58\dfrac{\sigma}{\sqrt{n}}$

$$= 64 \pm 2.58 \times \frac{3}{\sqrt{100}}$$

$$= 64.774, \ 63.226$$

$\therefore$ 99% confidence limits are 63.226 & 64.774.

(9) The mean IQ of a sample of 1600 children was 99. Is it likely that this was a random sample form a population with mean I.Q 100 and standard deviation 15?

Solution:

Given: n=1600, $\bar{x}=99,\ \mu=100,\ \sigma=100.$

(i) H_0: $\mu = 100$

H_1: $\mu \neq 100$ [Two tailed test]

(ii) Level of significance α =5% = 0.05

(iii) Critical value Z_α=1.96

(iv) Test statistic $Z=\dfrac{\bar{x}-\mu}{\sigma/\sqrt{n}}=\dfrac{99-100}{100/\sqrt{1600}}$

$=-2.67$

$\therefore\ |Z|=2.67$

(v) Here $|z|<z_\alpha$

$\therefore$ H_0 is accepted.

$\therefore$ The sample has not been drawn from a population with mean 100 & σ = 15.

EXERCISE

1) A sample of 400 items is taken from a normal population whose mean is 4 and variance is also 4. If the sample mean is 4.45. Can the sample be regarded as a truly random sample? Justify your answer.

Ans: $|Z|=4.5$

2) A sample of 1000 students from a university was taken and their average weight was found to be 112 kg with a S.D of 20 kg. Could the mean of students in the population be 120kg?

Ans: $|Z|=12.66$

3) A random sample of 200 measurements from a large population gave a mean value of 50 and S.D of 9. Determine 95% confidence interval for the mean of population

4) **A normal population has a mean 0.1 and S.D 2.1, find the probability that the mean of a sample of size 900 will be negative.**

Ans: $P\left[\bar{x} < 0\right] = P\left[z < \frac{-0.1}{0.07}\right] = 0.0764$

5) **400 workers were selected at random from a district. Their mean income was Rs.140.5 per month with S.D of Rs. 25.2. Do you believe that the average income of the workers community in the district is Rs. 150?**

Ans: $|Z| = 6.01$

6) **The guaranteed average life of a certain type of bulbs is 1000 hrs with a S.D of 125 hrs. It is decided to sample the output so as to ensure that 90% of the bulbs do not fall short of the guaranteed average by more than 2.5%. What must be the minimum size of the sample?**

Ans: n=41.

1.2.2 Test of Significance for Difference of Means

Let $\overline{x_1}$ be the mean of a sample of size n_1 from a population with mean μ_1 and variance σ_1^2. Let $\overline{x_2}$ be the mean of a sample of size n_2 from a population with mean μ_2 and variance σ_2^2.

To test whether there is any significant difference between $\overline{x_1}$ and $\overline{x_2}$.

Working Rule

(i) H_0: There is no significant difference between two sample means (or) Two samples have been drawn from the same population.

ie, $H_0: \mu_1 = \mu_2$

H_1: $\mu_1 \neq \mu_2$ [Two tailed test] (or)

$\mu_1 > \mu_2$ [Right tailed test] (or)

$\mu_1 < \mu_2$ [Left tailed] test]

(ii) Choose the appropriate level of significance.

(iii) Find the critical value.

(iv) Compute test statistic.

$$Z = \frac{\overline{x_1} - \overline{x_2}}{\sqrt{\frac{s_1^2}{n_1} + \frac{s_2^2}{n_2}}}$$ [if s_1 & s_2 are given]

(or)

$$Z = \frac{\overline{x_1} - \overline{x_2}}{\sqrt{\frac{\sigma_1^2}{n_1} + \frac{\sigma_2^2}{n_2}}}$$ [If σ_1 & σ_2 are given]

(v) Compare the computed value of Z with significant value Z_α. Write your conclusion.

EXAMPLES

1) Intelligence tests were given to two groups of boys and girls.

	Mean	S.D	Size
Girls	75	8	60
Boys	73	10	100

Examine if the difference between mean scores is significant.

Solution:

Given $n_1=60$, $\overline{x_1} = 75$, $s_1=8$

$n_2=100$, $\overline{x_2} = 73$, $s_2=10$.

(i) H_0: $\mu_1 = \mu_2$ (or) $\overline{x_1} = \overline{x_2}$

H_1: $\overline{x_1} \neq \overline{x_2}$ [Two tailed test]

(ii) Level of significance α=5%

(iii) Critical value at α=5% level is Z_α=1.96

(iv) Test statistic $Z = \frac{\overline{x_1} - \overline{x_2}}{\sqrt{\frac{s_1^2}{n_1} + \frac{s_2^2}{n_2}}}$

$$= \frac{75 - 73}{\sqrt{\frac{64}{60} + \frac{100}{100}}} = 1.3912$$

(v) Here $|Z| = 1.3912$

$\therefore \; |Z| < Z_\alpha$

$\therefore$ H_0 is accepted.

$\therefore$ There is no significant difference between mean scores.

2) The average income of persons was Rs. 210 with a S.D of Rs. 10 in a sample of 100 people of a city. For another sample of 150 persons, the average income was Rs. 220 with S.D of Rs. 12. The S.D of income of the people of the city was Rs.11. Test whether there is any significant difference between the average income of the localities.

Solution:

Given n_1=100, $\overline{x_1}$=210, s_1=10

n_2=150, $\overline{x_2}$=220, s_2=12

(i) H_0: $\mu_1 = \mu_2$

H_1: $\mu_1 \neq \mu_2$ [Two tailed test]

(ii) Level of significance α=5%

(iii) Critical value at α=5% level is Z_α=1.96

(iv) Test statistic $Z = \dfrac{\overline{x_1} - \overline{x_2}}{\sqrt{\dfrac{s_1^2}{n_1} + \dfrac{s_2^2}{n_2}}}$

$$= \frac{210 - 220}{\sqrt{\dfrac{10^2}{100} + \dfrac{12^2}{150}}} = -7.1428$$

(v) Here $|Z| = 7.1428$

$|Z| > Z_\alpha$

$\therefore$ H_0 is rejected and H_1 is accepted.

$\therefore$ There is significant difference between the average income of the localities.

3) The means of two large sample of size 2000 and 1000 are 68.0 and 67.5 gms respectively. Can the sample be regarded as drawn from the same population of S.D 2.25gm?

Solution:

Given n_1 =2000, $\overline{x_1}$=68.0

n_2=1000, $\overline{x_2}$ =67.5, $\sigma_1 = \sigma_2$= 2.25

(i) H_0: $\mu_1 = \mu_2$

H_1: $\mu_1 \neq \mu_2$ [Two tailed test]

(ii) Level of significance α=5%

(iii) Critical value Z_α=1.96

(iv) Test statistic $Z = \dfrac{\overline{x_1} - \overline{x_2}}{\sqrt{\dfrac{\sigma_1^2}{n_1} + \dfrac{\sigma_2^2}{n_2}}}$

$$= \frac{68.0 - 67.5}{\sqrt{\dfrac{(2.25)^2}{2000} + \dfrac{(2.25)^2}{1000}}} = 5.7378$$

(v) Here $|Z| = 5.7378$

$\therefore \ |Z| > Z_\alpha$

$\therefore$ H_0 is rejected and H_1 is accepted. The sample are not drawn from the same population of S.D 2.25 gm.

4) A simple sample of heights of 6,400 Englishmen has a mean of 170 inches and a S.D of 6.4 inches, while a simple sample of heights of 1600 Australians has a mean of 172 inches and a S.D of 6.3 inches. Do the data indicate that Australians are on the average taller than Englishmen?

Solution:

Given n_1=6400, $\overline{x_1}$= 170, s_1=6.4

n_2=1600, $\overline{x_2}$ =172, s_2=6.3

(i) H_0: $\mu_1 = \mu_2$

H_1: $\mu_1 < \mu_2$ [Left tailed test]

(ii) Level of significance α=5%

(iii) Critical value Z_α= −1.645

(iv) Test Statistic $Z = \dfrac{\overline{x_1} - \overline{x_2}}{\sqrt{\dfrac{s_1^2}{n_1} + \dfrac{s_2^2}{n_2}}} = \dfrac{170 - 172}{\sqrt{\dfrac{(6.4)^2}{6400} + \dfrac{(6.3)^2}{1600}}} = -11.32$

(v) Here $|Z| = 11.32$

$\therefore \quad |Z| > Z_\alpha$

$\therefore$ We reject H_0 and accept H_1.

$\therefore$ The data indicate that Australian are the average taller than Englishmen.

5) A sample of 100 bulbs of brand A gave a mean lifetime of 1200 hours with a S.D of 70 hours, while another sample of 120 bulbs of brand B gave a mean lifetime of 1150 hours with a S.D of 85 hours. Can we conclude that brand A bulbs are superior to brand B bulbs?

Solution:

Given $n_1=100$, $\overline{x}_1=1200$, $s_1=70$

$n_2=120$, $\overline{x}_2=1150$, $s_2=85$

(i) $H_0: \mu_1 = \mu_2$

$H_1: \mu_1 > \mu_2$ [Right tailed test]

(ii) Level of significance $\alpha=5\%$

(iii) Critical value $Z_\alpha = 1.645$

(iv) Test Statistic $Z = \dfrac{\overline{x}_1 - \overline{x}_2}{\sqrt{\dfrac{s_1^2}{n_1} + \dfrac{s_2^2}{n_2}}}$

$$= \frac{1200 - 1150}{\sqrt{\dfrac{(70)^2}{100} + \dfrac{(85)^2}{120}}} = 4.79$$

(v) Here $|Z| = 4.79$

$\therefore \quad |Z| > Z_\alpha$

$\therefore$ We reject H_0 and accept H_1.

$\therefore$ Brand A bulbs are superior to brand B bulbs.

6) In an investigation of the attitude of the purchasing nature. 400 shoppers are chosen at random in a locality A of a city. Their average weekly food expenditure was Rs. 250 with a S.D of Rs. 40. For another set of 400 shoppers chosen at random in another locality in the same city, the average weekly food expenditure was Rs. 220 with a S.D of Rs. 55. Test at 1% level of significance, whether the average weekly food expenditure of the two populations of shoppers are equal.

Solution:

Given $n_1=400$, $\overline{x_1}=250$, $s_1=40$

$n_2=400$, $\overline{x_2}=220$, $s_2=55$

(i) $H_0: \mu_1=\mu_2$

$H_1: \mu_1\neq\mu_2$ [Two tailed test]

(ii) Level of significance $\alpha=1\%$

(iii) Critical value $Z_\alpha= 2.58$

(iv) Test Statistic $Z=\dfrac{\overline{x_1}-\overline{x_2}}{\sqrt{\dfrac{s_1^2}{n_1}+\dfrac{s_2^2}{n_2}}}$

$$=\frac{250-220}{\sqrt{\dfrac{(40)^2}{400}+\dfrac{(55)^2}{400}}}=8.8226$$

(v) Here $|Z|=8.8226$

$\therefore\ |Z|>Z_\alpha$

$\therefore H_0$ is rejected and H_1 is accepted. The average weekly food expenditure of the two populations are not equal.

EXERCISE

1) **The mean produce of wheat of a sample of 100 fields comes to 200kg per acre and another sample of 150 fields gives the mean of 220kg. Assuming the S.D of the yield at 11kg for the universe. Test if there is a significant different between the means of the samples.**

[Ans: $|Z|=14.0835$]

2) **From the data given below, compute the standard error of the difference of the two sample means and find out if the two means significantly differ at 5% level of of significance.**

	No of items	Mean	S.D
Group I	50	181.5	3.0
Group II	75	179.0	3.6

[Ans: $|Z|=4.2089$]

3) **The average marks scored by 32 boys is 72 with a S.D of 8, while that for 36 girls is 70 with a S.D of 6. Test at 1% level of significance whether the boys perform better than girls.**

   [Ans: $|Z| = 1.15$]

4) **The sales manager of a large company conducted a sample survey in states A and B taking 400 samples in each case. The results were in the following table. Test whether the average sales is the same in the two states at 1% level.**

	State A	**State B**
Average Sales	Rs. 2500	Rs. 2200
S.D	Rs.400	Rs.550

   [Ans: $|Z| = 8.82$]

5) **The mean breaking strength of the cables supplied by a manufactures is 1800 with a S.D 100. By a new technique in the manufacturing process, it is claimed that the breaking strength of the cables have increased. In order to this claim, a sample of 50 cables is tested. It is found that the mean breaking strength 1850. Can we support the claim at 1% level of significance.**

   [Ans: $|Z| = 3.53$]

1.2.3 Test of Significance for Sigle Proportion

Suppose a large sample of size 'n is taken form a normal population. To set the significant difference between the sample proportion 'p' and the population proportion 'p'

Working rule:

(i) H_0 : The sample has been drawn from a population with population proportion P.

i.e, $H_0 : P = p$.

$H1 : p \neq P$ [Two tailed test]

(ii) Choose the appropriate Level of Significance 'α'.

(iii) Find the Critical value Z_α

(iv) Test Statistic $Z = \dfrac{p-P}{\sqrt{\dfrac{PQ}{n}}}$ Where $Q = 1 - P$

(v) Compare the computed value of Z with significant value Z_α.

(vi) The confidence (or) fiducial limits are $p \pm 3\sqrt{\dfrac{pq}{n}}$ Where $q = 1 - p$.

EXAMPLES

1) A manufacturer claimed that atleast 95% of the equipment which he supplied to a factory conformed to specifications. An examination of a sample of 200 pieces of equipment revealed that 18 were faulty. Test his claim at 5% and 1% level of significance.

Solution:

Given Sample size n=200

P = proportion of population = 95% = 0.95

Q = 1–P=0.05.

Number of pieces conforming to specification = 200–18=182.

∴ p = Proportion of pieces conforming specification.

$$= \frac{182}{200} = 0.91$$

(a) (i) $H_0 : p=0.95$

$H_1 : p<0.95$ [Left Tailed Test]

(ii) Level of significance α=5%.

(iii) Critical value $Z_\alpha=1.645$.

(iv) Test Statistic $Z = \dfrac{p-P}{\sqrt{\dfrac{PQ}{n}}}$ $Q = 1-P$

$$= \frac{0.91-0.95}{\sqrt{\dfrac{0.95\times0.05}{200}}} = -2.6$$

$\therefore |Z| = 2.6$.

(v) Here $|Z| > Z_\alpha$.

∴ H_0 is rejected and H_1 is accepted at 5% level significance.

∴ The manufacture claim is rejected.

(b) At 1% level of significance, $Z_\alpha = 2.33$ Here $|Z| = 2.6,\ Z_\alpha = 2.33$

$\therefore |Z| > Z_\alpha$

H_0 is rejected and H_1 is accepted.

∴ The manufacturer claim is rejected at 1% level of significance.

2) In a big city 325 men out of 600 men were found to be smokers. Does this information support the conclusion that the majority of men in this city are smokers?

Solution:

Given n=600

p = Sample proportion of smokers

$$= \frac{325}{600} = 0.5417$$

P = Population proportion of smokers

$$= \frac{1}{2} = 0.5$$

$$Q = 1 - P = 0.5$$

(i) H_0 : P=0.5

H_1: P > 0.5 [Right tailed test]

(ii) Level of Significance α =5%

(iii) Critical value Z_α=1.645.

(iv) Test Statistic $Z = \dfrac{p-P}{\sqrt{\dfrac{PQ}{n}}} = \dfrac{0.5417-0.5}{\sqrt{\dfrac{0.5\times 0.5}{600}}} = 2.04$

$\therefore |Z| = 2.04$

(v) Here $|Z| > Z_\alpha$

$\therefore$ H_0 is rejected and H_1 is accepted.

$\therefore$ The majority of men in the city are smokers.

3) A die was thrown 9000 times and out of these 3220 yielded a 3 or 4 is this consistent with the hypothesis that the die was unbiased?

Solution:

Given n=9000

p = Proportion of successes of getting 3 or 4 in 9000 throws

$$p = \frac{3220}{9000} = 0.3578$$

P = Population proportion of successes

= P [getting 3 or 4]

$$=\frac{1}{6}+\frac{1}{6}=\frac{2}{6}=\frac{1}{3}=0.3333$$

$\therefore Q = 1 - P = 0.6667$

(i) $H_0: P=\frac{1}{3}$ (i.e) H_0: The die is unbiased

$H_1: P\neq\frac{1}{3}$, (i.e) H_1: The die is biased. [Two tailed test]

(ii) Level of significance α=5% = 0.05

(iii) Critical value Z_α=1.96.

(iv) Test Statistic $Z=\frac{p-P}{\sqrt{\frac{PQ}{n}}}=\frac{0.3578-0.3333}{\sqrt{\frac{0.3333\times0.6667}{9000}}}=4.94$

$\therefore |Z|=4.94$

(v) Here $|Z|>Z_\alpha$

$\therefore$ H_0 is rejected.

$\therefore$ The die is biased.

4) A coin was tossed 400 times and the head turned up 216 times. Test the hypothesis that the coin is unbiased.

Solution:

Here n=400

p = proportion of success $=\frac{216}{400}=0.54$

P= proportion of population=$\frac{1}{2}$

$Q=1-P=1-\frac{1}{2}=0.5$

(i) H_0 : The coin is unbiased i.e, P=0.5

H_1 : The coin is biased i.e., P≠0.5 [Two tailed test]

(ii) Level of significance α=5%=0.05

(iii) Critical value Z_α=1.96.

(iv) Test Statistic $Z = \dfrac{p-P}{\sqrt{\dfrac{PQ}{n}}} = \dfrac{0.54-0.5}{\sqrt{\dfrac{0.5\times 0.5}{400}}} = 1.6$

$|Z| = 1.6$

(v) Here $|Z| < Z_\alpha$

∴ H_0 is accepted.

∴ The coin is unbiased.

5) A machine is producing bolts of which a certain fraction is defective. A random sample of 400 is taken from a large batch and is land to contain 30 defective bolts. Does this indicate that the proportion of defective is larger than that claimed by the manufacturer where the manufacturer claims that only 5% of his product are defective. Find 95% confidence limits of the proportion of defective bolts in batch.

Solution:

Here n=400

p = Proportion of sample $= \dfrac{30}{400} = 0.075$

P = proportion of population $= \dfrac{5}{100} = 0.05$

Q=1–P=0.95

(i) H_0: The manufacture claim is accepted

i.e, H_0 : P=0.05

H_1 : P>0.05 [Right Tailed test]

(ii) Level of significance α=5%=0.05

(iii) Critical value Z_α=1.645.

(iv) Test Statistic $Z = \dfrac{p-P}{\sqrt{\dfrac{PQ}{n}}} = \dfrac{0.075-0.05}{\sqrt{\dfrac{0.05\times 0.95}{400}}} = 2.2941$

$\therefore |Z| = 2.2941$

(v) Here $|Z| > Z_\alpha$.

∴ H_0 is rejected and H_1 is accepted.

∴ The proportion of defectives is larger than that claimed by the manufacture claim.

(vi) 95% confidence limits of the proportion

$$= P \pm Z_{\alpha}\sqrt{\frac{PQ}{n}}$$

$$= 0.05 + 1.645\sqrt{\frac{0.05 \times 0.95}{400}}$$

$$= 0.07136,\ 0.02865$$

6) In a random sample of 400 persons from a large population, 120 are females. Can it be said that males and females are in the ratio 5:3 in the population? Use 10% level of significance.

Solution:

Here n=400

$$\text{p} = \text{Proportion of sample } = \frac{120}{400} = 0.30$$

$$\text{P} = \text{Proportion of population } = \frac{3}{5+3} = 0.375$$

$$Q = 1 - P = 0.625$$

(i) H_0 : P=0.375

H_1: P≠0.375 [Two tailed test]

(ii) Level of significance α=10%=0. 1

(iii) Critical value Z_{α}=1.645.

(iv) Test Statistic $Z = \dfrac{p-P}{\sqrt{\dfrac{PQ}{n}}} = \dfrac{0.30 - 0.375}{\sqrt{\dfrac{0.375 \times 0.625}{400}}} = -3.125$

$\therefore |Z| = 3.125$

(v) Here $|Z| > Z_{\alpha}$.

∴ H_0 is rejected and H_1 is accepted.

∴ The males and females in the population are not in the ratio 5:3

7) In a sample of 1000 people in Tamilnadu 540 are rice eaters and the rest are wheat eaters. Can we assume that both rice and wheat are equally popular in this state at 5% level of significance?

Solution:

Here n=1000.

$$p = \text{Proportion of rice eaters} = \frac{540}{1000} = 0.54$$

$$P = \text{Proportion of population } = \frac{1}{2} = 0.5$$

$$Q = 1 - P = 0.5$$

(i) H_0: Both rice and wheat are equally popular in the state

i.e., H_0 : P=0. 5

H_1: P≠0. 5 [Two tailed test]

(ii) Level of significance α=5%=0. 05

(iii) Critical value Z_α=1.96.

(iv) Test Statistic $Z = \frac{p-P}{\sqrt{\frac{PQ}{n}}} = \frac{0.54-0.5}{\sqrt{\frac{0.5\times0.5}{1000}}} = 2.532$

$\therefore |Z| = 2.532$

(v) Here $|Z| > Z_\alpha$.

∴ H_0 is rejected and H_1 is accepted.

∴ Both rice and wheat are not equal popular in the state.

EXERCISE

1) **A coin is tossed 900 times and heads appear 490 times. Does this result support the hypothesis that the coin is unbiased.**

   [Ans: |Z| = 2.39]

2) **A manufacturer claimed that atleast 95% of bulbs which he supplied to a factory conformed to specifications. An examination of a sample of 600 bulbs, 39 were defective. Test is claim at 5 % level of significance.**

   [Ans: |Z| = 1.69]

3) **A die was thrown 400 times and sin resulted 80 times. Do the data justify the hypothesis of a unbiased dice?**

   [Ans: |Z| = 1.79]

4) In a sample of 400 burners there were 12 whose internal diameters were not within tolerance. Is this sufficient evidence for concluding that the manufacturing process is turning out more than 2% defective burners?

[Ans: |Z| = 1.429]

1.2.4 Test of significance for difference of proportions.

Suppose two large samples of sized n_1 and n_2 are taken respectively from two different populations. To test the significant difference between the sample proportions p_1 and p_2

Working rule:

(i) H_0 : the two samples have been drawn from the same population.

i.e., $H_0 : P_1=P_2$

$H_1 : P_1 \neq P_2$

(ii) Choose the appropriate level of significance α

(iii) Find the critical value Z_α

(iv) Test Statistic $Z = \dfrac{p_1 - p_2}{\sqrt{\dfrac{p_1 q_1}{n_1} + \dfrac{p_2 q_2}{n_2}}}$

Where $q_1=1-p_1$ and $q_2=1-p_2$.

Test Statistic $Z = \dfrac{p_1 - p_2}{\sqrt{pq\left[\dfrac{1}{n_1} + \dfrac{1}{n_2}\right]}}$

Where $p = \dfrac{n_1 p_1 + n_2 p_2}{n_1 + n_2}$

EXAMPLE

1) A machine produced 16 defective articles in a batch of 500. After over hauling it produced 3 defectives in a batch of 100. Has the machine improved?

Solution:

Here $n_1=500$, $n_2=100$;

$$p_1 = \frac{16}{500} = 0.032, \qquad p_2 = \frac{3}{100} = 0.03$$

(i) H_0 : The machine has not improved

i.e., $H_0 : p_1 = p_2$

$H_1 : p_1 > p_2$ [Right Tailed test]

(ii) Level of significance α=5%=0.05

(iii) Critical region Z_α=1.645

(iv) Test Statistic $Z = \dfrac{p_1 - p_2}{\sqrt{pq\left(\dfrac{1}{n_1} + \dfrac{1}{n_2}\right)}}$

Where $p = \dfrac{n_1 p_1 + n_2 p_2}{n_1 + n_2} = \dfrac{500 \times 0.032 + 100 \times 0.03}{500 + 100}$

$=0.032$

$\therefore q = 1 - p = 0.968$

$$\therefore Z = \frac{0.032 - 0.03}{\sqrt{0.032 \times 0.968\left(\dfrac{1}{500} + \dfrac{1}{100}\right)}} = 0.104$$

$|Z| = 0.104$

(v) Here $|Z| < Z_\alpha$

$\therefore$ H_0 is accepted.

$\therefore$ The machine has not improved.

2) In a sample of 600 men from a certain city, 450 men are found to be smokers in a sample of 900 from another city, 450 are found to be smokers. Do the data indicate that the two cities are significantly differ with respect to prevalence of smoking habits among men?

Solution:

Here n_1=600, n_2=900;

$p_1 = \dfrac{450}{600} = 0.75,$ $p_2 = \dfrac{450}{900} = 0.5$

(i) H_0 : There is no significant difference in the smoking habits of two cities.

i.e., $H_0 : p_1 = p_2$

$H_1 : p_1 \neq p_2$ [Two Tailed test]

(ii) Level of significance α=5%=0.05

(iii) Critical region Z_α=1.96

(iv) Test Statistic $Z = \dfrac{p_1 - p_2}{\sqrt{pq\left(\dfrac{1}{n_1}+\dfrac{1}{n_2}\right)}}$

Where $p = \dfrac{n_1p_1 + n_2p_2}{n_1 + n_2} = \dfrac{450+450}{600+900} = 0.6$

$\therefore q = 1 - p = 0.4$

$$\therefore Z = \frac{0.75-0.5}{\sqrt{0.6\times 0.4\left(\dfrac{1}{600}+\dfrac{1}{900}\right)}} = 9.7$$

$|Z| = 9.7$

(v) Here $|Z| > Z_\alpha$

$\therefore$ H_0 is rejected and H_1 is accepted.

$\therefore$ There is a significant difference in the smoking habits among men of two cities.

3) Before an increase in excise duty on tea 800 people out of a sample of 1000 persons were found to be tea drinker. After an increase in the duty, 800 persons were known to be tea drinkers in a sample of 1200 people. Do you think that there has been a significant decrease in the consumption of tea after the increase in the excise duty?

Solution:

Here n_1=1000, n_2=1200;

$p_1 = \dfrac{800}{1000} = 0.8,$ $p_2 = \dfrac{800}{1200} = 0.6667$

(i) H_0 : There is no significant difference in the consumption of tea before and after increase of excise duty.

i.e., $H_0 : p_1 = p_2$

$H_1 : p_1 > p_2$ [Right Tailed test]

(ii) Level of significance α=5%

(iii) Critical region Z_α=1.645

(iv) Test Statistic $Z = \dfrac{p_1 - p_2}{\sqrt{pq\left(\dfrac{1}{n_1} + \dfrac{1}{n_2}\right)}}$

Where $p = \dfrac{n_1 p_1 + n_2 p_2}{n_1 + n_2} = \dfrac{800+800}{1000+1200} = \dfrac{8}{11}$

$\therefore q = 1 - p = \dfrac{3}{11}$

$\therefore Z = \dfrac{0.8 - 0.6667}{\sqrt{\dfrac{8}{11} \times \dfrac{3}{11}\left(\dfrac{1}{1000} + \dfrac{1}{1200}\right)}} = 6.842$

$|Z| = 6.842$

(v) Here $|Z| > Z_\alpha$

$\therefore$ H_0 is rejected.

$\therefore$ There is significant decrease in the consumption of tea due to increase in excise duty.

4) On a certain day, 64 trains were arriving on time at Chennai station during the rush hours and 86 were late. At Hyderabad there were 65 on time and 105 late Is there any difference in the proportions arriving on time at the two stations?

Solution:

Here n_1=64+86=150, n_2=65+105=170;

$p_1 = \dfrac{64}{150} = 0.427$, $p_2 = \dfrac{65}{170} = 0.382$

(i) H_0 : There is no difference of arriving on time at the two stations.

i.e., $H_0 : p_1 = p_2$

$H_1 : p_1 \neq p_2$ [Two Tailed test]

(ii) Level of significance α=5%

(iii) Critical region Z_α=1.96

(iv) Test Statistic $Z = \dfrac{p_1 - p_2}{\sqrt{pq\left(\dfrac{1}{n_1} + \dfrac{1}{n_2}\right)}}$

Where $p = \dfrac{n_1 p_1 + n_2 p_2}{n_1 + n_2} = \dfrac{64 + 65}{150 + 170} = 0.4031$

$\therefore q = 1 - p = 0.5969$

$$\therefore Z = \frac{0.427 - 0.382}{\sqrt{0.4031 \times 0.5969\left(\dfrac{1}{150} + \dfrac{1}{170}\right)}} = 0.8189$$

$\therefore |Z| = 0.8189$

(v) Here $|Z| < Z_\alpha$

$\therefore$ H_0 is accepted.

$\therefore$ There is no significant difference of train arriving on time at the two cities.

5) In two large populations, here are 30% and 25 % respectively of fair haired people. Is this difference likely to be hidden in samples of 1200 and 900 respectively from the two populations.

Solution:

Here $n_1=1200$, $n_2=900$;

$$P_1 = 30\% = \frac{30}{100} = 0.3,\ P_2 = 25\% = \frac{25}{100} = 0.25$$

(i) H_0 : There is no difference between the two population.

i.e., $H_0 : P_1 = P_2$

$H_1 : P_1 \neq P_2$ [Two Tailed test]

(ii) Level of significance α=5%

(iii) Critical region Z_α=1.96

(iv) Test Statistic $Z = \dfrac{P_1 - P_2}{\sqrt{\dfrac{P_1 Q_1}{n_1} + \dfrac{P_2 Q_2}{n_2}}}$

$$= \frac{0.3 - 0.25}{\sqrt{\frac{0.3 \times 0.7}{1200} + \frac{0.25 \times 0.75}{900}}} = 2.55$$

$\therefore |Z| = 2.55$

(v) Here $|Z| > Z_\alpha$

$\therefore$ H_0 is rejected and H_1 is accepted.

$\therefore$ There is difference in population propositions.

EXERCISE

1) **A machine produced 20 defective articles in a batch of 400. After overhauling it produced 10 defectives in a batch of 300. Has the machine being improved after overhauling?**

   [Ans: |Z| = 1.103]

2) **In a random sample of 600 and 1000 men from two cities 400 and 600 are found to be literate. Do the data indicate at 5% level of significance that the population are significantly different in the percentage of literacy?**

   [Ans: |Z| = 2.67]

3) **In an infantile paralysis epidemic persons contracted the disease. 300 received n serum treatment and of them 75 serum treatment 65 became paralysed was the serum treatment effective?**

   [Ans: |Z| = 1.83]

4) **In a town a, there are 956 births of which 52.5% wee males while in towns a combined this proportion in total of 1406 births was 0.496. Is there any significant difference in the proportion of male births in the two towns?**

   [Ans: |Z| = 1.26]

1.3 TEST OF SIGNIFICANCE OF SMALL SAMPLES

When the size of the sample (n) is less than 30 then that sample is called a small sample.

The following are some important tests for small samples

(i) Student's 't' test

(ii) F- test

(iii) χ^2 – test

1.4 STUDENT'S 't'-TEST

The t- test is used when sample size n<30 and the population S.D is unknown.

Applications of t- distribution

It is used to test

(i) The significance of the difference of the mean of a random sample and the mean of the population.

(ii) The significance of the difference between two sample means

(iii) The significance of observed partial and multiple correlation coefficients.

(iv) The significance of an observed sample correlation coefficients and sample regression coefficients.

't' – Table:

The t – table given at the end is the probability integral of t- distribution. The t- distribution has different values for each degrees of freedom and when the d.f are infinite large, the t-distribution is equivalent to normal distribution and the probabilities shows the normal distribution tables are applicable.

1.4.1 t- test of significance for single mean

(i) Null hypothesis H_0: $\mu = \mu_0$

Alternative hypothesis H_1: $\mu \neq \mu_0$ [Two tailed test] (or)

$\mu > \mu_0$ [Right tailed test] (or)

$\mu < \mu_0$ [Left tailed test]

(ii) Write appropriate level of significance and d.f $=n-1$

(iii) Find critical values of 't' [ie, t_α] at the level of significance 'α' with $(n-1)$ d.f

(iv) Test Statistic $t = \dfrac{\bar{x}-\mu}{s/\sqrt{n-1}}$

(v) Compare the calculated value of 't' with critical value.

If $|t| < t_\alpha$ then H_0 is accepted.

If $|t| > t_\alpha$ then H_0 is rejected and H_1 is accepted.

Write the conclusion.

Confidence (or) fiducial limits

It t_α is the value of 't' at level of significance α at (n-1) degrees of freedom then the confidence limits are $\bar{x} \pm t_\alpha \dfrac{s}{\sqrt{n}}$

EXAMPLE

1) A sample of 20 items has mean 42 units and S.D 5 units. Test the hypothesis that it is a random sample from a normal population with mean 45 units.

Solution:

Given n=20, $\bar{x}$=42, s=5, μ=45

(i) H_0: μ=45

H_1: μ≠45 [Two tailed Test]

(ii) Level of significance α=0.05=5%, degrees of freedom $d.f = n - 1$=19

(iii) Critical value at 5% level with 19 d.f is $t_\alpha = 2.093$

(iv) Test statistic $t = \dfrac{\bar{x} - \mu}{s/\sqrt{n-1}}$

$$= \frac{42-45}{5/\sqrt{20-1}} = -2.615$$

(v) Here $|t| = 2.615$

$\therefore \quad |t| > t_\alpha$

∴ H_0 is rejected and H_1 is accepted. Therefore a random sample can not drawn from the normal population with mean 45 units.

2) A random sample of size 16 has 53 as mean. The sum of squares of the derivation from mean is 135. Can this sample be regarded as taken from the population having 56 as mean? Obtain 95% and 99% confidence limits of the mean of the population.

Solution:

Given n=16, $\bar{x}$=53, $\sum(x-\bar{x})^2$= 135, μ=56

(i) H_0: μ=56

H_1: μ≠56 [Two tailed test]

(ii) Level of significance α=5% = 0.05 and d.f = 15

(iii) Critical value at 5% level with 15 d.f is t_α=1.753

(iv) Test statistic $t = \dfrac{\bar{x} - \mu}{s/\sqrt{n-1}}$

Where $s^2 = \frac{\Sigma(x-\bar{x})^2}{n} = \frac{135}{16} = 8.4375 \Rightarrow$ s=2.9047 ,

$$\therefore\ t = \frac{53-56}{2.9047/\sqrt{15}} = -4$$

(v) Here $|t| = 4$

$\therefore\ |t| > t_\alpha$

$\therefore$ H_0 is rejected and H_1 is accepted. $\therefore$ The sample can not be regarded as taken from the population having 56 as mean

(vi) 95% confidence limits of the population mean $= \bar{x} \pm t_{0.05}\frac{s}{\sqrt{n}}$

$$= 53 \pm 1.753 \times \frac{2.9047}{\sqrt{16}}$$

$$= 53 \pm 1.2729$$

$$= (51.7271, 54.2729)$$

(vii) 99% confidence limits of the population mean $= \bar{x} \pm t_{0.01}\frac{s}{\sqrt{n}}$

$$= 53 \pm 2.602 \times \frac{2.9047}{\sqrt{16}}$$

$$= 53 \pm 1.8895$$

$$=(51.1105, 54.8895)$$

3) Test whether the sample having the values 63,63,64,55,66,69,70,70 and 71 has been choosen from a population with mean of 65 at 5% level of significance.

Solution:

Here n=9, α=5%, μ=65

(i) H_0: μ=65

H_1: $\mu \neq 65$ [Two tailed test]

(ii) Level of significance α=5% = 0.05 and d.f= n–1=8

(iii) Critical value at 5% level with 8 d.f is t_α= 2.31

(iv) Test Statistic $t = \dfrac{\bar{x} - \mu}{s/\sqrt{n-1}}$

Where $\bar{x} = \dfrac{\Sigma x}{n}$, $s^2 = \dfrac{\Sigma(x-\bar{x})^2}{n}$

x	$x-\bar{x}$	$(x-\bar{x})^2$
63	–2.66	7.0756
63	–2.66	7.0756
64	–1.66	2.7556
55	–10.66	113.6356
66	0.34	0.1156
69	3.34	11.1556
70	4.34	18.8356
70	4.34	18.8356
71	5.34	28.5156
591		208.0004

$$\bar{x} = \frac{591}{9} = 65.66$$

$$s^2 = \frac{208.0004}{9} = 23.1111$$

$\therefore$ s = 4.8074

$$\therefore\ t = \frac{65.66 - 65}{23.1111/\sqrt{8}} = 0.08077$$

(v) Here $|t| = 0.08077$

$\therefore |t| < t_\alpha$

$\therefore$ H_0 is accepted.

$\therefore$ The sample has been drawn from a population with mean 65.

4) A random sample of 10 boys had the following I.Q's: 70, 120, 110, 101, 88, 83, 95, 98, 107, 100. Do those data support the assumption of a population mean I.Q of 100? Find a reasonable range in which most of the mean I.Q values of samples of 10 boys lie.

Solution:

Given n=10, μ=100

(i) H_0: μ=100

H_1: μ≠100 [Two tailed test]

(ii) Level of significance α=5%, =0.05, d.f=n–1=9

(iii) Critical value at 5% level with 9 d.f is

$$t_\alpha = 2.262$$

(iv) Test Statistic $t = \dfrac{\bar{x} - \mu}{s/\sqrt{n-1}}$

Where $\bar{x} = \dfrac{\Sigma x}{n}$, $\quad s^2 = \dfrac{\Sigma(x-\bar{x})^2}{n}$ (or) $s^2 = \dfrac{\Sigma x^2}{n} - (\bar{x})^2$

x	70	120	110	101	88	83	95	98	107	100	Total 972
x^2	4900	14400	12100	10201	7744	6889	9025	9604	11449	10000	96312

$$\therefore \quad \bar{x} = \frac{972}{10} = 97.2$$

$$s^2 = \frac{96312}{10} - (97.2)^2 = 183.36$$

$$\Rightarrow \quad s = 13.5$$

$$\therefore \quad t = \frac{97.2 - 100}{13.5/\sqrt{9}} = -0.62$$

(v) Here $|t| = 0.62$

$\therefore |t| < t_\alpha$

∴ H_0 is accepted.

∴ The data support the assumption of a population I.Q of 100.

(vi) 95% confidence limits are $\bar{x} \pm t_{0.05} \dfrac{s}{\sqrt{n}}$

$$= 97.2 \pm 2.262 \times \frac{13.5}{\sqrt{10}}$$

=87.54, 106.86

∴ 95% confidence limits with in which the mean I.Q values of sample of 10 boys will lie is [86.99, 107.41]

5) The mean lifetime of a sample of 25 bulbs is found as 1550 hours with a S.D of 120 hours. The company manufacturing the bulbs claims that the average life of their bulbs is 1600 hours. Is the claim acceptable at 5% level of significance?

Solution:

Given $n=25$, $\bar{x}=1550$, $s=120$, $\mu=1600$

(i) $H_0: \mu=1600$

$H_1: \mu<1600$ [left tailed test]

(ii) Level of significance $\alpha=5\% =0.05$, $d.f = n-1 = 24$

(iii) Critical value at 5% level with 24 d.f is $t_\alpha = -1.711$.

(iv) Test statistic $t = \dfrac{\bar{x}-\mu}{s/\sqrt{n-1}}$

$$= \frac{1550-1600}{120/\sqrt{24}} = -2.04$$

(v) Here $|t| = 2.04$

$\therefore |t| > t_\alpha$

$\therefore H_0$ is rejected and H_1 is accepted.

$\therefore$ The claim of the company cannot be accepted at 5% level of significance.

6) Sandal powder is packed into packets by a machine. A random sample of 12 packets is drawn and their weights are found to be (in kg) 0.49, 0.48, 0.47, 0.48, 0.49, 0.50, 0.51, 0.49, 0.48, 0.50, 0.51 and 0.48. Test if the average weight of the packing can be taken as 0.5 kg.

Solution:

Given $n=12$, $\mu=0.5$

(i) $H_0: \mu=0.5$

$H_1: \mu\neq 0.5$ [Two tailed test]

(ii) Level of significance $\alpha=5\%$, $=0.05$, $d.f = n-1 = 11$

(iii) Critical value at 5% level with 11 d.f is $t_\alpha = 2.201$.

(iv) Test statistic $t = \dfrac{\bar{x}-\mu}{s/\sqrt{n-1}}$

Where $\bar{x} = \dfrac{\Sigma x}{n}$, $s^2 = \dfrac{\Sigma(x-\bar{x})^2}{n}$ (or) $s^2 = \dfrac{\Sigma x^2}{n} - (\bar{x})^2$

													Total
x	0.49	0.48	0.47	0.48	0.49	0.50	0.51	0.49	0.48	0.50	0.51	0.48	5.58
x^2	$(0.49)^2$	$(0.48)^2$	$(0.47)^2$	$(0.48)^2$	$(0.49)^2$	$(0.5)^2$	$(0.51)^2$	$(0.49)^2$	$(0.48)^2$	$(0.5)^2$	$(0.51)^2$	$(0.48)^2$	2.883

$$\bar{x} = \frac{5.88}{12} = 0.49$$

$$s^2 = \frac{2.883}{12} - (0.49)^2 = 0.00015 \Rightarrow s = 0.012$$

$$t = \frac{(0.49-0.5)}{0.012/\sqrt{11}} = -2.76$$

(v) Here $|t| = 2.76$

$\therefore$ $|t| > t_\alpha$

$\therefore$ H_0 is rejected and H_1 is accepted.

$\therefore$ The average packing cannot be taken as 0.5 kg.

7) The heights of 10 males of a given locality are found to be 70, 67, 62, 68, 61, 68, 70, 64, 64, 66 inches. Test at 5% level of significance. Is it reasonable to believe that the average height is greater than 64 inches?

Solution:

Given n=10, μ=64, α=5%

(i) H_0: μ=64

H_1: μ>64 [Right tailed test]

(ii) Level of significance α=5%, =0.05, d.f = n–1 = 9

(iii) Critical value at 5% significance level and 9 d.f is t_α= 1.833.

(iv) Test statistic $t = \dfrac{\bar{x}-\mu}{s/\sqrt{n-1}}$

Where $\bar{x} = \dfrac{\Sigma x}{n}$, $s^2 = \dfrac{\Sigma(x-\bar{x})^2}{n}$ (or) $s^2 = \dfrac{\Sigma x^2}{n} - (\bar{x})^2$

x	70	67	62	68	61	68	70	64	64	66	Total 660
x^2	$(70)^2$	$(67)^2$	$(62)^2$	$(68)^2$	$(61)^2$	$(68)^2$	$(70)^2$	$(64)^2$	$(64)^2$	$(66)^2$	43650

$$\therefore \bar{x} = \frac{660}{10} = 66$$

$$s^2 = \frac{43650}{10} - (66)^2 = 9$$

$$\therefore s=3$$

$$\therefore \quad t = \frac{66-64}{3/\sqrt{9}} = 2$$

(v) Here $|t| = 2$

$$\therefore |t| > t_\alpha$$

$\therefore$ We reject H_0 and accepted H_1.

$\therefore$ The average height is greater than 64 inches.

8) The lifetime of electric bulbs for a random sample of 10 from a large consignment gave the following data.

Item	**1**	**2**	**3**	**4**	**5**	**6**	**7**	**8**	**9**	**10**
Life time in hrs (Thousand)	**4.2**	**4.6**	**3.9**	**4.1**	**5.2**	**3.8**	**3.9**	**4.3**	**4.4**	**5.6**

Can we accept the hypothesis that the average lifetime of bulb is 4000 hrs?

Solution:

Given n=10, μ=4.

(i) $H_0 : \mu=4$

$H_1 : \mu\neq4$ [Two tailed test]

(ii) Level of significance α=5% and d.f=n–1=9.

(iii) Critical value t_α=2.26

(iv) Test Statistic $Z = \dfrac{\bar{x}-\mu}{s/\sqrt{n-1}}$

Where $\bar{x} = \dfrac{\sum x}{n}$

$$s^2 = \frac{\Sigma(x-\bar{x})^2}{n} \text{ (or) } \frac{\Sigma x^2}{n} - (\bar{x})^2$$

											Total
x:	4.2	4.6	3.9	4.1	5.2	3.8	3.9	4.3	4.4	5.6	44
$x-\bar{x}$:	–0.2	0.2	–0.5	–0.3	0.8	–0.6	–0.5	–0.1	0	1.2	
$(x-\bar{x})^2$:	0.04	0.04	0.25	0.09	0.64	0.36	0.25	0.01	0	1.44	3.12

$$\bar{x} = \frac{\Sigma x}{n} = \frac{44}{10} = 4.4$$

$$s^2 = \frac{\Sigma\left(x-\bar{x}\right)^2}{n} = \frac{3.12}{10} = 0.312$$

$\Rightarrow \quad s = 0.5586$

$$\therefore t = \frac{4.4-4}{0.5586/\sqrt{9}} = 2.148$$

$$\therefore |t| = 2.148$$

(v) Here $|t| < t_\alpha$

$\therefore$ H_0 is accepted.

$\therefore$ The average lifetime of bulbs could be 4000 hours.

9) A fertiliser mixing machine is set to give 12 kg of nitrate for every quintal bag of fertiliser. Ten 100 kg bags are examined. The percentage of nitrate are 15,14,13,12,13,12,13,14,11,12. Is there reason to believe that the machine is defective?

Solution:

Given n=10, $\mu = 12$

(i) $H_0 : \mu = 12$

$H_1 : \mu \neq 12$ [Two tailed test]

(ii) Level of significance α=5% and d.f=n–1=9.

(iii) Critical value t_α=2.26

(iv) Test Statistic $Z = \dfrac{\bar{x} - \mu}{s/\sqrt{n-1}}$

Where $\bar{x} = \dfrac{\sum x}{n}$

$s^2 = \dfrac{\sum(x-\bar{x})^2}{n}$ (or) $\dfrac{\sum x^2}{n} - (\bar{x})^2$

											Total
x:	15	14	13	12	13	12	13	14	11	12	30
$x-\bar{x}$:	2	1	0	−1	0	−1	0	1	−2	0	
$(x-\bar{x})^2$:	4	1	0	1	0	1	0	1	4	0	12

$\bar{x} = \dfrac{130}{10} = 13.0$

$s^2 = \dfrac{12}{10} = 1.2$

$\therefore s = 1.095$

$\therefore t = \dfrac{13-12}{1.095/\sqrt{9}} = 2.7397$

$\therefore |t| = 2.7397$

(v) Here $|t| > t_\alpha$

$\therefore$ H_0 is rejected and H_1 is accepted.

$\therefore$ There is same region to believe that machine is defective

10) A salesman is expected to effect an average sales of Rs. 3500 a sample test revealed that a particular salesman had made the following sales. Rs.2000 Rs.2500 Rs.3000 Rs.3400. Rs 3700 Rs 5200. Test whether his work is below standard or not.

Solution.

Here n=6, $\mu = 3500$

(i) $H_0 : \mu=3500$

$H_1 : \mu<3500$

							Total
x:	2000	2500	3000	3400	3700	5200	19800
$x-\bar{x}$:	–1300	–800	–300	100	400	1900	
$(x-\bar{x})^2$:	1690000	640000	90000	10000	160000	3610000	6200000

$$\bar{x} = \frac{\Sigma x}{n} = \frac{19800}{6} = 3300$$

$$s^2 = \frac{\Sigma\left(x-\bar{x}\right)^2}{n} = \frac{6200000}{6} = 1033333.33$$

$$\Rightarrow \quad s = 1016.53$$

$$\therefore t = \frac{3300-3500}{1016.53/\sqrt{5}} = 0.4399$$

$$\therefore |t| = 0.4399$$

(v) Here $|t| < t_\alpha$

∴ H_0 is accepted.

∴ The salesman work is standard.

EXERCISE

1) The following resuslts are obtained from a sample of 10 boxes of biscuits. Mean weight content = 490 gms, S.D of the weight = 9gm, could the sample come from a population having a mean of 500 gm?

[Ans: |t|= 3.3333]

2) The average breaking strength of steel rods is specified to be 17.5 (in units of 1000 kg). To test this sample of 14 rods were tested and gave the following results: 15, 18, 16, 21, 19, 21, 17, 17, 15, 17, 20, 19, 17, 18. Is the result of the experiment significant? Also obtain the 95% confidence interval for average breaking strength.

[Ans: |t|= 0.6833]

3) A random sample of 16 values from a normal population showed a mean of 41.5 inches and the sum of squares of derivations from this mean equal to 135 square inches. Show that the assumption of a mean of 43.5 inches for the population is not reasonable. Obtain 95% and 99% fiducial limits for the same

[Ans: |t|=2.67]

4) The mean weekly sales of powder in supermarket was 146.3 tins. After a special advertising campaign the mean weekly sales is 22 branches in a week increased to 153.7 tins and showed a S.D of 17.2 tins. Was the advertising campaign successful?

[Ans: $|t|$= 1.9716]

1.4.2 t-test of significance for difference of Means

The following assumptions are made in using this test.

(i) Parent populations, from which the samples have been drawn are normally distributed.

(ii) Population variances are equal and unknown

(iii) The two samples are random and independent.

Working procedure

(i) Null hypothesis $H_0:\mu_1 = \mu_2$

Alternative hypothesis H_1: $\mu_1 = \mu_2$ [Two tailed test] or $\mu_1 > \mu_2$ [Right tailed test] or $\mu_1 < \mu_2$ [Left tailed test]

(ii) Choose the appropriate level of significance

Degrees of freedom d.f = $n_1 + n_2 - 2$

(iii) Find the critical value t_α

(iv) Compute the test statistic $t = \dfrac{\overline{x_1} - \overline{x_2}}{\sqrt{S^2\left[\dfrac{1}{n_1} + \dfrac{1}{n_2}\right]}}$

Where $S^2 = \dfrac{n_1 s_1^2 + n_2 s_2^2}{n_1 + n_2 - 2}$

s_1 and s_2 are sample standard deviations.

(v) Compare the value of t with t_α. Write your conclusion

EXAMPLE

1) The average number of articles produced by two machines per day are 200 and 250 and S.D 20 and 25 respectively on the basis of records of 25 days production. Can you regard both the machine equally efficient at 1% level of significance?

Solution:

Given n_1=25, n_2=25, $\overline{x_1}$ =200, $\overline{x_2}$ =250, s_1=20, s_2=25

(i) $H_0: \mu_1 = \mu_2$

$H_1: \mu_1 \neq \mu_2$ [Two tailed test]

(ii) Level of significance α=1%, =0.01, d.f = n_1+n_2-2 =48

(iii) Critical value at 1% significance level with 48 d.f is t_α= 2.58.

(iv) Test statistic $t = \dfrac{\overline{x_1} - \overline{x_2}}{\sqrt{S^2\left[\dfrac{1}{n_1} + \dfrac{1}{n_2}\right]}}$

Where $S^2 = \dfrac{n_1 s_1^2 + n_2 s_2^2}{n_1 + n_2 - 2}$

$$= \frac{25(20)^2 + 25(25)^2}{25+25-2} = 533.854$$

$$\therefore \quad t = \frac{200-250}{\sqrt{533.854\left[\dfrac{1}{25}+\dfrac{1}{25}\right]}} = -7.657$$

(v) Here $|t|$ = 7.657

$\therefore |t| > t_\alpha$

$\therefore$ H_0 is rejected and H_1 is accepted

$\therefore$ The machines are not equally efficient.

2) Two salesman A & B work in a certain district from a sampling curry conducted by the head office. The following results were obtained. State whether there is any significant difference in the average sales between the two salesman.

	A	B
No of sales:	20	18
Average sales (in Rs.):	170	205
Standard deviation (in Rs.):	20	25

Solution:

Given n_1=20, n_2=18

$\overline{x_1} = 170$, $\overline{x_2} = 205$

$s_1 = 20, \qquad s_2 = 25$

(i) $H_0 : \mu_1 = \mu_2$

$H_1 : \mu_1 \neq \mu_2$ [Two tailed test]

(ii) Level of significance $\alpha=5\%$ & $d.f = n_1+n_2-2=36$

(iii) Critical value $t_\alpha=1.96$

(iv) Test Statistic $t = \dfrac{\overline{x_1} + \overline{x_2}}{\sqrt{S^2\left[\dfrac{1}{n_1} + \dfrac{1}{n_2}\right]}}$

$$\text{Where } S^2 = \frac{n_1 s_1^2 + n_2 s_2^2}{n_1 + n_2 - 2} = \frac{20(20)^2 + 18(25)^2}{20 + 18 - 2} = 534.72$$

$$\therefore t = \frac{170 - 205}{\sqrt{534.72\left(\dfrac{1}{20} + \dfrac{1}{18}\right)}} = -4.6587$$

$\therefore |t| = 4.6587$

(v) Here $|t| > t_\alpha$.

$\therefore$ H_0 is rejected and H_1 is accepted.

$\therefore$ There is significant difference in the average sales between the two salesman.

3) A group of 7 week old chicken reared on a high protein diet weight 12,15,11,16,14,14 and 16 ounces. A second group of fire chickens similarly treated except that they receive a low protein diet, weight 8,10,14,10 and 13 ounces test whether there is evidence that additional protein has increased the weight of the chicken. (The table value of t for v=10 at 5% level of significance is 2.33).

Solution:

Given $n_1=7$, $n_2=5$.

(i) $H_0 : \mu_1 = \mu_2$

$H_1 : \mu_1 > \mu_2$ [Right tailed test]

(ii) Level of significance $\alpha=5\%$ & $d.f = n_1+n_2-2$

(iii) Critical value $t_\alpha=2.33$

(iv) Test Statistic $t = \dfrac{\overline{x_1} - \overline{x_2}}{\sqrt{S^2\left[\dfrac{1}{n_1} + \dfrac{1}{n_2}\right]}}$

Where $S^2 = \dfrac{n_1 s_1^2 + n_2 s_2^2}{n_1 + n_2 - 2}$

								Total
x_1:	12	15	11	16	14	14	16	98
x_2:	8	10	14	10	13			55
x_1^2:	144	225	121	256	196	196	256	1394
x_2^2:	64	100	196	100	169			629

$\overline{x_1} = \dfrac{98}{7} = 14$

$\overline{x_2} = \dfrac{55}{5} = 11$

$s_1^2 = \dfrac{\Sigma x_1^2}{n_1} - \left(\overline{x_1}\right)^2 = \dfrac{1394}{7} - (14)^2 = 3.1429$

$s_2^2 = \dfrac{\Sigma x_2^2}{n_2} - \left(\overline{x_2}\right)^2 = \dfrac{629}{5} - (11)^2 = 4.8$

$\therefore\ S^2 = \dfrac{7 \times 3.1429 + 5 \times 4.8}{7 + 5 - 2} = 4.6$

$\therefore\ t = \dfrac{14 - 11}{\sqrt{4.6\left(\dfrac{1}{7} + \dfrac{1}{5}\right)}} = 2.3888$

$\therefore |t| = 2.38888$

(v) Here $|t| > t_\alpha$.

$\therefore$ H_0 is rejected and H_1 is accepted.

$\therefore$ The additional protein has increased the weight of the chicken

4) Two horses A and B were tested according to the time (in seconds) to run a particular race with the following results.

Horse A	28	30	32	33	33	29	34
Horse B	29	30	30	24	27	29	

Test whether the horse A is running faster than horse B at 5% level.

Solution:

Given n_1=7, n_2=6, α=5%

(i) H_0: $\mu_1 = \mu_2$

H_1: $\mu_1 > \mu_2$ [Right tailed test]

(ii) Level of significance α=5%, and degrees of freedom = n_1+n_2-2= 11

(iii) Critical value t_α= 1.796.

(iv)

x_1	x_2	x_1^2	x_2^2
28	29	784	841
30	30	900	900
32	30	1024	900
33	24	1089	576
33	27	1089	729
29	29	841	841
34		1156	
219	169	6883	4787

$$\therefore \quad \overline{x_1} = \frac{\Sigma x_1}{n_1} = \frac{219}{7} = 31.29$$

$$\overline{x_2} = \frac{\Sigma x_2}{n_2} = \frac{169}{6} = 28.17$$

$$s_1^2 = \frac{\Sigma x_1^2}{n_1} - \left(\overline{x_1}\right)^2 = \frac{6883}{7} - (31.29)^2 = 4.23$$

$$s_2^2 = \frac{\Sigma x_2^2}{n_2} - \left(\overline{x_2}\right)^2 = \frac{4787}{6} - (28.17)^2 = 4.28$$

$$\therefore \quad S^2 = \frac{n_1 s_1^2 + n_2 s_2^2}{n_1 + n_2 - 2} = \frac{7 \times 4.23 + 6 \times 4.28}{7+6-2} = 5.03$$

$$\therefore \text{ Test statistic } t = \frac{\overline{x_1} - \overline{x_2}}{\sqrt{S^2\left[\frac{1}{n_1} + \frac{1}{n_2}\right]}} = \frac{31.29 - 28.17}{\sqrt{5.03\left[\frac{1}{7} + \frac{1}{6}\right]}} = 2.498$$

(v) Here $|t| = 2.498$

$\therefore |t| > t_\alpha$

$\therefore$ H_0 is rejected and H_1 is accepted.

$\therefore$ Horse A is running faster than Horse B.

5) To compare the prices of a certain product in two cities, ten shops were selected at random in each town. The prices were noted below.

City I:	61	63	56	63	56	63	59	56	44	61
City II:	54	54	47	59	51	61	57	55	64	58

Test whether the average prices can said to be the same in two cities.

Solution:

Given $n_1=10, n_2=10$

(i) $H_0: \mu_1 = \mu_2$

$H_1: \mu_1 \neq \mu_2$ [Two tailed test]

(ii) Level of significance $\alpha=5\%, =0.05$, $d.f = n_1+n_2-2 = 18$

(iii) Critical value at 5% significance level with 18 d.f is $t_\alpha = 2.10$.

(iv) Test statistic $t = \dfrac{\overline{x_1} - \overline{x_2}}{\sqrt{S^2\left[\dfrac{1}{n_1} + \dfrac{1}{n_2}\right]}}$

Where $S^2 = \dfrac{n_1 s_1^2 + n_2 s_2^2}{n_1 + n_2 - 2}$

x_1	61	63	56	63	56	63	59	56	44	61	582
x_1^2	3721	3969	3136	3969	3136	3969	3481	3136	1936	3721	34174
x_2	54	54	47	59	51	61	57	55	64	58	560
x_2^2	2916	2916	2209	3481	2601	3721	3249	3025	4096	3364	31578

$$\overline{x_1} = \frac{\Sigma x_1}{n_1} = \frac{582}{10} = 58.2$$

$$\overline{x_2} = \frac{\Sigma x_2}{n_2} = \frac{560}{10} = 56$$

$$s_1^2 = \frac{\Sigma x_1^2}{n_1} - \left(\overline{x_1}\right)^2 = \frac{34174}{10} - (58.2)^2 = 30.16$$

$$s_2^2 = \frac{\Sigma x_2^2}{n_2} - \left(\overline{x_2}\right)^2 = \frac{31578}{10} - (56)^2 = 21.8$$

$$\therefore \quad S^2 = \frac{n_1 s_1^2 + n_2 s_2^2}{n_1 + n_2 - 2} = \frac{10 \times 30.16 + 10 \times 21.8}{10 + 10 - 2} = 28.8667$$

$$\therefore \quad t = \frac{\overline{x_1} - \overline{x_2}}{\sqrt{S^2\left[\frac{1}{n_1} + \frac{1}{n_2}\right]}} = \frac{58.2 - 56}{\sqrt{28.8667\left[\frac{1}{10} + \frac{1}{10}\right]}} = 0.9156$$

(v) Here $|t| = 0.9156$

$\therefore \; |t| < t_\alpha$

$\therefore$ H_0 is accepted

$\therefore$ The average price is same in both cities.

6) Twelve students were given intensive coaching and tests were given before and after coaching. Is there any improvement due to coaching?

Marks in I test [before]	50	42	51	26	35	42	60	41	70	55	62	38
Marks in II test [after]	62	40	61	35	30	52	68	51	84	63	72	50

Solution:

Given $n_1=12$, $n_2=12$.

(i) $H_0: \mu_1 = \mu_2$

$H_1: \mu_1 < \mu_2$ [Left tailed test]

(ii) Level of significance $\alpha=5\%$, $=0.05$, d.f $= n_1+n_2-2 = 22$.

(iii) Critical value $t_\alpha = -1.717$.

(iv) Test statistic $t = \frac{\overline{x_1} - \overline{x_2}}{\sqrt{S^2\left[\frac{1}{n_1} + \frac{1}{n_2}\right]}}$

Where $S^2 = \frac{n_1 s_1^2 + n_2 s_2^2}{n_1 + n_2 - 2}$

												Total
x_1	50	42	51	26	35	42	60	41	70	55	62	38	572
x_1^2	2500	1764	2601	676	1225	1764	3600	1681	4900	3025	3844	1444	29024
x_2	62	40	61	35	30	52	68	51	84	63	72	50	668
x_2^2	3844	1600	3721	1225	900	2704	4624	2601	7056	3969	5184	2500	39928

$$\therefore\ \overline{x_1} = \frac{\Sigma x_1}{n_1} = \frac{572}{12} = 47.67$$

$$\overline{x_2} = \frac{\Sigma x_2}{n_2} = \frac{668}{12} = 55.67$$

$$s_1^2 = \frac{\Sigma x_1^2}{n_1} - \left(\overline{x_1}\right)^2 = 146.24$$

$$s_2^2 = \frac{\Sigma x_2^2}{n_2} - \left(\overline{x_2}\right)^2 = 228.18$$

$$\therefore\ S^2 = \frac{n_1 s_1^2 + n_2 s_2^2}{n_1 + n_2 - 2} = \frac{12 \times 146.24 + 12 \times 228.18}{12 + 12 - 2} = 204.23$$

$$\therefore\ t = \frac{47.67 - 55.67}{\sqrt{204.23\left[\frac{1}{12} + \frac{1}{12}\right]}} = -1.3712$$

(v) Here $|t| = 1.3712$

$|t| > t_\alpha$

∴ H_0 is rejected and H_1 is accepted.

∴ There is improvement due to coaching.

7) A group of 10 rats fed on diet A and another group of 8 rats fed on diet B recorded the following increase in weight (gms).

Diet A:	5	6	8	1	12	4	3	9	6	10
Diet B:	2	3	6	8	10	1	2	8		

Does this show superiority of diet A over diet B.

Solution:

Given $n_1=10$, $n_2=8$.

(i) $H_0: \mu_1=\mu_2$

$H_1: \mu_1>\mu_2$ [Right tailed test]

(ii) Level of significance $\alpha=5\%=0.05$, $d.f = n_1+n_2-2$

(iii) Critical value $t_\alpha=1.746$

(iv) Test statistic $t=\dfrac{\overline{x_1}-\overline{x_2}}{\sqrt{S^2\left[\dfrac{1}{n_1}+\dfrac{1}{n_2}\right]}}$

Where $S^2=\dfrac{n_1 s_1^2+n_2 s_2^2}{n_1+n_2-2}$

											Total
x_1	5	6	8	1	12	4	3	9	6	10	64
x_1^2	25	36	64	1	144	16	9	81	36	100	512
x_2	2	3	6	8	10	1	2	8	–	–	40
x_2^2	4	9	36	64	100	1	4	64	–	–	282

$$\therefore \quad \overline{x_1}=\frac{\Sigma x_1}{n_1}=\frac{64}{10}=6.4$$

$$\overline{x_2}=\frac{\Sigma x_2}{n_2}=\frac{40}{8}=5$$

$$s_1^2=\frac{\Sigma x_1^2}{n_1}-\left(\overline{x_1}\right)^2=\frac{512}{10}-(6.4)^2=10.24$$

$$s_2^2=\frac{\Sigma x_2^2}{n_2}-\left(\overline{x_2}\right)^2=\frac{282}{8}-(5)^2=10.25$$

$$\therefore \quad S^2=\frac{10\times 10.24+8\times 10.25}{10+8-2}=11.525$$

$$\therefore \quad t=\frac{6.4-5}{\sqrt{11.525\left[\frac{1}{10}+\frac{1}{8}\right]}}=0.8694$$

(v) Here $|t|=0.8694$

$|t|>t_\alpha$

∴ H_0 is accepted.

∴ Diet A is superior to diet B.

EXERCISE

1) The sample of sodium vapour bulbs were tested for length of life and following results were got.

	Size	Sample Mean	Sample S.D
Type – I	8	1234 hrs	36 hrs
Type – II	7	1036 hrs	40 hrs

Is the difference in the means significant to generalize that Type-I is superior to Type-II regarding length of life

[Ans : $|t| = 18.148$]

2) Two independent samples from normal populations with equal variances gave the following.

Sample	Size	Mean	S.D
1	16	23.4	2.5
2	12	24.9	2.8

Is the difference between the means significant?

[Ans: $|t|= 1.4377$]

3) A group of 5 patients treated with medicine 'A' weigh 42, 39, 48, 60 and 41 kg. A second group of 7 patients from the same hospital treated with medicine 'B' weigh 38, 42, 56, 64, 68, 69 and 62kg. Do you agree with the claim that medicine B increases the weight significantly?

[Ans: $|t| = 1.7036.$]

4) The following table gives the values of protein from Kangeyam cow's milk and buffalo's milk. Examine if these differences are significantly.

Cow's Milk	1.90	1.95	2.00	2.02	1.85	1.80
Buffalo's Milk	2.12	2.00	2.20	2.45	2.20	2.10

[Ans: $|t| = 3.641$]

5) Two independent schools are chosen from two schools A and B, a common test is given in a subject. The scores of the students as follows.

School A	76	68	70	43	94	68	33	
School B	40	48	92	85	70	76	68	22

Can we conclude that students of school A performed better that students of school B?

[Ans: |t| = 0.173]

1.5 TEST BASED ON χ^2-TEST : [CHI-SQUARE TEST]

I-Application (or) uses of χ^2 distribution

(i) To test the goodness of fit.

(ii) To test the independence of attributes.

(iii) To test the hypothetical value of the population variance.

(iv) To test the homogeneity of independent estimates of the population variance.

(v) To test the homogenity of independent estimates of the population correlation coefficient.

II- Conditions for validity of χ^2-test:

This is an approximate test for large values of 'n'. For the validity of χ^2-test of goodness of fit between theory and experiment, the following conditions must be satisfied.

(i) The sample observations should be independent.

(ii) Constraints on the cell frequencies, if any, must be linear.

(iii) N, the total frequency, should be reasonably large, say greater than 50.

(iv) No theoretical cell frequency should be less than 5. If theoretical frequency is less than 5, then for the application of χ^2-test, it is pooled with the succeeding (or) preceding so that the pooled frequency is more than 5.

III- Degrees of Freedom:

(i) In the case of fitting a Binomial distribution, d.f = n–1

(ii) In the case of fitting a Poisson distribution d.f = n–2

(iii) In the case of fitting a Normal distribution d.f = n–3

1.5.1 χ^2-Test for goodness of fit

χ^2-test of goodness of fit is a test to find if the deviation of the experiment from theory is just by chance or it is due to the inadequacy of the theory to fit the observed data.

By this test, we test whether differences between observed and expected frequencies are significant or not.

$$\text{Test statistic } \chi^2 = \sum \frac{(O-E)^2}{E}$$

Where O – Observed frequency

E – Expected frequency

EXAMPLE

1) A coin were tossed 160 times and the following results were obtained.

No.of. Heads	0	1	2	3	4
Observed frequencies	17	52	54	31	6

Under the assumption that the coins are unbiased, find the expected frequencies of getting 0,1,2,3,4 heads and test goodness of fit.

Solution:

(i) H_0 : The coins are unbiased

H_1 : The coins are biased.

(ii) Level of significance $\alpha = 0.05$, d.f = n–1 = 4

(iii) Critical value of χ^2 is $\chi_\alpha^2 = 9.488$

(iv) Test Statistic $\chi^2 = \sum \frac{(O-E)^2}{E}$

$$\text{Probability of getting head } p = \frac{1}{2}$$

$$\text{Probability of getting tail } q = \frac{1}{2}$$

$\therefore$ Expected frequencies are

$$P(x) = nC_x p^x q^{n-x}, \quad x = 0, 1, 2, 3, 4$$

$$\therefore P(0) = 4C_0 \left(\frac{1}{2}\right)^0 \left(\frac{1}{2}\right)^4 = 0.0625$$

$$P(1) = 4C_1 \left(\frac{1}{2}\right)^1 \left(\frac{1}{2}\right)^3 = 0.250$$

$$P(2) = 4C_2\left(\frac{1}{2}\right)^2\left(\frac{1}{2}\right)^2 = 0.375$$

$$P(3) = 4C_3\left(\frac{1}{2}\right)^3\left(\frac{1}{2}\right)^1 = 0.25$$

$$P(4) = 4C_4\left(\frac{1}{2}\right)^4\left(\frac{1}{2}\right)^0 = 0.0625$$

No of heads	Observed frequency (O)	Expected frequency (E) [160×P(x)]	$\frac{(O-E)^2}{E}$
0	17	160×0.0625=10	4.9
1	52	160×0.25=40	3.6
2	54	160×0.375=60	0.6
3	31	160×0.25=40	2.025
4	6	160×0.0625=10	1.6
Total	160	160	12.725

$\therefore \chi^2 = 12.725$

(v) Here $\chi^2 > \chi_\alpha^2$

$\therefore$ We reject H_0 and accept H_1

$\therefore$ The coins are biased.

2) Records taken of the number of male and Female births in 800 families having four children are as follows.

No. of male births:	0	1	2	3	4
No. of female births:	4	3	2	1	0
No. of families:	32	178	290	206	94

Test whether the data are consistent with the hypothesis that the Binomial law holds and the chance of male birth is equal to that of female birth namely $p = q = \frac{1}{2}$

Solution:

Here n=5

(i) H_0: The data are consistent with the hypothesis that the Binomial law holds of equal probability for male and female births. ie. p=q=1/2

H_1: The data are inconsistent.

(ii) Level of significance α=5%, d.f = n–1 = 5–1 =4

(iii) Critical value χ_α^2=9.488

(iv) Test statistic $\chi^2 = \sum \frac{(O-E)^2}{E}$

We use binomial distribution to calculate theoretical frequency

$$P(X=x) = nC_x p^x q^{n-x}, \quad x = 0,1,2,3,4$$

$$P(x=0) = 4C_0 \left(\frac{1}{2}\right)^0 \left(\frac{1}{2}\right)^4 = 0.0625$$

$$P(x=1) = 4C_1 \left(\frac{1}{2}\right)^1 \left(\frac{1}{2}\right)^3 = 0.250$$

$$P(x=2) = 4C_2 \left(\frac{1}{2}\right)^2 \left(\frac{1}{2}\right)^2 = 0.375$$

$$P(x=3) = 4C_3 \left(\frac{1}{2}\right)^3 \left(\frac{1}{2}\right)^1 = 0.25$$

$$P(x=4) = 4C_4 \left(\frac{1}{2}\right)^4 \left(\frac{1}{2}\right)^0 = 0.0625$$

No of male	**Observed frequency (O)**	**Expected frequency (E) [N×P(*x*)]**	$\frac{(O-E)^2}{E}$
0	32	800×0.0625=50	6.48
1	178	800×0.25=200	2.42
2	290	800×0.375=300	0.333
3	206	800×0.25=200	0.18
4	94	800×0.0625=50	38.72
Total	800	800	47.467

$\therefore \chi^2 = 47.467$

(v) Here $\chi^2 > \chi_\alpha^2$

∴ H_0 is rejected and H_1 is accepted.

∴ The data are not consistent.

3) A die is thrown 270 times and the results of these throws are given below.

No. appeared on the die	1	2	3	4	5	6
Frequency	40	32	29	59	57	59

Test whether the die is biased or not.

Solution:

(i) H_0: The die is unbiased

H_1: The die is biased.

(ii) Level of significance α=5%, d.f = n–1 =5

(iii) Critical value $\chi_\alpha^2 = 11.070$

(iv) Test statistic $\chi^2 = \sum \frac{(O-E)^2}{E}$

	O	E	$\frac{(O-E)^2}{E}$
	40	46	0.7826
	32	46	4.2609
	29	46	6.2826
	59	46	3.6739
	57	46	2.6304
	59	46	3.6739
Total	276	276	21.30

$\therefore$ Expected frequency $= \frac{276}{6} = 46$

$\therefore \quad \chi^2$=21.30.

(v) Here $\chi^2 > \chi_\alpha^2$

$\therefore$ H_0 is rejected and H_1 is accepted.

$\therefore$ The die is biased.

4) Verify whether Poisson distribution can be assumed from the data given:

No. of defects	0	1	2	3	4	5
Frequency	6	13	13	8	4	3

Solution:

Here n=6

(i) H_0: Poisson fit is a good fit to the data

H_1: Poisson fit is not a good fit to the data.

(ii) Level of significance α=5 %, d.f = n–2=4

(iii) Critical value $\chi_{\alpha}^{2} = 9.488$

(iv) Test statistic $\chi^2 = \sum \frac{(O-E)^2}{E}$

$$\text{Mean } \bar{x} = \frac{\Sigma f_i x_i}{\Sigma f_i} = \frac{94}{47} = 2$$

To fit a Poisson distribution we require λ.

$\therefore$ Parameter $\lambda = \bar{x} = 2$

$\therefore$ Probability $P(X = x) = \frac{e^{-\lambda}\lambda^x}{x!} = \frac{e^{-2}.2^x}{x!}$

$$P(X=0) = \frac{e^{-2}.2^0}{0!} = e^{-2}$$

$$P(X=1) = \frac{e^{-2}.2^1}{1!} = 2e^{-2}$$

$$P(X=2) = \frac{e^{-2}.2^2}{2!} = 2e^{-2}$$

$$P(X=3) = \frac{e^{-2}.2^3}{3!} = \frac{4}{3}e^{-2}$$

$$P(X=4) = \frac{e^{-2}.2^4}{4!} = \frac{2}{3}e^{-2}$$

$$P(X=5) = \frac{e^{-2}.2^5}{5!} = \frac{4}{15}e^{-2}$$

X	O	$P(X=x)$	$E=N.\ P(X=x)$	$\frac{(O-E)^2}{E}$
0	6	e^{-2}	6.3608	0.2037
1	13	$2e^{-2}$	12.7215	0.00616
2	13	$2e^{-2}$	12.7215	0.00616
3	8	$\frac{4}{3}e^{-2}$	8.481	0.02716
4	4	$\frac{2}{3}e^{-2}$	4.2405	0.0135
5	3	$\frac{4}{15}e^{-2}$	1.6962	1.0026
Total	47			1.2864

$\therefore\ \chi^2 = 1.2864$

(v) Here $\chi^2 < \chi_\alpha^{\ 2}$

$\therefore$ H_0 is accepted

$\therefore$ Poisson distribution provides a good fit to the data.

5) The table below gives the number of aircraft accidents that occurred during the various days of the week. Test whether the accidents are uniformly distributed over the week.

Days	**Mon**	**Tue**	**Wed**	**Thu**	**Fri**	**Sat**
No.of.Accidents	**14**	**18**	**12**	**11**	**15**	**14**

Solution:

(i) H_0: The accidents are uniformly distributed over the week.

H_1: The accidents are not uniformly distributed over the week.

(ii) Levels of significance α=5%, d.f = n–1

(iii) Critical value $\chi_\alpha^{\ 2}$=11.07

(iv) Test statistic $\chi^2 = \sum \frac{(O-E)^2}{E}$

	O	E	O–E	$(O-E)^2$	$\frac{(O-E)^2}{E}$
	14	14	0	0	0
	18	14	4	16	1.143
	12	14	–2	4	0.286
	11	14	–3	9	0.643
	15	14	1	1	0.071
	14	14	0	0	0
Total	84	84			2.143

Here N=total frequency = 84

$\therefore$ Expected frequency = 84/6 = 14

$\therefore \ \chi^2 = 2.143$

(v) Here $\chi^2 < \chi_\alpha^2$

$\therefore$ H_0 is accepted

$\therefore$ The accidents are uniformly distributed over the week.

6) The following table gives the number of aircraft accidents that occurred during the various days of the week. Find whether the accidents are uniformly distributed over the week.

Days	**Sun**	**Mon**	**Tue**	**Wed**	**Thu**	**Fri**	**Sat**
No.of.Accidents	**14**	**16**	**08**	**12**	**11**	**09**	**14**

Solution:

(i) H_0 : The accidents are uniformly distributed over the week.

H_1: The accidents are not uniformly distributed over the week.

(ii) Level of significance α=5%, d.f=n–1=6

(iii) Critical value χ_α^2=12.592

(iv) Test Statistic $\chi^2 = \sum \frac{(O-E)^2}{E}$

Here Total frequency = 84

$\therefore$ Expected frequency $= \frac{84}{7} = 12$

	O	E	O–E	$(O-E)^2$	$\frac{(O-E)^2}{E}$
	14	12	2	4	0.333
	16	12	4	16	1.333
	8	12	–4	16	1.333
	12	12	0	0	0
	11	12	–1	1	0.083
	9	12	–3	9	0.75
	14	12	2	4	0.333
Total	84	84			4.165

$\therefore \chi^2 = 4.165$

(v) Here $\chi^2 < \chi_\alpha^2$

$\therefore$ H_0 is accepted

$\therefore$ The accidents are uniformly distributed over the week.

7) The theory predicts the proportion of beans in the four groups G_1, G_2, G_3, G_4 should be in the ratio 9:3:3:1. In an experiment with 1600 beans the numbers in the four groups were 882, 313, 287, 118. Does the experimental result support the theory?

Solution

(i) H_0 : The experimental result supports the theory.

H_1: The experimental result does not support the theory.

(ii) Level of significance $\alpha=5\%$, d.f=n–1=3

(iii) Critical value $\chi_\alpha^2 = 7.815$

(iv) Test statistic $\chi^2 = \sum \frac{(O-E)^2}{E}$

The observed frequencies are 882, 313, 287, 118.

$\therefore$ Total Frequency = 1600

∴ Expected frequencies are

$$E(G_1) = \frac{1600 \times 9}{16} = 900$$

$$E(G_2) = \frac{1600 \times 3}{16} = 300$$

$$E(G_3) = \frac{1600 \times 3}{16} = 300$$

$$E(G_4) = \frac{1600 \times 1}{16} = 100$$

	O	E	O–E	$(O-E)^2$
	882	900	324	0.36
	313	300	169	0.5633
	287	300	169	0.5633
	118	100	324	3.24
Total	1600	1600		4.7266

$\therefore\ \chi^2 = 4.7266$

(v) Here $\chi^2 < \chi_\alpha{}^2$

∴ H_0 is accepted

∴ The experimental result supports the theory.

8) In 90 throws of a die, face, 1 turned 9 time face 2 and 3 turned 27 times, face 4 or 5 turned 36 times and 6 turned 18 times. Test at 10% level if the die is honest, at being given that χ^2 for 3 d.f = 6.25 at 10% level of significance.

Solution:

(i) H_0: The die is honest

H_1: The die is not honest

(ii) Level of significance α=10%

(iii) Critical value $\chi_\alpha^2 = 6.25$

(iv) Test Statistic $\chi_\alpha^2 = \Sigma \frac{(O-E)^2}{E}$

Face turned	Observed Frequency (O_i)	Expected frequency (E_i)	$\frac{(O-E)^2}{E}$
1	9	15	2.4
2(or)3	27	30	0.3
4 (or) 5	36	30	1.2
6	18	15	0.6
Total	90	90	4.5

$\therefore$ Expected frequency $= \frac{\Sigma O_i}{6} = \frac{90}{6} = 15$

$\therefore \ \chi^2 = 4.5$

(v) Here $\chi^2 < \chi^2_\alpha$

$\therefore$ H_0 is accepted

$\therefore$ The die is honest.

9) Among 64 offsprings of a certain cross between guinea pigs, 32 were red, 10 were black and 22 were white. According to the genetic model, these numbers should be in the ratio 9:3:4. Are the data consistent with the model at 5% level?

Solution:

(i) H_0: Data are consistent with the model.

H_1: Data are not consistent with the model.

(ii) Level of Significance α=5% and d.f=n–1=2

(iii) Critical value $\chi^2_\alpha = 5.991$

(iv) Test Statistic $\chi^2_\alpha = \Sigma \frac{(O-E)^2}{E}$

The observed frequencies are 32,10, 22.

$\therefore$ Expected frequencies are

$$E(\text{Red}) = \frac{9 \times 64}{16} = 36$$

$$E(\text{Black}) = \frac{3}{16} \times 64 = 12$$

$$E(\text{White}) = \frac{4}{16} \times 64 = 16$$

O_i	E_i	$\frac{O_i - E_i}{E_i}$
32	36	0.4444
10	12	0.3333
22	16	2.25
		3.0277

$\therefore\ \chi^2 = 3.0277$

(v) Here $\chi^2 < \chi^2_\alpha$

$\therefore$ H_0 is accepted

$\therefore$ Data are consistent with the model.

EXERCISE

1) In 120 throws of a single die, the following distribution of faces was observed.

Face:	1	2	3	4	5	6
Frequency:	30	25	18	10	22	15

Can you say that the die is biased.

[Ans: $\chi_\alpha^{\ 2}$ = 12.9; $\chi_\alpha^{\ 2}$=11.07]

2) A sample analysis of examination results of 500 students was made. It was found that 220 students have failed, 170 have scored a third class, 90 have secured a second class and the rest a first class so do these figures support the general belief that the above categories are in the ratio 4:3:2:1 respectively?

[Ans : χ^2 = 23.667]

3) Fit a Poisson distribution to the following data and test the goodness of fit.

x:	0	1	2	3	4	5	6
f:	275	72	30	7	5	2	1

[Ans: χ^2=40.938]

1.5.2 Chi-Square Test of Independence of Attributes

Let us consider two attributes A and B. A is divided in 'r' classes $A_1, A_2, \ldots A_r$ and B is divided in 's' classes $B_1, B_2, \ldots B_s$. If this expressed as r×s matrix, the matrix is called r × s contingency table.

Suppose A is divided into two classes and B is divided in two classes. The various cell frequencies can be expressed in the following table known as 2×2 contingence table.

		B		**Total**
		B_1	**B_2**	
A	**A_1**	a	b	a+b
	A_2	c	d	c+d
Total		a+c	b+d	a+b+c+d=N

The expected frequencies are given by

$E(a)=\dfrac{(a+b)(a+c)}{N}$	$E(b)=\dfrac{(a+b)(b+d)}{N}$	a+b
$E(c)=\dfrac{(a+c)(c+d)}{N}$	$E(d)=\dfrac{(b+d)(c+d)}{N}$	c+d
a+c	b+d	N=a+b+c+d

In this χ^2 test we test if two attributes A and B under consideration are independent or not.

Degrees of freedom d.f = (r–1) (s–1)

Where r – number of rows

s – number of columns

EXAMPLE

1) What are the expected frequencies of 2×2 contingency tables given below

(i)

a	b
c	d

(ii)

2	10
6	6

Solution:

(i) Observed frequencies

a	b	a+b
c	d	c+d
a+c	b+d	a+b+c+d=N

Expected frequencies

$\frac{(a+b)(a+c)}{N}$	$\frac{(a+b)(b+d)}{N}$	a+b
$\frac{(a+c)(c+d)}{N}$	$\frac{(b+d)(c+d)}{N}$	c+d
a+c	b+d	N

(ii) Observed frequencies

2	10	12
6	6	12
8	16	24

Expected frequencies

$\frac{8\times 12}{24}=4$	$\frac{16\times 12}{24}=8$	12
$\frac{8\times 12}{24}=4$	$\frac{16\times 12}{24}=8$	12
8	16	24

2) On the basis of information noted below, find out whether the new treatment is comparatively superior to the conventional one.

	Favourable	Non-Favourable	Total
Conventional	40	70	110
New	60	30	90
Total	100	100	200

Solution:

(i) H_0: The two treatments are independent.

H_1: The two treatments are dependent.

(ii) Level of significance α=5%

$$d.f=(r-1)(s-1)=(2-1)(2-1)=1$$

(iii) Critical value $\chi_{\alpha}^{2}=3.841$

(iv) Test statistic $\chi^2=\sum\frac{(O-E)^2}{E}$

The expected frequencies are

$\frac{110\times100}{200}=55$	$\frac{110\times100}{200}=55$
$\frac{90\times100}{200}=45$	$\frac{90\times100}{200}=45$

$$\therefore \quad \chi_\alpha^{\ 2}=\frac{(40-55)^2}{55}+\frac{(70-55)^2}{55}+\frac{(60-45)^2}{45}+\frac{(30-45)^2}{45}=18.1818$$

(v) Here $\chi^2 > \chi_\alpha^{\ 2}$

$\therefore$ H_0 is rejected and H_1 is accepted.

$\therefore$ The treatments are dependent.

3) From the following table regarding the colour of eyes of father and son. Test if the colour of son's eye is associated with that of the father.

		Eye Colour of son	
		Light	**Not Light**
Eye colour of father	**Light**	**471**	**51**
	Not light	**148**	**230**

Solution:

The observed frequencies are

		B		Total
		B_1	B_2	
A	A_1	471	51	522
	A_2	148	230	378
Total		619	281	900

The excepted frequencies are

		B		Total
		B_1	B_2	
A	A_1	$\frac{619\times522}{900}=359.02$	$\frac{289\times522}{900}=162.98$	522
	A_2	$\frac{619\times378}{900}=259.98$	$\frac{289\times378}{900}=118.02$	378
Total		619	281	900

(i) H_0: The colour of eyes of father and sons are independent.

H_1 : The colour of eyes of father and sons are dependent.

(ii) Level of significance α=5%

D.f = (r–1) (s –1) = (2 – 1)(2–1)=1.

(iii) Critical value $\chi_\alpha^2 = 3.841$

(iv).Test Statistic $\chi^2 = \sum \frac{(O-E)^2}{E}$

$$= \frac{(471-359.02)^2}{359.02} + \frac{(51-162.98)^2}{162.98} + \frac{(148-259.98)^2}{259.98} + \frac{(230-118.02)^2}{118.02}$$

=266.366

(v) Here $\chi^2 > \chi_\alpha^2$

∴ H_0 is rejected and H_1 is accepted.

∴ The colour of eyes of father and sons are dependent.

4) Two researchers A and B adopted different techniques while rating the students level. Can you say that the techniques adopted by them are significant?

Researches	Below average	Average	Above Average	Genius	Total
A	40	33	25	2	100
B	86	60	44	10	200
Total	126	93	69	12	300

Solution:

(i) H_0: There is no significant difference between the techniques of the two researches.

H_1: There is significant difference between the techniques of the two researches

(ii) Level of significance α=5%

d.f = (r–1) (s–1) = (2–1) (4–1) = 3

(iii) Critical value $\chi_\alpha^2 = 7.815$

(iv).Test Statistic $\chi^2 = \sum \frac{(O-E)^2}{E}$

The expected frequencies are

Researches	Below average	Average	Above Average	Genius	Total
A	$\frac{100\times126}{300}=42$	$\frac{100\times93}{300}=31$	$\frac{69\times100}{300}=23$	$\frac{12\times100}{300}=4$	100
B	$\frac{126\times200}{300}=84$	$\frac{200\times93}{300}=62$	$\frac{200\times69}{300}=46$	$\frac{12\times200}{300}=8$	200
Total	126	93	69	12	300

$$\chi^2=\frac{(40-42)^2}{42}+\frac{(33-31)^2}{31}+\frac{(25-23)^2}{23}+\frac{(2-4)^2}{4}$$

$$+\frac{(86-84)^2}{84}+\frac{(60-62)^2}{62}+\frac{(44-46)^2}{46}+\frac{(10-8)^2}{8}$$

$$=2.0971$$

(v) Here $\chi^2<\chi^2_\alpha$

$\therefore$ H_0 is accepted

$\therefore$ There is no significant difference between the techniques of two researchers.

5) 1000 students at college level were graded according to their IQ and their economic conditions. What conclusion can you draw from the following data?

Economic conditions	I.Q Level		Total
	High	Low	
Rich	460	140	600
Poor	240	160	400
Total	700	300	1000

Solution:

(i) H_0: The given attributes are independent

H_1: The attributes are dependent.

(ii) Level of significance α=5%

D.f = (r–1)(s–1) = (2–1) (2–1) =1

(iii) Critical value $\chi_\alpha{}^2=3.841$

(iv) Test statistic $\chi^2 = \sum \frac{(O-E)^2}{E}$

The expected frequencies are

Economic conditions	I.Q Level		Total
	High	Low	
Rich	$\frac{600\times700}{1000}=420$	$\frac{600\times300}{1000}=180$	600
Poor	$\frac{400\times700}{1000}=280$	$\frac{400\times300}{1000}=120$	400
Total	700	300	1000

$$\therefore \quad \chi^2 = \frac{(460-420)^2}{420} + \frac{(140-180)^2}{180} + \frac{(240-280)^2}{280} + \frac{(160-120)^2}{120}$$

$=31.7373$

(v) Here $\chi^2 > \chi_\alpha^2$

∴ H_0 is rejected and H_1 is accepted.

∴ The attributes are dependent.

6) Two sample polls of votes for two candidates A and B for a public office are taken one from among residents of rural areas. The results are given below. Examine whether the nature of the area is related to voting preference in this election.

Area\Votes	A	B	Total
Rural	**620**	**380**	**1000**
Urban	**550**	**450**	**1000**
Total	**1170**	**830**	**2000**

Solution:

(i) H_0: The attributes are independent

H_1: The attributes are dependent

(ii) Level of significance α=5%

D.f= (r–1) (s–1) = (2–1) (2–1) =1

(iii) Critical value $\chi_\alpha^2 = 3.841$

(iv) Test statistic $\chi^2 = \sum \frac{(O-E)^2}{E}$

The expected frequencies are

Area\Votes	A	B	Total
Rural	$\frac{1000\times1170}{2000}=585$	$\frac{1000\times830}{2000}=415$	1000
Urban	$\frac{1000\times1170}{2000}=585$	$\frac{1000\times830}{2000}=415$	1000
Total	1170	830	2000

$$\therefore \chi^2 = \frac{(620-585)^2}{585} + \frac{(380-415)^2}{415} + \frac{(550-585)^2}{585} + \frac{(450-415)^2}{415}$$

$=10.0916$

(v) Here $\chi^2 > \chi_\alpha^2$

$\therefore$ H_0 is rejected and H_1 is accepted.

$\therefore$ The attributes are dependent.

7) Using the data given in the following table to test at 0.01 level of significance whether a person's ability in Mathematics is independent of his/her interest in Statistics

		Ability in Mathematics		
		Low	**Average**	**High**
Interest in Statistics	**Low**	**63**	**42**	**15**
	Average	**58**	**61**	**31**
	High	**14**	**47**	**29**

Solution:

(i) H_0: Ability in Mathematics and interest in Statistics are independent.

H_1: They are dependent

(ii) Level of Significance α=1% =0.01 and d.f=(r–1)(s–1)=(3–1)(3–1)=4

(iii) Critical Value $\chi_\alpha^2 = 13.277$

(iv) Test Statistic $\chi^2_\alpha = \sum \frac{(O-E)^2}{E}$

The observed frequencies are

	Ability in Mathematics				
		Low	**Average**	**High**	**Total**
Interest in Statistics	**Low**	63	42	15	120
	Average	58	61	31	150
	High	14	47	29	90
	Total	135	150	75	360

The expected frequencies are

	Ability in Mathematics				
		Low	**Average**	**High**	**Total**
Interest in Statistics	**Low**	$\frac{120\times135}{360}=45$	$\frac{120\times150}{360}=50$	$\frac{120\times75}{360}=25$	120
	Average	$\frac{150\times135}{360}=56.25$	62.5	31.25	150
	High	$\frac{90\times135}{360}=33.75$	39.5	18.75	90
	Total	135	150	75	360

$$\therefore \chi^2 = \frac{(63-45)^2}{45} + \frac{(42-50)^2}{50} + \frac{(15-25)^2}{25} + \frac{(58-56.25)^2}{56.25} + \frac{(61-62.5)^2}{62.5} + \frac{(31-31.25)^2}{31.25} + \frac{(14-33.75)^2}{33.75} + \frac{(47-39.5)^2}{39.5} + \frac{(29-18.75)^2}{18.75}$$

$$= 32.14$$

(v) Here $\chi^2 > \chi^2_\alpha$

$\therefore$ H_0 is rejected and H_1 is accepted.

$\therefore$ They are dependent.

8) Given the following contingency table for hair colour and eye colour, find the value of χ^2. Is there a good association between the two?

	Hair Colour			
		Brown	**Black**	**Total**
Eye colour	**Blue**	**70**	**50**	**120**
	Grey	**80**	**20**	**100**
	Brown	**35**	**45**	**80**
	Total	**185**	**115**	**300**

Solution:

(i) H_0: There is a good association between hair colour & eye colour

H_1: There is no good association between hair and eye colour.

(ii) Level of Significance α=5% and d.f = (r–1)(s–1)=(3–1)(2–1)=2

(iii) Critical value $\chi^2_\alpha = 5.991$

(iv) Test Statistic $\chi^2_\alpha = \Sigma \dfrac{(O-E)^2}{E}$

The expected frequencies are

	Hair Colour			
		Brown	**Black**	**Total**
Eye colour	**Brown**	$\dfrac{185\times120}{200}=74$	$\dfrac{115\times120}{300}=46$	120
	Grey	$\dfrac{185\times100}{300}=61.67$	$\dfrac{115\times100}{300}=38.33$	100
	Brown	$\dfrac{185\times80}{300}=49.33$	$\dfrac{115\times80}{300}=30.67$	80
	Total	185	115	300

$$\therefore \chi^2 = \frac{(70-74)^2}{74}+\frac{(50-46)^2}{46}+\frac{(80-61.67)^2}{61.67}+$$
$$\frac{(20-38.33)^2}{38.33}+\frac{(35-49.33)^2}{49.33}+\frac{(45-30.67)^2}{30.67}$$
$$= 25.636$$

(v) Here $\chi^2 > \chi^2_\alpha$

$\therefore$ H_0 is rejected.

$\therefore$ There is no good association between hair colour and eye colour.

EXERCISE

1) The following table gives a classification of a sample of 160 plants of their flower colour and flatness of leaf.

	Flat leaves	Curled leaves	Total
White flower	99	36	135
Red Flower	20	5	25
Total	119	41	160

[Ans: χ^2 =0.4919]

2) From the following information, state whether the two attributes viz condition of house and condition of child are independent.

Condition of child	Condition of house		Total
	Clean	Dirty	
Clean	69	51	120
Fairly clean	81	20	101
Dirty	35	44	79
Total	185	115	300

[Ans: χ^2 =25.639]

3) From the data given below, compare the association between literacy and unemployment among males using χ^2-test. Total 250. Literate 100, unemployed 50, Literate and unemployed 30.

4) Given the following contingency table, for hair color and eye color. Find the values of χ^2. Is there good association between the two.

		Hair colour			Total
		Fair	Brown	Black	
Eye colour	Blue	15	5	20	40
	Grey	20	10	20	50
	Brown	25	15	20	60
	Total	60	30	60	150

[Ans: χ^2 =3.6458]

1.6 F- TEST (OR) SNEDECOR'S VARIANCE RATIO TEST

To test whether if there is any significant difference between two estimates of population variance. (or)

To test if the two samples have come from the same population, we use F-test. In this case, before applying the t-test for the significance of the difference of two means, we have to test the equality of population variance by using F-test.

Assumptions:

(i) The populations for each sample must be normally distributed.

(ii) The samples must be random and independent.

(iii) The ratio of σ_1^2 and σ_2^2 should be equal to 1 (or) greater than 1. That is why we take the large variance in the numerator of the ratio.

Applications:

F test is used to test.

(i) Whether two independent samples have been drawn from the normal populations with the same variance σ^2.

(ii) Whether the two independent estimates of the population variance are homogeneous or not.

Working Procedure

(i) $H_0: \sigma_1^2=\sigma_2^2$. i.e the two independent samples have been drawn from the normal population with the same variance. (or) there is no significant difference between population variance

$H_1:\sigma_1^2\neq\sigma_2^2$.

(ii) Test statistic $F=\frac{S_1^2}{S_2^2}$ if $S_1^2 > S_2^2$

(or) $F=\frac{S_2^2}{S_1^2}$ if $S_2^2 > S_1^2$

Where $S_1^2=\frac{n_1 s_1^2}{n_1-1}$ *and* $S_2^2=\frac{n_2 s_2^2}{n_2-1}$

s_1^2, s_2^2 are sample variances

(iii) Choose the appropriate level of significance, degrees of freedom d.f=(n_1-1, n_2-1).

(iv) Find the critical value F_α

(v) Compare the value of F with F_α

If $F< F_\alpha$ then H_0 is accepted.

If $F> F_\alpha$ then H_0 is rejected.

EXAMPLE

1) Test whether the samples could have come from the same normal population.

Solution:

If we want to test the samples from the same normal population, we have to test.

(a) The equality of population variances (using F-test)

(b) The equality of population means (using t-test).

(a) F-test:

Given $n_1=10$, $n_2=12$, $\overline{x_1}=15$, $\overline{x_2}=14$

$$\Sigma(x_1-\overline{x_1})^2=90, \qquad \Sigma(x_2-\overline{x_2})^2=108$$

$$\therefore \quad s_1^2=\frac{\Sigma(x_1-\overline{x_1})^2}{n_1}=\frac{90}{10}=9$$

$$s_2^2=\frac{\Sigma(x_2-\overline{x_2})^2}{n_2}=\frac{108}{12}=9$$

$$\therefore \quad S_1^2=\frac{n_1s_1^2}{n_1-1}=\frac{10\times 9}{10-1}=10$$

$$S_2^2=\frac{n_2s_2^2}{n_2-1}=\frac{12\times 9}{12-1}=9.8181$$

(i) $H_0: \sigma_1^2=\sigma_2^2$

$H_1: \sigma_1^2\neq\sigma_2^2$

(ii) Test Statistic $\quad F=\dfrac{S_1^2}{S_2^2} \qquad \left[\because S_1^2>S_2^2\right]$

$$=\frac{10}{9.8181}=1.019$$

(iii) Level of Significance $\alpha = 5\%$

D.f = $(n_1-1, n_2-1) = (9, 11)$

(iv) Critical value $F_\alpha = 2.90$

(v) Here $F < F_\alpha$

$\therefore$ H_0 is accepted.

(b) t-Test:

(i) $H_0: \mu_1 = \mu_2$

$H_1: \mu_1 \neq \mu_2$ [Two tailed Test]

(ii) Level of significance $\alpha = 5\%$

d.f = $n_1+n_2-2 = 20$

(iii) Critical value $t_\alpha = 2.086$

(iv) Test statistic $t = \dfrac{\overline{x_1} - \overline{x_2}}{\sqrt{S^2\left[\dfrac{1}{n_1} + \dfrac{1}{n_2}\right]}}$

Where $S^2 = \dfrac{n_1 s_1^2 + n_2 s_2^2}{n_1 + n_2 - 2} = \dfrac{10 \times 9 + 12 \times 9}{10 + 12 - 2} = 10.9$

$$\therefore \quad t = \frac{15-14}{\sqrt{10.9\left[\frac{1}{10} + \frac{1}{12}\right]}} = 0.707$$

(v) Here $|t| = 0.707$

$\therefore$ $|t| < t_\alpha$

$\therefore$ H_0 is accepted.

$\therefore$ The samples have come from the same normal population.

Note:

If F-test failed then t-test should not be used

2) In the sample of 8 observations, the sum of the squares of deviations of the sample values from the sample mean was 94.5 and in another sample of 10 observations, it was found to be 101.7. Test whether the difference of variance is significant.

Solutions:

Given $n_1=8$, $\Sigma(x_1-\overline{x_1})^2=94.5$

$n_2=10$, $\Sigma(x_2-\overline{x_2})^2=101.7$

(i) $H_0: \sigma_1^2=\sigma_2^2$ [The difference of variance is not Significant]

$H1: \sigma_1^2 \neq \sigma_2^2$

(ii) Test statistic $F=\frac{S_1^2}{S_2^2}$ if $S_1^2>S_2^2$

Where $S_1^2=\frac{n_1 s_1^2}{n_1-1}$, $S_2^2=\frac{n_2 s_2^2}{n_2-1}$

$$s_1^2=\frac{\Sigma(x_1-\overline{x_1})^2}{n_1}=\frac{94.5}{8}=11.8125$$

$$\therefore S_1^2=\frac{8\times 11.8125}{8-1}=13.5$$

$$s_2^2=\frac{\Sigma(x_2-\overline{x_2})^2}{n_2}=\frac{101.7}{10}=10.17$$

$$\therefore S_2^2=\frac{10\times 10.17}{10-1}=11.3$$

Here $S_1^2>S_2^2$

$$\therefore F=\frac{13.5}{11.3}=1.195$$

(iii) Level of Significance $\alpha=5\%$

$D.f=(n_1-1, n_2-1)=(7,9)$

(iv) Critical Value $F_\alpha=3.29$

(v) Here $F<F_\alpha$

$\therefore$ H_0 is accepted.

$\therefore$ The difference of variances is not significant.

3) Pumpkins were grown under two experimental conditions two random samples of 11 and 9 pumpkins show the sample standard deviations of their weights as 0.8 and 0.5 respectively. Assuming that the weight distributions are normal, test the hypothesis that the two variances are equal [use α=10%]

Solution:

Given $n_1=11$, $n_2=9$

$s_1=0.8$, $s_2=0.5$.

(i) H_0: The two variances are equal

H_1: The two variances are not equal.

(ii) W.K.T $S_1^2 = \frac{n_1 s_1^2}{n_1 - 1} = \frac{11 \times (0.8)^2}{10} = 0.704$

$$S_2^2 = \frac{n_2 s_2^2}{n_2 - 1} = \frac{9 \times (0.5)^2}{8} = 0.28125$$

Here $S_1^2 > S_2^2$

$\therefore$ Test Statistic $F = \frac{S_1^2}{S_2^2}$

$$= \frac{0.704}{0.28125} = 2.5$$

(iii) Level of Significance α=10% and d.f=(n_1-1, n_2-1)=(10, 8)

(iv) Critical value $F_\alpha = 3.25$

(v) Here $F < F_\alpha$

$\therefore$ H_0 is accepted.

$\therefore$ The two variances are equal.

4) From the following two sample values find out whether they have come from the same population.

Sample I	17	27	18	25	27	29	27	23	17
Sample II	16	16	20	16	20	17	15	21	

Solution:

If we want to test the samples have come from the same normal population, we have to find

(a) The equality of population variances [Using F-test]

(b) The equality population means [Using t-test]

(a) F-test:

Given n_1=9, n_2=8

(i) H_0: $\sigma_1^2=\sigma_2^2$

H_1: $\sigma_1^2\neq\sigma_2^2$

(ii) W.K.T $S_1^2 = \frac{n_1 s_1^2}{n_1 - 1}$ $\quad S_2^2 = \frac{n_2 s_2^2}{n_2 - 1}$

$$s_1^2 = \frac{\Sigma x_1^2}{n_1} - \left(\overline{x_1}\right)^2, \quad s_2^2 = \frac{\Sigma x_2^2}{n_2} - \left(\overline{x_2}\right)^2$$

										Total
x_1:	17	27	18	25	27	29	27	23	17	210
x_1^2:	289	729	324	625	729	841	729	529	289	5084
x_2:	16	16	20	16	20	17	15	21		141
x_2^2	256	256	400	256	400	289	225	441		2523

$$\therefore \quad \overline{x_1} = \frac{\Sigma x_1}{n_1} = \frac{210}{9} = 23.33$$

$$\overline{x_2} = \frac{\Sigma x_2}{n_2} = \frac{141}{8} = 17.63$$

$$\therefore \quad s_1^2 = \frac{5084}{9} - (23.33)^2 = 20.6$$

$$s_2^2 = \frac{2523}{8} - (17.63)^2 = 4.5581$$

$$\therefore \quad S_1^2 = \frac{9 \times 20.6}{9-1} = 23.175$$

$$S_2^2 = \frac{8 \times 4.5581}{8-1} = 5.2093$$

$$F = \frac{S_1^2}{S_2^2} = \frac{23.175}{5.2093} \qquad [\because S_1^2 > S_2^2]$$

$=4.4488$

(iii) Level of Significance $\alpha = 5\%$

D.f = $(n_1-1, n_2-1) = (8, 7)$

(iv) Critical value $F_\alpha = 3.73$

(v) Here $F > F_\alpha$

$\therefore$ H_0 is rejected.

$\therefore$ The population variances can not be taken as equal.

$\therefore$ t-test can not be applied here.

Hence they have not come from the same populations.

5) It is known that the mean diameters of rivets produced by two firms A and B are practically the same but the S.D may differ. For 22 rivets produced by firm A, the S.D is 2.9 mm, while for 16 rivets manufactured by firm B, the S.D is 3.8mm. Compute the statistic you would use to test whether the products of firm A have the same variability as those of firm B and test its significance.

Solution:

Given n_1=22, n_2=16, s_1=2.9, s_2=3.8.

(i) $H_0: \sigma_1^2=\sigma_2^2$

$H_1: \sigma_1^2\neq\sigma_2^2$

(iii) W.K.T $S_1^2 = \frac{n_1 s_1^2}{n_1 - 1}$ $\qquad S_2^2 = \frac{n_2 s_2^2}{n_2 - 1}$

$= \frac{22\times(2.9)^2}{22-1}$ $\qquad = \frac{16\times(3.8)^2}{15}$

$=8.8105$ $\qquad =15.403$

Here $S_2^2 > S_1^2$

$\therefore$ Test statistic $F = \frac{S_2^2}{S_1^2} = \frac{15.403}{8.8105} = 1.75$

(iii) Level of significance α=5%

$D.f=(n_2-1, n_1-1) = (15, 21)$

(iv) Critical value of F with (15, 21) d.f at 5% level of significance is 2.20. i.e, F_α=2.20.

(v) Here $F < F_\alpha$

$\therefore$ H_0 is accepted.

$\therefore$ The products of both the firms A and B have the same variability.

6) In a Laboratory experiment, two samples of blood gave the following results.

Sample Size	**10**	**12**
Sample mean	**15**	**14**
Sum of squares of deviations from mean	**90**	**108**

Test the equality of sample variances at 5% level of significance.

Solution:

Given $n_1=10$, $n_2=12$

$\overline{x_1}=15,\quad \overline{x_2}=14$

(i) $H_0: \sigma_1^2=\sigma_2^2$

$H_1: \sigma_1^2 \neq \sigma_2^2$

(ii) W.K.T $S_1^2=\dfrac{n_1 s_1^2}{n_1-1}$ and $S_2^2=\dfrac{n_2 s_1^2}{n_2-1}$

Where $s_1^2=\dfrac{\Sigma(x_1-\overline{x_1})^2}{n_1}=\dfrac{90}{10}=9$

$$s_2^2=\frac{\Sigma(x_2-\overline{x_2})^2}{n_2}=\frac{108}{12}=9$$

$$S_1^2=\frac{10\times 9}{9}=10$$

$$S_2^2=\frac{12\times 9}{11}=9.82$$

Here $S_1^2 > S_2^2$

$\therefore$ Test Statistic $F=\dfrac{S_1^2}{S_2^2}=\dfrac{10}{9.82}=1.018$

(iii) Level of Significance $\alpha=5\%$ and d.f $=(n_1-1, n_2-1)=(9,11)$

(iv) Critical value $F_\alpha=2.90$

(v) Here $F<F_\alpha$

$\therefore$ H_0 is accepted.

$\therefore$ The two experiments have same variances.

7) A group of 10 rats fed on diet A and another group of 8 rats fed on diet B, recorded the following increase in weight.

Diet A	5	6	8	1	12	4	3	9	6	10
Diet B	2	3	6	8	10	1	2	8		

Find if the variances are significantly different.

Solution:

Given $n_1=10$, $n_2=8$

(i) $H_0: \sigma_1^2=\sigma_2^2$

$H_1: \sigma_1^2 \neq \sigma_2^2$

(ii) W.K.T $S_1^2 = \frac{n_1 s_1^2}{n_1 - 1}$ $\qquad S_2^2 = \frac{n_2 s_2^2}{n_2 - 1}$

Where $s_1^2 = \frac{\Sigma x_1^2}{n_1} - \left(\overline{x_1}\right)^2, \quad s_2^2 = \frac{\Sigma x_2^2}{n_2} - \left(\overline{x_2}\right)^2$

											Total
x_1:	5	6	8	1	12	4	3	9	6	10	64
x_1^2:	25	36	64	1	144	16	9	81	36	100	512
x_2:	2	3	6	8	10	1	2	8			40
x_2^2	4	9	36	64	100	1	4	64			282

$$\overline{x_1} = \frac{\Sigma x_1}{n_1} = \frac{64}{10} = 6.4$$

$$\overline{x_2} = \frac{\Sigma x_2}{n_2} = \frac{40}{8} = 5$$

$$\therefore\ s_1^2 = \frac{512}{10} - (6.4)^2 = 10.24$$

and $$s_2^2 = \frac{282}{8} - (5)^2 = 10.25$$

$$\therefore\ S_1^2 = \frac{10 \times 10.24}{10 - 1} = 11.3777$$

$$S_2^2 = \frac{8 \times 10.25}{8 - 1} = 11.7143$$

Here $S_2^2 > S_1^2$

$$\therefore\ \text{Test statistic F} = \frac{S_2^2}{S_1^2} = \frac{11.7143}{11.3777} = 1.02958$$

(iii) Level of Significance $\alpha = 5\%$

D.f = $(n_2-1, n_1-1) = (7, 9)$

(iv) Critical value at 5% level of significance with (7, 9) d.f is F_α=3.29

(v) Here $F < F_\alpha$

$\therefore$ H_0 is accepted.

$\therefore$ The difference of variances is not significant.

8) Two horses A and B were tested according to the time (in seconds) to run a particular track with the following results.

Horse A	28	30	32	33	33	29	34
Horse B	29	30	30	24	27	29	

Test whether the two horses have the same capacity.

Solution:

Here n_1=7, n_2=6

(i) $H_0: \sigma_1^2=\sigma_2^2$

$H_1: \sigma_1^2\neq\sigma_2^2$

(ii) W.K.T $\quad S_1^2 = \dfrac{n_1 s_1^2}{n_1 - 1} \qquad S_2^2 = \dfrac{n_2 s_2^2}{n_2 - 1}$

Where $\quad s_1^2 = \dfrac{\Sigma x_1^2}{n_1} - \left(\overline{x_1}\right)^2, \quad s_2^2 = \dfrac{\Sigma x_2^2}{n_2} - \left(\overline{x_2}\right)^2$

								Total
x_1:	28	30	32	33	33	29	34	219
x_1^2:	784	900	1024	1089	1089	841	1156	6883
x_2:	29	30	30	24	27	29	–	169
x_2^2	841	900	900	576	729	841	–	4787

$$\overline{x_1} = \frac{\Sigma x_1}{n_1} = \frac{219}{7} = 31.28$$

$$\overline{x_2} = \frac{\Sigma x_2}{n_2} = \frac{169}{6} = 28.2$$

and $\quad s_1^2 = \dfrac{6883}{7} - (31.28)^2 = 4.8473$

$$s_2^2 = \frac{4787}{6} - (28.2)^2 = 2.5933$$

$$\therefore \quad S_1^{\,2} = \frac{7 \times 4.8473}{7-1} = 5.6552$$

$$S_2^{\,2} = \frac{6 \times 2.5933}{6-1} = 3.1119$$

Here $S_1^2 > S_2^2$

$$\therefore \quad \mathrm{F} = \frac{S_1^2}{S_2^2} = \frac{5.6552}{3.1119} = 1.8173$$

(iii) Level of Significance $\alpha = 5\%$

$$\mathrm{D.f} = (n_1 - 1, n_2 - 1) = (6, 5)$$

(iv) Critical value $F_\alpha = 4.95$

(v) Here $F < F_\alpha$

$\therefore$ H_0 is accepted.

$\therefore$ The two horses have same capacity.

Two random samples give the following results.

Sample	Size	Mean	Sum of squares of deviations from mean
I	10	15	90
II	12	14	108

EXERCISE

1) The following data relate to a random sample of government employees in two states of the Indian Union.

	State - I	State - II
Sample size	16	25
Mean monthly income of the employees	440	460
Variance	40	42

Test whether the sample come from the same normal Population.

[Ans: F = 1.05, |t| = 9.73]

2) The samples are drawn from the two normal populations. From the following data test whether the two samples have the same variance at 5% level

Sample I	60	65	71	74	76	82	85	87		
Sample II	61	66	67	85	78	63	85	86	88	91

[Ans: F = 1.467]

3) The nicotine contents in milligrams in two samples of tobacco were found to be as follows

Sample A	24	27	26	21	25	
Sample B	27	30	28	31	22	36

Can it be said that two samples come from same normal population.

[Ans: F=4.07, |t| = 1.92]

PART-A

QUESTIONS WITH ANSWERS

1) Define parameter and statistics.

Solution:

A Statistical measure obtained from the population is known as population parameter (or) parameter.

For example, Population mean (μ), population variance (σ^2) etc, are parameters

A statistical measure obtained from the sample is known as statistics (or) sample statistics.

For example, Sample mean ($\bar{x}$), sample variance (s^2) etc, are statistics.

2) Define Null and Alternate hypothesis

Solution:

Null hypothesis is a hypothesis of no difference and it is denoted by H_0.

Any hypothesis which is complementary to the null hypothesis H_0 is called an alternate hypothesis and it is denoted by H_1.

3) Define Type-I and Type –II error.

Solution:

Type –I error:

If H_0 is rejected, while it should have been accepted

Type- II Error:

If H_0 is accepted, while it should have been rejected.

4) Define critical region and level of significance.

Solution:

Critical region

A region corresponding to a test statistic in the sample space which tends to rejection of H_0 is called critical region or region of rejection.

Level of significance:

The probability that the value of the statistic lies in the critical region is called the level of significance.

5) State the procedure followed in testing of hypothesis.

Solution:

Procedure for testing of hypothesis are

(i) Null and Alternative hypothesis

(ii) Level of Significance α

(iii) Critical value

(iv) Test statistic

(v) Conclusion.

6) Write any two applications of t-test

Solution:

(i) It is used to test the significance of the difference of the mean of a random sample and the mean of the population.

(ii) It is used to test the significance of the difference between two sample means.

7) Define Chi-Square test for goodness of fit.

Solution:

χ^2 test of goodness of fit is a test whether difference between observed and expected frequencies are significant.

$$\text{Test Statistic} \quad \chi^2 = \Sigma \frac{(O-E)^2}{E}$$

Where O –Observed Frequency.

E –Expected Frequency.

8) Write any two applications of χ^2 distribution.

Solution:

(i) To test the goodness of fit.

(ii) To test the independence of attributes.

9) What are the expected frequencies of 2×2 contingency table

a	b
c	d

Solution:

Expected frequency table is

$\frac{(a+b)(a+c)}{N}$	$\frac{(a+b)(b+d)}{N}$
$\frac{(a+c)(c+d)}{N}$	$\frac{(c+d)(b+d)}{N}$

Where N=a+b+c+d

10) What is the value of χ^2 for a 2×2 contingency table

a	**b**
c	**d**

Solution:

$$\chi 2 = \frac{(a+b+c+d)(ad-bc)^2}{(a+c)(b+d)(a+b)(c+d)}$$

11) What are the uses of F-distribution?

Solution:

F-test is used to

(i) test whether the two independent samples have been drawn from the normal populations with the same variance σ^2.

(ii) test whether the two independent estimates of the population variances are homogeny or not

12) A sample of 100students is taken from a large population. The mean height of the students in this sample is 160cm. can it be reasonably regard that, in the population, the mean height is 165cm and the S.D is 10cm?

Solution:

Given n=100, μ=165, s=10, $\bar{x}$=160

(i) H_0: μ = 165

H_1: μ ≠ 165 [Two tailed test]

(ii) Level of significant α=5%

(iii) Critical value (or) table value is Z_α=1.96

(iv) Test statistic $Z = \frac{\bar{x}-\mu}{s/\sqrt{n}}$

$$= \frac{100 - 165}{10/\sqrt{100}} = -5$$

(v) Here $|Z| = 5$

$\therefore$ $|Z| > Z_\alpha$

$\therefore$ H_0 is rejected and H_1 is accepted.

13) In a large City A, 20%of a random sample of 900 school boys had a slight physical defect. In another large city B, 18.5 % of random sample of 1600 school boys had the same defect. Is the difference between the proportions significant.

Solution:

Given $n_1=900$, $n_2=1600$.

$$p_1 = \frac{20}{100} = 0.2, \qquad p_2 = \frac{18.5}{100} = 0.185$$

(i) H_0: $p_1 = p_2$

H_1: $p_1 \neq p_2$

(ii) Level of Significance $\alpha=5\%$

(iii) Critical value $Z_\alpha = 1.96$

(iv) Test Statistic $Z = \dfrac{p_1 - p_2}{\sqrt{pq\left(\dfrac{1}{n_1} + \dfrac{1}{n_2}\right)}}$

Where

$$p = \frac{n_1 p_1 + n_2 p_2}{n_1 + n_2}$$

$$= \frac{900(0.2) + 1600(0.185)}{900 + 1600}$$

$$= 0.1904$$

$$q = 1 - p = 1 - 0.1904 = 0.8096$$

$$\therefore Z = \frac{0.2 - 0.185}{\sqrt{(0.1904)(0.8096)\left[\dfrac{1}{900} + \dfrac{1}{1600}\right]}} = 0.9375$$

(v) Here $|Z|>Z_\alpha$

$\therefore$ H_0 is accepted.

$\therefore$ The difference between two proportions are not significant.

14) A sample of size, 13 gave an estimated population variance of 3.0, while another sample of size 15 gave an estimate of 2.5. Could both samples be from populations with the same variance?

Solution:

Given : $n_1=13$, $n_2=15$.

$S_1^2 = 3.0$, $S_2^2 = 2.5$

(i) H_0: The two variances are equal

H_1: The two variances are not equal

(ii) Test statistic $F = \frac{S_1^2}{S_2^2}$, $\left[\because S_1^2 > S_2^2\right]$

$$= \frac{3.0}{2.5} = 1.2$$

(iii) Level of Significance $\alpha=5\%$

d.f$=(n_1-1, n_2-1) = (12, 14)$

(iv) Critical value $F_\alpha = 2.53$

(v) Here $F < F_\alpha$

$\therefore$ H_0 is accepted.

$\therefore$ The two variances are equal.

UNIT - 2

DESIGN OF EXPERIMENTS

Basic Principles in the Design of Experiment

There are three basic principles of an experimental design. They are

1) Randomization
2) Replication
3) Local Control

Complete Block Designs

There are three such designs. They are

1) Completely Randomized design (CRD)
2) Randomized Block design (RBD)
3) Latin Square design (LSD)

2.1 ANALYSIS OF VARIANCE

Definition: In small samples, to test the single or equality of means of two populations, we use t-test. If there are more than two samples, t-test cannot be used. In such cases we use a new technique called Analysis of Variance. So the main aim of Analysis of Variance is to test the equality of several means. It is shortly written as ANOVA.

2.2 ONE –WAY CLASSIFICATION – COMPLETELY RANDOMIZED DESIGN (CRD)

Definition: It is a Design of Experiment in which treatments are allocated at random to the entire experimental units.

Working Procedure (One Way Classification CRD)

H_0 : There is no significant difference between the treatments.

H_1: There is significant difference between the treatments.

Step 1 : Find N i.e., The number of observations.

Step 2 : Find T i.e., The total value of all observations.

Step 3 : Find $\frac{T^2}{N}$ i.e., the correction factor.

Step 4 : Calculate the total sum of squares.

$$\text{TSS} = \Sigma X_1^2 + \Sigma X_2^2 + \ldots - \frac{T^2}{N}$$

Step 5 : Calculate the column /row sum of squares

$$\text{SSC} = \frac{(\Sigma X_1)^2}{n_1} + \frac{(\Sigma X_2)^2}{n_1} + \frac{(\Sigma X_3)^2}{n_1} + \ldots - \frac{T^2}{N}$$

Here n_1 is the number of elements in each column.

(or)

$$\text{SSR} = \frac{(\Sigma Y_1)^2}{n_2} + \frac{(\Sigma Y_2)^2}{n_2} + \frac{(\Sigma Y_3)^2}{n_2} + \ldots - \frac{T^2}{N}$$

Here n_2 is the number of elements in each row.

Step 6 : Find SSE = TSS – SSC

Step 7 : Prepare the ANOVA table to calculate F-ratio

Analysis of Variance Table

Source of Variation	**Sum of squares**	**Degrees of freedom**	**Mean sum of squares**	**Variance ratio**
Between columns	SSC	$c - 1$	$\text{MSC} = \frac{\text{SSC}}{c-1}$	$F = \frac{\text{MSC}}{\text{MSE}}$
Error	SSE	$N - c$	$\text{MSE} = \frac{\text{SSE}}{N-c}$	*(or)*
Total	TSS	$N - 1$		$F = \frac{\text{MSE}}{\text{MSC}}$

The F- ratio should be calculated in such a way that F>1

Step 8 : Find the table value

Step 9 : Conclusion

EXAMPLE

1) The following are the numbers of mistakes made in 5 successive days of 4 technicians working for a photographic laboratory :

Technician I (X_1)	Technician II (X_2)	Technician III (X_3)	Technician IV (X_4)
6	14	10	9
14	9	12	12
10	12	7	8
8	10	15	10
11	14	11	11

Test at the level of significance $\alpha = 0.01$, whether the difference among the 4 sample means, can be attributed to chance.

Solution :

H_0 : There is no significant difference between the technicians.

H_1: There is significant difference between the technicians.

X_1	X_2	X_3	X_4	Total	X_1^2	X_2^2	X_3^2	X_4^2
6	14	10	9	39	36	196	100	81
14	9	12	12	47	196	81	144	144
10	12	7	8	37	100	144	49	64
8	10	15	10	43	64	100	225	100
11	14	11	11	47	121	196	121	121
49	59	55	50	213	517	717	639	510

Step 1 : N=20

Step 2 : T=213

Step 3 : $\frac{T^2}{N} = \frac{(213)^2}{20} = 2268.45$

Step 4 : $\text{TSS} = \Sigma X_1^2 + \Sigma X_2^2 + \Sigma X_3^2 + \Sigma X_4^2 - \frac{T^2}{N}$

$= 517+717+639+510 - 2268.45 = 114.55$

Step 5 : $SSC = \frac{(\Sigma X_1)^2}{n_1} + \frac{(\Sigma X_2)^2}{n_1} + \frac{(\Sigma X_3)^2}{n_1} + \frac{(\Sigma X_4)^2}{n_1} - \frac{T^2}{N}$

$n_1 \rightarrow$ number of elements in each column.

$$= \frac{(49)^2}{5} + \frac{(59)^2}{5} + \frac{(55)^2}{5} + \frac{(50)^2}{5} - 2268.45$$

$$= 480.2 + 696.2 + 605 + 500 - 2268.45$$

$$= 12.95$$

Step 6 : SSE = TSS – SSC

$$= 114.55 - 12.95 = 101.6$$

Step 7 : ANOVA Table

Source of variation	**Sum of squares**	**Degrees of freedom**	**Mean sum of squares**	**Variance ratio**	**Table value at 1% level**
Between columns	SSC=12.95	c–1= 4–1 =3	$MSC=\frac{SSC}{c-1}$ $MSC=\frac{12.95}{3}$ MSC=4.317	$F_c=\frac{MSE}{MSC}$ $=\frac{6.35}{4.317}$ $=1.471>1$ Since $\frac{MSC}{MSE}<1$	$F_c(16,3)$ $=26.9$
Error	SSE=101.6	N–c=20–4 =16	$MSE=\frac{SSE}{N-c}$ $MSE=\frac{101.6}{16}$ MSE=6.35		
Total	TSS=114.55				

Step 8 : Conclusion

Cal Fc < Tab F_C , So we accept H_0 .

It is concluded that there is no significant difference between the technicians at 1% level of significance.

2) There are three main brands of a certain powder. A set of 120 sample values is examined and found to be allocated among four groups (A,B,C and D) and three brands (I,II,III) as shown under.

Brands	Groups			
	A	B	C	D
I	0	4	8	15
II	5	8	13	6
III	8	19	11	13

Is there any significant difference in brands preference? Answer at 5% level.

Solution :-

H_0 : There is no significant difference in brands.

H_1 : There is significant difference in brands.

Brands	Groups				Total	X_1^2	X_2^2	X_3^2	X_4^2
	A (X_1)	B (X_2)	C (X_3)	D (X_4)					
I (Y_1)	0	4	8	15	27	0	16	64	225
II (Y_2)	5	8	13	6	32	25	64	169	36
III (Y_3)	8	19	11	13	51	64	361	121	169
Total	13	31	32	34	110	89	441	354	430

Step 1 : N = 12

Step 2 : T=110

Step 3 : $\frac{T^2}{N} = \frac{(110)^2}{12} = 1008.3$

Step 4 : $TSS = \Sigma X_1^2 + \Sigma X_2^2 + \Sigma X_3^2 + \Sigma X_4^2 - \frac{T^2}{N}$

$= 89 + 441 + 354 + 430 - 1008.3$

$= 305.7$

Step 5 $SSR = \frac{(\Sigma Y_1)^2}{n_2} + \frac{(\Sigma Y_2)^2}{n_2} + \frac{(\Sigma Y_3)^2}{n_2} - \frac{T^2}{N}$

$n_2 \rightarrow$ No. of elements in each row.

$= \frac{(27)^2}{4} + \frac{(32)^2}{4} + \frac{(51)^2}{4} - 1008.3$

$= 182.25 + 256 + 650.25 - 1008.3$

$= 80.2$

Step 6 : SSE = TSS – SSR

$= 305.7 - 80.2$

SSE = 225.50

Step 7 : ANOVA Table

Source of Variation	Sum of Squares	d.f	Mean sum of Squares	Variance ratio	Table value at 5% level
between rows	SSR = 80.2	r–1=3–1= 2	$MSR=\frac{SSR}{r-1} = \frac{80.2}{2}$ MSR=40.1	$F_R=\frac{MSR}{MSE} = \frac{40.1}{20.06}$ $F_R=1.999$	$F_R(2,9)=4.26$
Error	SSE = 225.5	N–r =12–3 = 9	$MSE=\frac{SSE}{N-r} = \frac{225.5}{9}$ MSE=20.06		
Total	TSS = 305.7				

Step 8 : Conclusion :

Cal F_R < Tab F_R, so we accept H_0.

3) The following table shows the lives in hours of four brands of electric lamps.

Brand A :	1610	1610	1650	1680	1700	1720	1800	
B :	1580	1640	1640	1700	1750			
C :	1460	1550	1600	1620	1640	1660	1740	1820
D :	1510	1520	1530	1570	1600	1680		

Perform an analysis of variance test the homogeneity of the mean lives of the four brands of Lamps.

Solution :-

H_0: There is no significant difference between the four brands.

H_1: There is significant difference between the four brands.

Subtract 1600 and then divide by 10, we get

X_1 A	X_2 B	X_3 C	X_4 D	Total	X_1^2	X_2^2	X_3^2	X_4^2
1	–2	–14	–9	–24	1	4	196	81
1	4	–5	–8	–8	1	16	25	64
5	4	0	–7	2	25	16	0	49
8	10	2	–3	17	64	100	4	9
10	15	4	0	29	100	225	16	0
12	–	6	8	26	144	–	36	64
20	–	14	–	34	400	–	196	–
–	–	22	–	22	–	–	484	–
57	31	29	–19	98	735	361	957	267

Step 1 : N=26

Step 2 : T = 98

Step 3 : $\frac{T^2}{N} = \frac{9604}{26} = 369.39$

Step 4 : $TSS = \Sigma X_1^2 + \Sigma X_2^2 + \Sigma X_3^2 + \Sigma X_4^2 - \frac{T^2}{N}$

$= 735 + 361 + 957 + 267 - 369.39$

$= 1950.61$

Step 5 : $SSC = \frac{(\Sigma X_1)^2}{n_1} + \frac{(\Sigma X_2)^2}{n_1} + \frac{(\Sigma X_3)^2}{n_1} + \frac{(\Sigma X_4)^2}{n_1} - \frac{T^2}{N}$

n_1 → number of elements in corresponding column.

$= \frac{(57)^2}{7} + \frac{(31)^2}{5} + \frac{(29)^2}{8} + \frac{(-19)^2}{6} - 369.39$

$= \frac{3249}{7} + \frac{961}{5} + \frac{841}{8} + \frac{361}{6} - 369.39$

$= 464.14 + 192.2 + 105.13 + 60.17 - 369.39 = 452.25$

Step 6 : SSE = TSS – SSC

$= 1950.61 - 452.25 = 1498.36$

Step 7 : ANOVA TABLE

Source of Variation	Sum of Squares	d.f	Mean sum of Square	Variance ratio	Table value at 5% level
Between columns	SSC = 452.25	$c-1$ $=4-1$ $=3$	$MSC=\frac{SSC}{c-1}$ $=\frac{452.25}{3}$ MSC=150.75	$F_C=\frac{MSE}{MSC}$ $=\frac{150.75}{68.11}$ =2.21>1	$F_c(3, 22)=3.05$
Error	SSE= 1498.36	$N-c$ $=26-4$ $=22$	$MSE=\frac{SSE}{N-c}$ $=\frac{1498.36}{22}$ MSE=68.11	Since MSE< MSC	
Total	TSS = 1950.61				

Step 8 : Conclusion.

Cal F_c < Tab F_c, so we accept H_0.

4) A completely randomised design experiment with 10 plots and 3 treatments gave the following result.

Plat no:	1	2	3	4	5	6	7	8	9	10
Treatment:	A	B	C	A	C	C	A	B	A	B
Yield:	5	4	3	7	5	1	3	4	1	7

Solution:

H_0 : There is no significant difference among the average yields in the three treatments.

H_1: There is significant difference among the average yields in the three treatments.

Treatments	Yields from pots			
A	5	7	3	1
B	4	4	7	–
C	3	5	1	–

X_1	X_2	X_3	Total	X_1^2	X_2^2	X_3^2
5	4	3	12	25	16	9
7	4	5	16	49	16	25

	3	7	1	11	9	49	1
	3	7	1	11	9	49	1
	1	–	–	1	1	–	–
Total	16	15	9	**40**	84	81	35

Step 1: N=10

Step 2: T= 40

Step 3: $C.F = \frac{T^2}{N} = \frac{1600}{10} = 160$

Step 4: $TSS = \sum X_1^2 + \sum X_2^2 + \sum X_3^2 - \frac{T^2}{N}$

$= 84 + 81 + 35 - 160$

$= 40$

Step 5: $SSC = \frac{(\sum X_1)^2}{n_1} + \frac{(\sum X_2)^2}{n_1} + \frac{(\sum X_3)^2}{n_1} - \frac{T^2}{N}$

$= \frac{(16)^2}{4} + \frac{(15)^2}{3} + \frac{(9)^2}{3} - 160$

$= 6$

Step 6: $SSF = TSS - SSC$

$= 40 - 6$

$= 34$

Step 7: ANOVA TABLE

Source of variation	**Sum of squares**	**Degrees of freedom**	**Mean sum of squares**	**Variance ratio (F)**	**Table value (F_α)**
Between Columns	SSC = 6	c–1=2	$MSC = \frac{SSC}{d.f}$ =3	$F = \frac{MSF}{MSC}$ =1.62	$F_\alpha(7,2)$ =19.35
Error	SSE = 34	N–c=10–3 =7	$MSF = \frac{SSF}{d.f}$ =4.86		
Total	TSS = 40				

Step 8: Here $F_c < F_\alpha$

$\therefore$ H_0 is accepted.

$\therefore$ The treatments are not significant.

5) Four machines A,B,C and D are used to produce a certain kind of cotton fabric. Sample of size 4 with each unit as 100 square meters are selected from the output of the machines at random and the number of flows is each 100 square meters is counted with the following result.

A	B	C	D
8	6	14	20
9	8	12	22
11	10	18	25
12	4	9	23

Do you think that there is a significance difference in the performance of the four machines ? test at 1% level of significance.

Solution:

H_0: There is no significance difference in the performance of the four machines.

H_1: There is significance difference in the performance of the four machines.

	X_1	X_2	X_3	X_4	Total	X_1^2	X_2^2	X_3^2	X_4^2
	8	6	14	20	48	64	36	196	400
	9	8	12	22	51	81	64	144	484
	11	10	18	25	64	121	100	324	625
	12	4	9	23	48	144	16	84	529
Total	40	28	53	90	**211**	410	216	745	2038

Step 1: N = 16

Step 2: T = 211

Step 3: $C.F = \frac{T^2}{N} = 2782.56$

Step 4: $TSS = \Sigma X_1^2 + \Sigma X_2^2 + \Sigma X_3^2 + \Sigma X_4^2 - \frac{T^2}{N}$

$= 410 + 216 + 745 + 2038 - 2782.56$

$= 626.44$

Step 5: $SSC = \frac{(\Sigma X_1)^2}{n_1} + \frac{(\Sigma X_2)^2}{n_1} + \frac{(\Sigma X_3)^2}{n_1} + \frac{(\Sigma X_4)^2}{n_1} - \frac{T^2}{N}$

$= \frac{(40)^2}{4} + \frac{(28)^2}{4} + \frac{(53)^2}{4} + \frac{(90)^2}{4} - 2782.56$

$= 540.69$

Step 6: $SSF = TSS - SSC$

$= 626.44 - 540.69$

$= 85.75$

Step 7: ANOVA TABLE

Source of variation	Sum of squares	Degrees of freedom	Mean sum of squares	Variance ratio (F)	Table value (F_α)
Between Columns	SSC = 540.69	c–1=3	$MSC = \frac{SSC}{d.f}$ =180.23	$F = \frac{MSC}{MSE}$ =25.207	$F_\alpha(3,12)$ =5.95
Error	SSE = 85.75	N–c=12	$MSE = \frac{SSE}{d.f}$ =7.15		
Total	TSS = 626.44				

Step 8: Here $F > F_\alpha$

∴ H_0 is rejected and H_1 is accepted.

∴ There is a significant difference in the performance of four machines.

6) **In order to determine there is significant difference in the durability of 3 makes of computers, samples of size 5 are selected from each make and the frequency of repair during the first year of purchase is observed. The results are as follows.**

Makes	Values of x_i				
A	5	6	8	9	7
B	8	10	11	12	4
C	7	3	5	4	1

Perform analysis of variance and state your conclusion.

Solution:

H_0: There is no significant difference in the durability of 3 makes of computers

H_1: There is significant difference in the durability of 3 makes of computers.

	X_1	X_2	X_3	Total	X_1^2	X_2^2	X_3^2
	5	8	7	20	25	64	49
	6	10	3	19	36	100	9
	8	11	5	24	64	121	25
	9	12	4	25	81	144	16
	7	4	1	12	49	16	1
Total	35	45	20	**100**	255	445	100

Step 1: N = 15

Step 2: T =100

Step 3: $C.F = \frac{T^2}{N} = \frac{(100)^2}{15} = 666.67$

Step 4: $TSS = \Sigma X_1^2 + \Sigma X_2^2 + \Sigma X_3^2 - \frac{T^2}{N}$

$$= 255 + 445 + 100 - 666.67$$

$$= 133.33$$

Step 5: $SSC = \frac{(\Sigma X_1)^2}{n_1} + \frac{(\Sigma X_2)^2}{n_1} + \frac{(\Sigma X_3)^2}{n_1} - \frac{T^2}{N}$

$$= \frac{(35)^2}{5} + \frac{(45)^2}{5} + \frac{(20)^2}{5} - 666.67$$

$$= 63.33$$

Step 6: $SSF = TSS - SSC$

$$= 133.33 - 63.33$$

$$= 70$$

Step 7: ANOVA TABLE

Source of variation	Sum of squares	Degrees of freedom	Mean sum of squares	Variance ratio (F)	Table value (F_α)
Between Columns	SSC = 63.33	c–1=2	$MSC = \frac{SSC}{d.f}$ =31.67	$F = \frac{MSC}{MSE}$ =5.43	$F_\alpha(7,2)$ =3.88
Error	SSE = 70	N–c=12	$MSE = \frac{SSE}{d.f}$ =5.83		
Total	TSS = 133.33				

Step 8: Here $F > F_\alpha$

$\therefore$ H_0 is rejected and H_1 is accepted.

$\therefore$ There is significant difference in the durability of 3 makes of computers.

EXERCISE

1) A set of data involving 4 tropical food stuffs A,B,C,D tried on 20 chicks is given below. All the 20 chicks are treated alike in all respects expect the feeding treatments and each feeding treatment is given to 5 chicks. Analyze the data.

A	55	49	42	21	52
B	61	112	30	89	63
C	42	97	81	95	92
D	169	137	169	85	154

2) Weekly sales in Rs., in small shops in 3 towns, A, B and C are as follows

A :	620	600	740	800	
B :	410	380	350		
C :	920	870	1040	1030	1010

Can we conclude that the shops in the 3 towns have the same average sales? Test at 5% level.

2.3 TWO-WAY CLASSIFICATIONS – RANDOMIZED BLOCK DESIGN (RBD)

Definition : If the given experimental area is not homogenous, it can be divided into many subgroups which are homogenous among themselves. Such groups are called Blocks. If the treatments are applied at random to these blocks, this design is known as Randomized Block Design (RBD).

Working Procedure : (Two – Way Classification, RBD)

H_0 : There is no significant difference

H_1 : There is significant difference

Step 1: Find N

Step 2 : Find T

Step 3 : Find $\frac{T^2}{N}$

Step 4 : Find TSS

Step 5 : Find SSC

Step 6 : Find SSR

Step 7 : SSE = TSS – SSC - SSR

Step 8 : Prepare the ANOVA Table.

Source of Variation	Sum of Squares	Degrees of freedom	Mean sum of Squares	Variance ratio
Column treatments	SSC	(c–1)	$MSC=\frac{SSC}{c-1}$	$F_c=\frac{MSC}{MSE}$
Row treatments	SSR	(r–1)	$MSR=\frac{SSR}{r-1}$	$F_R=\frac{MSR}{MSE}$
Error	SSE	(N–c-r+1)	$MSE=\frac{SSE}{(N-c-r+1)}$	
Total	TSS	rc–1		

Note: The F- ratios Fc, FR are calculated in a such way that they are each greater than one.

For example, if $\frac{MSC}{MSE}<1$, then take $F_c=\frac{MSE}{MSC}$

Step 9 : Find Table F_C and F_R

Step10 : Conclusion.

EXAMPLE

1) An experiment was designed to study the performance of 4 different detergents for cleaning fuel injectors. The following "Cleanliness" readings were obtained with specially designed equipment for 12 tanks of gas distributed over 3 different modes of engines.

	Engine 1	Engine 2	Engine 3	Total
Detergent A	45	43	51	139
Detergent B	47	46	52	145
Detergent C	48	50	55	153
Detergent D	42	37	49	128
Total	182	176	207	565

Perform the ANOVA and test at 0.01 level of significance, whether there are differences in the detergents or in the engines.

Solution :

The above data are classified according to criteria (i) Detergent (ii) Engine.

In order to simplify calculations, we code the data by subtracting 50 from each figure.

Detergent	Engine			Total	X_1^2	X_2^2	X_3^2
	(X_1)	(X_2)	(X_3)				
A (Y_1)	–5	–7	1	–11	25	49	1
B (Y_2)	–3	–4	2	–5	9	16	4
C (Y_3)	–2	0	5	3	4	0	25
D (Y_4)	–8	–13	–1	–22	64	169	1
Total	–18	–24	7	–35	102	234	31

1) H_0 : There is no significant difference between Detergents and Engines

2) H_1: There is significant difference between Detergents and Engines.

Step 1 : N = 12 [Total Number of entries]

Step 2 : T = –35

Step 3 : $\frac{T^2}{N} = \frac{(-35)^2}{12} = 102.08$

Step 4 : $TSS = \Sigma X_1^2 + \Sigma X_2^2 + \Sigma X_3^2 - \frac{T^2}{N}$

$= (102) + (234) + (31) - 102.08$

$= 367 - 102.08 = 264.92$

Step 5 : $SSC = \frac{(\Sigma X_1)^2}{n_1} + \frac{(\Sigma X_2)^2}{n_1} + \frac{(\Sigma X_3)^2}{n_1} - \frac{T^2}{N}$

($n_1 \rightarrow$ No of elements in each column)

$= \frac{(-18)^2}{4} + \frac{(-24)^2}{4} + \frac{(7)^2}{4} - 102.08$

$= 81 + 144 + 12.25 - 102.08 = 135.17$

Step 6 : $SSR = \frac{(\Sigma Y_1)^2}{n_2} + \frac{(\Sigma Y_2)^2}{n_2} + \frac{(\Sigma Y_3)^2}{n_2} + \frac{(\Sigma Y_4)^2}{n_2} - \frac{T^2}{N}$

($n_2 \rightarrow$ No of elements in each row)

$$= \frac{(-11)^2}{3} + \frac{(-5)^2}{3} + \frac{(3)^2}{3} + \frac{(-22)^2}{3} - 102.08$$

$$= 40.33 + 8.33 + 3 + 161.33 - 102.08$$

$$SSR = 110.91$$

Step 7 :

$$SSE = TSS - SSC - SSR$$

$$= 264.92 - 135.17 - 110.91$$

$$SSE = 18.84$$

Step 8 : Table of Analysis of Variance

Source of Variation	**Sum of Squares**	**Degree of freedom**	**Mean sum of Squares**	**Variance ratio**	**Table value at 1% level**
Between Columns	SSC = 135.17	c–1 = 3–1=2	$MSC=\frac{SSC}{c-1}$ $=\frac{135.17}{2}$ MSC=67.585	$F_C=\frac{MSC}{MSE}$ $=\frac{67.585}{3.14}$ F_C=21.52	$F_c(2,6)$ = 10.92
Between Rows	SSR = 110.91	r–1 = 4–1 =3	$MSR=\frac{SSR}{r-1}$ $=\frac{110.91}{3}$ MSR=36.97	$F_R=\frac{MSR}{MSE}$ $=\frac{36.97}{3.14}$ F_R=11.77	$F_R(3,6)$ = 9.78
Error	SSE = 18.84	N–-c-r+1 = 12–3-4+1 = 6	$MSE=\frac{SSE}{N-c-r+1}$ $=\frac{18.84}{6}$ MSE=3.14		
Total	TSS = 264.92	rc–1=3×4–1 =11			

Step 8 : Conclusion

Cal F_c > Table F_c, so we reject H_0.

Cal F_R > Table F_R, so we reject H_0.

2) Analyse the following RBD and find your conclusion.

		Treatments			
Blocks		T_1	T_2	T_3	T_4
	B_1	12	14	20	22
	B_2	17	27	19	15
	B_3	15	14	17	12
	B_4	18	16	22	12
	B_5	19	15	20	14

Solution :-

H_0 : There is no significant difference between blocks and treatments.

H_1 : There is significant difference between blocks and treatments

Subtract 15 from each number we get

	X_1	X_2	X_3	X_4	Total	X_1^2	X_2^2	X_3^2	X_4^2
Y_1	–3	–1	5	7	8	9	1	25	49
Y_2	2	12	4	0	18	4	144	16	0
Y_3	0	–1	2	–3	–2	0	1	4	9
Y_4	3	1	7	–3	8	9	1	49	9
Y_5	4	0	5	–1	8	16	0	25	1
Total	6	11	23	0	40	38	147	119	68

Step 1 : N= 20

Step 2 : T = 40

Step 3 : $\frac{T^2}{N} = \frac{(40)^2}{20} = 80$

Step 4 : $TSS = \Sigma X_1^2 + \Sigma X_2^2 + \Sigma X_3^2 + \Sigma X_4^2 - \frac{T^2}{N}$

$= 38 + 147 + 119 + 68 - 80$

TSS= 292

Step 5 : $SSC = \frac{(\Sigma X_1)^2}{n_1} + \frac{(\Sigma X_2)^2}{n_1} + \frac{(\Sigma X_3)^2}{n_1} + \frac{(\Sigma X_4)^2}{n_1} - \frac{T^2}{N}$

($n_1 \rightarrow$ No of elements in each column)

$$= \frac{(6)^2}{5} + \frac{(11)^2}{5} + \frac{(23)^2}{5} + 0 - 80$$

SSC = 57.2

Ste 6 : $$SSR = \frac{(\Sigma Y_1)^2}{n_2} + \frac{(\Sigma Y_2)^2}{n_2} + \frac{(\Sigma Y_3)^2}{n_2} + \frac{(\Sigma Y_4)^2}{n_2} + \frac{(\Sigma Y_5)^2}{n_2} - \frac{T^2}{N}$$

($n_2 \rightarrow$ No of elements in each row)

$$= \frac{8^2}{4} + \frac{18^2}{4} + \frac{(-2)^2}{4} + \frac{8^2}{4} + \frac{8^2}{4} - 80$$

SSR = 50

Step 7 : SSE = TSS – SSC – SSR

= 292 – 57.2 – 50

SSE = 184.8

Step 8 : ANOVA Table

Source of Variation	**Sum of Squares**	**Degree of freedom**	**Mean sum of Squares**	**Variance ratio**	**Table value at 1% level**
Between Columns	SSC = 57.2	c–1 = 4–1=3	$MSC = \frac{SSC}{c-1} = \frac{57.2}{3}$ MSC=19.1	$F_C = \frac{MSC}{MSE} = \frac{19.1}{15.4}$ F_C=1.24	F_c (3,12) = 3.49
Between Rows	SSR = 50	r–1 = 5–1 =4	$MSR = \frac{SSR}{r-1} = \frac{50}{4}$ MSR=12.5	$F_R = \frac{MSE}{MSR} = \frac{15.4}{12.5}$ F_R =1.23	F_R (12,4) = 5.91
Error	SSE = 184.8	N-c-r+1 = 20-4–5+1 = 12	$MSE = \frac{SSE}{N-c-r+1} = \frac{184.8}{12}$ MSE=15.4		
Total	TSS = 292				

Step 9 : Conclusion.

Cal Fc < Table Fc, so we accept H_0.

Cal F_R < Table F_R, so we accept H_0.

3) Four varieties A,B,C,D of a fertilizer are tested in a randomized block design with 4 replications. The plot yields in pounds are as follows :-

Column Row	1	2	3	4
1	A (12)	D (20)	C (16)	B (10)
2	D (18)	A (14)	B (11)	C (14)
3	B (12)	C (15)	D (19)	A (13)
4	C (16)	B (11)	A (15)	D (20)

Analyse the experimental yield.

Solution :-

Calculation of correction factor

Variety	Block				Total Varieties	X_1^2	X_2^2	X_3^2	X_4^2
	1 (X_1)	2 (X_2)	3 (X_3)	4 (X_4)					
A	12	14	15	13	54	144	196	225	169
B	12	11	11	10	44	144	121	121	100
C	16	15	16	14	61	256	225	256	196
D	18	20	19	20	77	324	400	361	400
	58	60	61	57	236	868	942	963	865

H_0 : Four varieties are similar

H_1 : Four varieties are not similar

Step 1 : N = 16

Step 2 : T = 236

Step 3 : $\frac{T^2}{N} = \frac{(236)^2}{16} = 3481$

Step 4 : $TSS = \Sigma X_1^2 + \Sigma X_2^2 + \Sigma X_3^2 + \Sigma X_4^2 - \frac{T^2}{N}$

$= 868 + 942 + 963 + 865 - 3481$

$\text{TSS} = 157$

Step 5 : Sum of squares between columns (SSC)

$$\text{SSC} = \frac{(\Sigma X_1)^2}{n_1} + \frac{(\Sigma X_2)^2}{n_1} + \frac{(\Sigma X_3)^2}{n_1} + \frac{(\Sigma X_4)^2}{n_1} - \frac{T^2}{N}$$

($n_1 \rightarrow$ No of elements in each column)

$$= \frac{(58)^2}{4} + \frac{(60)^2}{4} + \frac{(61)^2}{4} + \frac{(57)^2}{4} - 3481$$

$$= 841 + 900 + 930 + 812 - 3481$$

$$= 2$$

Step 6 : $$\text{SSR} = \frac{(\Sigma Y_1)^2}{n_2} + \frac{(\Sigma Y_2)^2}{n_2} + \frac{(\Sigma Y_3)^2}{n_2} + \frac{(\Sigma Y_4)^2}{n_2} - \frac{T^2}{N}$$

($n_2 \rightarrow$ No of elements in each row)

$$= \frac{(54)^2}{4} + \frac{(44)^2}{4} + \frac{(61)^2}{4} + \frac{(77)^2}{4} - 3481$$

$$= \frac{2916}{4} + \frac{1936}{4} + \frac{3721}{4} + \frac{5929}{4} - 3481$$

$$= 729 + 484 + 930.25 + 1482.25 - 3481$$

$\text{SSR} = 144.5$

Step 7 : $\text{SSE} = \text{TSS} - \text{SSC} - \text{SSR}$

$= 157 - 2 - 144.5$

$\text{SSE} = 10.5$

Step 8 : ANOVA Table

Source of Variation	**Sum of Squares**	**Degree of freedom**	**Mean sum of Squares**	**Variance ratio**	**Table value at 5% level**
Between Columns	SSC = 2	c–1 = 3	$\text{MSC} = \frac{\text{SSC}}{c-1}$ $= \frac{2}{3}$ MSC=0.67	$F_c = \frac{\text{MSE}}{\text{MSC}}$ $= \frac{1.17}{0.67}$ $F_c = 1.75$	Fc (9,3) = 8.81

Between Rows	SSR = 144.5	r–1 = 3	$MSR=\frac{SSR}{r-1}$ $=\frac{144.5}{3}$ MSR=48.17	$F_R=\frac{MSR}{MSE}$ $=\frac{48.17}{1.17}$ F_R=41.17	F_R (3,9) = 3.86
Error	SSE = 10.5	N–c-r+1 = 9	$MSE=\frac{SSE}{N-c-r+1}$ $=\frac{10.5}{9}$ MSE=1.17		
Total	TSS = 157				

Step 9 : Conclusion.

Cal Fc < Table Fc, so we accept H_0.

Cal F_R > Table F_R, so we reject H_0.

4) The following data represent the number of units production per day turned out by different workers, using 4 different types of machines.

		Machine type			
Workers		**A**	**B**	**C**	**D**
	1	44	38	47	36
	2	46	40	52	43
	3	34	36	44	32
	4	43	38	46	33
	5	38	42	49	39

Test whether the five men differ with respect to mean productivity and test whether the mean productivity is the same for the four different machine types.

Solution :

Code the data by subtracting 40 from each value.

	X_1	X_2	X_3	X_4	Total	X_1^2	X_2^2	X_3^2	X_4^2
Y_1	4	–2	7	–4	5	16	4	49	16
Y_2	6	0	12	3	21	36	0	144	9
Y_3	–6	–4	4	–8	–14	36	16	16	64
Y_4	3	–2	6	–7	0	9	4	36	49
Y_5	–2	2	9	–1	8	4	4	81	1
Total	5	-6	38	–17	T = 20	101	28	326	139

H_0 : There is no significant difference between workers and machine types.

H_1 : There is significant difference between workers and machine types.

Step 1 : $N = 20$

Step 2 : $T = 20$

Step 3 : $\frac{T^2}{N} = \frac{400}{20} = 20$

Step 4 : $TSS = \Sigma X_1^2 + \Sigma X_2^2 + \Sigma X_3^2 + \Sigma X_4^2 - \frac{T^2}{N}$

$= 101 + 28 + 326 + 139 - 20$

$TSS = 574$

Step 5 : $SSC = \frac{(\Sigma X_1)^2}{n_1} + \frac{(\Sigma X_2)^2}{n_1} + \frac{(\Sigma X_3)^2}{n_1} + \frac{(\Sigma X_4)^2}{n_1} - \frac{T^2}{N}$

$= \frac{5^2}{5} + \frac{(-6)^2}{5} + \frac{(38)^2}{5} + \frac{(-17)^2}{5} - 20$

$= 5 + 7.2 + 288.8 + 57.8 - 20$

$= 338.8$

Step 6 : $SSR = \frac{(\Sigma Y_1)^2}{n_2} + \frac{(\Sigma Y_2)^2}{n_2} + \frac{(\Sigma Y_3)^2}{n_2} + \frac{(\Sigma Y_4)^2}{n_2} + \frac{(\Sigma Y_5)^2}{n_2} - \frac{T^2}{N}$

($n_2 \rightarrow$ No of elements in each row)

$= \frac{5^2}{4} + \frac{(21)^2}{4} + \frac{(-14)^2}{4} + \frac{0^2}{4} + \frac{8^2}{4} - 20$

$= \frac{25}{4} + \frac{441}{4} + \frac{196}{4} + \frac{64}{4} - 20$

$= 6.25 + 110.25 + 49 + 16 - 20$

$SSR = 161.5$

Step 7 : $SSE = TSS - SSC - SSR$

$= 574 - 338.8 - 161.5$

$SSE = 73.7$

Step 8 : ANOVA Table

Source of Variation	Sum of Squares	Degree of freedom	Mean sum of Squares	Variance ratio	Table value at 5% level
Between Columns	SSC = 338.8	c–1 = 4–1=3	$MSC=\frac{SSC}{c-1}$ $=\frac{338.8}{3}$ MSC=112.933	$F_C=\frac{MSC}{MSE}$ $=\frac{112.933}{6.142}$ F_C=18.38	F_C (3,12) = 3.49
Between Rows	SSR = 161.5	r–1 = 5–1 = 4	$MSR=\frac{SSR}{r-1}$ $=\frac{161.5}{4}$ MSR=40.375	$F_R=\frac{MSR}{MSE}$ $=\frac{40.375}{6.142}$ F_R=6.574	F_R (4,12) = 3.26
Error	SSE = 73.7	N–c–r+1 = 12	$MSE=\frac{SSE}{N-c-r+1}$ $=\frac{73.7}{2}$ MSR=6.142		
Total	TSS = 574				

Step 9 : Conclusion.

Cal Fc > Table Fc, so we reject H_0.

Cal F_R > Table F_R, so we reject H_0.

5) Four different, though supposedly equivalent, forms of a standardized reading achievements test were given to each of 5 students, and the following are the score which they obtained.

	Student				
Form	**1**	**2**	**3**	**4**	**5**
A	**75**	**73**	**59**	**69**	**84**
B	**83**	**72**	**56**	**70**	**92**
C	**86**	**61**	**53**	**72**	**88**
D	**73**	**67**	**62**	**79**	**95**

Perform a two – way analysis of variance to test at the level of significance α=0.01, whether it is reasonable to treat the four forms as equivalent.

Solution:

H_0: There is no significant difference between forms and students.

H_1: There is significant difference between forms and students.

Code the data by subtracting 80from each value.

	X_1	X_2	X_3	X_4	X_5	Total	X_1^2	X_2^2	X_3^2	X_4^2	X_5^2
Y_1	–5	–7	–21	–11	4	–40	25	49	441	121	16
Y_2	3	–8	–24	–10	12	–27	9	64	576	100	144
Y_3	6	–19	–27	–8	8	–40	36	361	729	64	64
Y_4	–7	–13	–18	–1	15	–24	49	169	324	1	225
Total	–3	–47	–90	–30	39	**–131**	119	643	2070	286	449

Step 1: $N = 20$

Step 2: $T = -131$

Step 3: $C.F = \frac{T^2}{N} = \frac{(-131)^2}{20} = 858.05$

Step 4: $TSS = \Sigma X_1^2 + \Sigma X_2^2 + \Sigma X_3^2 + \Sigma X_4^2 + \Sigma X_5^2 - \frac{T^2}{N}$

$$= 119 + 643 + 2070 + 286 + 449 - 858.05$$
$$= 2708.95$$

Step 5: $SSC = \frac{(\Sigma X_1)^2}{n_1} + \frac{(\Sigma X_2)^2}{n_1} + \frac{(\Sigma X_3)^2}{n_1} + \frac{(\Sigma X_4)^2}{n_1} + \frac{(\Sigma X_5)^2}{n_1} - \frac{T^2}{N}$

$$= \frac{(-3)^2}{4} + \frac{(-47)^2}{4} + \frac{(-90)^2}{4} + \frac{(-30)^2}{4} + \frac{(39)^2}{4} - 858.05$$
$$= 2326.7$$

Step 6: $SSR = \frac{(\Sigma Y_1)^2}{n_2} + \frac{(\Sigma Y_2)^2}{n_2} + \frac{(\Sigma Y_3)^2}{n_2} + \frac{(\Sigma Y_4)^2}{n_2} - \frac{T^2}{N}$

$$= \frac{(-40)^2}{5} + \frac{(-27)^2}{5} + \frac{(-40)^2}{5} + \frac{(-24)^2}{5} - 858.05$$
$$= 42.95$$

Step 7: $SSF = TSS - SSC - SSR$

$= 2708.95 - 42.95 - 2326.7$

$= 339.30$

Step 8: ANOVA TABLE

Source of variation	Sum of squares	Degrees of freedom	Mean sum of squares	Variance ratio (F)	Table value (F_α)
Between Columns	2326.7	c–1=5–1=4	581.675	$F_c = \frac{MSC}{MSE}$ =20.572	$F_\alpha(4,12)$ =5.41
Between Rows	42.95	r–1=4–1=3	14.317	$F_R = \frac{MSE}{MSR}$ =1.975	$F_\alpha(12,3)$ =27.05
Error	339.30	N–c–r+1=12	28.275		
Total	2708.95	19			

Step 9:

(i) Here calculates F_c < Table value of F_c

∴ H_0 is accepted and the means for the students are not the same.

(ii) Here calculated F_R < Table value of F_R.

∴ H_0 is accepted and there is no form effect.

6) To study the performance of three detergents and three different water temperatures, the following whiteness readings were obtained with specially designed equipment.

Water Temp	Detergent A	Detergent B	Detergent C
Cold water	57	55	67
Warm water	49	52	68
Hot water	54	46	58

Perform a two-way analysis of variance, using 5% level of significance.

Solution:

H_0: There is no significant difference between detergents and water temperatures

H_1: There is significant difference between detergents and water temperatures.

Code the data by subtracting each value by 50.

	X_1	X_2	X_3	Total	X_1^2	X_2^2	X_3^2
Y_1	7	5	17	29	49	25	289
Y_2	–1	2	18	19	1	4	324
Y_3	4	–4	8	8	16	16	64
Total	10	3	43	**56**	66	45	677

Step 1: N = 9

Step 2: T = 56

Step 3: $C.F = \frac{T^2}{N} = 348.44$

Step 4: $TSS = \sum X_1^2 + \sum X_2^2 + \sum X_3^2 - \frac{T^2}{N}$

$$= 66 + 45 + 677 - 348.44$$
$$= 439.56$$

Step 5: $SSC = \frac{(\sum X_1)^2}{n_1} + \frac{(\sum X_2)^2}{n_1} + \frac{(\sum X_3)^2}{n_1} - \frac{T^2}{N}$

$$= \frac{(10)^2}{3} + \frac{(3)^2}{3} + \frac{(43)^2}{3} - 348.44$$
$$= 304.22$$

Step 6: $SSR = \frac{(\sum Y_1)^2}{n_2} + \frac{(\sum Y_2)^2}{n_2} + \frac{(\sum Y_3)^2}{n_2} - \frac{T^2}{N}$

$$= \frac{(29)^2}{3} + \frac{(19)^2}{3} + \frac{(8)^2}{3} - 348.44$$
$$= 73.55$$

Step 7: $SSF = TSS - SSC - SSR$

$$= 439.56 - 304.22 - 73.55$$
$$= 61.79$$

Step 8: ANOVA TABLE

Source of variation	Sum of squares	Degrees of freedom	Mean sum of squares	Variance ratio (F)	Table value (F_α)
Between Columns	304.22	c–1=2	152.11	$F_c = \frac{MSC}{MSE}$ =9.85	$F_\alpha(2,4)$ =6.94
Between Rows	73.55	r–1=2	36.775	$F_R = \frac{MSE}{MSR}$ =2.38	$F_\alpha(2,4)$ =6.94
Error	61.79	N–c–r+1=4	15.445		
Total	439.56	8			

Step 9:

(i) Here calculated $F_c >$ table value of F_c .

$\therefore$ H_0 is rejected and H_1 is accepted.

$\therefore$ There is significant difference between the detergents.

(ii) Here calculated $F_R <$ table value of F_R.

$\therefore$ H_0 is accepted

$\therefore$ There is no significant difference between water temperatures.

EXERCISE

1) Set up two-way ANOVA Table for the data given below without any interpretation.

Plots of Land	**Treatment**			
	A	**B**	**C**	**D**
I	**30**	**27**	**31**	**30**
II	**35**	**30**	**29**	**31**
III	**34**	**32**	**35**	**28**

Use coding method su1btracting 30 from the given numbers.

2) A tea company appoints four salesman A,B,C and D and observes their sales in three Seasons – Summer, Winter and Monsoon. The figures (in lakhs) are given in the following table.

Seasons	Salesmen				Season's Total
	A	B	C	D	
Summer	36	36	21	35	128
Winter	28	29	31	32	120
Monsoon	26	28	29	29	112
Salesmen's Total	90	93	81	96	360

(i) Do the salesmen significanty differ in performance ?

(ii) Is there significant difference between the seasons ?

3) Three varieties A,B and C of a crop are tested in a randomized block design with four replications. The plot yield in pounds are as follows :-

A	6	C	5	A	8	B	9
C	8	A	4	B	6	C	9
B	7	B	6	C	10	A	6

Analyse the experimental yield and state your conclusion.

4) Four doctors each test four treatments for a certain disease and observe the no. of days each patient takes to recover. The results are as follows. (Recovery time in days)

Doctor	Treatment			
	1	2	3	4
A	10	14	19	20
B	11	15	17	21
C	9	12	16	19
D	8	13	17	20

Discuss the difference between (a) doctors and (b) treatment

2.4 LATIN SQUARE DESIGN (LSD)

Definition :- The design of experiment having equal number of replications and treatments is known as Latin Square Design. Here the data is classified in the form of a square matrix. It controls the experimental error in two perpendicular directions.

Working Rule :

Step 1: Find N

Step 2 : Find T

Step 3 : Find $\frac{T^2}{N}$

Step 4 : Find TSS

Step 5 : Find SSC

Step 6 : Find SSR,

Step7: Find SSK

Step 8: Find SSE

Step 9 : ANOVA Table

Step 10 : Conclusion

Preparation of ANOVA Table

Source of Variation	Sum of Squares	Degree of freedom	Mean Sum of Squares	Variance ratio
Between Columns	SSC	K–1	$MSC=\frac{SSC}{K-1}$	$F_C=\frac{MSC}{MSE}$
Between Rows	SSR	K–1	$MSR=\frac{SSR}{K-1}$	$F_R=\frac{MSR}{MSE}$
Between treatments	SSK	K–1	$MSK=\frac{SSK}{K-1}$	$F_T=\frac{MSK}{MSE}$
Error	SSE	(K–1)(K–2)	$MSE=\frac{SSE}{(K-1)(K-2)}$	
Total	TSS	K^2-1		

The F-ratios F_C, F_R, F_T are calculated in a such way that they are each greater than one.

For eg, if $\frac{MSC}{MSE} < 1$, then take $F_C=\frac{MSE}{MSC}$.

EXAMPLE

1) The following is a Latin Square of a design, when 4 varieties of seeds are being tested. Set up the analysis of variance table and state your conclusion . You may carry out suitable change of origin and scale.

A	105	B	95	C	125	D	115
C	115	D	125	A	105	B	105
D	115	C	95	B	105	A	115
B	95	A	135	D	95	C	115

Solution :

Subtract 100 and then divide by 5, we get

A	1	B	–1	C	5	D	3
C	3	D	5	A	1	B	1
D	3	C	–1	B	1	A	3
B	–1	A	7	D	–1	C	3

H_0 : There is no significant difference

H_1 : There is significant difference

	X_1	X_2	X_3	X_4	Total	X_1^2	X_2^2	X_3^2	X_4^2
Y_1	1	–1	5	3	8	1	1	25	9
Y_2	3	5	1	1	10	9	25	1	1
Y_3	3	–1	1	3	6	9	1	1	9
Y_4	–1	7	–1	3	8	1	49	1	9
Total	6	10	6	10	T = 32	20	76	28	28

Step 1 : N = 16

Step 2 : T = 32

Step 3 : $\frac{T^2}{N} = \frac{(32)^2}{16} = 64$

Step 4 : $TSS = \Sigma X_1^2 + \Sigma X_2^2 + \Sigma X_3^2 + \Sigma X_4^2 - \frac{T^2}{N}$

$$= 20 + 76 + 28 + 28 - 64 = 88$$

TSS = 88

Step 5 $SSC = \frac{(\Sigma X_1)^2}{n_1} + \frac{(\Sigma X_2)^2}{n_1} + \frac{(\Sigma X_3)^2}{n_1} + \frac{(\Sigma X_4)^2}{n_1} - \frac{T^2}{N}$

($n_1 \rightarrow$ No of elements in each column)

$$= \frac{6^2}{4} + \frac{10^2}{4} + \frac{6^2}{4} + \frac{10^2}{4} - 64$$

$$= 9 + 25 + 9 + 25 - 64$$

$$SSC = 4$$

Step 6 $SSR = \frac{(\Sigma Y_1)^2}{n_2} + \frac{(\Sigma Y_2)^2}{n_2} + \frac{(\Sigma Y_3)^2}{n_2} + \frac{(\Sigma Y_4)^2}{n_2} - \frac{T^2}{N}$

($n_2 \rightarrow$ No of elements in each row)

$$= \frac{8^2}{4} + \frac{10^2}{4} + \frac{6^2}{4} + \frac{8^2}{4} - 64$$

$$= 16 + 25 + 9 + 16 - 64$$

$$SSR = 2$$

Step 7 : To find SSK

Arrange the elements in the order of treatments.

					Total
A	1	1	3	7	12
B	–1	1	1	–1	0
C	5	3	–1	3	10
D	3	5	3	–1	10

$$SSK = \frac{(12)^2}{4} + \frac{0^2}{4} + \frac{(10)^2}{4} + \frac{(10)^2}{4} - \frac{T^2}{N}$$

$$= 36 + 0 + 25 + 25 - 64$$

$$SSK = 22$$

Step 8 : $SSE = TSS - SSC - SSR - SSK$

$$= 88 - 4 - 2 - 22$$

$$SSE = 60$$

Step 9 : ANOVA Table

Source of Variation	Sum of Squares	Degree of freedom	Mean sum of Squares	Variance ratio	Table value at 5% level
Between Rows	SSR = 2	K–1=3	$MSR=\frac{SSR}{K-1}$ $=0.67$	$F_R=\frac{MSR}{MSE}$ $=\frac{10}{0.67}$ $F_R=14.9$	$F_R(6,3)$ = 8.94
Between Columns	SSC = 4	K–1=3	$MSC=\frac{SSC}{K-1}$ $=1.33$	$F_C=\frac{MSE}{MSC}$ $=\frac{10}{1.33}$ $F_C=7.52$	$F_C(6,3)$ = 8.94
Between treatments	SSK=22	K–1=3	$MSK=\frac{SSK}{K-1}$ $=7.33$	$F_T=\frac{MSE}{MSK}$ $=\frac{10}{7.33}$ $F_T=1.36$	$F_T(6,3)$ = 8.94
Error	SSE=60	(K–1) (K–2)= 6	$MSE=\frac{SSE}{(K-1)(K-2)}$ $=10$		
Total	TSS=88	15			

Step 10 : Conclusion.

Here Cal Fc < Table Fc, so we accept H_0.

Cal F_R > Table F_R, so we reject H_0.

Cal F_T < Table F_T, so we accept H_0.

2) A farmer wishes to test the effects of four different fertilizers A,B,C,D on the yield of wheat. In order to eliminate sources of error due to variability in soil fertility he uses the fertilizers in a Latin Square arrangement as indicated in the following table, where the numbers indicate yields in bushels per unit area.

A 18	C 21	D 25	B 11
D 22	B 12	A 15	C 19
B 15	A 20	C 23	D 24
C 22	D 21	B 10	A 17

Perform an analysis of variance to determine, If there is a significant difference between the fertilizers at $\alpha = 0.05$ level of significance.

Solution : -

Subtract 20 we get

A	–2	C	1	D	5	B	-9
D	2	B	-8	A	-5	C	-1
B	-5	A	0	C	3	D	4
C	2	D	1	B	-10	A	-3

H_0 : There is no significant difference

H_1 : There is significant difference

	X_1	X_2	X_3	X_4	**Total**	X_1^2	X_2^2	X_3^2	X_4^2
Y_1	–2	1	5	–9	–5	4	1	25	81
Y_2	2	–8	–5	–1	–12	4	64	25	1
Y_3	–5	0	3	4	2	25	0	9	16
Y_4	2	1	–10	–3	–10	4	1	100	9
Total	–3	–6	–7	–9	–25	37	66	159	107

Step 1 : N = 16

Step 2 : T = –25

Step 3 : $\frac{T^2}{N} = \frac{(-25)^2}{16} = \frac{625}{16} = 39.06$

Step 4 : $TSS = \Sigma X_1^2 + \Sigma X_2^2 + \Sigma X_3^2 + \Sigma X_4^2 - \frac{T^2}{N}$

$= 37 + 66 + 159 + 107 - 39.06$

$= 369 - 39.06 = 329.94$

TSS = 329.94

Step 5 : $SSC = \frac{(\Sigma X_1)^2}{n_1} + \frac{(\Sigma X_2)^2}{n_1} + \frac{(\Sigma X_3)^2}{n_1} + \frac{(\Sigma X_4)^2}{n_1} - \frac{T^2}{N}$

($n_1 \rightarrow$ No of elements in each column)

$$= \frac{9}{4} + \frac{36}{4} + \frac{49}{4} + \frac{81}{4} - 39.06$$

$$= \frac{175}{4} - 39.06 = 4.69$$

SSC = 4.69

Step 6 : $SSR = \frac{(\Sigma Y_1)^2}{n_2} + \frac{(\Sigma Y_2)^2}{n_2} + \frac{(\Sigma Y_3)^2}{n_2} + \frac{(\Sigma Y_4)^2}{n_2} - \frac{T^2}{N}$

($n_2 \rightarrow$ No of elements in each row)

$$= \frac{(-5)^2}{4} + \frac{(-12)^2}{4} + \frac{(2)^2}{4} + \frac{(-10)^2}{4} - 39.06$$

$$= \frac{273}{4} - 39.06 = 29.19$$

SSR = 29.19

Step 7 : To find SSK

Arrange the elements in the order of treatments.

					Total
A	–2	–5	0	–3	–10
B	–9	–8	–5	–10	–32
C	1	–1	3	2	5
D	5	2	4	1	12

$$SSK = \frac{(-10)^2}{4} + \frac{(-32)^2}{4} + \frac{(5)^2}{4} + \frac{(12)^2}{4} - \frac{T^2}{N}$$

$$= \frac{100}{4} + \frac{1024}{4} + \frac{25}{4} + \frac{144}{4} - 39.06$$

SSK = 284.19

Step 7 : SSE = TSS – SSC – SSR - SSK

= 329.94 – 4.69 – 29.19 – 284.19

SSE = 11.87

Step 8 : ANOVA Table

Source of Variation	Sum of Squares	Degree of freedom	Mean sum of Squares	Variance ratio	Table value at 5% level
Between Rows	SSR = 29.19	K–1=3	$MSR=\frac{SSR}{K-1}$ $=9.73$	$F_R=\frac{MSR}{MSE}$ $F_R=4.91$	$F_R(3,6)$ $=4.76$
Between Columns	SSC = 4.69	K–1=3	$MSC=\frac{SSC}{K-1}$ $=1.56$	$F_C=\frac{MSE}{MSC}$ $F_C=1.26$	$F_C(6,3)$ $=8.94$
Between treatments	SSK=284.19	K–1=3	$MSK=\frac{SSK}{K-1}$ $=94.73$	$F_T=\frac{MSK}{MSE}$ $F_T=47.8$	$F_T(3,6)$ $=4.76$
Error	SSE=11.87	(K–1)(K–2)= 6	$MSE=\frac{SSE}{(K-1)(K-2)}$ $=1.98$		
Total	TSS=329.94	15			

Step 10 : Conclusion.

Here Cal Fc < Table Fc, so we accept H_0.

Cal F_R > Table F_R, so we reject H_0.

Cal F_T > Table F_T, so we reject H_0.

3) In a Latin Square experiment given below are the yields in quintals per acre on the paddy crop carried out for testing the effect of five fertilizers A,B,C,D,E. Analyze the data for variations.

B	25	A	18	E	27	D	30	C	27
A	19	D	31	C	29	E	26	B	23
C	28	B	22	D	33	A	18	E	27
E	28	C	26	A	20	B	25	D	33
D	32	E	25	B	23	C	28	A	20

Solution :

It is a 5×5 Latin Square. Let us subtract 25 from all the items.

	X_1	X_2	X_3	X_4	X_5	Total	X_1^2	X_2^2	X_3^2	X_4^2	X_5^2
Y_1	0	–7	2	5	2	2	0	49	4	25	4
Y_2	–6	6	4	1	–2	3	36	36	16	1	4
Y_3	3	–3	8	–7	2	3	9	9	64	49	4
Y_4	3	1	–5	0	8	7	9	1	25	0	64
Y_5	7	0	–2	3	–5	3	49	0	4	9	25
Total	7	–3	7	2	5	18	103	95	113	84	101

H_0 : There is no significant difference

H_1 : There is significant difference

Step 1 : N = 25

Step 2 : T = 18

Step 3 : $\frac{T^2}{N} = \frac{(18)^2}{25} = 12.96$

Step 4 : $TSS = \Sigma X_1^2 + \Sigma X_2^2 + \Sigma X_3^2 + \Sigma X_4^2 + \Sigma X_5^2 - \frac{T^2}{N}$

$= 103 + 95 + 113 + 84 + 101 - 12.96$

$TSS = 483.04$

Step 5 : $SSC = \frac{(\Sigma X_1)^2}{n_1} + \frac{(\Sigma X_2)^2}{n_1} + \frac{(\Sigma X_3)^2}{n_1} + \frac{(\Sigma X_4)^2}{n_1} + \frac{(\Sigma X_5)^2}{n_1} - \frac{T^2}{N}$

($n_1 \rightarrow$ No of elements in each column)

$= \frac{49}{5} + \frac{9}{5} + \frac{49}{5} + \frac{4}{5} + \frac{25}{5} - 12.96$

$SSC = 14.24$

Step 6 : $SSR = \frac{(\Sigma Y_1)^2}{n_2} + \frac{(\Sigma Y_2)^2}{n_2} + \frac{(\Sigma Y_3)^2}{n_2} + \frac{(\Sigma Y_4)^2}{n_2} + \frac{(\Sigma Y_5)^2}{n_2} - \frac{T^2}{N}$

($n_2 \rightarrow$ No of elements in each row)

$= \frac{4}{5} + \frac{9}{5} + \frac{9}{5} + \frac{49}{5} + \frac{9}{5} - 12.96$

$SSR = 3.04$

Step 7 : To find SSK

Arrange the elements in the order of treatments.

Treatment	1	2	3	4	5	Total
A	–6	–7	–5	–7	–5	–30
B	0	–3	–2	0	–2	–7
C	3	1	4	3	2	13
D	7	6	8	5	8	34
E	3	0	2	1	2	8

$$SSK = \frac{1}{5}[(-30)^2 + (-7)^2 + (13)^2 + (34)^2 + (8)^2] - \frac{T^2}{N}$$

$$= \frac{1}{5}[900 + 49 + 169 + 1156 + 64] - 12.96$$

$$= 454.64$$

Step 7 : SSE = TSS – SSC – SSR - SSK

= 483.04 – 14.24 – 3.04 – 454.64

SSE = 11.12

Step 8 : ANOVA Table

Source of Variation	**Sum of Squares**	**Degree of freedom**	**Mean sum of Squares**	**Variance ratio**	**Table value at 5% level**
Between Columns	SSC = 14.24	K–1=5–1=4	$MSC = \frac{SSC}{K-1}$ $= \frac{14.24}{4}$ $= 3.56$	$F_C = \frac{MSC}{MSE}$ $= \frac{3.56}{0.927}$ $F_C = 3.84$	F_C (4,12) = 3.26
Between Rows	SSR = 3.04	K–1=5–1=4	$MSR = \frac{SSR}{K-1}$ $= \frac{3.04}{4}$ $= 0.76$	$F_R = \frac{MSE}{MSR}$ $= \frac{0.927}{0.76}$ $F_R = 1.22$	F_R (12,4) = 5.91
Between treatments	SSK=454.64	K–1=5–1=4	$MSK = \frac{SSK}{K-1}$ $= \frac{454.64}{4}$ $= 113.66$	$F_T = \frac{MSK}{MSE}$ $= \frac{113.66}{0.927}$ $F_T = 122.6$	F_T (4,12) = 3.26

Error	SSE=11.12	(K–1) (K–2) = 12	$MSE=\frac{SSE}{(K-1)(K-2)}$ $=\frac{11.12}{12}=0.927$		
Total	TSS=483.04	24			

Step 10 : Conclusion.

Here Cal Fc > Table Fc, (There is significant difference)

Cal F_R < Table F_R, (There is no significant difference)

Cal F_T > Table F_T, (There is significant difference)

4) The following is the Latin square design when four varieties of seeds are tested. Setup the analysis of variance and state your conclusion.

D122 A121 C122 B122

B124 C123 A122 D125

A120 B119 D120 C121

C122 D123 B121 A122

Solution:

H_0 : There is no significant difference.

H_1 : There is significant difference.

We subtract 120 from given values

	X_1	X_2	X_3	X_4	Total	X_1^2	X_2^2	X_3^2	X_4^2
Y_1	2	1	3	2	8	4	1	9	4
Y_2	4	3	2	5	14	16	9	4	25
Y_3	0	–1	0	1	0	0	1	0	1
Y_4	2	3	1	2	8	4	9	1	4
Total	8	6	6	10	**30**	24	20	14	34

Step 1: N = 16

Step 2: T = 30

Step 3: $C.F=\frac{T^2}{N}=56.25$

Step 4: $\text{TSS} = \Sigma X_1^2 + \Sigma X_2^2 + \Sigma X_3^2 + \Sigma X_4^2 - \frac{T^2}{N}$

$$= 24 + 20 + 14 + 34 - 56.25$$
$$= 35.75$$

Step 5: $\text{SSC} = \frac{(\Sigma X_1)^2}{n_1} + \frac{(\Sigma X_2)^2}{n_1} + \frac{(\Sigma X_3)^2}{n_1} + \frac{(\Sigma X_4)^2}{n_1} - \frac{T^2}{N}$

$$= \frac{(8)^2}{4} + \frac{(6)^2}{4} + \frac{(6)^2}{4} + \frac{(10)^2}{4} - 56.25$$
$$= 2.75$$

Step 6: $\text{SSR} = \frac{(\Sigma Y_1)^2}{n_2} + \frac{(\Sigma Y_2)^2}{n_2} + \frac{(\Sigma Y_3)^2}{n_2} + \frac{(\Sigma Y_4)^2}{n_2} - \frac{T^2}{N}$

$$= \frac{(8)^2}{4} + \frac{(14)^2}{4} + \frac{(0)^2}{4} + \frac{(8)^2}{4} - 56.25$$
$$= 24.75$$

Step 7: To find SSK

Arrange the elements in the order of treatments.

					Total
A	1	2	0	2	5
B	2	4	–1	1	6
C	3	3	1	2	9
D	2	5	0	3	10

$$\text{SSK} = \frac{(\Sigma A)^2}{n_3} + \frac{(\Sigma B)^2}{n_3} + \frac{(\Sigma C)^2}{n_3} + \frac{(\Sigma D)^2}{n_3} - \frac{T^2}{N}$$

$$\therefore \text{SSK} = \frac{(5)^2}{4} + \frac{(6)^2}{4} + \frac{(9)^2}{4} + \frac{(10)^2}{4} - 56.25$$
$$= 4.25$$

Step 8: SSE = TSS – SSC –SSR–SSK

$$= 35.75 – 2.75 – 24.75 – 4.25$$

$$=4$$

Step 9: ANOVA TABLE

Source of variation	Sum of squares	Degrees of freedom	Mean sum of squares	Variance ratio (F)	Table value (F_α)
Between Columns	SSC = 2.75	c–1=3	$MSC=\frac{SSC}{d.f}$ =0.92	$F_c=\frac{MSC}{MSE}$ =1.373	$F_\alpha(3,6)$ =4.76
Between Rows	SSR = 24.75	r–1=2	$MSR=\frac{SSR}{d.f}$ =8.25	$F_R=\frac{MSR}{MSE}$ =12.313	$F_\alpha(3,6)$ =4.76
Between Treatments	SSK = 4.25	k–1= 3	$MSK=\frac{SSK}{d.f}$ =1.42	$F_T=\frac{MSK}{MSE}$ =2.119	$F_\alpha(3,6)$ =4.76
Error	SSE = 4	(k–1)(k–2) =6	$MSE=\frac{SSE}{d.f}$ =0.67		
Total	TSS = 35.75	15			

Step: 10

(i) Here calculated F_C < Table value of F_C

∴ H_0 is accepted..

∴ There is no significant difference between columns

(ii) Here calculated F_R > Table value of F_R

∴ H_0 is rejected and H_1 is accepted.

∴ There is significant difference between rows.

(iii) Here calculated F_T < Table value of F_T

∴ H_0 is accepted.

∴ There is no significant difference between treatments.

5) Analysis the variance in the following Latin square.

A16	**B17**	**C20**
B16	**C21**	**A15**
C15	**A12**	**B13**

Solution:

H_0 : There is no significance difference.

H_1 : There is significance difference.

We subtract the values by 15.

	X_1	X_2	X_3	Total	X_1^2	X_2^2	X_3^2
Y_1	1	2	5	8	1	4	25
Y_2	1	6	0	7	1	36	0
Y_3	0	–3	–2	–5	0	9	4
Total	2	6	3	**10**	2	49	29

Step 1: N = 9

Step 2: T = 10

Step 3: $C.F = \frac{T^2}{N} = 11.11$

Step 4: $TSS = \Sigma X_1^2 + \Sigma X_2^2 + \Sigma X_3^2 - \frac{T^2}{N}$

$$= 2 + 49 + 29 - 11.11$$

$$= 68.89$$

Step 5: $SSC = \frac{(\Sigma X_1)^2}{n_1} + \frac{(\Sigma X_2)^2}{n_1} + \frac{(\Sigma X_3)^2}{n_1} - \frac{T^2}{N}$

$$= \frac{(2)^2}{3} + \frac{(5)^2}{3} + \frac{(3)^2}{3} - 11.11$$

$$= 1.560$$

Step 6: $SSR = \frac{(\Sigma Y_1)^2}{n_2} + \frac{(\Sigma Y_2)^2}{n_2} + \frac{(\Sigma Y_3)^2}{n_2} - \frac{T^2}{N}$

$$= \frac{(8)^2}{3} + \frac{(7)^2}{3} + \frac{(-5)^2}{3} - 11.11$$

$$= 34.89$$

Step 7: To find SSK

Arrange the elements in the order of treatments

				Total
A	1	0	–3	–2
B	2	1	–2	1
C	5	6	0	11

$$\therefore \text{SSK} = \frac{(\Sigma A)^2}{n_3} + \frac{(\Sigma B)^2}{n_3} + \frac{(\Sigma C)^2}{n_3} - \frac{T^2}{N}$$

$$= \frac{(-2)^2}{3} + \frac{(1)^2}{3} + \frac{(11)^2}{3} - 11.11$$

$$= 30.89$$

Step 8: SSE = TSS – SSC –SSR –SSK

= 68.89 – 1.56 –34.89 – 30.89

= 1.55

Step 9: ANOVA TABLE

Source of variation	**Sum of squares**	**Degrees of freedom**	**Mean sum of squares**	**Variance ratio (F)**	**Table value (F_α)**
Between Columns	SSC = 1.56	c–1=2	$MSC=\frac{SSC}{d.f}$ =0.78	$F_c=\frac{MSC}{MSE}$ =1.01	$F_\alpha(2,2)$ =19.00
Between Rows	SSR = 34.89	r–1=2	$MSR=\frac{SSR}{d.f}$ =17.445	$F_R=\frac{MSR}{MSE}$ =22.51	$F_\alpha(2,2)$ =19.00
Between Treatments	SSK = 30.89	K–1=2	$MSK=\frac{SSK}{d.f}$ =15.445	$F_T=\frac{MSK}{d.f}$ =19.93	$F_\alpha(2,2)$ =19.00
Error	SSE = 1.55	(k–1)(k–2)=2	$MSE=\frac{SSE}{d.f}$ =0.775		
Total	TSS = 68.89	8	–		

Step 10:

(i) Here calculated F_c < Table value of F_c .

$\therefore$ H_0 is accepted.

∴ There is no significant difference between columns

(ii) Here cal $F_R <$ Table F_R

∴ H_0 is accepted.

∴ There is no significant difference between rows.

(iii) Here cal $F_T <$ Table F_T

∴ H_0 is accepted.

∴ There is no significant difference between Treatments

6) The following results were obtained in a textile equipment to compare the effects of sizing treatments. A, B, C, D on the number of warps breaking per hour. Is the difference between the treatments significant?

A54	B31	C70	D45
B59	A23	D100	C32
C40	D41	B74	A33
D83	C29	A100	B28

Solution:

H_0 : There is no significant difference.

H_1 : There is significant difference.

	X_1	X_2	X_3	X_4	**Total**	X_1^2	X_2^2	X_3^2	X_4^2
Y_1	54	31	70	45	200	2916	961	4900	2025
Y_2	59	23	100	22	204	3481	529	10000	484
Y_3	40	41	74	33	188	1600	1681	5476	1089
Y_4	83	29	100	28	240	6889	841	10000	784
Total	236	124	344	128	**832**	14886	4012	30376	4382

Step 1: N = 16

Step 2: T = 832

Step 3: $C.F = \frac{T^2}{N} = \frac{(832)^2}{16} = 43264$

Step 4: $\text{TSS} = \Sigma X_1^2 + \Sigma X_2^2 + \Sigma X_3^2 + \Sigma X_4^2 - \dfrac{T^2}{N}$

$$= 14886 + 4012 + 30376 + 4382 - 43264$$
$$= 10392$$

Step 5: $\text{SSC} = \dfrac{(\Sigma X_1)^2}{n_1} + \dfrac{(\Sigma X_2)^2}{n_1} + \dfrac{(\Sigma X_3)^2}{n_1} + \dfrac{(\Sigma X_4)^2}{n_1} - \dfrac{T^2}{N}$

$$= \frac{(236)^2}{4} + \frac{(124)^2}{4} + \frac{(344)^2}{4} + \frac{(128)^2}{4} - 43264$$
$$= 8184$$

Step 6: $\text{SSR} = \dfrac{(\Sigma Y_1)^2}{n_2} + \dfrac{(\Sigma Y_2)^2}{n_2} + \dfrac{(\Sigma Y_3)^2}{n_2} + \dfrac{(\Sigma Y_4)^2}{n_2} - \dfrac{T^2}{N}$

$$= \frac{(200)^2}{4} + \frac{(204)^2}{4} + \frac{(188)^2}{4} + \frac{(240)^2}{4} - 43264$$
$$= 376$$

Step 7: To find SSK

Arrange the elements in the order of treatments.

					Total
A	54	23	33	100	210
B	31	59	74	28	192
C	70	22	40	29	161
D	45	100	41	83	269

$$\therefore \text{SSK} = \frac{(\Sigma A)^2}{n_3} + \frac{(\Sigma B)^2}{n_3} + \frac{(\Sigma C)^2}{n_3} + \frac{(\Sigma D)^2}{n_3} - \frac{T^2}{N}$$

$$\therefore \text{SSK} = \frac{(210)^2}{4} + \frac{(192)^2}{4} + \frac{(161)^2}{4} + \frac{(269)^2}{4} - 43264$$
$$= 1547.5$$

Step 8: SSE = TSS – SSC –SSR–SSK

= 10392–8184–376–1547.5

=284.5

Step 9: ANOVA TABLE

Source of variation	Sum of squares	Degrees of freedom	Mean sum of squares	Variance ratio (F)	Table value (F_α)
Between Columns	SSC = 8184	c–1=3	$MSC=\frac{SSC}{d.f}$ =2728	$F_c=\frac{MSC}{MSE}$ =28.77	$F_\alpha(3,6)$ =4.76
Between Rows	SSR = 376	r–1=3	$MSR=\frac{SSR}{d.f}$ =125.33	$F_R=\frac{MSR}{MSE}$ =1.322	$F_\alpha(3,6)$ =4.76
Between Treatments	SSK = 1547.5	k–1= 3	$MSK=\frac{SSK}{d.f}$ =515.83	$F_T=\frac{MSK}{MSE}$ =5.439	$F_\alpha(3,6)$ =4.76
Error	SSE = 284.5	(k–1)(k–2) =6	$MSE=\frac{SSE}{d.f}$ =94.83		
Total	TSS = 10392	15			

Step: 10

(i) Here calculated $F_C <$ Table value of F_C, we accept H_0.

Calculate $F_R >$ Table F_R, we reject H_0.

Calculate $F_T >$ Table F_T, we accept H_0.

EXERCISE

1) Illustration : Analyze the following of Latin Square experiment.

Row \ Column	1	2	3	4
1	**A (12)**	**D (20)**	**C (16)**	**B (10)**
2	**D (18)**	**A (14)**	**B (11)**	**C (14)**
3	**B (12)**	**C (15)**	**D (19)**	**A (13)**
4	**C (16)**	**B (11)**	**A (15)**	**D (20)**

The letters A,B,C,D denote the treatments and the figures in brackets denote the observations.

2) A variable trial was conducted on wheat with 4 varieties in a Latin Square Design. The plan of the experiment and the per plot yield are given below:

C	25	B	23	A	20	D	20
A	19	D	19	C	21	B	18
B	19	A	14	D	17	C	20
D	17	C	20	B	21	A	15

Analyze the data and interpret the result.

3) The following data relate to the results of a Latin Square experiments of four varieties of Paddy A,B,C,D

1.	B	17.6	A	20.9	D	22.5	C	15.4
2.	A	21.2	B	15.8	C	14.7	D	24.7
3.	C	13.3	D	21.8	A	20.0	B	16.9
4.	D	22.4	C	14.16	B	17.4	A	20.1

Analyze the results and offer your comments.

2.5 2^2 FACTORIAL DESIGN

Definition : The Design of experimental in which "K" factors are applied each at 2 levels (presence and absence) is called 2^2 Factorial Design.

EXAMPLE

1) Find out the main effects and interactions in the following 2^2 factorial experiment and write down the Analysis of Variance table.

	(1) 00	a 10	b 01	ab 11
Block I	64	25	30	6
II	75	14	50	33
III	76	12	41	17
IV	75	33	25	10

Solution :

Taking deviation from y = 37, we get

Treatment Combination	I X_1	II X_2	III X_3	IV X_4	Total	X_1^2	X_2^2	X_3^2	X_4^2
(Y_1) (1)	27	38	39	38	142	729	1444	1521	1444
(Y_2) a	-12	-23	-25	-4	-64	144	529	625	16
(Y_3) b	-7	13	4	-12	-2	49	169	16	144
(Y_4) ab	-31	-4	-20	-27	-82	961	16	400	729
Total	-23	24	-2	-5	-6	1883	2158	2562	2333

Step 1 : N = 16

Step 2 : T = – 6

Step 3 : Correction Factor = $\frac{T^2}{N} = \frac{36}{16} = 2.25$

Step 4 : $TSS = \Sigma X_1^2 + \Sigma X_2^2 + \Sigma X_3^2 + \Sigma X_4^2 - \frac{T^2}{N}$

$= 1883 + 2158 + 2562 + 2333 - 2.25$

TSS = 8933.75

Step 5 : $SSC = \frac{(\Sigma X_1)^2}{n_1} + \frac{(\Sigma X_2)^2}{n_1} + \frac{(\Sigma X_3)^2}{n_1} + \frac{(\Sigma X_4)^2}{n_1} - \frac{T^2}{N}$

($n_1 \rightarrow$ No of elements in each column)

$= \frac{(-23)^2}{4} + \frac{(24)^2}{4} + \frac{(-2)^2}{4} + \frac{(-82)^2}{4} - 2.25$

$= \frac{529}{4} + \frac{576}{4} + \frac{4}{4} + \frac{25}{4} - 2.25$

SSC = 281.25

Step 6 : $SSR = \frac{(\Sigma Y_1)^2}{n_2} + \frac{(\Sigma Y_2)^2}{n_2} + \frac{(\Sigma Y_3)^2}{n_2} + \frac{(\Sigma Y_4)^2}{n_2} - \frac{T^2}{N}$

($n_2 \rightarrow$ No of elements in each row)

$= \frac{(142)^2}{4} + \frac{(-64)^2}{4} + \frac{(-2)^2}{4} + \frac{(-82)^2}{4} - 2.25$

$= \frac{20164}{4} + \frac{4096}{4} + \frac{4}{4} + \frac{6724}{4} - 2.25$

SSR = 7744.75

Step 7 : SSE = TSS – SSC – SSR

= 8933.75 – 281.25 – 7744.75

SSE = 907.75

For 2^2 experiment

Contrast A = [a + ab - b- (1)]

= –64 – 82 + 2 – 142 = – 286

Contrast B = [b + ab –a – (1)]

= –2 – 82 + 64 – 142 = – 162

Contrast AB = [ab + (1) – a – b]

= – 82 + 142 + 64 + 2 = 126

Main effect A = ½ [a+ ab – b– (1)]

= – 143

B = ½ [b + ab – a – (1)]

= – 81

AB = ½ [ab + (1) –a– b]

= 63

$$SS_A = \frac{[a+ab-b-(1)]^2}{16}$$

$$= \frac{(-286)^2}{16} = 5112.25$$

$$SS_B = \frac{[b+ab-a-(1)]^2}{16}$$

$$= \frac{(-162)^2}{16} = 1640.25$$

$$SS_{AB} = \frac{[ab+(1)-a-b]^2}{16}$$

$$= \frac{(126)^2}{16} = 992.25$$

Analysis of variance table for the 2^2 experiment

S.V	d.f	S.S	MSS	Variance ratio	Table value of F	
					5%	1%
Blocks	3	281.5	93.83	$F_c = \frac{100.86}{93.83} = 1.075$	$F_C(9,3) = 8.81$	27.35
Treatment	3	7744.75	2581.58	$F_R = \frac{2581.58}{100.86} = 25.60$	$F_R(3,9) = 3.86$	6.99
A	1	5112.25	5112.25	$\frac{5112.25}{100.86} = 50.69$	$F_A(1,9) = 5.12$	6.99
B	1	1640.25	1640.25	$\frac{1640.25}{100.86} = 16.26$	$F_B(1,9) = 5.12$	6.99
AB	1	992.25	992.25	$\frac{992.25}{100.86} = 9.84$	$F_{AB}(1,9) = 5.12$	6.99
Error	9	907.75	100.86			

$$\begin{aligned}\text{Error (d.f)} &= N-c-r+1 \\ &= 16 - 4 - 4 + 1 \\ &= 9\end{aligned}$$

Conclusion.

Here Cal $F_A >$ Table F_A

Cal $F_B >$ Table F_B

Cal $F_{AB} >$ Table F_{AB}

2) An experiment was planned to study the effect of sulphate of potash and super phosphate on the yield of potatoes. The (y_{70})yields [lb. per plot =(y_{70})] acre obtained are given in the table. Analyse the data and give your conclusions.

Block	Yields (lbs per plot)			
I	(1) 23	a 25	b 22	ab 38
II	b 40	(1) 26	a 36	ab 38
III	(1) 29	a 20	ba 30	b 20
IV	ab 34	a 31	b 24	(1) 28

Solution:

Treatment combination		Blocks				Total	X_1^2	X_2^2	X_3^2	X_4^2
		X_1	X_2	X_3	X_4					
Y_1	(1)	–6	–3	0	1	–10	36	9	0	1
Y_2	a	–4	7	–9	2	–4	16	49	81	4
Y_3	b	–7	11	–9	–5	–10	49	121	81	25
Y_4	ab	9	9	1	5	24	81	81	1	25
Total		–8	24	–17	1	0	182	260	163	55

Step 1: N=16

Step 2: T=0

Step 3: $CF=\frac{T^2}{N}=0$

Step 4: $TSS=\Sigma X_1^2+\Sigma X_2^2+\Sigma X_3^2+\Sigma X_4^2-\frac{T^2}{N}$

=182+260+163+55–0

=660

Step 5: $SSC=\frac{(\Sigma X_1)^2}{n_1}+\frac{(\Sigma X_2)^2}{n_1}+\frac{(\Sigma X_3)^2}{n_1}+\frac{(\Sigma X_4)^2}{n_1}-\frac{T^2}{N}$

$=\frac{64}{4}+\frac{576}{4}+\frac{289}{4}+\frac{1}{4}-0$

=232.5

Step 6: $SSR=\frac{(\Sigma Y_1)^2}{n_2}+\frac{(\Sigma Y_2)^2}{n_2}+\frac{(\Sigma Y_3)^2}{n_2}+\frac{(\Sigma Y_4)^2}{n_2}-\frac{T^2}{N}$

$=\frac{100}{4}+\frac{16}{4}+\frac{100}{4}+\frac{576}{4}-0$

=198

Step 7: SSE = TSS–SSC–SSR

= 660–232.5–198

= 229.50

For 2^2 Experiment

Contrast A = [a+ab–b–(1)]

= [–4+24+10+10]

A=40

Contrast B =[b+ab–a–(1)]

=[–10+24+4+10]

B = 28

Contrast AB = [ab+(1)–a–b]

= [24–10+4+10]

AB = 28

$$SS_A = \frac{[a+ab-b-(1)]^2}{16}$$

$$= \frac{40^2}{16} = 100$$

$$SS_B = \frac{[b+ab-a-(1)]^2}{16}$$

$$= \frac{(28)^2}{16} = 49$$

$$SS_{AB} = \frac{[ab+(1)-a-b]^2}{16}$$

$$= \frac{(28)^2}{16} = 49$$

Analysis of variance table for the 2^2 experiment.

S.V	**d.t**	**S.S**	**MSS**	**Variance ratio**	**Table value of F**	
					5%	1%
Blocks	3	232.5	$\frac{232.5}{3} = 77.5$	$F_C = \frac{77.5}{25.5} = 3.04$	$F_C(3.9)=3.86$	6.99
Treatments	3	198.00	$\frac{198}{3} = 66.00$	$F_R = \frac{66}{25.5} = 2.59$	$F_R(3,9)=3.86$	6.99
A	1	100	$\frac{100}{1} = 100$	$F_A = \frac{100}{25.5} = 3.92$	$F_A(1,9) = 5.12$	10.56
B	1	49	$\frac{49}{1} = 49$	$F_B = \frac{49}{25.5} = 1.92$	$F_B(1,9) = 5.12$	10.56
AB	1	49	$\frac{49}{1} = 49$	$F_{AB} = \frac{49}{25.5} = 1.92$	$F_{AB}(1,9) = 5.12$	10.56
Error	9	229.5	$\frac{229.5}{9} = 25.5$			

Error (d.f)=N–c–r+1

=16–4–4+1

=17–8

=9

As in each of the cases, the computed value of F is less than the corresponding tabulated value, there are no significant difference.

EXERCISE

1) The following data are obtained from a 2^2 factorial experiment replicated three times. Evaluate the sum of squares for all factorial effects by contrast method. Draw conclusions.

Treatment	Replicate 1	Replicate 2	Replicate 3
(1)	17	25	21
a	16	19	19
b	24	23	29
ab	28	25	20

2) From the following data, evaluate the sum of squares all factorial effects by contrast method and draw conclusions using 0.05 level of significance

Treatment	Replicate 1	Replicate 2	Replicate 3	Replicate 4
(1)	68	57	73	61
a	83	94	91	86
b	72	81	63	59
ab	92	68	75	87

PART – A

QUESTION AND ANSWERS

1) What are the assumptions in analysis of variance?

(1).Each of the sample is drawn from a normal population.

(2) The variances for the population from which samples have been drawn are equal.

(3) The variation of each value around its own grand mean should be independent for each value.

2) What are the basic steps in ANOVA?

1. One estimate of the population variance from the variance among the sample means.
2. Determine a second estimate of the population variance from the variance within the sample.
3. Compare these two estimates if they are approximately equal in value, accept the null hypothesis.

3) Define mean sum of squares.

Mean sum of squares (M.S.S): The sum of square divided by its degrees of freedom gives the corresponding variance or the mean sum of squares (MSS), thus

$$\frac{\text{SST}}{(\text{K}-1)} = S_t^2 \text{ (say) is the MSS due to treatments.}$$

$$\frac{\text{SSE}}{(\text{N}-\text{K})} = S_E^2 \text{ (say) is the MSS due to error.}$$

4) What are the advantages of completely randomized block design?

The advantages of a completely randomized experimental design are as follows:

(a) Easy to layout

(b) Allows flexibility

(c) Simple statistical analysis

(d) The lots of information due to missing data is smaller than with any other design

5) Define Replication:

To estimate the magnitude of an effect in an experiment the principle of randomisation and replication are applied. Randomisation by itself is not necessarily sufficient to yield a valid experiment.

The replication or repetition of an experiment or experimental unit is also necessary. Randomisation must be invariably accompanied by sufficient replication so as to ensure validity in an experiment.

6) State the advantages of Latin Square design:

Advantages of LSD over other designs are

(a) Latin square controls more of the variation than the completely randomized block design with a two way stratification.

(b) The analysis is simple

(c) Even with missing data the analysis remains relatively simple.

7) Why a 2×2 Latin Square is not possible? Explain:

In a Latin square, the formula for degrees of freedom for residual (SSE) is

$$df=(n-1)(n-2)$$

Substituting n=2, df=0

$$MSE=\infty$$

There fore 2×2 Latin square is not possible.

8) Write the differences between RBD and LSD

Randomized Block Design	Latin Square Design
• Available for a wide range of treatments • No restriction on the number of replications • Flexible and easier to manage • Can be accommodated in a field of any shape	• More efficient when there is diagonal trend of fertility • Suitable only in the special cases where the land exhibits marked trends in fertility • Suitable mainly for 5 or 10 treatments • Shape of the field should be approximately square or rectangular.

9) State the advantages of a factorial experiment over a simple experiment.

Factorial design are frequently used in experiments involving several factors where it is necessary to the joint effect of the factors on a response.

10) Compare one-way classification model with two-way classification model.

S.No	One way	Two way
1.	We cannot test two sets of hypothesis	Two sets of hypothesis can be tested
2.	Data are classified according to one factor	Data are classified according to two different factors

11) Write down the ANOVA TABLE for Randomised block design.

Source of variation	Sum of squares	Degrees of freedom	Mean sum of squares	Variance ratio (F)	Table value (F_α)
Columns	SSC	c–1	$MSC=\frac{SSC}{c-1}$	$F=\frac{MSC}{MSE}$	F_α
Rows	SSR	r–1	$MSR=\frac{SSR}{r-1}$	$F=\frac{MSR}{MSE}$	F_α
Error	SSE	(c–1)(r–1) (or) N–c–r+1	$MSE=\frac{SSE}{d.f}$		
Total	TSS	–	–		

12) What are the basic principles of design of experiment?

(i) Replication

(ii) Randomization

(iii) Local control

13) How do you find correction factor in L.S.D?

$C.F=\frac{T^2}{N}$, Where T - Grand Total

N - Number of observations

14) Name three basic designs of experiment

(i) Completely randomized design

(ii) Randomized block design

(iii) Lation square.

15) Write the advantages of RBD

Advantages:

(i) Accuracy

(ii) Flexibility

(iii) Easy to analyse

Disadvantage:

It is not suitable for large number of treatment.

UNIT - 3

SOLUTION OF EQUATION AND EIGEN VALUE PROBLEMS

IMPORTANT TERMS TO REMEMBER

1) *Iterative formula for N–R method is,*

$$x_{n+1} = x_n - \frac{f(x_n)}{f'(x_n)}$$

2) *The rate of convergence of N–R method is of order 2 (or) N–R method is convergent quadratically.*

3) *Condition for convergence of N–R method is,*

$$|f(x)f''(x)| < |f'(x)|^2$$

4) *Condition for the convergence of iteration method for x=g(x) is* $|g'(x)| < 1$

5) *The two types of pivoting are*

   (i) Partial pivoting

   (ii) Complete pivoting

6) *Numerical methods of solving linear simultaneous equations are of two types:*

   (i) Direct

   (ii) Indirect (or) iterative

7) Gauss Elimination and Gauss-Jordan are direct methods while Gauss-Seidel and Gauss-Jacobi are *iterative* methods.

8) *In Gauss-Jordan method the co-efficient matrix is transformed into diagonal matrix.*

9) *In Gauss-elimination method the co-efficient matrix is transformed into upper Triangular Matrix.*

10) *Condition for Gauss-Jacobi and Gauss-Seidel method to converge is "The co-efficient of matrix should be diagonally dominant."*

11) *The convergence in the Gauss-Seidel method is twice as fast as in Jacobi's method.*

12) *Power method is usually used to find the dominant (or) largest Eigen value.*

3.1 NUMERICAL SOLUTION OF ALGEBRAIC AND TRANSCENDENTAL EQUATIONS

(1) Newton's Method (or) Newton-Raphson [N–R] Method

Newton Raphson Method is also known as Method of iteration (Newton's Iteration Method)

The rate of convergence in N–R method is of order 2.

The condition for convergence is $|f(x)f''(x)| < |f'(x)|^2$

Iterative formula for N–R method is,

$$\boxed{x_{n+1} = x_n - \frac{f(x_n)}{f'(x_n)}}$$

Problem Based on N-R method.

1. Using Newton's iterative method find the root b/w 0 and 1 of $x^3 = 6x - 4$ correct to 2-decimal place.

Solution:

Let $f(x) = x^3 - 6x + 4$

$$f'(x) = 3x^2 - 6$$
$$f(0) = (0)^3 - 6(0) + 4 = 0 - 0 + 4 = 4 = '+'\text{ve}$$
$$f(1) = (1)^3 - 6(1) + 4 \Rightarrow 1 - 6 + 4 \Rightarrow -1 = '-'\text{ve}$$

$\therefore$ The root lies between 0 and 1.

Take $x_0 = 0.5$

The N–R formula is,

$$x_{n+1} = x_n - \frac{f(x_n)}{f'(x_n)} \qquad \rightarrow (1)$$

Put n=0 in (1) then we get

$$x_1 = x_0 - \frac{f(x_0)}{f'(x_0)}$$

$$= 0.5 - \frac{f(0.5)}{f'(0.5)}$$

$$= 0.5 - \left[\frac{(0.5)^3 - 6(0.5) + 4}{3(0.5)^2 - 6}\right]$$

$$\boxed{x_1 = 0.71}$$

Put n=1 in (1) then,

$$x_2 = x_1 - \frac{f(x_1)}{f'(x_1)}$$

$$= 0.71 - \frac{f(0.71)}{f'(0.71)}$$

$$\boxed{x_2 = 0.73}$$

Put n=2 in (1) then

$$x_3 = x_2 - \frac{f(x_2)}{f'(x_2)}$$

$$= 0.73 - \frac{f(0.73)}{f'(0.73)}$$

$$\boxed{x_3 = 0.73}$$

$$x_2 = x_3$$

∴ The better approximation root is x= 0.73

2. Find the positive root of $x^4 - x = 10$ correct to 3-decimal places using N–R method.

Solution:

Let $f(x) = x^4 - x - 10$

$f'(x) = 4x^3 - 1$

$f(0) = 0 - 0 - 10 = -10 = '-'\text{ve}$

$$f(1) = 1 - 1 - 10 = -10 = '-'\text{ve}$$
$$f(2) = 16 - 2 - 10 = 4 = '+'\text{ve}$$

$\therefore$ The positive root lies between 1 & 2

Take x_0=1.5

$$x_{n+1} = x_n - \frac{f(x_n)}{f'(x_n)} \qquad \rightarrow (1)$$

Put n=0 in (1) we get

$$x_1 = x_0 - \frac{f(x_0)}{f'(x_0)}$$

$$x_1 = 1.5 - \frac{f(1.5)}{f'(1.5)}$$

$$\boxed{x_1 = 2.015}$$

Put n=1 in (1) we get

$$x_2 = x_1 - \frac{f(x_1)}{f'(x_1)}$$

$$x_2 = 2.02 - \frac{f(2.02)}{f'(2.02)}$$

$$\boxed{x_2 = 1.874}$$

Put n=2 in (1) we get

$$x_3 = x_2 - \frac{f(x_2)}{f'(x_2)}$$

$$x_3 = 1.874 - \frac{f(1.874)}{f'(1.874)}$$

$$\boxed{x_3 = 1.856}$$

Put n=3 in (1) we get

$$x_4 = x_3 - \frac{f(x_3)}{f'(x_3)}$$

$$x_4 = 1.856 - \frac{f(1.856)}{f'(1.856)}$$

$$\boxed{x_4 = 1.856}$$

Hence $x_3 = x_4$

$\therefore$ The better approximation root is $x = 1.856$

3. Find the positive root of $3x - \cos x - 1 = 0$ by Newton's method correct to 6 decimal places.

Solution:

Let
$$f(x) = 3x - \cos x - 1$$
$$f'(x) = 3 + \sin x$$
$$f(0) = 3(0) - \cos(0) - 1 = -2 = '-'\text{ve}$$
$$f(1) = 3 - \cos(1) - 1 = 1.459698 = '+'\text{ve}$$

The root lies between 0 & 1

Take $x_0 = 0.5$

The N–R formula is,

$$x_{n+1} = x_n - \frac{f(x_n)}{f'(x_n)} \qquad \rightarrow (1)$$

Put n = 0 in (1) we get

$$x_1 = x_0 - \frac{f(x_0)}{f'(x_0)}$$

$$= 0.5 - \frac{f(0.5)}{f'(0.5)}$$

$$\boxed{x_1 = 0.608519}$$

Put n = 1 in (1) we get

$$x_2 = x_1 - \frac{f(x_1)}{f'(x_1)}$$

$$= 0.608519 - \frac{f(0.608519)}{f'(0.608519)}$$

$$\boxed{x_2 = 0.607102}$$

Put n = 2 in (1) we get

$$x_3 = x_2 - \frac{f(x_2)}{f'(x_2)}$$

$$= 0.607102 - \frac{f(0.607102)}{f'(0.607102)}$$

$$\boxed{x_3 = 0.607102}$$

$\therefore\ x_2 = x_3$

$\therefore$ The required root is $x = 0.607102$

4. Find the root of $\log_{10} x = 1.2$ by N–R method.

Solution:

Let $f(x) = \log_{10} x - 1.2$

$f(x) = \log_{10} x - 1.2$

$f'(x) = \frac{1}{x}\log e$

$f(15) = \log_{10} 15 - 1.2 = -0.0239 = '-'\text{ve}$

$f(16) = \log_{10} 16 - 1.2 = +0.0041 = '+'\text{ve}$

The roots lies between 15 & 16

Take x_0=15.5

The N–R method is,

$$x_{n+1} = x_n - \frac{f(x_n)}{f'(x_n)} \quad \rightarrow (1)$$

Put n = 0 in (1) we get

$$x_1 = x_0 - \frac{f(x_0)}{f'(x_0)}$$

$$= 15.5 - \frac{f(15.5)}{f'(15.5)}$$

$$\boxed{x_1 = 15.8451}$$

Put n = 1 in (1) we get

$$x_2 = x_1 - \frac{f(x_1)}{f'(x_1)}$$

$$= 15.8451 - \frac{f(15.8451)}{f'(15.8451)}$$

$$\boxed{x_2 = 15.8489}$$

Put n = 2 in (1) we get

$$x_3 = x_2 - \frac{f(x_2)}{f'(x_2)}$$

$$= 15.8489 - \frac{f(15.8489)}{f'(15.8489)}$$

$$\boxed{x_3 = 15.8489}$$

$\therefore \quad x_2 = x_3$

$\therefore$ The best root is $x = 15.8489$

5. Find a root of $x\log_{10} x - 1.2 = 0$ by N–R method correct to 3-decimal places.

Solution:

Let $f(x) = x\log_{10} x - 1.2$

$$f'(x) = x.\frac{1}{x}\log e + \log_{10} x - 0$$

$$f'(x) = \log_{10} e + \log_{10} x$$

$$f(0) = 0\log_{10} 0 - 1.2 = -1.2 = '-'\text{ve}$$

$$f(1) = 1\log_{10} 1 - 1.2 = -1.2 = '-'\text{ve}$$

$$f(2) = 2\log_{10} 2 - 1.2 = -0.598 = '-'\text{ve}$$

$$f(3) = 3\log_{10} 3 - 1.2 = 0.231 = '+'\text{ve}$$

So the root lies between 2 & 3

The N–R formula is,

$$x_{n+1} = x_n - \frac{f(x_n)}{f'(x_n)} \quad \rightarrow (1)$$

Take $x_0=2.5$

Put n =0 in (1) we get

$$x_1 = x_0 - \frac{f(x_0)}{f'(x_0)}$$

$$= 2.5 - \frac{f(2.5)}{f'(2.5)}$$

$$\boxed{x_1 = 2.747}$$

Put n = 1 in (1) we get

$$x_2 = x_1 - \frac{f(x_1)}{f'(x_1)}$$

$$= 2.747 - \frac{f(2.747)}{f'(2.747)}$$

$$\boxed{x_2 = 2.741}$$

Put n = 2 in (1) we get

$$x_3 = x_2 - \frac{f(x_2)}{f'(x_2)}$$

$$= 2.741 - \frac{f(2.741)}{f'(2.741)}$$

$$\boxed{x_3 = 2.741}$$

$\therefore \quad x_2 = x_3$

$\therefore$ Hence, the best approximation root is $x = 2.741$

6. Obtain Newton Raphson iterative formula for finding $\sqrt{N}$ where N is a positive real number. Hence evaluate $\sqrt{5}$

Solution:

Let $x = \sqrt{N}$

$x^2 = N$

$f(x) = x^2 - N$

$f'(x) = 2x$

N–R formula is,

$$x_{n+1} = x_n - \frac{f(x_n)}{f'(x_n)}$$

$$= x_n - \left[\frac{x_n^2 - N}{2x_n}\right]$$

$$= x_n - \frac{x_n}{2} + \frac{N}{2x_n}$$

$$= \frac{x_n}{2} + \frac{N}{2x_n}$$

$$x_{n+1} = \frac{1}{2}\left[x_n + \frac{N}{x_n}\right] \qquad \rightarrow (1)$$

To find $\sqrt{5}$

$$f(x) = x^2 - 5$$
$$f(0) = -5 = '-'\text{ve}$$
$$f(1) = -4 = '-'\text{ve}$$
$$f(2) = -1 = '-'\text{ve}$$
$$f(3) = 4 = '+'\text{ve}$$

The root lies between 2 & 3

Put n = 0 in (1) we get and x_0=2.5

$$x_1 = \frac{1}{2}\left[x_0 + \frac{N}{x_0}\right]$$

$$= \frac{1}{2}\left[2.5 + \frac{5}{2.5}\right]$$

$$\boxed{x_1 = 2.25}$$

Put n = 1 in (1) we get

$$x_2 = \frac{1}{2}\left[x_1 + \frac{N}{x_1}\right]$$

$$= \frac{1}{2}\left[2.25 + \frac{5}{2.25}\right]$$

$$\boxed{x_2 = 2.2361}$$

Put n = 2 in (1) we get

$$x_3 = \frac{1}{2}\left[x_2 + \frac{N}{x_2}\right]$$

$$= \frac{1}{2}\left[2.2361 + \frac{5}{2.2361}\right]$$

$$\boxed{x_3 = 2.2361}$$

$$\therefore \; x_2 = x_3$$

Hence the better approximation root is $x = 2.2361$

7. Derive the iterative formula to find the value of $\frac{1}{N}$ where N is real Number by N–R method. Hence evaluate $\frac{1}{26}$ Correct to 4-decimal.

Solution:

Let $x = \frac{1}{N}$

$$N = \frac{1}{x}$$

$$f(x) = \frac{1}{x} - N$$

$$f'(x) = \frac{-1}{x^2}$$

N–R formula is,

$$x_{n+1} = x_n - \frac{f(x_n)}{f'(x_n)}$$

$$= x_n - \frac{\left(\frac{1}{x_n} - N\right)}{\left(\frac{-1}{x_n^2}\right)}$$

$$x_{n+1} = x_n + \frac{x_n^2}{x_n} - Nx_n^2$$

$$= x_n + x_n - Nx_n^2$$

$$= 2x_n - Nx_n^2$$

$$x_{n+1} = x_n[2 - x_n N] \qquad \rightarrow (1)$$

To find $\frac{1}{26}$ Take N = 26

$$f(x) = \frac{1}{x} - N$$

$$f(0) = -26 = '-'\text{ve}$$

$$f(0.1) = 0.06 = '+'\text{ve}$$

The root lies between 0 & 0.1. take x_0=0.04

Put n =0 in (1) we get

$$x_1 = x_0[2 - 26x_0]$$

$$= 0.04[2 - 26(0.04)]$$

$$\boxed{x_1 = 0.0384}$$

Put n =1 in (1)

$$x_2 = x_1\ (2 - 26(x_1))$$

$$= 0.0384\ (2 - 26(0.0384))$$

$$\boxed{x_2 = 0.0385}$$

Put n =2 in (1)

$$x_3 = x_2\ (2 - 26(x_2))$$

$$= 0.0385\ (2 - 26(0.0385))$$

$$\boxed{x_3 = 0.0385}$$

$$\therefore\ x_2 = x_3$$

Hence, the better approximation root is $x = 0.0385$

(8) Find the Least root of $xe^{-2x} = 0.5\ sinx$. Correct to three decimal place using N-R Method.

Solution:

Let $f(x) = xe^{-2x} - 0.5\ sinx$

$$f'(x) = x[-2e^{-2x}] + e^{-2x}(1) - 0.5\cos x$$

$$f'(x) = e^{-2x}[1-2x] - 0.5\cos x$$

$$f(0) = 0$$

$$f(1) = -0.285 \quad = '-'ve$$

$$f(2) = -0.418 \quad = '-'ve$$

$$f(3) = -0.063 \quad = '-'ve$$

$$f(4) = 0.380 \quad = '+'ve$$

So, the root lies between 3 & 4

$$\boxed{x_0 = 3.5}$$

The N.R Formula is

$$x_{n+1} = x_n - \frac{f(x_n)}{f'(x_n)} \quad \rightarrow (1)$$

Take n=0 in equ (1)

$$x_1 = x_0 - \frac{f(x_0)}{f'(x_0)}$$

$$= 3.5 - \frac{f(3.5)}{f'(3.5)}$$

$$\boxed{x_1 = 3.114}$$

Put n=1 in equ (1)

$$x_2 = x_1 - \frac{f(x_1)}{f'(x_1)}$$

$$= 3.114 - \frac{f(3.114)}{f'(3.114)}$$

$$\boxed{x_2 = 3.130}$$

Put n=2 in equ (1)

$$x_3 = x_2 - \frac{f(x_2)}{f'(x_2)}$$

$$= 3.130 - \frac{f(3.130)}{f'(3.130)}$$

$$\boxed{x_3 = 3.130}$$

Here $x_2 = x_3$

So, the better approximation root is 3.130

(9) Find the root if $\cos x = xe^x$ by N-R Method. Take x_0=0.5

Solution:

Given $\cos x = xe^x$

$$\cos x - xe^x = 0$$

Let $f(x) = \cos x - xe^x$

$$f'(x) = -\sin x - xe^x - e^x(1)$$

$$x_0 = 0.5$$

Put n=0 in (1)

$$x_1 = x_0 - \frac{f(x_0)}{f'(x_0)}$$

$$= 0.5 - \frac{f(0.5)}{f'(0.5)}$$

$$\boxed{x_1 = 0.5180}$$

Put n=1 in (1)

$$x_2 = x_1 - \frac{f(x_1)}{f'(x_1)}$$

$$= 0.5180 - \frac{f(0.5180)}{f'(0.5180)}$$

$$\boxed{x_2 = 0.5178}$$

Put n=2 in (1)

$$x_3 = x_2 - \frac{f(x_2)}{f'(x_2)}$$

$$= 0.5178 - \frac{f(0.5178)}{f'(0.5178)}$$

$$\boxed{x_3 = 0.5178}$$

The better approximation root is 0.5178

(10) Find the root of $x = 2\sin x$ near 1.9, correct to three decimal places by applying N-R Method twice.

Solution:

Given: $x = 2\sin x$

Let $f(x) = x - 2\sin x,\ f'(x) = 1 - 2\cos x$

Given $x_0 = 1.9$

N-R Formula: $x_{n+1} = x_n - \frac{f(x_n)}{f'(x_n)}$

Take n=0

$$x_1 = x_0 - \frac{f(x_0)}{f'(x_0)}$$

$$= 1.9 - \frac{f(1.9)}{f'(1.9)}$$

$$= 1.9 - \frac{1.9 - 2\sin(1.9)}{1 - 2\cos(1.9)}$$

$$\boxed{x_1 = 1.896}$$

Take n=0

$$x_2 = x_1 - \frac{f(x_1)}{f'(x_1)}$$

$$= 1.896 - \frac{f(1.896)}{f'(1.896)}$$

$$= 1.896 - \frac{1.896 - 2\sin(1.896)}{1 - 2\cos(1.896)}$$

$$= 1.896 - \frac{0.0008}{1.639}$$

$$\boxed{x_2 = 1.896}$$

Here $x_1 = x_2 = 1.896$

Hence, the better approximate roots 1.896.

3.2 NUMERICAL SOLUTION OF LINEAR SYSTEM OF EQUATIONS

There are two types of methods to solve simultaneous linear algebraic equations with many unknowns.

1) Direct Methods
   - (i) Gauss-Elimination
   - (ii) Gauss-Jordan
   - (iii) Crout's method
2) Indirect/Iterative Method
   - (i) Gauss-Jacobi
   - (ii) Gauss-Seidel

3.2.1 Gauss-Elimination Method

Gauss Elimination method is a direct method which consists of transforming the given system of simultaneous equations to an equivalent upper triangular system. From this system the required solution can be obtained by the method of back substitution.

3.2.2 Gauss-Jordan Method

In this method, the co-efficient matrix A of the system AX=B is brought to a diagonal matrix or unit matrix.

(1) Solve the system of equations $x - 2y = 0,\ 2x + y = 5$ by Gauss Elimination and Gauss Jordan methods.

Solution:

(i) Gauss Elimination Method:

The given system is equivalent to

$$\begin{bmatrix} 1 & -2 \\ 2 & 1 \end{bmatrix} \begin{bmatrix} x \\ y \end{bmatrix} = \begin{bmatrix} 0 \\ 5 \end{bmatrix} \Rightarrow \text{AX=B}$$

Augmented matrix is

$$[A,B]=\left[\begin{array}{cc|c}1 & -2 & 0\\ 2 & 1 & 5\end{array}\right]$$

$$\sim\left[\begin{array}{cc|c}1 & -2 & 0\\ 0 & 5 & 5\end{array}\right] R_2 \to R_2 - 2R_1$$

By back substitution method

$$5y=5$$
$$y=1$$
$$x-2y=0$$
$$x-2=0$$
$$x=2$$

Result: $\boxed{x=2 \ \& \ y=1}$

(ii) Gauss - Jordan Method:

$$[A,B]=\left[\begin{array}{cc|c}1 & -2 & 0\\ 0 & 5 & 5\end{array}\right]$$

$$\sim\left[\begin{array}{cc|c}5 & 0 & 10\\ 0 & 5 & 5\end{array}\right] R_1 \to 5R_1 + 2R_2$$

$$5y=5$$
$$\boxed{y=1}$$
$$5x=10$$
$$\boxed{x=2}$$

Result: $\boxed{x=2 \ \& \ y=1}$

(2) 2x+3y–z=5, 4x+4y–3z=3 & 2x–3y+2z=2; Solve this system of equations by Gauss Elimination and Gauss Jordan methods.

Solution:

(i) Gauss Elimination Method:

The given system is equivalent to

$$\begin{bmatrix}2 & 3 & -1\\ 4 & 4 & -3\\ 2 & -3 & 2\end{bmatrix}\begin{bmatrix}x\\ y\\ z\end{bmatrix}=\begin{bmatrix}5\\ 3\\ 2\end{bmatrix} \Rightarrow AX=B$$

Augmented matrix is,

$$[A,B]=\left[\begin{array}{ccc|c}2 & 3 & -1 & 5\\ 4 & 4 & -3 & 3\\ 2 & -3 & 2 & 2\end{array}\right]$$

Now, we will make upper triangular matrix

$$\sim\left[\begin{array}{ccc|c}2 & 3 & -1 & 5\\ 4 & 4 & -3 & 3\\ 2 & -3 & 2 & 2\end{array}\right]$$

$$\sim\left[\begin{array}{ccc|c}2 & 3 & -1 & 5\\ 0 & -2 & -1 & -7\\ 0 & -6 & 3 & -3\end{array}\right]\begin{array}{l}\\ R_2\to R_2-2R_1\\ R_3\to R_3-R_1\end{array}$$

$$\sim\left[\begin{array}{ccc|c}2 & 3 & -1 & 5\\ 0 & -2 & -1 & -7\\ 0 & 0 & 6 & 18\end{array}\right]\begin{array}{l}\\ \\ R_3\to R_3-3R_2\end{array}$$

$$\Rightarrow \quad 6z=18$$

$$\boxed{z=3}$$

$$\Rightarrow \quad -2y-z=-7$$

$$-2y-3=-7$$

$$-2y=-4$$

$$\boxed{y=2}$$

$$\Rightarrow \quad 2x+3(2)-3=5$$

$$2x+6-3=5$$

$$2x+3=5$$

$$2x=2$$

$$\boxed{x=1}$$

Hence the solution is x=1, y=2, z =3

(ii) Gauss-Jordan Method

$$[A,B]=\left[\begin{array}{ccc|c} 2 & 3 & -1 & 5 \\ 0 & -2 & -1 & -7 \\ 0 & 0 & 6 & 18 \end{array}\right]$$

$$\sim\left[\begin{array}{ccc|c} 2 & 5 & 0 & 12 \\ 0 & -12 & 0 & -24 \\ 0 & 0 & 6 & 18 \end{array}\right]\begin{array}{l} R_1 \to R_1 - R_2 \\ R_2 \to 6R_2 + R_3 \\ \end{array}$$

$$\sim\left[\begin{array}{ccc|c} 24 & 0 & 0 & 24 \\ 0 & -12 & 0 & -24 \\ 0 & 0 & 6 & 18 \end{array}\right] R_1 \to 12R_1 + 5R_2$$

$$\sim\left[\begin{array}{ccc|c} 1 & 0 & 0 & 1 \\ 0 & 1 & 0 & 2 \\ 0 & 0 & 1 & 3 \end{array}\right]\begin{array}{l} R_1/24 \\ R_2/-12 \\ R_3/6 \end{array}$$

$\therefore$ Solution is x=1, y=2, z=3

(3) Solve the following system of equations by (i) Gauss-Elimination (ii) Gauss-Jordan method.

$$\mathbf{10x - 2y + 3z = 23}$$
$$\mathbf{2x + 10y - 5z = -33}$$
$$\mathbf{3x - 4y + 10z = 41}$$

Solution:

(i) Gauss Elimination method:

The given system is equivalent to

$$\begin{bmatrix} 10 & -2 & 3 \\ 2 & 10 & -5 \\ 3 & -4 & 10 \end{bmatrix}\begin{bmatrix} x \\ y \\ z \end{bmatrix}=\begin{bmatrix} 23 \\ -33 \\ 41 \end{bmatrix}$$

$\Rightarrow$ AX=B

$$[A,B]=\left[\begin{array}{ccc|c} 10 & -2 & 3 & 23 \\ 2 & 10 & -5 & -33 \\ 3 & -4 & 10 & 41 \end{array}\right]$$

Now, we will make the matrix A as a upper triangular

$$[A,B] \sim \left[\begin{array}{ccc|c} 10 & -2 & 3 & 23 \\ 0 & 52 & -28 & -188 \\ 0 & -34 & 91 & 341 \end{array}\right] \begin{array}{l} \\ R_2 \to 5R_2 - R_1 \\ R_3 \to 10R_3 - 3R_1 \end{array}$$

$$\sim \left[\begin{array}{ccc|c} 10 & -2 & 3 & 23 \\ 0 & 52 & -28 & -188 \\ 0 & 0 & 3780 & 11340 \end{array}\right] \begin{array}{l} \\ \\ R_3 \to 52R_3 + 34R_2 \end{array}$$

This is an upper triangular matrix.

Now, we use back substitution method.

$3780z = 11340$	$52y - 28z = -188$	$10x - 2y + 3z = 23$
$z = 3$	$52y - 84 = -188$	$10x + 4 + 9 = 23$
	$52y = -104$	$10x = 23 - 13$
	$y = -2$	$x = \frac{10}{10} = 1$

$\therefore$ Solution is $x = 1, y = -2, z = 3$.

(ii) Gauss-Jordan method:

$$(A, B) \sim \left[\begin{array}{ccc|c} 10 & -2 & 3 & 23 \\ 0 & 52 & -28 & -188 \\ 0 & 0 & 3780 & 11340 \end{array}\right]$$

Now we will make the matrix A is a diagonal matrix.

$$\sim \left[\begin{array}{ccc|c} 12600 & -2520 & 0 & 17640 \\ 0 & 7020 & 0 & -14040 \\ 0 & 0 & 3780 & 11340 \end{array}\right] \begin{array}{l} R_1 \to 1260R_1 - R_3 \\ R_2 \to 135R_2 + R_3 \\ \\ \end{array}$$

$$\sim \left[\begin{array}{ccc|c} 88452000 & 0 & 0 & 88452000 \\ 0 & 7020 & 0 & -14040 \\ 0 & 0 & 3780 & 11340 \end{array}\right] \begin{array}{l} R_1 \to 7020R_1 + 2520R_2 \\ \\ \\ \end{array}$$

$$\sim \left[\begin{array}{ccc|c} 1 & 0 & 0 & 1 \\ 0 & 1 & 0 & -2 \\ 0 & 0 & 1 & 3 \end{array}\right] \begin{array}{l} R_1 \to R_1 / 88452000 \\ R_2 \to R_2 / 7020 \\ R_3 \to R_3 / 3780 \end{array}$$

Hence solution is, $x = 1, y = -2, z = 3$.

(4) 3x+4y+5z=18, 2x–y+8z=13, 5x–2y+7z=20 solve this system of equations by Gauss-Elimination and Gauss-Jordan method.

Solution:

(i) Gauss Elimination Method:

The given system is equivalent to

$$\begin{bmatrix} 3 & 4 & 5 \\ 2 & -1 & 8 \\ 5 & -2 & 7 \end{bmatrix}\begin{bmatrix} x \\ y \\ z \end{bmatrix} = \begin{bmatrix} 18 \\ 13 \\ 20 \end{bmatrix} \Rightarrow \text{AX=B}$$

Now, we will make the matrix A as a upper triangular.

$$[\text{A, B}] = \left[\begin{array}{ccc|c} 3 & 4 & 5 & 18 \\ 2 & -1 & 8 & 13 \\ 5 & -2 & 7 & 20 \end{array}\right]$$

$$\sim \left[\begin{array}{ccc|c} 3 & 4 & 5 & 18 \\ 0 & -11 & 14 & 3 \\ 0 & -26 & -4 & -30 \end{array}\right] \begin{array}{l} \\ R_2 \to 3R_2 - 2R_1 \\ R_3 \to 3R_3 - 5R_1 \end{array}$$

$$\sim \left[\begin{array}{ccc|c} 3 & 4 & 5 & 18 \\ 0 & -11 & 14 & 3 \\ 0 & 0 & -408 & -408 \end{array}\right] \begin{array}{l} \\ \\ R_3 \to 11R_3 - 26R_2 \end{array}$$

By back substitution method,

$-408z = -408$

$z = 1$

$-11y + 14(z) = 3$

$-11y + 14 = 3$

$\Rightarrow y = 1$

$3x + 4y + 5z = 18$

$3x + 4(1) + 5(1) = 18$

$3x = 9$

$\Rightarrow x = 3$

Solution $x = 3, \quad y = 1, \quad z = 1$

(ii) Gauss-Jordan Method:

$$[\text{A, B}] \sim \left[\begin{array}{ccc|c} 3 & 4 & 5 & 18 \\ 0 & -11 & 14 & 3 \\ 0 & 0 & -408 & -408 \end{array}\right]$$

$$\sim\left[\begin{array}{ccc|c} -42 & -111 & 0 & -237 \\ 0 & 4488 & 0 & 4488 \\ 0 & 0 & -408 & 408 \end{array}\right] \begin{array}{l} R_1 \to -14R_1 + 5R_2 \\ R_2 \to -408R_2 - 14R_3 \\ \end{array}$$

$$\sim\left[\begin{array}{ccc|c} -42 & -111 & 0 & -237 \\ 0 & 4488 & 0 & 4488 \\ 0 & 0 & -408 & -408 \end{array}\right] \begin{array}{l} R_1 \to -14R_1 + 5R_2 \\ R_2 \to -408R_2 - 14R_3 \\ \end{array}$$

$$\sim\left[\begin{array}{ccc|c} 1 & 0 & 0 & 3 \\ 0 & 1 & 0 & 1 \\ 0 & 0 & 1 & 1 \end{array}\right] \begin{array}{l} R_1/_{-188496} \\ R_2/_{4488} \\ R_3/_{-408} \end{array}$$

Hence the solution is $x = 3, \quad y = 1, \quad z = 1$.

(5) Using the Gauss Jordan Method solve the following

$$\mathbf{10x + y + z = 12}$$
$$\mathbf{2x + 10y + z = 13}$$
$$\mathbf{x + y + 5z = 7}$$

Solution:

Given system of equation is equivalent to

$$AX=B$$

$$\begin{bmatrix} 10 & 1 & 1 \\ 2 & 10 & 1 \\ 1 & 1 & 5 \end{bmatrix}\begin{bmatrix} x \\ y \\ z \end{bmatrix} = \begin{bmatrix} 12 \\ 13 \\ 7 \end{bmatrix}$$

$$[A, B] = \begin{bmatrix} 10 & 1 & 1 & 12 \\ 2 & 10 & 1 & 13 \\ 1 & 1 & 5 & 7 \end{bmatrix}$$

$$\sim\begin{bmatrix} 10 & 1 & 1 & 12 \\ 0 & 49 & 4 & 53 \\ 0 & 9 & 49 & 58 \end{bmatrix} \begin{array}{l} \\ R_2 \to 5R_2 - R_1 \\ R_3 \to 10R_3 - R_1 \end{array}$$

$$\sim\begin{bmatrix} 10 & 1 & 1 & 12 \\ 0 & 49 & 4 & 53 \\ 0 & 0 & 2365 & 2365 \end{bmatrix} \begin{array}{l} \\ \\ R_3 \to 49R_3 - 9R_2 \end{array}$$

$$\sim\begin{bmatrix} 2365 & 2365 & 0 & 26015 \\ 0 & 115885 & 0 & 115885 \\ 0 & 0 & 2365 & 2365 \end{bmatrix} \begin{matrix} R_1 \to 2365R_1 - R_3 \\ R_2 \to 2365R_2 - 4R_3 \\ \end{matrix}$$

$$\sim\begin{bmatrix} 2740680250 & 0 & 0 & 2740680250 \\ 0 & 115885 & 0 & 115885 \\ 0 & 0 & 2365 & 2365 \end{bmatrix} R_1 \to 115885R_1 - 2365R_3$$

The Solutions are

z=1

y=1

x=1

(6) Using Gauss-Elimination Method, Solve the system.

$$\mathbf{3.15x - 1.96y + 3.85z = 12.95}$$
$$\mathbf{2.13x + 5.12y - 2.89z = -8.61}$$
$$\mathbf{5.92x + 3.05y + 2.15z = 6.88}$$

Solution:

The Given system is equivalent to

$$\begin{bmatrix} 3.15 & -1.96 & 3.85 \\ 2.13 & 5.12 & -2.89 \\ 5.92 & 3.05 & 2.15 \end{bmatrix} \begin{bmatrix} x \\ y \\ z \end{bmatrix} = \begin{bmatrix} 12.95 \\ -8.61 \\ 6.88 \end{bmatrix}$$

$$[A, B] = \begin{bmatrix} 3.15 & -1.96 & 3.85 & 12.95 \\ 2.13 & 5.12 & -2.89 & -8.61 \\ 5.92 & 3.05 & 2.15 & 6.88 \end{bmatrix}$$

$$\sim\begin{bmatrix} 3.15 & -1.96 & 3.85 & 12.95 \\ 0 & 20.3028 & -17.304 & -54.705 \\ 0 & 21.2107 & -16.0195 & -54.992 \end{bmatrix} \begin{matrix} \\ R_2 \to 3.15R_2 - 2.13R_1 \\ R_3 \to 3.15R_3 - 5.92R_1 \end{matrix}$$

$$\sim\begin{bmatrix} 3.15 & -1.96 & 3.85 & 12.95 \\ 0 & 20.3028 & -17.304 & -54.705 \\ 0 & 0 & 41.7812 & 43.8398 \end{bmatrix} R_3 \to 20.3028R_3 - 21.2107R_2$$

This is an upper triangular matrix. Now using back substitution method.

$$41.7892\ z = 43.8398$$

$$\boxed{z = 1.049}$$

Substitution z value in above equations

$$20.3028y - 17.304z = -54.705$$

$$20.3028y - (17.304)(1.049) = -54.705$$

$$20.3028y - 18.1519 = -54.705$$

$$20.3028y = -54.705 + 18.1519$$

$$\boxed{y = -1.800}$$

$$3.15x - 1.96y + 3.85z = 12.95$$

$$3.15x - 1.96(-1.8) + 3.85(1.049) = 12.95$$

$$3.15x = 12.95 - 7.56665$$

$$= 5.38335$$

$$\boxed{x = 1.709}$$

Hence, the solution is $x = 1.709,\ y = -1.800,\ z = 1.049.$

3.2.3 Iterative Methods of Gauss Jacobi and Gauss Seidel

Iterative method (or) Indirect method

1) Gauss-Jacobi
2) Gauss-Seidel

Gauss-Jacobi (or) Jacobi method of iteration

Consider the system of equations:

$$a_1x + b_1y + c_1z = d_1$$
$$a_2x + b_2y + c_2z = d_2$$
$$a_3x + b_3y + c_3z = d_3$$

The condition for these 2 methods to converge is

$$|a_1| > |b_1| + |c_1|$$
$$|b_2| > |a_2| + |c_2|$$
$$|c_3| > |a_3| + |b_3|$$

So the process of iteration by Gauss-Seidel and Gauss-Jacobi method will converge, if in each system of equation the absolute value of the largest co-efficient is greater than the sum of absolute value of the remaining co-efficient. That is ***the co-efficient matrix should be diagonally dominant***.

> ***Note:***
>
> **Gauss-Jacobi:**
>
> Start the iteration with x=0, y=0, z=0. For successive iterations use old values of x, y, z and continue the iterations till any two adjacent values coincide.
>
> **Gauss-Seidel:**
>
> Proceed as in Gauss-Jacobi but use the latest values of x, y, z.

(1) Solve the following system of equations by Gauss-Jacobi method and Gauss-Seidel method.

$$\mathbf{27x+6y-z=85}$$
$$\mathbf{x+y+54z=110}$$
$$\mathbf{6x+15y+2z=72}$$

Solution:

Here the co-efficient matrix is not diagonally dominant. So rewrite the equation as follows:

$$27x+6y-z=85$$
$$6x+15y+2z=72$$
$$x+y+54z=110$$

Now the diagonal elements are dominant in the co-efficient matrix.

So we write x, y, z as follows

$$x=\frac{1}{27}[85-6y+z]$$
$$y=\frac{1}{15}[72-6x-2z]$$
$$z=\frac{1}{54}[110-x-y]$$

(i) Gauss-Jacobi method:

Let the initial values be x=0, y=0, z=0.

Iteration No	$x=\frac{1}{27}(85-6y+z)$	$y=\frac{1}{15}(72-6x-2z)$	$z=\frac{1}{54}(110-x-y)$
1	3.148	4.8	2.037
2	2.157	3.269	1.890
3	2.492	3.685	1.937

4	2.401	3.545	1.923
5	2.432	3.583	1.927
6	2.423	3.570	1.926
7	2.426	3.574	1.926
8	2.425	3.573	1.926
9	2.425	3.573	1.926

$\therefore$ Solution is $x=2.425, \quad y=3.573, \quad z=1.926$

(ii) Gauss-Seidel Method:

Initial values are $y=0, \ z=0$

Iteration No	$x=\frac{1}{27}(85-6y+z)$	$y=\frac{1}{15}(72-6x-2z)$	$z=\frac{1}{54}(110-x-y)$
1	3.148	3.541	1.913
2	2.432	3.572	1.926
3	2.426	3.573	1.926
4	2.425	3.573	1.926
5	2.425	3.573	1.926

Hence the solution is $x=2.425, \quad y=3.573, \quad z=1.926$

(2) Solve the following system of equations by Gauss-Jacobi and Gauss Seidel method:

$$4x+2y+z=14$$
$$x+5y-z=10$$
$$x+y+8z=20$$

Solution:

The given system of equations is diagonally dominant,

So express x, y, z as follows

$$x=\frac{1}{4}[14-2y-z]$$
$$y=\frac{1}{5}[10-x+z]$$
$$z=\frac{1}{8}[20-x-y]$$

(i) Gauss-Jacobi method:

Initial condition are x=y=z=0

Iteration No	x	y	z
1	3.5	2.000	2.5
2	1.8750	1.8000	1.8125
3	2.1468	1.9875	2.8406
4	1.9961	1.9787	1.9832
5	2.0148	1.9974	2.0031
6	2.0005	1.9976	1.9984
7	2.0016	1.9995	2.0002
8	2.0002	1.9997	1.9999
9	2.0002	1.9999	2.0000
10	2.0001	2.0000	2.0000
11	2.0000	2.0000	2.0000
12	2.0000	2.0000	2.0000

$\therefore$ ***Solution:*** $x=2, \quad y=2, \quad z=2$

(ii) Gauss Seidel method

Initial values are y = z = 0

Iteration No	x	y	z
1	3.5	1.3	1.9
2	2.3750	1.9060	1.9649
3	2.0558	1.9818	1.9953
4	2.0103	1.9970	1.9991
5	2.0017	1.9995	1.9999
6	2.0003	1.9999	2.0000
7	2.0001	2	2
8	2	2	2

$\therefore$ ***Solution:*** $x=2, \quad y=2, \quad z=2$

(3) Solve the system of equations given below and Gauss-Jacobi and Gauss-Seidel methods

$$20x + y - 2z = 17$$

$$3x + 20y - z = -18$$

$$2x - 3y + 20z = 25$$

Solution:

The given system of equations is diagonally dominant

So, express x, y, z as follows

$$x = \frac{1}{20}[17 - y + 2z]$$

$$y = \frac{1}{20}[-18 - 3x + z]$$

$$z = \frac{1}{20}[25 - 2x + 3y]$$

(i) Gauss-Jacobi method

Initial conditions are $x = 0, \quad y = 0, \quad z = 0$

Iteration No	*x*	*y*	*z*
1	0.8500	–0.9	1.25
2	1.0200	–0.9650	1.0300
3	1.0013	–1.0015	1.0033
4	1.0004	–1.0000	0.9996
5	1.0000	–1.0001	1.0000
6	1	–1	1
7	1	–1	1

Solution : $x = 1, \quad y = -1, \quad z = 1$

(ii) Gauss-Seidel method:

Initial conditions are $y = 0, \quad z = 0$

Iteration No	*x*	*y*	*z*
1	0.85	–1.0275	1.0109
2	1.0025	–0.9998	0.9998
3	1.0000	–1.0000	1.0000
4	1.0000	–1.0000	1.0000

Solution : $x = 1, \quad y = -1, \quad z = 1$

(4) Solve the following system by applying first two iterations Gauss- Jacobi method and continue using the Gauss-Seidal method.

$$3x_1 - x_2 + x_3 = 1,\ \ 3x_1 + 6x_2 + 2x_3 = 0,\ \ 3x_1 + x_2 + 7x_3 = 4.$$

Solution:

The given system of equations is diagonally dominant.

So, x_1, x_2, x_3 as follows,

$$x_1 = \frac{1}{3}[1 + x_2 - x_3]$$

$$x_2 = \frac{1}{6}[-3x_1 - 2x_3]$$

$$x_3 = \frac{1}{7}[4 - 3x_1 - 3x_2]$$

First two Iteration used Gauss-Jacobi method and continue using the Seidal Method.

Initial conditions are $x_1 = 0, x_2 = 0, x_3 = 0$

Iteration No	x_1	x_2	x_3
1	0.3333	0	0.5714
2	0.1429	–0.3571	0.4286
3	0.0714	–0.1786	0.6174
4	0.0680	–0.2398	0.6451
5	0.0384	–0.2342	0.6553
6	0.0368	–0.2368	0.6571
7	0.0354	–0.2367	0.6577
8	0.0352	–0.2368	0.6578
9	0.0351	–0.2368	0.6579
10	0.0351	–0.2368	0.6579

The Solutions are

$$x_1 = 0.0351$$
$$x_2 = -0.2368$$
$$x_3 = 0.6579$$

(5) Using the Gauss-Jacobi and Gauss- Seidal Method, solve the following system start with $x=1,\ y=-2,\ z=3$

$$x+3y+52z=173.61$$
$$x-27y+2z=71.31$$
$$41x-2y+3z=65.46$$

Solution:

The given system of equation is not diagonally dominant as it is

We rewrite the equation

$$41x-2y+3z=65.46$$

$$x-27y+2z=71.31$$

$$x+3y+52z=173.61$$

Now the system of equation is diagonally dominant.

We write *x, y, z* as follows

$$x=\frac{1}{41}[65.46+2y-3z]$$

$$y=\frac{-1}{27}[71.31-x-2z]$$

$$z=\frac{1}{52}[173.61-x-3y]$$

The initial values are $x=1,\ y=-2,\ z=3$

Iteration. No	x	y	z
1	1.280	–2.382	3.146
2	1.250	–2.496	3.451
3	1.222	–2.339	3.459
4	1.229	–2.340	3.450
5	1.230	–2.340	3.450
6	1.230	–2.340	3.450

The solutions are,

$$x=1.230$$
$$y=-2.340$$
$$z=3.450$$

Gauss-Seidel Method

Initial values are $x = 1,\ y = -2, z = 3$

Iteration. No	x	y	z
1	1.2795	–2.3715	3.4509
2	1.2284	–2.340	3.450
3	1.230	–2.340	3.450
4	1.230	–2.340	3.450

The Solutions are

$$x = 1.230$$
$$y = -2.340$$
$$z = 3.450$$

3.3 DOMINANT EIGEN VALUE OF A MATRIX BY POWER METHOD

(1) Find the numerically largest Eigen value and corresponding eigen vector of

$$\mathbf{A} = \begin{bmatrix} \mathbf{25} & \mathbf{1} & \mathbf{2} \\ \mathbf{1} & \mathbf{3} & \mathbf{0} \\ \mathbf{2} & \mathbf{0} & \mathbf{-4} \end{bmatrix}$$

Solution:

Given

$$A = \begin{bmatrix} 25 & 1 & 2 \\ 1 & 3 & 0 \\ 2 & 0 & -4 \end{bmatrix}$$

Let $X_1 = \begin{bmatrix} 1 \\ 0 \\ 0 \end{bmatrix}$ be an arbitrary initial Eigen vector.

$$AX_1 = \begin{bmatrix} 25 & 1 & 2 \\ 1 & 3 & 0 \\ 2 & 0 & -4 \end{bmatrix}\begin{bmatrix} 1 \\ 0 \\ 0 \end{bmatrix} = \begin{bmatrix} 25 \\ 1 \\ 2 \end{bmatrix}$$

$$= 25\begin{bmatrix} 1 \\ 0.04 \\ 0.08 \end{bmatrix}$$

$$=25X_2$$

$$AX_2 = \begin{bmatrix} 25 & 1 & 2 \\ 1 & 3 & 0 \\ 2 & 0 & -4 \end{bmatrix}\begin{bmatrix} 1 \\ 0.04 \\ 0.08 \end{bmatrix} = \begin{bmatrix} 25.2 \\ 1.12 \\ 1.68 \end{bmatrix} = 25.2\begin{bmatrix} 1 \\ 0.044 \\ 0.067 \end{bmatrix} = 25.2X_3$$

$$AX_3 = \begin{bmatrix} 25 & 1 & 2 \\ 1 & 3 & 0 \\ 2 & 0 & -4 \end{bmatrix}\begin{bmatrix} 1 \\ 0.044 \\ 0.067 \end{bmatrix} = \begin{bmatrix} 25.178 \\ 1.132 \\ 1.732 \end{bmatrix} = 25.178\begin{bmatrix} 1 \\ 0.045 \\ 0.069 \end{bmatrix} = 25.178X_4$$

$$AX_4 = \begin{bmatrix} 25 & 1 & 2 \\ 1 & 3 & 0 \\ 2 & 0 & -4 \end{bmatrix}\begin{bmatrix} 1 \\ 0.045 \\ 0.069 \end{bmatrix} = \begin{bmatrix} 25.183 \\ 1.135 \\ 1.724 \end{bmatrix} = 25.183\begin{bmatrix} 1 \\ 0.045 \\ 0.068 \end{bmatrix} = 25.183X_5$$

$$AX_5 = \begin{bmatrix} 25 & 1 & 2 \\ 1 & 3 & 0 \\ 2 & 0 & -4 \end{bmatrix}\begin{bmatrix} 1 \\ 0.045 \\ 0.068 \end{bmatrix} = \begin{bmatrix} 25.181 \\ 1.135 \\ 1.728 \end{bmatrix} = 25.181\begin{bmatrix} 1 \\ 0.045 \\ 0.068 \end{bmatrix}$$

$\therefore$ The largest Eigen value is =25.181 and the Eigen vector is $\begin{bmatrix} 1 \\ 0.045 \\ 0.068 \end{bmatrix}$.

2) Determine the largest Eigen value and the corresponding Eigen vector of the matrix $\begin{bmatrix} 1 & 1 \\ 1 & 1 \end{bmatrix}$ correct to two decimal places using power method.

Solution:

Given $$A = \begin{bmatrix} 1 & 1 \\ 1 & 1 \end{bmatrix}$$

Let $X_1 = \begin{bmatrix} 1 \\ 0 \end{bmatrix}$

$$AX_1 = \begin{bmatrix} 1 & 1 \\ 1 & 1 \end{bmatrix}\begin{bmatrix} 1 \\ 0 \end{bmatrix} = \begin{bmatrix} 1 \\ 1 \end{bmatrix} = X_2$$

$$AX_2 = \begin{bmatrix} 1 & 1 \\ 1 & 1 \end{bmatrix}\begin{bmatrix} 1 \\ 1 \end{bmatrix} = \begin{bmatrix} 2 \\ 2 \end{bmatrix} = 2X_3$$

$$AX_3 = \begin{bmatrix} 1 & 1 \\ 1 & 1 \end{bmatrix}\begin{bmatrix} 1 \\ 1 \end{bmatrix} = \begin{bmatrix} 2 \\ 2 \end{bmatrix} = 2\begin{bmatrix} 1 \\ 1 \end{bmatrix} = 2$$

$\therefore$ This shows that the largest Eigen value = 2.

The corresponding Eigen vector = $\begin{bmatrix} 1 \\ 1 \end{bmatrix}$

3) Find the numerically largest Eigen value of $A = \begin{bmatrix} 1 & -3 & 2 \\ 4 & 4 & -1 \\ 6 & 3 & 5 \end{bmatrix}$ by power method.

Solution:

Given $A = \begin{bmatrix} 1 & -3 & 2 \\ 4 & 4 & -1 \\ 6 & 3 & 5 \end{bmatrix}$

Let $X_1 = \begin{bmatrix} 1 \\ 0 \\ 0 \end{bmatrix}$

$$AX_1 = \begin{bmatrix} 1 & -3 & 2 \\ 4 & 4 & -1 \\ 6 & 3 & 5 \end{bmatrix}\begin{bmatrix} 1 \\ 0 \\ 0 \end{bmatrix} = \begin{bmatrix} 1 \\ 4 \\ 6 \end{bmatrix} = 6\begin{bmatrix} 0.167 \\ 0.667 \\ 1 \end{bmatrix} = 6X_2$$

$$AX_2 = \begin{bmatrix} 1 & -3 & 2 \\ 4 & 4 & -1 \\ 6 & 3 & 5 \end{bmatrix}\begin{bmatrix} 0.167 \\ 0.667 \\ 1 \end{bmatrix} = \begin{bmatrix} 0.166 \\ 2.336 \\ 8.003 \end{bmatrix} = 8.003\begin{bmatrix} 0.021 \\ 0.292 \\ 1 \end{bmatrix} = 8.003X_3$$

$$AX_3 = \begin{bmatrix} 1 & -3 & 2 \\ 4 & 4 & -1 \\ 6 & 3 & 5 \end{bmatrix}\begin{bmatrix} 0.021 \\ 0.292 \\ 1 \end{bmatrix} = \begin{bmatrix} 1.145 \\ 0.252 \\ 6.002 \end{bmatrix} = 6.002\begin{bmatrix} 0.191 \\ 0.042 \\ 1 \end{bmatrix} = 6.002X_4$$

$$AX_4 = \begin{bmatrix} 1 & -3 & 2 \\ 4 & 4 & -1 \\ 6 & 3 & 5 \end{bmatrix}\begin{bmatrix} 0.191 \\ 0.042 \\ 1 \end{bmatrix} = \begin{bmatrix} 2.065 \\ -0.068 \\ 6.272 \end{bmatrix} = 6.272\begin{bmatrix} 0.329 \\ -0.011 \\ 1 \end{bmatrix} = 6.272X_5$$

$$AX_5 = \begin{bmatrix} 1 & -3 & 2 \\ 4 & 4 & -1 \\ 6 & 3 & 5 \end{bmatrix}\begin{bmatrix} 0.329 \\ -0.011 \\ 1 \end{bmatrix} = \begin{bmatrix} 2.362 \\ 0.272 \\ 6.941 \end{bmatrix} = 6.941\begin{bmatrix} 0.340 \\ 0.039 \\ 1 \end{bmatrix} = 6.941X_6$$

$$AX_6 = \begin{bmatrix} 1 & -3 & 2 \\ 4 & 4 & -1 \\ 6 & 3 & 5 \end{bmatrix}\begin{bmatrix} 0.340 \\ 0.039 \\ 1 \end{bmatrix} = \begin{bmatrix} 2.223 \\ 0.516 \\ 7.157 \end{bmatrix} = 7.157\begin{bmatrix} 0.311 \\ 0.072 \\ 1 \end{bmatrix} = 7.157X_7$$

$$AX_7 = \begin{bmatrix} 1 & -3 & 2 \\ 4 & 4 & -1 \\ 6 & 3 & 5 \end{bmatrix}\begin{bmatrix} 0.311 \\ 0.072 \\ 1 \end{bmatrix} = \begin{bmatrix} 2.095 \\ 0.532 \\ 7.082 \end{bmatrix} = 7.082\begin{bmatrix} 0.296 \\ 0.075 \\ 1 \end{bmatrix} = 7.082X_8$$

$$AX_8 = \begin{bmatrix} 1 & -3 & 2 \\ 4 & 4 & -1 \\ 6 & 3 & 5 \end{bmatrix}\begin{bmatrix} 0.296 \\ 0.075 \\ 1 \end{bmatrix} = \begin{bmatrix} 2.071 \\ 0.484 \\ 7.001 \end{bmatrix} = 7.001\begin{bmatrix} 0.296 \\ 0.069 \\ 1 \end{bmatrix} = 7.001X_9$$

$$AX_9 = \begin{bmatrix} 1 & -3 & 2 \\ 4 & 4 & -1 \\ 6 & 3 & 5 \end{bmatrix}\begin{bmatrix} 0.296 \\ 0.069 \\ 1 \end{bmatrix} = \begin{bmatrix} 2.089 \\ 0.460 \\ 6.983 \end{bmatrix} = 6.983\begin{bmatrix} 0.299 \\ 0.066 \\ 1 \end{bmatrix} = 6.983X_{10}$$

$$AX_{10} = \begin{bmatrix} 1 & -3 & 2 \\ 4 & 4 & -1 \\ 6 & 3 & 5 \end{bmatrix}\begin{bmatrix} 0.299 \\ 0.066 \\ 1 \end{bmatrix} = \begin{bmatrix} 2.101 \\ 0.460 \\ 6.992 \end{bmatrix} = 6.992\begin{bmatrix} 0.3 \\ 0.066 \\ 1 \end{bmatrix} = 6.992X_{11}$$

$$AX_{11} = \begin{bmatrix} 1 & -3 & 2 \\ 4 & 4 & -1 \\ 6 & 3 & 5 \end{bmatrix}\begin{bmatrix} 0.3 \\ 0.06 \\ 1 \end{bmatrix} = \begin{bmatrix} 2.102 \\ 0.464 \\ 6.998 \end{bmatrix} = 6.998\begin{bmatrix} 0.3 \\ 0.066 \\ 1 \end{bmatrix} = 6.998X_{12}$$

$$AX_{12} = \begin{bmatrix} 1 & -3 & 2 \\ 4 & 4 & -1 \\ 6 & 3 & 5 \end{bmatrix}\begin{bmatrix} 0.3 \\ 0.066 \\ 1 \end{bmatrix} = \begin{bmatrix} 2.102 \\ 0.464 \\ 6.998 \end{bmatrix} = 6.998\begin{bmatrix} 0.3 \\ 0.066 \\ 1 \end{bmatrix}$$

Result:

(i) Dominant Eigen value = 6.998

(ii) Eigen Vector = $\begin{bmatrix} 0.3 \\ 0.066 \\ 1 \end{bmatrix}$

(4) Find the dominant Eigen value and the corresponding Eigen vector of $A = \begin{bmatrix} 1 & 6 & 1 \\ 1 & 2 & 0 \\ 0 & 0 & 3 \end{bmatrix}$ by power method, find also the least latent root and hence find the third Eigen value.

Solution:

Given $$A = \begin{bmatrix} 1 & 6 & 1 \\ 1 & 2 & 0 \\ 0 & 0 & 3 \end{bmatrix}$$

Let $$X_1 = \begin{bmatrix} 1 \\ 0 \\ 0 \end{bmatrix}$$

$$AX_1 = \begin{bmatrix} 1 & 6 & 1 \\ 1 & 2 & 0 \\ 0 & 0 & 3 \end{bmatrix}\begin{bmatrix} 1 \\ 0 \\ 0 \end{bmatrix} = \begin{bmatrix} 1 \\ 1 \\ 0 \end{bmatrix} = 1\begin{bmatrix} 1 \\ 1 \\ 0 \end{bmatrix} = X_2$$

$$AX_2 = \begin{bmatrix} 1 & 6 & 1 \\ 1 & 2 & 0 \\ 0 & 0 & 3 \end{bmatrix}\begin{bmatrix} 1 \\ 1 \\ 0 \end{bmatrix} = \begin{bmatrix} 7 \\ 3 \\ 0 \end{bmatrix} = 7\begin{bmatrix} 1 \\ 0.4286 \\ 0 \end{bmatrix} = 7X_3$$

$$AX_3 = \begin{bmatrix} 1 & 6 & 1 \\ 1 & 2 & 0 \\ 0 & 0 & 3 \end{bmatrix}\begin{bmatrix} 1 \\ 0.4286 \\ 0 \end{bmatrix} = \begin{bmatrix} 3.5714 \\ 1.8572 \\ 0 \end{bmatrix} = 3.5714\begin{bmatrix} 1 \\ 0.52 \\ 0 \end{bmatrix} = 3.5714X_4$$

$$AX_4 = \begin{bmatrix} 1 & 6 & 1 \\ 1 & 2 & 0 \\ 0 & 0 & 3 \end{bmatrix}\begin{bmatrix} 1 \\ 0.52 \\ 0 \end{bmatrix} = \begin{bmatrix} 4.12 \\ 2.04 \\ 0 \end{bmatrix} = 4.12\begin{bmatrix} 1 \\ 0.4951 \\ 0 \end{bmatrix} = 4.12X_5$$

$$AX_5 = \begin{bmatrix} 1 & 6 & 1 \\ 1 & 2 & 0 \\ 0 & 0 & 3 \end{bmatrix}\begin{bmatrix} 1 \\ 0.4951 \\ 0 \end{bmatrix} = \begin{bmatrix} 3.9706 \\ 1.9902 \\ 0 \end{bmatrix} = 3.9706\begin{bmatrix} 1 \\ 0.5012 \\ 0 \end{bmatrix} = 3.9706X_6$$

$$AX_6 = \begin{bmatrix} 1 & 6 & 1 \\ 1 & 2 & 0 \\ 0 & 0 & 3 \end{bmatrix}\begin{bmatrix} 1 \\ 0.5012 \\ 0 \end{bmatrix} = \begin{bmatrix} 4.0072 \\ 2.0024 \\ 0 \end{bmatrix} = 4.0072\begin{bmatrix} 1 \\ 0.4997 \\ 0 \end{bmatrix} = 4.0072X_7$$

$$AX_7 = \begin{bmatrix} 1 & 6 & 1 \\ 1 & 2 & 0 \\ 0 & 0 & 3 \end{bmatrix}\begin{bmatrix} 1 \\ 0.4997 \\ 0 \end{bmatrix} = \begin{bmatrix} 3.9982 \\ 1.9994 \\ 0 \end{bmatrix} = 3.9982\begin{bmatrix} 1 \\ 0.5 \\ 0 \end{bmatrix} = 3.9982X_8$$

$$AX_8 = \begin{bmatrix} 1 & 6 & 1 \\ 1 & 2 & 0 \\ 0 & 0 & 3 \end{bmatrix}\begin{bmatrix} 1 \\ 0.5 \\ 0 \end{bmatrix} = \begin{bmatrix} 4 \\ 2 \\ 0 \end{bmatrix} = 4\begin{bmatrix} 1 \\ 0.5 \\ 0 \end{bmatrix} = 4X_9$$

$$AX_9 = \begin{bmatrix} 1 & 6 & 1 \\ 1 & 2 & 0 \\ 0 & 0 & 3 \end{bmatrix}\begin{bmatrix} 1 \\ 0.5 \\ 1 \end{bmatrix} = \begin{bmatrix} 4 \\ 2 \\ 0 \end{bmatrix} = 4\begin{bmatrix} 1 \\ 0.5 \\ 0 \end{bmatrix}$$

Hence, the largest Eigen value = 4

$$\text{Eigen Vector} = \begin{bmatrix} 1 \\ 0.5 \\ 0 \end{bmatrix}$$

To find the least Eigen value

Let B = A–4I Since $\lambda_1 = 4$

$$B = \begin{bmatrix} 1 & 6 & 1 \\ 1 & 2 & 0 \\ 0 & 0 & 3 \end{bmatrix} - \begin{bmatrix} 4 & 0 & 0 \\ 0 & 4 & 0 \\ 0 & 0 & 4 \end{bmatrix}$$

$$B = \begin{bmatrix} -3 & 6 & 1 \\ 1 & -2 & 2 \\ 0 & 0 & -2 \end{bmatrix}$$

We will find the dominant Eigen value of B

Let $Y_1 = \begin{bmatrix} 1 \\ 0 \\ 0 \end{bmatrix}$

$$BY_1 = \begin{bmatrix} -3 & 6 & 1 \\ 1 & -2 & 2 \\ 0 & 0 & -2 \end{bmatrix}\begin{bmatrix} 1 \\ 0 \\ 0 \end{bmatrix} = \begin{bmatrix} -3 \\ 1 \\ 0 \end{bmatrix} = -3\begin{bmatrix} 1 \\ -0.3333 \\ 0 \end{bmatrix} = -3Y_2$$

$$BY_2 = \begin{bmatrix} -3 & 6 & 1 \\ 1 & -2 & 2 \\ 0 & 0 & -2 \end{bmatrix} \begin{bmatrix} 1 \\ -0.3333 \\ 0 \end{bmatrix} = \begin{bmatrix} -5 \\ 1.6666 \\ 0 \end{bmatrix} = -5 \begin{bmatrix} 1 \\ -0.3333 \\ 0 \end{bmatrix} = -5Y_3$$

$$BY_3 = \begin{bmatrix} -3 & 6 & 1 \\ 1 & -2 & 2 \\ 0 & 0 & -2 \end{bmatrix} \begin{bmatrix} 1 \\ -0.3333 \\ 0 \end{bmatrix} = \begin{bmatrix} -5 \\ 1.6666 \\ 0 \end{bmatrix} = -5 \begin{bmatrix} 1 \\ -0.3333 \\ 0 \end{bmatrix}$$

Dominant Eigen Value of B is –5

$\therefore$ The smallest Eigen value of A = –5+4 = –1

Sum of Eigen values = Trace of A

$$4+(-1)+\lambda_3 = 1+2+3$$

$$3+\lambda_3 = 6$$

$$\lambda_3 = 3$$

Result: All the three Eigen values are 4, 3, –1

(5) Using power method, find all the Eigen value of $A = \begin{bmatrix} 5 & 0 & 1 \\ 0 & -2 & 0 \\ 1 & 0 & 5 \end{bmatrix}$

Solution:

Given $A = \begin{bmatrix} 5 & 0 & 1 \\ 0 & -2 & 0 \\ 1 & 0 & 5 \end{bmatrix}$

Let $X_1 = \begin{bmatrix} 1 \\ 0 \\ 0 \end{bmatrix}$

$$AX_1 = \begin{bmatrix} 5 & 0 & 1 \\ 0 & -2 & 0 \\ 1 & 0 & 5 \end{bmatrix} \begin{bmatrix} 1 \\ 0 \\ 0 \end{bmatrix} = \begin{bmatrix} 5 \\ 0 \\ 1 \end{bmatrix} = 5 \begin{bmatrix} 1 \\ 0 \\ 0.2 \end{bmatrix} = 5X_2$$

$$AX_2 = \begin{bmatrix} 5 & 0 & 1 \\ 0 & -2 & 0 \\ 1 & 0 & 5 \end{bmatrix} \begin{bmatrix} 1 \\ 0 \\ 0.2 \end{bmatrix} = \begin{bmatrix} 5.2 \\ 0 \\ 2 \end{bmatrix} = 5.2 \begin{bmatrix} 1 \\ 0 \\ 0.39 \end{bmatrix} = 5.2X_3$$

$$AX_3 = \begin{bmatrix} 5 & 0 & 1 \\ 0 & -2 & 0 \\ 1 & 0 & 5 \end{bmatrix} \begin{bmatrix} 1 \\ 0 \\ 0.39 \end{bmatrix} = \begin{bmatrix} 5.39 \\ 0 \\ 2.95 \end{bmatrix} = 5.39 \begin{bmatrix} 1 \\ 0 \\ 0.55 \end{bmatrix} = 5.2X_4$$

$$AX_4 = \begin{bmatrix} 5 & 0 & 1 \\ 0 & -2 & 0 \\ 1 & 0 & 5 \end{bmatrix} \begin{bmatrix} 1 \\ 0 \\ 0.55 \end{bmatrix} = \begin{bmatrix} 5.55 \\ 0 \\ 3.75 \end{bmatrix} = 5.55 \begin{bmatrix} 1 \\ 0 \\ 0.68 \end{bmatrix} = 5.55X_5$$

$$AX_5 = \begin{bmatrix} 5 & 0 & 1 \\ 0 & -2 & 0 \\ 1 & 0 & 5 \end{bmatrix} \begin{bmatrix} 1 \\ 0 \\ 0.68 \end{bmatrix} = \begin{bmatrix} 5.68 \\ 0 \\ 4.4 \end{bmatrix} = 5.68 \begin{bmatrix} 1 \\ 0 \\ 0.78 \end{bmatrix} = 5.68X_6$$

$$AX_6 = \begin{bmatrix} 5 & 0 & 1 \\ 0 & -2 & 0 \\ 1 & 0 & 5 \end{bmatrix} \begin{bmatrix} 1 \\ 0 \\ 0.78 \end{bmatrix} = \begin{bmatrix} 5.78 \\ 0 \\ 4.9 \end{bmatrix} = 5.78 \begin{bmatrix} 1 \\ 0 \\ 0.85 \end{bmatrix} = 5.78X_7$$

$$AX_7 = \begin{bmatrix} 5 & 0 & 1 \\ 0 & -2 & 0 \\ 1 & 0 & 5 \end{bmatrix} \begin{bmatrix} 1 \\ 0 \\ 0.85 \end{bmatrix} = \begin{bmatrix} 5.85 \\ 0 \\ 5.25 \end{bmatrix} = 5.85 \begin{bmatrix} 1 \\ 0 \\ 0.9 \end{bmatrix} = 5.85X_8$$

$$AX_8 = \begin{bmatrix} 5 & 0 & 1 \\ 0 & -2 & 0 \\ 1 & 0 & 5 \end{bmatrix} \begin{bmatrix} 1 \\ 0 \\ 0.9 \end{bmatrix} = \begin{bmatrix} 5.9 \\ 0 \\ 5.5 \end{bmatrix} = 5.9 \begin{bmatrix} 1 \\ 0 \\ 0.93 \end{bmatrix} = 5.9X_9$$

$$AX_9 = \begin{bmatrix} 5 & 0 & 1 \\ 0 & -2 & 0 \\ 1 & 0 & 5 \end{bmatrix} \begin{bmatrix} 1 \\ 0 \\ 0.93 \end{bmatrix} = \begin{bmatrix} 5.93 \\ 0 \\ 5.65 \end{bmatrix} = 5.93 \begin{bmatrix} 1 \\ 0 \\ 0.95 \end{bmatrix} = 5.93X_{10}$$

$$AX_{10} = \begin{bmatrix} 5 & 0 & 1 \\ 0 & -2 & 0 \\ 1 & 0 & 5 \end{bmatrix} \begin{bmatrix} 1 \\ 0 \\ 0.95 \end{bmatrix} = \begin{bmatrix} 5.95 \\ 0 \\ 5.75 \end{bmatrix} = 5.95 \begin{bmatrix} 1 \\ 0 \\ 1 \end{bmatrix} = 5.95X_{11}$$

$$AX_{11} = \begin{bmatrix} 5 & 0 & 1 \\ 0 & -2 & 0 \\ 1 & 0 & 5 \end{bmatrix} \begin{bmatrix} 1 \\ 0 \\ 1 \end{bmatrix} = \begin{bmatrix} 6 \\ 0 \\ 6 \end{bmatrix} = 6 \begin{bmatrix} 1 \\ 0 \\ 1 \end{bmatrix}$$

$$AX_{12} = \begin{bmatrix} 5 & 0 & 1 \\ 0 & -2 & 0 \\ 1 & 0 & 5 \end{bmatrix} \begin{bmatrix} 1 \\ 0 \\ 1 \end{bmatrix} = 6 \begin{bmatrix} 1 \\ 0 \\ 1 \end{bmatrix}$$

$$x_1 = 6; \text{ Eigen vector} = \begin{bmatrix} 1 \\ 0 \\ 1 \end{bmatrix}$$

$$B = A - 6I = \begin{bmatrix} -1 & 0 & 1 \\ 0 & -8 & 0 \\ 1 & 0 & -1 \end{bmatrix} \quad \text{Take } y_1 = \begin{bmatrix} 1 \\ 0 \\ 0 \end{bmatrix}$$

$$B\,y_1 = \begin{bmatrix} -1 & 0 & 1 \\ 0 & -8 & 0 \\ 1 & 0 & -1 \end{bmatrix}\begin{bmatrix} 1 \\ 0 \\ 0 \end{bmatrix} = \begin{bmatrix} -1 \\ 0 \\ 1 \end{bmatrix} = -1\begin{bmatrix} 1 \\ 0 \\ -1 \end{bmatrix} = -y_2$$

$$B\,y_2 = \begin{bmatrix} -1 & 0 & 1 \\ 0 & -8 & 0 \\ 1 & 0 & -1 \end{bmatrix}\begin{bmatrix} 1 \\ 0 \\ -1 \end{bmatrix} = \begin{bmatrix} -2 \\ 0 \\ 2 \end{bmatrix} = -2\begin{bmatrix} 1 \\ 0 \\ -1 \end{bmatrix} = -2y_3$$

$$B\,y_3 = \begin{bmatrix} -1 & 0 & 1 \\ 0 & -8 & 0 \\ 1 & 0 & -1 \end{bmatrix}\begin{bmatrix} 1 \\ 0 \\ -1 \end{bmatrix} = \begin{bmatrix} +2 \\ 0 \\ -2 \end{bmatrix} = -2\begin{bmatrix} 1 \\ 0 \\ -1 \end{bmatrix}$$

Greater Eigen value of B = –2

Smallest Eigen Value of A = –2+6=4

W.K.T Sum of Eigen values = Sum of Diagonal elements

$$\lambda_1 + \lambda_2 + \lambda_3 = 5 - 2 + 5$$

$$6 + 4 + \lambda_3 = 8$$

$$\lambda_3 = 8 - 10$$
$$\lambda_3 = -2$$

∴ Eigen Values are 6, 4, –2.

3.4 MATRIX INVERSION BY GAUSS-JORDAN METHOD

(1) Using Gauss-Jordan method find the inverse of $A = \begin{bmatrix} 1 & 1 & 3 \\ 1 & 3 & -3 \\ -2 & -4 & -4 \end{bmatrix}$

Solution:

$$\text{Let}\quad [A, I] \sim \left[\begin{array}{ccc|ccc} 1 & 1 & 3 & 1 & 0 & 0 \\ 1 & 3 & -3 & 0 & 1 & 0 \\ -2 & -4 & -4 & 0 & 0 & 1 \end{array}\right]$$

$$\sim \left[\begin{array}{ccc|ccc} 1 & 1 & 3 & 1 & 0 & 0 \\ 0 & 2 & -6 & -1 & 1 & 0 \\ 0 & -2 & 2 & 2 & 0 & 1 \end{array}\right] \begin{array}{l} \\ R_2 \to R_2 - R_1 \\ R_3 \to R_3 + 2R_1 \end{array}$$

$$\sim \left[\begin{array}{ccc|ccc} 1 & 1 & 3 & 1 & 0 & 0 \\ 0 & 1 & -3 & -0.5 & 0.5 & 0 \\ 0 & -2 & 2 & 2 & 0 & 1 \end{array}\right] R_2 \to R_2/2$$

$$\sim \left[\begin{array}{ccc|ccc} 1 & 0 & 6 & 1.5 & -0.5 & 0 \\ 0 & 1 & -3 & -0.5 & 0.5 & 0 \\ 0 & 0 & -4 & 1 & 1 & 1 \end{array}\right] \begin{array}{l} R_1 \to R_1 - R_2 \\ \\ R_3 \to R_3 + 2R_2 \end{array}$$

$$\sim \left[\begin{array}{ccc|ccc} 1 & 0 & 6 & 1.5 & -0.5 & 0 \\ 0 & 1 & -3 & -0.5 & 0.5 & 0 \\ 0 & 0 & 1 & -0.25 & -0.25 & -0.25 \end{array}\right] R_3 \to R_3/-4$$

$$\sim \left[\begin{array}{ccc|ccc} 1 & 0 & 0 & 3 & 1 & 1.5 \\ 0 & 1 & 0 & -1.25 & -0.25 & -0.75 \\ 0 & 0 & 1 & -0.25 & -0.25 & -0.25 \end{array}\right] \begin{array}{l} R_1 \to R_1 - 6R_3 \\ R_2 \to R_2 + 3R_3 \\ \\ \end{array}$$

$$\therefore \quad A^{-1} = \begin{bmatrix} 3 & 1 & 1.5 \\ -1.25 & -0.25 & -0.75 \\ -0.25 & -0.25 & -0.25 \end{bmatrix}$$

(2) Using Gauss-jordan Method find the Inverse of $A = \begin{bmatrix} 2 & 2 & 6 \\ 2 & 6 & -6 \\ 4 & -8 & -8 \end{bmatrix}$

Solution:

$$\text{Given} \qquad A = \begin{bmatrix} 2 & 2 & 6 \\ 2 & 6 & -6 \\ 4 & -8 & -8 \end{bmatrix}$$

$$= \begin{bmatrix} 1 & 1 & 3 \\ 1 & 3 & -3 \\ 1 & -2 & -2 \end{bmatrix} \begin{matrix} R_1/2 \\ R_2/2 \\ R_3/4 \end{matrix}$$

$$[A, I] \sim \left[\begin{array}{ccc|ccc} 1 & 1 & 3 & 1 & 0 & 0 \\ 1 & 3 & -3 & 0 & 1 & 0 \\ 1 & -2 & -2 & 0 & 0 & 1 \end{array}\right]$$

$$\sim \left[\begin{array}{ccc|ccc} 1 & 1 & 3 & 1 & 0 & 0 \\ 0 & 2 & -6 & -1 & 1 & 0 \\ 0 & -3 & -5 & -1 & 0 & 1 \end{array}\right] \begin{matrix} \\ R_2 \to R_2 - R_1 \\ R_3 \to R_3 - R_1 \end{matrix}$$

$$\sim \left[\begin{array}{ccc|ccc} 1 & 1 & 3 & 1 & 0 & 0 \\ 0 & 1 & -3 & -0.5 & 0.5 & 0 \\ 0 & 0 & 4.67 & 0.83 & -0.5 & -0.33 \end{array}\right] \begin{matrix} R_1 \to R_1 - R_2 \\ \\ R_3 \to R_3 - R_2 \end{matrix}$$

$$\sim \left[\begin{array}{ccc|ccc} 1 & 0 & 6 & 1.5 & -0.5 & 0 \\ 0 & 1 & -3 & -0.5 & 0.5 & 0 \\ 0 & 0 & 1 & 0.18 & -0.10 & -0.07 \end{array}\right] \begin{matrix} \\ \\ R_3 \to R_3 / 4.67 \end{matrix}$$

$$\sim \left[\begin{array}{ccc|ccc} 1 & 0 & 0 & 0.42 & 0.16 & 0.42 \\ 0 & 1 & 0 & 0.04 & 0.17 & -0.21 \\ 0 & 0 & 1 & 0.18 & -0.10 & -0.07 \end{array}\right] \begin{matrix} R_1 \to R_1 - 6R_3 \\ R_2 \to R_3 + 3R_3 \\ \\ \end{matrix}$$

$$\therefore \; A^{-1} = \begin{bmatrix} 0.42 & 0.16 & 0.42 \\ 0.04 & 0.17 & -0.21 \\ 0.18 & -0.10 & -0.07 \end{bmatrix}$$

(3) Using Gauss-Jordan method, find the inverse of the matrix $\begin{bmatrix} \mathbf{2} & \mathbf{2} & \mathbf{3} \\ \mathbf{2} & \mathbf{1} & \mathbf{1} \\ \mathbf{1} & \mathbf{3} & \mathbf{5} \end{bmatrix}$

Solution:

Given
$$A = \begin{bmatrix} 2 & 2 & 3 \\ 2 & 1 & 1 \\ 1 & 3 & 5 \end{bmatrix}$$

Let
$$[A, I] \sim \left[\begin{array}{ccc|ccc} 2 & 2 & 3 & 1 & 0 & 0 \\ 2 & 1 & 1 & 0 & 1 & 0 \\ 1 & 3 & 5 & 0 & 0 & 1 \end{array}\right]$$

$$\sim\left[\begin{array}{ccc|ccc} 1 & 1 & 3/2 & 1/2 & 0 & 0 \\ 2 & 1 & 1 & 0 & 1 & 0 \\ 1 & 3 & 5 & 0 & 1 & 1 \end{array}\right] R_1 \to R_1/2$$

$$\sim\left[\begin{array}{ccc|ccc} 1 & 1 & 3/2 & 1/2 & 0 & 0 \\ 0 & -1 & -2 & -1 & 1 & 0 \\ 0 & 2 & 7/2 & -1/2 & 0 & 1 \end{array}\right] \begin{array}{l} R_2 \to R_2 - 2R_1 \\ R_3 \to R_3 - R_1 \end{array}$$

$$\sim\left[\begin{array}{ccc|ccc} 1 & 1 & 3/2 & 1/2 & 0 & 0 \\ 0 & 1 & 2 & 1 & -1 & 0 \\ 0 & 2 & 7/2 & -1/2 & 0 & 1 \end{array}\right] R_2 \to R_2/-1$$

$$\sim\left[\begin{array}{ccc|ccc} 1 & 0 & 1/2 & -1/2 & 1 & 0 \\ 0 & 1 & 2 & 1 & -1 & 0 \\ 0 & 0 & -1/2 & -5/2 & 2 & 1 \end{array}\right] \begin{array}{l} R_1 \to R_1 - R_2 \\ \\ R_3 \to R_3 - 2R_1 \end{array}$$

$$\sim\left[\begin{array}{ccc|ccc} 1 & 0 & -1/2 & -1/2 & 1 & 0 \\ 0 & 1 & 2 & 1 & -1 & 0 \\ 0 & 0 & 1 & 5 & -4 & -2 \end{array}\right] R_3 \to R_3 \times (-2)$$

$$\sim\left[\begin{array}{ccc|ccc} 1 & 0 & 0 & 2 & -1 & -1 \\ 0 & 1 & 0 & -9 & 7 & 4 \\ 0 & 0 & 1 & 5 & -4 & -2 \end{array}\right] \begin{array}{l} R_1 \to R_1 + \frac{1}{2}R_3 \\ R_2 \to R_2 - 2R_3 \end{array}$$

$$\therefore \quad A^{-1} = \begin{bmatrix} 2 & -1 & -1 \\ -9 & 7 & 4 \\ 5 & -4 & -2 \end{bmatrix}$$

Verification:

$$AA^{-1} = I$$

$$\begin{bmatrix} 2 & 2 & 3 \\ 2 & 1 & 1 \\ 1 & 3 & 5 \end{bmatrix}\begin{bmatrix} 2 & -1 & -1 \\ -9 & 7 & 4 \\ 5 & -4 & -2 \end{bmatrix} = \begin{bmatrix} 1 & 0 & 0 \\ 0 & 1 & 0 \\ 0 & 0 & 1 \end{bmatrix}$$

(4) Find the inverse of the co-efficient matrix by Gauss-Jordan method:

$$5x-2y=10$$
$$3x+4y=12$$

Solution:

$$A=\begin{bmatrix}5 & -2\\ 3 & 4\end{bmatrix}$$

$$[A, I]=\left[\begin{array}{cc|cc}5 & -2 & 1 & 0\\ 3 & 4 & 0 & 1\end{array}\right]$$

$$=\left[\begin{array}{cc|cc}1 & -2/5 & 1/5 & 0\\ 3 & 4 & 0 & 1\end{array}\right] R_1 \to R_1/5$$

$$\sim\left[\begin{array}{cc|cc}1 & -2/5 & 1/5 & 0\\ 0 & 26/5 & -3/5 & 1\end{array}\right] R_2 \to R_2-3R_1$$

$$\sim\left[\begin{array}{cc|cc}1 & -2/5 & 1/5 & 0\\ 0 & 1 & -3/26 & 5/26\end{array}\right] R_2 \to R_2\times 5/26$$

$$\sim\left[\begin{array}{cc|cc}1 & 0 & 2/13 & 1/13\\ 0 & 1 & -3/26 & 5/26\end{array}\right] R_1 \to R_1+2/5\,R_2$$

$$A^{-1}\sim\begin{bmatrix}2/13 & 1/13\\ -3/26 & 5/26\end{bmatrix}$$

$$\therefore \quad A^{-1}=\frac{1}{26}\begin{bmatrix}4 & 2\\ -3 & 5\end{bmatrix}$$

3.5 STATEMENT OF FIXED POINT THEOREM-FIXED POINT ITERATION *x=g(x)* METHOD.

3.5.1 Fixed point iteration: *x=g(x)* method.

Let $f(x)=0$ be the given equation whose actual root is r. The equation $f(x)=0$ be written as $x=g(x)$. let I be the interval containing the root $x=r$. if $|g'(x)|<1$ for all x in I, then the sequence of approximations $x_0, x_1, x_2, \ldots x_n$ will converge to r, if the initial starting value x_0 is chosen in I.

> ***Note 1:*** Since $|x_n - r| \le K|x_{n-1} - r|$ where K is a constant the convergence is linear and the convergence is of order 1.
>
> ***Note 2:*** The sufficient condition for the convergence is $|g'(x)| < 1$ for all x in I.

(1) Find a real root of the equation $x^3 + x^2 - 100 = 0$.

Solution:

Given $x^3 + x^2 - 100 = 0$

Let $f(x) = x^3 + x^2 - 100$

$$f(0) = -100 = -ve$$
$$f(1) = 1+1-100 = -98 = -ve$$
$$f(2) = 8+4-100 = -88 = -ve$$
$$f(3) = 27+9-100 = -64 = -ve$$
$$f(4) = 64+16-100 = -20 = -ve$$
$$f(5) = 125+25-100 = +50 = +ve$$

So, a root lies between 4 and 5.

The given equation can be written as

$$x^2(x+1) = 100$$

$$x^2 = \frac{100}{x+1}$$

$$x = \frac{10}{\sqrt{x+1}} = g(x)$$

i.e., $g(x) = \dfrac{10}{\sqrt{x+1}}$

$$g'(x) = 10\frac{\left[-\frac{1}{2}\right]}{(x+1)^{3/2}} = \frac{-5}{(x+1)^{3/2}}$$

$$|g'(x)| = \frac{5}{(x+1)^{3/2}}$$

$$|g'(4)| = \frac{5}{5^{3/2}} < 1$$

$$|g'(5)| = \frac{5}{6^{3/2}} < 1$$

$\therefore$ $|g'(x)|$ is less than 1 in the internal (4, 5)

So, this method can be applied.

Let, x_0=4.2

$$x_1 = g(x_0) = \frac{10}{\sqrt{x_0 + 1}} = \frac{10}{\sqrt{4.2+1}} = 4.38529$$

$$x_2 = g(x_1) = \frac{10}{\sqrt{x_1 + 1}} = \frac{10}{\sqrt{4.38529+1}} = 4.30919$$

$$x_3 = g(x_2) = \frac{10}{\sqrt{x_2 + 1}} = \frac{10}{\sqrt{4.30919+1}} = 4.33996$$

$$x_4 = g(x_3) = \frac{10}{\sqrt{x_3 + 1}} = \frac{10}{\sqrt{4.33996+1}} = 4.32744$$

$$x_5 = g(x_4) = \frac{10}{\sqrt{x_4 + 1}} = 4.33252$$

$$x_6 = g(x_5) = \frac{10}{\sqrt{x_5 + 1}} = 4.33046$$

$$x_7 = g(x_6) = \frac{10}{\sqrt{x_6 + 1}} = 4.33129$$

$$x_8 = g(x_7) = \frac{10}{\sqrt{x_7 + 1}} = 4.33096$$

$$x_9 = g(x_8) = \frac{10}{\sqrt{x_8 + 1}} = 4.33109$$

$$x_{10} = g(x_9) = \frac{10}{\sqrt{x_9 + 1}} = 4.33104$$

$$x_{11} = g(x_{10}) = \frac{10}{\sqrt{x_{10} + 1}} = 4.33106$$

$$x_{12} = g(x_{11}) = \frac{10}{\sqrt{x_{11}+1}} = 4.33105$$

$$x_{13} = g(x_{12}) = \frac{10}{\sqrt{x_{12}+1}} = 4.33105$$

Here, $x_{12} = x_{13} = 4.33105$ correct to 5 decimal places.

Hence, the better approximate root is 4.33105.

(2) Find a real root of the equation $\cos x = 3x-1$ correct to 5 decimal places by fixed point iteration method.

Solution:

Given : $\cos x = 3x-1$

Let $f(x) = \cos x - 3x + 1 = 0$

$$f(0) = 1 - 0 + 1 = 2 = +ve$$

$$f(1) = \cos 1 - 3 + 1 = -1.4597 = -ve$$

So, a root lies between 0 and 1.

The given equation may be written as

$$x = \frac{1}{3}(1+\cos x) = g(x)$$

i.e., $g(x) = \frac{1}{3}(1+\cos x)$

$$g'(x) = -\frac{1}{3}\sin x$$

$$|g'(x)| = \frac{1}{3}\sin x$$

$$|g'(0)| = 0 < 1$$

$$|g'(1)| = \frac{1}{3}\sin 1 = 0.2804 < 1$$

So, the method can be applied.

Let $x_0 = 0.6$

$$x_1 = \frac{1}{3}[1+\cos x_0] = \frac{1}{3}[1+\cos(0.6)] = 0.60845$$

$$x_2 = \frac{1}{3}[1+\cos x_1] = 0.60684$$

$$x_3 = \frac{1}{3}[1+\cos x_2] = 0.60715$$

$$x_4 = \frac{1}{3}[1+\cos x_3] = 0.60709$$

$$x_5 = \frac{1}{3}[1+\cos x_4] = 0.60710$$

$$x_6 = \frac{1}{3}[1+\cos x_5] = 0.60710$$

Here, $x_5 = x_6 = 0.60710$

Hence, the better approximate root is 0.060710.

(3) Solve, $e^x - 3x = 0$ by the method of fixed point iteration.

Solution:

Given: $e^x - 3x = 0$

Let $f(x) = e^x - 3x$

$$f(0) = 1 = +ve$$

$$f(1) = e - 3 = -ve$$

So, a root lies between 0 and 1

The given equation may be written as

$$x = \frac{1}{3}e^x = g(x)$$

i.e., $g(x) = \frac{1}{3}e^x$

$$g'(x) = \frac{1}{3}e^x$$

$$|g'(x)| = \frac{1}{3}e^x$$

$$|g'(0)| = \frac{1}{3} < 1$$

$$|g'(1)| = \frac{1}{3}e < 1$$

In the interval (0,1), we get $|g'(x)| < 1$

So, the method can be applied

Let x_0=0.6

$$x_1 = \frac{1}{3}e^{x_0} = \frac{1}{3}e^{0.6} = 0.6074$$

$$x_2 = \frac{1}{3}e^{x_1} = 0.6119$$

$$x_3 = \frac{1}{3}e^{x_2} = 0.6146$$

$$x_4 = \frac{1}{3}e^{x_3} = 0.6163$$

$$x_5 = \frac{1}{3}e^{x_4} = 0.6174$$

$$x_6 = \frac{1}{3}e^{x_5} = 0.6180$$

$$x_7 = \frac{1}{3}e^{x_6} = 0.6184$$

$$x_8 = \frac{1}{3}e^{x_7} = 0.6187$$

$$x_9 = \frac{1}{3}e^{x_8} = 0.6188$$

$$x_{10} = \frac{1}{3}e^{x_9} = 0.6189$$

$$x_{11} = \frac{1}{3}e^{x_{10}} = 0.6190$$

$$x_{12} = \frac{1}{3}e^{x_{11}} = 0.6190$$

Here, $x_{11} = x_{12} = 0.6190$ correct to 4 decimal places.

Hence, the better approximate root is 0.6190.

(4) Find the negative root of the equation $x^3 - 2x + 5 = 0$.

Solution:

Given : $x^3 - 2x + 5 = 0$

Let $K(x) = x^3 - 2x + 5$

To find the negative root is nothing but to find the positive root of $K(-x) = -x^3 + 2x + 5 = 0$

(i.e.,) $x^3-2x-5=0$

Choose $f(x)=x^3-2x-5=0$

$$f(0)=-5=-ve$$
$$f(1)=1-2-5=-6=-ve$$
$$f(2)=8-4-5=-1=-ve$$
$$f(3)=27-6-5=16=+ve$$

So, a root lies between 2 and 3.

The equation *f(x)=0* may be written as *x=g(x)*

(i.e.,) $x=(2x+5)^{1/3}=g(x)$

$$g'(x)=\frac{1}{3}(2x+5)^{-2/3}2=\frac{2}{3}\frac{1}{(2x+5)^{2/3}}$$

$$|g'(x)|=\left|\frac{2}{3}\frac{1}{(2x+5)^{2/3}}\right|$$

$|g'(x)|<1$ in the internal (2,3)

So, the method can be applied.

Let $x_0=2.1$

$$x_1=g(x_0)=(2x_0+5)^{1/3}=[2(2.1)+5]^{1/3}=2.09538$$

$$x_2=g(x_1)=(2x_1+5)^{1/3}=2.09468$$

$$x_3=g(x_2)=(2x_2+5)^{1/3}=2.09457$$

$$x_4=g(x_3)=(2x_3+5)^{1/3}=2.09455$$

$$x_5=g(x_4)=(2x_4+5)^{1/3}=2.09455$$

Here, $x_4=x_5=2.09455$ correct to 5 decimal places.

So, the negative root of the given equation is –2.09455.

(5) Use the method of fixed point iteration to solve the equation $3x-\log_{10}x=6$

Solution:

Given $3x-\log_{10}x=6$

Let $f(x) = 3x - \log_{10} x - 6$

$f(2) = -0.3010 = '-'\text{ve}$

$f(3) = 2.5 = '+'\text{ve}$

The root lies between 2 and 3

The equation can be written as

$$x = \frac{1}{3}[6 + \log_{10} x] = g(x)$$

$$g(x) = \frac{1}{3}[6 + \log_{10} x]$$

$$g'(x) = \frac{1}{3}\left[\frac{\log_{10} e}{x}\right]$$

$|g'(x)| < 1$ in the interval (2,3)

Let $x_0 = 2$

$$x_1 = g(x_0) = \frac{1}{3}[6 + \log_{10} x_0] = \frac{1}{3}[6 + \log_{10} 2] = 2.1003$$

$$x_2 = g(x_1) = \frac{1}{3}[6 + \log_{10} x_1] = 2.1074$$

$$x_3 = g(x_2) = \frac{1}{3}[6 + \log_{10} x_2] = 2.1079$$

$$x_4 = g(x_3) = \frac{1}{3}[6 + \log_{10} x_3] = 2.1080$$

$$x_5 = g(x_4) = \frac{1}{3}[6 + \log_{10} x_4] = 2.1080$$

Here $x_4 = x_5 = 2.1080$

Hence, the better approximation root is 2.1080

SHORT QUESTIONS AND ANSWERS

1) What is the condition for applying the fixed point iteration method (successive approximation method) to find the real root of the equation *x=f(x)*.

Solution:

The condition for convergence is that in the neighbourhood of the root $|g'(x)| < 1$

2) What is the order of convergence for fixed point iteration?

Solution:

The convergence is linear and the convergence is of order 1.

3) Write sufficient condition for convergence of an iterative method for *f(x)=0* written as *x=g(x)*

Solution:

The sufficient condition for convergence is $|g'(x)| < 1$

EXERCISE

Solve the following by iteration method.

1) $x^3 + x^2 - 1 = 0$

   Ans: 0.7548

2) $3x - \log_{10} x = 6$

   Ans: 2.108

3) $\tan x = x$

   Ans: 4.4346

4) $x^3 - 10x - 5 = 0$

   Ans: 3.3876

3.6 EIGEN VALUES AND EIGEN VECTORS-JACOBI METHOD

1) Using Jacobi's method find all the eigen values and the eigen vectors of the matrix

$$A = \begin{bmatrix} 1 & \sqrt{2} & 2 \\ \sqrt{2} & 2 & \sqrt{2} \\ 2 & \sqrt{2} & 1 \end{bmatrix}$$

Solution

The largest non-diagonal element in A is $a_{13} = a_{31} = 2$. Also $a_{11} = 1$ and $a_{33} = 1$.

$$\tan 2\theta = \frac{2a_{13}}{a_{11} - a_{33}} = \frac{2 \times 2}{1 - 1} = \infty$$

$$2\theta = \frac{\pi}{2}$$

$$\theta = \frac{\pi}{4} \quad \text{Since } a_{13} > 0$$

Consider the orthogonal matrix

$$B_1 = \begin{bmatrix} \cos\theta & 0 & -\sin\theta \\ 0 & 1 & 0 \\ \sin\theta & 0 & \cos\theta \end{bmatrix}$$

$$B_1 = \begin{bmatrix} \frac{1}{\sqrt{2}} & 0 & \frac{-1}{\sqrt{2}} \\ 0 & 1 & 0 \\ \frac{1}{\sqrt{2}} & 0 & \frac{1}{\sqrt{2}} \end{bmatrix} \text{ and } B_1^{-1} = B_1^{T}$$

First rotation: The Matrix after first rotation

$$A_1 = B_1^{-1} A B_1 = \begin{bmatrix} \frac{1}{\sqrt{2}} & 0 & \frac{1}{\sqrt{2}} \\ 0 & 1 & 0 \\ \frac{-1}{\sqrt{2}} & 0 & \frac{1}{\sqrt{2}} \end{bmatrix} \begin{bmatrix} 1 & \sqrt{2} & 2 \\ \sqrt{2} & 3 & \sqrt{2} \\ 2 & \sqrt{2} & 1 \end{bmatrix} \begin{bmatrix} \frac{1}{\sqrt{2}} & 0 & \frac{-1}{\sqrt{2}} \\ 0 & 1 & 0 \\ \frac{1}{\sqrt{2}} & 0 & \frac{1}{\sqrt{2}} \end{bmatrix}$$

$$= \begin{bmatrix} 3 & 2 & 0 \\ 2 & 3 & 0 \\ 0 & 0 & -1 \end{bmatrix}$$

A_1 is not a diagonal matrix.

So, we have to perform second rotation.

In A_1 the largest non-diagonal element is

$$a_{12} = a_{21} = 2$$

Also $a_{11} = 3$ and $a_{33} = 3$

We choose θ to construct an orthogonal matrix B_2 such that

$$\tan 2\theta = \frac{2a_{12}}{a_{11} - a_{22}} = \infty$$

$$2\theta = \frac{\pi}{2}$$

$$\theta = \frac{\pi}{4}$$

∴ The orthogonal matrix is,

$$B_2 = \begin{bmatrix} \cos\theta & -\sin\theta & 0 \\ \sin\theta & \cos\theta & 0 \\ 0 & 0 & 1 \end{bmatrix}$$

$$\therefore B_2 = \begin{bmatrix} \frac{1}{\sqrt{2}} & \frac{-1}{\sqrt{2}} & 0 \\ \frac{1}{\sqrt{2}} & \frac{1}{\sqrt{2}} & 0 \\ 0 & 0 & 1 \end{bmatrix} \text{ and } B_2^{-1} = B_2^T$$

Second rotation: The matrix after second rotation

$$A_2 = B_2^{-1} A_1 B_2 = \begin{bmatrix} \frac{1}{\sqrt{2}} & \frac{1}{\sqrt{2}} & 0 \\ \frac{-1}{\sqrt{2}} & \frac{1}{\sqrt{2}} & 0 \\ 0 & 0 & 1 \end{bmatrix} \begin{bmatrix} 3 & 2 & 0 \\ 2 & 3 & 0 \\ 0 & 0 & -1 \end{bmatrix} \begin{bmatrix} \frac{1}{\sqrt{2}} & \frac{-1}{\sqrt{2}} & 0 \\ \frac{1}{\sqrt{2}} & \frac{1}{\sqrt{2}} & 0 \\ 0 & 0 & 1 \end{bmatrix}$$

$$= \begin{bmatrix} 5 & 0 & 0 \\ 0 & 1 & 0 \\ 0 & 0 & -1 \end{bmatrix} = D \text{ (diagonal matrix)}$$

$\therefore B_2^{-1} B_1^{-1} A B_1 B_2 = D \Rightarrow$ the eigen values of A are 5,1,–1. The corresponding eigen vectors are the columns of $B = B_1 B_2$

Now

$$B = \begin{bmatrix} \frac{1}{\sqrt{2}} & 0 & \frac{-1}{\sqrt{2}} \\ 0 & 1 & 0 \\ \frac{1}{\sqrt{2}} & 0 & \frac{1}{\sqrt{2}} \end{bmatrix} \begin{bmatrix} \frac{1}{\sqrt{2}} & \frac{-1}{\sqrt{2}} & 0 \\ \frac{1}{\sqrt{2}} & \frac{1}{\sqrt{2}} & 0 \\ 0 & 0 & 1 \end{bmatrix} = \begin{bmatrix} \frac{1}{\sqrt{2}} & \frac{-1}{2} & \frac{1}{\sqrt{2}} \\ \frac{1}{\sqrt{2}} & \frac{1}{\sqrt{2}} & 0 \\ \frac{1}{2} & \frac{-1}{2} & \frac{1}{\sqrt{2}} \end{bmatrix}$$

Hence the Eigen Vectors are $\left[\frac{1}{2}, \frac{1}{\sqrt{2}}, \frac{1}{2}\right]^T, \left[\frac{-1}{2}, \frac{1}{\sqrt{2}}, \frac{-1}{2}\right]^T$ and $\left[\frac{-1}{\sqrt{2}}, 0, \frac{1}{\sqrt{2}}\right]^T$.

2) Find the eigen values and eigen vectors of the matrix $A = \begin{bmatrix} 2 & 0 & 4 \\ 0 & 6 & 0 \\ 4 & 0 & 2 \end{bmatrix}$

Solution:

In A, the non-diagonal element is $a_{13} = a_{31} = 4$, $a_{11} = 2$ and $a_{33} = 2$.

For first rotation, the orthogonal matrix is taken as

$$B_1 = \begin{bmatrix} \cos\theta & 0 & -\sin\theta \\ 0 & 1 & 0 \\ \sin\theta & 0 & \cos\theta \end{bmatrix} \text{ where } \theta \text{ is given by}$$

$$\tan 2\theta = \frac{2a_{13}}{a_{11} - a_{33}}$$

$$\tan 2\theta = \frac{8}{2-2} = \infty$$

This given $\theta = \frac{\pi}{4}$ since $a_{13} > 0$

$$B_1 = \begin{bmatrix} \frac{1}{\sqrt{2}} & 0 & \frac{-1}{\sqrt{2}} \\ 0 & 1 & 0 \\ \frac{1}{\sqrt{2}} & 0 & \frac{1}{\sqrt{2}} \end{bmatrix}$$

The matrix after the first rotation is

$$A_1 = B_1^T A B_1 = \begin{bmatrix} \frac{1}{\sqrt{2}} & 0 & \frac{1}{\sqrt{2}} \\ 0 & 1 & 0 \\ \frac{-1}{\sqrt{2}} & 0 & \frac{1}{\sqrt{2}} \end{bmatrix} \begin{bmatrix} 2 & 0 & 4 \\ 0 & 6 & 0 \\ 4 & 0 & 2 \end{bmatrix} \begin{bmatrix} \frac{1}{\sqrt{2}} & 0 & \frac{-1}{\sqrt{2}} \\ 0 & 1 & 0 \\ \frac{1}{\sqrt{2}} & 0 & \frac{1}{\sqrt{2}} \end{bmatrix}$$

$$= \begin{bmatrix} \frac{6}{\sqrt{2}} & 0 & \frac{6}{\sqrt{2}} \\ 0 & 6 & 0 \\ \frac{2}{\sqrt{2}} & 0 & \frac{-2}{\sqrt{2}} \end{bmatrix} \begin{bmatrix} \frac{1}{\sqrt{2}} & 0 & \frac{-1}{\sqrt{2}} \\ 0 & 1 & 0 \\ \frac{1}{\sqrt{2}} & 0 & \frac{1}{\sqrt{2}} \end{bmatrix}$$

$$= \begin{bmatrix} 6 & 0 & 6 \\ 0 & 6 & 0 \\ 0 & 0 & -2 \end{bmatrix} = \text{Diagonal Matrix}$$

Hence the eigen values of A are 6,6,-2 and the corresponding eigen values are $\left[\frac{1}{\sqrt{2}}, 0, \frac{1}{\sqrt{2}}\right]^T$, $[0, 1, 0]^T$ and $\left[-\frac{1}{\sqrt{2}}, 0, \frac{1}{\sqrt{2}}\right]^T$.

(3) Using Jacobi method, find all the eigen values and eigen vectors of the matrix. $A = \begin{bmatrix} 1 & 0 & 0 \\ 0 & 3 & -1 \\ 0 & -1 & 3 \end{bmatrix}$

Solution:

Given $A = \begin{bmatrix} 1 & 0 & 0 \\ 0 & 3 & -1 \\ 0 & -1 & 3 \end{bmatrix}$

In A, consider the non-diagonal element $a_{23} = a_{32} = -1$

For first rotation, we consider the orthogonal matrix.

$$B_1 = \begin{bmatrix} 1 & 0 & 0 \\ 0 & \cos\theta & -\sin\theta \\ 0 & \sin\theta & \cos\theta \end{bmatrix}$$

Where $\tan 2\theta = \frac{2a_{23}}{a_{22} - a_{33}}$

$$\tan 2\theta = \frac{2(-1)}{3-3}$$

$$\tan 2\theta = \infty$$

$$\theta = -\frac{\pi}{4} \text{ Since } a_{23} < 0$$

$$B_1 = \begin{bmatrix} 1 & 0 & 0 \\ 0 & \frac{1}{\sqrt{2}} & \frac{1}{\sqrt{2}} \\ 0 & \frac{-1}{\sqrt{2}} & \frac{1}{\sqrt{2}} \end{bmatrix} \quad \text{and} \quad B_1^{-1} = B_1^T$$

The matrix after the first rotation is given by,

$$A_1 = B_1^{-1} A B_1 = \begin{bmatrix} 1 & 0 & 0 \\ 0 & \frac{1}{\sqrt{2}} & \frac{-1}{\sqrt{2}} \\ 0 & \frac{1}{\sqrt{2}} & \frac{1}{\sqrt{2}} \end{bmatrix} \begin{bmatrix} 1 & 0 & 0 \\ 0 & 3 & -1 \\ 0 & -1 & 3 \end{bmatrix} \times \begin{bmatrix} 1 & 0 & 0 \\ 0 & \frac{1}{\sqrt{2}} & \frac{1}{\sqrt{2}} \\ 0 & \frac{-1}{\sqrt{2}} & \frac{1}{\sqrt{2}} \end{bmatrix}$$

$$A_1 = \begin{bmatrix} 1 & 0 & 0 \\ 0 & \frac{4}{\sqrt{2}} & \frac{-4}{\sqrt{2}} \\ 0 & \frac{2}{\sqrt{2}} & \frac{2}{\sqrt{2}} \end{bmatrix} \begin{bmatrix} 1 & 0 & 0 \\ 0 & \frac{1}{\sqrt{2}} & \frac{1}{\sqrt{2}} \\ 0 & \frac{-1}{\sqrt{2}} & \frac{1}{\sqrt{2}} \end{bmatrix}$$

$$A_1 = \begin{bmatrix} 1 & 0 & 0 \\ 0 & 4 & 0 \\ 0 & 0 & 2 \end{bmatrix} = \text{a diagonal matrix}$$

The eigen values of A are 1,4,2. The corresponding eigen vectors are $[1, \ 0, \ 0]^T$, $\left[0, \ \frac{1}{\sqrt{2}}, \ \frac{-1}{\sqrt{2}}\right]^T$ and $\left[0, \ \frac{1}{\sqrt{2}}, \ \frac{1}{\sqrt{2}}\right]^T$.

(4) Find the eigen values and vectors of matrix $\begin{bmatrix} 1 & -1 & 0 \\ -1 & 1 & 0 \\ 0 & 0 & 1 \end{bmatrix}$ using Jacobi method.

Solution:

The given matrix is $A = \begin{bmatrix} 1 & -1 & 0 \\ -1 & 1 & 0 \\ 0 & 0 & 1 \end{bmatrix}$

In A, the non-diagonal element is $a_{12} = a_{21} = -1$

Also $a_{11} = 1, \ a_{22} = 1$

For first rotation, we consider the orthogonal matrix.

$$B_1 = \begin{bmatrix} \cos\theta & -\sin\theta & 0 \\ \sin\theta & \cos\theta & 0 \\ 0 & 0 & 1 \end{bmatrix} \quad \text{Where } \theta \text{ is given by}$$

$$\tan 2\theta = \frac{2a_{12}}{a_{11} - a_{22}}$$

$$\tan 2\theta = \frac{-2}{1-1} = \infty$$

$$\theta = -\frac{\pi}{4} \qquad \text{since } \ a_{12} < 0$$

$$B_1 = \begin{bmatrix} \frac{1}{\sqrt{2}} & \frac{1}{\sqrt{2}} & 0 \\ \frac{-1}{\sqrt{2}} & \frac{1}{\sqrt{2}} & 0 \\ 0 & 0 & 1 \end{bmatrix}$$

The matrix after the first rotation is given by $A_1 = B_1^{-1}AB_1 = B_1^T AB_1$

$$A_1 = \begin{bmatrix} \frac{1}{\sqrt{2}} & \frac{-1}{\sqrt{2}} & 0 \\ \frac{1}{\sqrt{2}} & \frac{1}{\sqrt{2}} & 0 \\ 0 & 0 & 1 \end{bmatrix} \begin{bmatrix} 1 & -1 & 0 \\ -1 & 1 & 0 \\ 0 & 0 & 1 \end{bmatrix} \begin{bmatrix} \frac{1}{\sqrt{2}} & \frac{1}{\sqrt{2}} & 0 \\ \frac{-1}{\sqrt{2}} & \frac{1}{\sqrt{2}} & 0 \\ 0 & 0 & 1 \end{bmatrix}$$

$$= \begin{bmatrix} \frac{2}{\sqrt{2}} & -\frac{2}{\sqrt{2}} & 0 \\ \frac{1}{\sqrt{2}} & \frac{1}{\sqrt{2}} & 0 \\ 0 & 0 & 1 \end{bmatrix} \begin{bmatrix} \frac{1}{\sqrt{2}} & \frac{1}{\sqrt{2}} & 0 \\ \frac{-1}{\sqrt{2}} & \frac{1}{\sqrt{2}} & 0 \\ 0 & 0 & 1 \end{bmatrix}$$

$$= \begin{bmatrix} 2 & 0 & 0 \\ 0 & 0 & 0 \\ 0 & 0 & 1 \end{bmatrix} = \text{diagonal matrix}$$

The diagonal elements are the eigen values of A.

The column vectors of B are the corresponding eigen vectors.

The eigen values of A are 2,0,1 and the corresponding eigen vectors are

$$\begin{bmatrix} \frac{1}{\sqrt{2}} \\ -\frac{1}{\sqrt{2}} \\ 0 \end{bmatrix}, \begin{bmatrix} \frac{1}{\sqrt{2}} \\ \frac{1}{\sqrt{2}} \\ 0 \end{bmatrix} \text{ and } \begin{bmatrix} 0 \\ 0 \\ 1 \end{bmatrix}$$

(5) Find all the eigen values and eigen vectors of $A = \begin{bmatrix} 2 & -1 & -1 \\ -1 & 2 & -1 \\ -1 & -1 & 2 \end{bmatrix}$ **by Jacobi's Method.**

Solution:

In A, the Largest non-diagonal element in magnitude is $a_{13} = -1 = a_{31}$. Also $a_{11} = a_{33} = 2$.

For the first rotation, we consider the orthogonal matrix $B_1 = \begin{bmatrix} \cos\theta & 0 & -\sin\theta \\ 0 & 1 & 0 \\ \sin\theta & 0 & \cos\theta \end{bmatrix}$

Where $\tan 2\theta = \dfrac{2a_{13}}{a_{11} - a_{33}} \Rightarrow \tan 2\theta = \infty$

$$\therefore \quad \theta = -\frac{\pi}{4} \quad \text{since} \quad a_{13} < 0$$

$$B_1 = \begin{bmatrix} \frac{1}{\sqrt{2}} & 0 & -\frac{1}{\sqrt{2}} \\ 0 & 1 & 0 \\ \frac{1}{\sqrt{2}} & 0 & \frac{1}{\sqrt{2}} \end{bmatrix} \quad \text{and } B_1^{-1} = B_1^T$$

$$B_1^{-1}AB_1 = \begin{bmatrix} \frac{1}{\sqrt{2}} & 0 & -\frac{1}{\sqrt{2}} \\ 0 & 1 & 0 \\ \frac{1}{\sqrt{2}} & 0 & \frac{1}{\sqrt{2}} \end{bmatrix} \begin{bmatrix} 2 & -1 & -1 \\ -1 & 2 & -1 \\ -1 & -1 & 2 \end{bmatrix} \begin{bmatrix} \frac{1}{\sqrt{2}} & 0 & \frac{1}{\sqrt{2}} \\ 0 & 1 & 0 \\ \frac{-1}{\sqrt{2}} & 0 & \frac{1}{\sqrt{2}} \end{bmatrix}$$

$$= \begin{bmatrix} \frac{3}{\sqrt{2}} & 0 & -\frac{3}{\sqrt{2}} \\ -1 & 2 & -1 \\ \frac{1}{\sqrt{2}} & \frac{-2}{\sqrt{2}} & \frac{1}{\sqrt{2}} \end{bmatrix} \begin{bmatrix} \frac{1}{\sqrt{2}} & 0 & \frac{1}{\sqrt{2}} \\ 0 & 1 & 0 \\ \frac{-1}{\sqrt{2}} & 0 & \frac{1}{\sqrt{2}} \end{bmatrix}$$

$$B_1^{-1}AB_1 = \begin{bmatrix} 3 & 0 & 0 \\ 0 & 2 & -\sqrt{2} \\ 0 & -\sqrt{2} & 1 \end{bmatrix}$$

In $B_1^{-1}AB_1 = A_1$ the largest non-diagonal element is $a_{23} = a_{32} = -\sqrt{2}$ and $a_{22} = 2$, $a_{33} = 1$.

For second rotation we construct the matrix $B_2 = \begin{bmatrix} 1 & 0 & 0 \\ 0 & \cos\theta & -\sin\theta \\ 0 & \sin\theta & \cos\theta \end{bmatrix}$

Where $\tan 2\theta = \dfrac{2a_{23}}{a_{22} - a_{33}} = -2\sqrt{2}$

$$\therefore \tan 2\theta = -2\sqrt{2} \Rightarrow \theta = \frac{1}{2}\tan^{-1}(-2\sqrt{2}) = -35°16'$$

$$B_2 = \begin{bmatrix} 1 & 0 & 0 \\ 0 & 0.8165 & 0.5773 \\ 0 & -0.5773 & 0.8165 \end{bmatrix} \text{ and } B_2^{-1} = B_2^T$$

$$B_2^{-1}A_1B_2 = \begin{bmatrix} 1 & 0 & 0 \\ 0 & 0.8165 & -0.5773 \\ 0 & 0.5773 & 0.8165 \end{bmatrix} \begin{bmatrix} 3 & 0 & 0 \\ 0 & 2 & -1.414 \\ 0 & -1.414 & 1 \end{bmatrix} \times \begin{bmatrix} 1 & 0 & 0 \\ 0 & 0.8165 & 0.5773 \\ 0 & -0.5773 & 0.8165 \end{bmatrix}$$

$$= \begin{bmatrix} 3 & 0 & 0 \\ 0 & 2.4493 & -1.7318 \\ 0 & 0 & 0 \end{bmatrix} \begin{bmatrix} 1 & 0 & 0 \\ 0 & 0.8165 & 0.5773 \\ 0 & -0.5773 & 0.8165 \end{bmatrix}$$

$$= \begin{bmatrix} 3 & 0 & 0 \\ 0 & 3 & 0 \\ 0 & 0 & 0 \end{bmatrix} = \text{a diagonal matrix}$$

The eigen values of A are 3, 3, 0.

The corresponding eigen vectors of A are the columns of $B = B_1B_2$

$$B = \begin{bmatrix} 0.7071 & 0 & 0.7071 \\ 0 & 1 & 0 \\ -0.7071 & 0 & 0.7071 \end{bmatrix} \begin{bmatrix} 1 & 0 & 0 \\ 0 & 0.865 & 0.5773 \\ 0 & 0.5773 & 0.8165 \end{bmatrix}$$

$$= \begin{bmatrix} 0.7071 & -0.4082 & 0.5773 \\ 0 & 0.815 & 0.5773 \\ -0.7071 & -0.4082 & 0.5773 \end{bmatrix}$$

The eigen values are 3,3, 0 and the corresponding eigen vectors are $(0.7071, 0, -0.7071)^T$ $(-0.4082, 0.8165, -0.4082)^T$ and $(0.5773, 0.5773, 0.5773)^T$

(6) Using Jacobi's Method, find all the eigen values and the eigen vectors of

$$A = \begin{bmatrix} 5 & 0 & 1 \\ 0 & -2 & 0 \\ 1 & 0 & 5 \end{bmatrix}$$

Solution:

In A, the largest non-diagonal element is $a_{13} = a_{31} = 1$ and $a_{11} = 5,\ a_{33} = 5$

For First rotation, we consider the orthogonal matrix $B_1 = \begin{bmatrix} \cos\theta & 0 & -\sin\theta \\ 0 & 1 & 0 \\ \sin\theta & 0 & \cos\theta \end{bmatrix}$

We choose θ such that

$$\tan 2\theta = \frac{2a_{13}}{a_{11} - a_{33}} = \frac{2}{5-5} = \infty$$

$$\therefore\ 2\theta = \frac{\pi}{2} \Rightarrow \theta = \frac{\pi}{4}\ \therefore (a_{13} > 0)$$

$$B_1 = \begin{bmatrix} \frac{1}{\sqrt{2}} & 0 & \frac{-1}{\sqrt{2}} \\ 0 & 1 & 0 \\ \frac{1}{\sqrt{2}} & 0 & \frac{1}{\sqrt{2}} \end{bmatrix} \qquad B_1^{-1} = B_2^{T}$$

$$\text{Now}\quad B_1^{-1}AB_1 = \begin{bmatrix} \frac{1}{\sqrt{2}} & 0 & \frac{1}{\sqrt{2}} \\ 0 & 1 & 0 \\ \frac{-1}{\sqrt{2}} & 0 & \frac{1}{\sqrt{2}} \end{bmatrix} \begin{bmatrix} 5 & 0 & 1 \\ 0 & -2 & 0 \\ 1 & 0 & 5 \end{bmatrix} \begin{bmatrix} \frac{1}{\sqrt{2}} & 0 & \frac{-1}{\sqrt{2}} \\ 0 & 1 & 0 \\ \frac{1}{\sqrt{2}} & 0 & \frac{1}{\sqrt{2}} \end{bmatrix}$$

$$= \begin{bmatrix} \frac{6}{\sqrt{2}} & 0 & \frac{6}{\sqrt{2}} \\ 0 & -2 & 0 \\ \frac{-4}{\sqrt{2}} & 0 & \frac{4}{\sqrt{2}} \end{bmatrix} \begin{bmatrix} \frac{1}{\sqrt{2}} & 0 & \frac{-1}{\sqrt{2}} \\ 0 & 1 & 0 \\ \frac{1}{\sqrt{2}} & 0 & \frac{1}{\sqrt{2}} \end{bmatrix}$$

$$= \begin{bmatrix} 6 & 0 & 0 \\ 0 & -2 & 0 \\ 0 & 0 & 4 \end{bmatrix}$$

$B_1^{-1}AB_1$ = a diagonal matrix

Hence the eigen values of A are 6, –2, 4 and the corresponding eigen vectors are $\left[\frac{1}{\sqrt{2}}, \; 0, \; \frac{1}{\sqrt{2}}\right]^T$, $[0, \; 1, \; 0]^T$ and $\left[\frac{-1}{\sqrt{2}}, \; 0, \; \frac{1}{\sqrt{2}}\right]^T$.

(The columns of B are the eigen vectors of A)

PART - A

QUESTION & ANSWERS

N–R METHODS

1) State the order of rate of convergence and convergence condition for Newton-Raphson method.

Solution:

The order of (rate of) convergence is 2

Condition for convergence is $|f(x)f''(x)| < |f'(x)|^2$

2) Newton Raphson method is also known as the method of

Solution: Tangents

3) N–R method is convergent

Solution: Quadratically

4) Write the iterative formula of N–R method

Solution:

$$x_{n+1} = x_n - \frac{f(x_n)}{f'(x_n)}$$

5) When should we not use N–R method?

The method should not be used in cases where the graph of the function when it crosses the X axis is nearly horizontal.

6) What is the criterion for the convergence in N–R method?

(i) $f'(x_0)$ should not be equal to zero. If $f'(x_0) = 0$ then initial approximation must be changed.

(ii) For better convergence the product $f(x_0)f''(x_0)$ should be positive.

7) Show that the N-R formula to find $\sqrt{a}$ can be expressed in the form $x_{n+1} = \frac{1}{2}\left[x_n + \frac{a}{x_n}\right]$, n=0, 1, 2, 3...

Solution

If $x = \sqrt{a}$ then $x^2 - a = 0$

Let $f(x) = x^2 - a$

$f'(x) = 2x$

N–R formula is,

$$x_{n+1} = x_n - \frac{f(x_n)}{f'(x_n)}$$

$$= x_n - \frac{x_n^2 - a}{2x_n}$$

$$= \frac{2x_n^2 - x_n^2 + a}{2x_n}$$

$$= \frac{x_n^2 + a}{2x_n}$$

$$x_{n+1} = \frac{1}{2}\left[x_n + \frac{a}{x_n}\right], \text{ n=0, 1, 2, 3...}$$

EXERCISE

[NEWTON'S METHOD]

1) **Find the positive root of $x^3 - 2x - 5 = 0$ correct to three decimal places using N–R Method**

   Solution: 2.0946

2) **Solve by Newton's method, a root of $e^x - 4x = 0$**

   Solution: 0.3574

3) **Find the least positive root of $xe^{-2x} = 0.5\sin x$ correct to three decimal places using N–R**

   Solution: –1.9338

4) **Using N–R, solve $x\log_{10} x = 12.34$ start with x_0=10**

   Solution: 11.5949

5) **Obtain Newton's iterative formula for finding $\sqrt{N}$ where N is a positive real number. Hence evaluate $\sqrt{142}$.**

   Solution: 11.9164

6) **(i) $4x - e^x = 0$ between 2 & 3 (ii) $2x^3 - 3x - 6 = 0$ Between 1&2 by N–R**

SOLUTION OF LINEAR SYSTEM OF EQUATION BY GAUSSIAN ELIMINATION AND GAUSS-JORDAN METHODS

1) For solving a linear system. Compare Gaussian Elimination method and Gauss-Jordan method.

Gaussian-Elimination	*Gauss-Jordan*
1. Direct method	Direct method
2. Co-efficient matrix is transformed into upper triangular matrix	Co-efficient matrix is transformed into diagonal matrix
3. We obtain the solutions by back-substitution method	No need of back substitution method

2) State the principle used in Gauss-Jordan method.

Co-efficient matrix is transformed into diagonal matrix.

3) In what form is the co-efficient matrix transformed into when AX=B is solved by Gauss-Elimination method.

Solution: Upper triangular matrix.

4) In what form is the co-efficient matrix transformed into when AX=B is solved by Gauss-Jordan method.

Solution: Diagonal Matrix.

5) The numerical methods of solving linear equations are of two types : one is direct and the other is .

Solution: Iterative (Indirect)

6) Explain the term "pivot Elements"

Solution:

In an augmented matrix $\left[\begin{array}{cccc|c} a_{11} & a_{12} & \cdots & a_{1n} & b_1 \\ a_{21} & a_{22} & \cdots & a_{2n} & b_2 \\ \cdots & \cdots & \cdots & \cdots & \cdots \\ a_{n1} & a_{n2} & \cdots & a_{nn} & b_n \end{array}\right]$ the elements a_{11}, a_{22}, …a_{nn} which have been assumed to be non-zero are called pivot elements.

7) Explain the term pivoting

In the elimination process, it any one of the pivot elements a_{11}, a_{22}… a_{nn} vanishes (or) becomes very small compared to other elements. In that column, then we attempt to rearrange the remaining row so as to obtain a non-vanishing pivot or to avoid the multiplication by a large number. This strategy is called pivoting.

The pivoting is of two types.

(1) Partial pivoting

(2) Complete pivoting.

8) Give two direct methods to solve a system of linear equations.

Solution:

(i) Gauss-Elimination Methods

(ii) Gauss-Jordan Method

9) When Gauss-Elimination method fails.

This method fails if the elements in the top of the first column is zero. We can rectify this by interchanging the rows of the matrix.

10) Solve the following system of equations by Gauss-Jordan method 5x+4y=15, 3x+7y=12.

Solution:

The given system is equivalent to

$$\begin{bmatrix} 5 & 4 \\ 3 & 7 \end{bmatrix}\begin{bmatrix} x \\ y \end{bmatrix} = \begin{bmatrix} 15 \\ 12 \end{bmatrix}$$

$$\text{AX} = \text{B}$$

$$[\text{A}, \text{B}] = \begin{bmatrix} 5 & 4 \\ 3 & 7 \end{bmatrix}\begin{bmatrix} 15 \\ 12 \end{bmatrix}$$

$$\sim \left[\begin{array}{cc|c} 5 & 4 & 15 \\ 0 & 23 & 15 \end{array}\right] \text{R}_2 \to 5\text{R}_2 - 3\text{R}_1$$

$$\sim \left[\begin{array}{cc|c} 115 & 0 & 285 \\ 0 & 23 & 15 \end{array}\right] \text{R}_1 \to 23\text{R}_1 - 4\text{R}_2$$

$115x=285$

$\boxed{x = 2.4783}$

$2xy = 15$

$\boxed{y = 0.6522}$

EXERCISE

1) Using the Gauss-Jordan method solve the following equations

$$10x + y + z = 12$$
$$2x + 10y + z = 13$$
$$x + y + 5z = 7$$

Solution: $x = 1, y = 1, z = 1$

2) Solve $x+3y+3z=16$, $x+4y+3z=18$, $x+3y+4z=19$ by Gauss-Jordan method.

Solution: $x=1, y=2, z=3$

3) Using Gauss Elimination method: solve the system

$$3.15x-1.96y+3.85z=12.95$$
$$2.13x+5.12y-2.89z=-8.61$$
$$5.92x+3.05y+2.15z=6.88$$

Solution: $x=1.709, y=-1.800, z=1.049$

4) Using Gauss Elimination method, and Gauss-Jordan solve the system

$$x+y+z=9$$
$$2x-3y+4z=13$$
$$3x+4y+5z=40$$

Solution: $x=1,\ y=3,\ z=5$

5) By Gauss Jordan method

$$2x-y+3z=8$$
$$-x+2y+z=4$$
$$3x+y-4z=0$$

Solution: $x=2,\ y=2,\ z=2$

6) Solve the following system by Gauss-Jordan method

$$5x_1+x_2+x_3+x_4=4$$
$$x_1+7x_2+x_3+x_4=12$$
$$x_1+x_2+6x_3+x_4=-5$$
$$x_1+x_2+x_3+x_4=-6$$

Solution: $x_1=1,\ x_2=2,\ x_3=-1,\ x_4=-2$

7) Solve the following system by Gauss-Jordan method

$$5x_1-x_2=9$$
$$-x_1+5x_2-x_3=4$$
$$-x_2+5x_3=-6$$

Solution: $x=2,\ y=1,\ z=-1$

GAUSS-JACOBI AND GAUSS-SEIDEL METHOD

1) Give two indirect methods to solve a system of linear equations.

Solution:

(i) Gauss-Jacobi method

(ii) Gauss-Seidel method

2) Compare Gauss-Jacobi and Gauss-Seidel methods

Solution:

Gauss-Jacobi	Gauss-Seidel
1. Convergence rate is slow	1. The rate of convergence of Gauss-Seidel method is roughly twice that of Gauss-Jacobi
2. Indirect method	2. Indirect Method
3. Condition for convergence is the co-efficient matrix is diagonally dominant	3. Condition for convergence is the co-efficient matrix is diagonally dominant.

3) Write a sufficient condition for Gauss-Seidel method to converge (or) sufficient condition for Gauss- Jacobi method to converge.

The process of iteration by Gauss-Seidel method will converge. If in each equation of the system, the absolute value of the largest co-efficient is greater than the sum of the absolute values of the remaining co-efficients.

[The co-efficient of matrix should be diagonally dominant.]

4) Is the iteration method, a self-correcting method always?

In general iteration is a self-correcting method, since the round off error is smaller.

5) Distinguish between direct and indirect method of solving simultaneous equations.

Solution:

Direct method	Iterative method
1. We get exact solution	Approximate solution
2. Simple take less time	Time consuming laborious

EXERCISE

1) **Solve the following system by applying first two iterations Gauss Jacobi methods and continue using the Gauss-Seidel method.** $3x_1 - x_2 + x_3 = 1$, $3x_1 + 6x_2 + 2x_3 = 0$, $3x_1 + 3x_2 + 7x_3 = 4$

   Solution: $x_1 = 0.0354,\ x_2 = -0.2367,\ x_3 = 0.6577$

2) **Using Gauss-Seidel method start with x=1, y=–2, z=3.**

   $$x + 3y + 52z = 173.661$$
   $$x - 27y + 2z = 71.31$$
   $$41x - 2y + 3z = 65.46$$

   Solution: $x = 1.23,\ y = -2.34,\ z = 3.45$

3) **Using Jacobi & Seidel** $8x - 3y + 2z = 20$, $4x + 11y - z = 33$, $6x + 3y + 12z = 35$

   Solution: $x = 3.0168,\ y = 1.9859,\ z = 0.9118$

4) **Solve Jocobi & Seidel** $28x + 4y - z = 32$, $x + 3y + 10z = 24$, $2x + 17y + 4z = 35$

   Solution: $x = 0.9936,\ y = 1.507,\ z = 1.8486$

MATRIX INVERSION BY GAUSS-JORDAN METHOD

1) **State the basic Principle involved for finding A^{-1} by Gauss-Jordan method?**

   If we reduce the augmented matrix (A, I) in the form (I, X), then $X = A^{-1}$

EXERCISE

1) **Find by Gauss-Jordan Method, the Inverse of the following.**

   (i) $A = \begin{bmatrix} 3 & 1 & 2 \\ 2 & -3 & -1 \\ 1 & 2 & 1 \end{bmatrix}$

   Solution:

   $$A^{-1} = \begin{bmatrix} -1 & 3 & 5 \\ -3 & 1 & 7 \\ 7 & -5 & -11 \end{bmatrix}$$

(ii) $A = \begin{bmatrix} 1 & 1 & 2 \\ 1 & 2 & 3 \\ 2 & 3 & 1 \end{bmatrix}$

Solution:

$$A^{-1} = \frac{1}{4}\begin{bmatrix} 7 & -5 & 1 \\ -5 & 3 & 1 \\ 1 & 1 & -1 \end{bmatrix}$$

(iii) $A = \begin{bmatrix} 3 & 2 & 4 \\ 2 & 1 & 1 \\ 1 & 3 & 5 \end{bmatrix}$

Solution:

$$A^{-1} = \begin{bmatrix} 1/4 & 1/4 & -1/4 \\ -9/8 & 11/8 & 5/8 \\ 5/8 & -7/8 & -1/8 \end{bmatrix}$$

EIGEN VALUES OF A MATRIX BY POWER METHOD

1) Find the power method, the largest Eigen value of $\begin{bmatrix} 4 & 1 \\ 1 & 3 \end{bmatrix}$ correct to two decimal places, chase $[1, 1]^T$ as the initial eigen vector

Solution:

Let $X_1 = \begin{bmatrix} 1 \\ 1 \end{bmatrix}$

$$AX_1 = \begin{bmatrix} 4 & 1 \\ 1 & 3 \end{bmatrix}\begin{bmatrix} 1 \\ 1 \end{bmatrix} = \begin{bmatrix} 5 \\ 4 \end{bmatrix} = 5\begin{bmatrix} 1 \\ 0.8 \end{bmatrix} = 5X_2$$

$$AX_2 = \begin{bmatrix} 4 & 1 \\ 1 & 3 \end{bmatrix}\begin{bmatrix} 1 \\ 0.8 \end{bmatrix} = \begin{bmatrix} 4.8 \\ 3.4 \end{bmatrix} = 4.8\begin{bmatrix} 1 \\ 0.71 \end{bmatrix} = 4.8X_3$$

$$AX_3 = \begin{bmatrix} 4 & 1 \\ 1 & 3 \end{bmatrix}\begin{bmatrix} 1 \\ 0.71 \end{bmatrix} = \begin{bmatrix} 4.71 \\ 3.13 \end{bmatrix} = 4.71\begin{bmatrix} 1 \\ 0.67 \end{bmatrix} = 4.71X_4$$

$$AX_4 = \begin{bmatrix} 4 & 1 \\ 1 & 3 \end{bmatrix} \begin{bmatrix} 1 \\ 0.67 \end{bmatrix} = \begin{bmatrix} 4.67 \\ 3.01 \end{bmatrix} = 4.67 \begin{bmatrix} 1 \\ 0.65 \end{bmatrix} = 4.67X_5$$

$$AX_5 = \begin{bmatrix} 4 & 1 \\ 1 & 3 \end{bmatrix} \begin{bmatrix} 1 \\ 0.65 \end{bmatrix} = \begin{bmatrix} 4.65 \\ 2.95 \end{bmatrix} = 4.65 \begin{bmatrix} 1 \\ 0.63 \end{bmatrix} = 4.65X_6$$

$$AX_6 = \begin{bmatrix} 4 & 1 \\ 1 & 3 \end{bmatrix} \begin{bmatrix} 1 \\ 0.63 \end{bmatrix} = \begin{bmatrix} 4.63 \\ 2.89 \end{bmatrix} = 4.63 \begin{bmatrix} 1 \\ 0.62 \end{bmatrix} = 4.63X_7$$

$$AX_7 = \begin{bmatrix} 4 & 1 \\ 1 & 3 \end{bmatrix} \begin{bmatrix} 1 \\ 0.62 \end{bmatrix} = \begin{bmatrix} 4.62 \\ 2.86 \end{bmatrix} = 4.62 \begin{bmatrix} 1 \\ 0.62 \end{bmatrix} = 4.62X_8$$

$\therefore$ The Eigen value = 4.62

The Eigen Vector = $\begin{bmatrix} 1 \\ 0.62 \end{bmatrix}$

2) The power method will work satisfactorily only if a has a _____ eigen value.

Solution: Dominant

3) If the Eigen values of a A are –3, 3, 1 then the dominant eigen value of A is ______

Solution: No dominant eigen value

4) If the eigen value of A are 1, 3, 4 then the dominant eigen value of A is ______

Solution: 4

5) If the eigen value of A are –4, 3, 1 then the dominant eigen value of A is ______

Solution: –4

6) What types of eigen value can be obtained using power method.

Solution: The dominant eigen value can be obtained by power method.

7) Find the Dominant Eigen value of $A=\begin{bmatrix} 1 & 2 \\ 3 & 4 \end{bmatrix}$ by power method?

Solution:

Let $X_1 = \begin{bmatrix} 1 \\ 1 \end{bmatrix}$

$$AX_1 = \begin{bmatrix} 1 & 2 \\ 3 & 4 \end{bmatrix} \begin{bmatrix} 1 \\ 1 \end{bmatrix} = \begin{bmatrix} 3 \\ 7 \end{bmatrix} = 7 \begin{bmatrix} 0.43 \\ 1 \end{bmatrix} = 7X_2$$

$$AX_2 = \begin{bmatrix} 1 & 2 \\ 3 & 4 \end{bmatrix} \begin{bmatrix} 0.43 \\ 1 \end{bmatrix} = \begin{bmatrix} 2.43 \\ 5.29 \end{bmatrix} = 5.29 \begin{bmatrix} 0.46 \\ 1 \end{bmatrix} = 5.29X_3$$

$$AX_3 = \begin{bmatrix} 1 & 2 \\ 3 & 4 \end{bmatrix} \begin{bmatrix} 0.46 \\ 1 \end{bmatrix} = \begin{bmatrix} 2.46 \\ 5.38 \end{bmatrix} = 5.38 \begin{bmatrix} 0.46 \\ 1 \end{bmatrix} = 5.38X_4$$

$\therefore$ The Eigen value = 5.38

The Eigen Vector = $\begin{bmatrix} 0.46 \\ 1 \end{bmatrix}$

8) When do use the power method?

Solution:

We use the power method to find the largest eigen value in magnitude the corresponding Eigen vector of A.

9) What is the use of power method?

Solution: To find the numerically largest eigen value of a given matrix

EXERCISE

Find The Dominant Eigen Value And Eigen Vector of The Following Matrices By Power Method.

1) $A = \begin{bmatrix} -4 & -5 \\ 1 & 2 \end{bmatrix}$

Solution:

Eigen Value = –3

Eigen Vector = $\begin{bmatrix} 1 \\ -1/5 \end{bmatrix}$

2) $\begin{bmatrix} 1 & 3 & -1 \\ 3 & 2 & 4 \\ -1 & 4 & 10 \end{bmatrix}$

Solution:

Eigen Value = 11.66

Eigen Vector = $\begin{bmatrix} 0.025 \\ 0.422 \\ 1 \end{bmatrix}$

3) $\begin{bmatrix} 2 & -1 & 0 \\ -1 & 2 & -1 \\ 0 & -1 & 2 \end{bmatrix}$

Solution:

Eigen Value = 3

$$\text{Eigen Vector} = \begin{bmatrix} 0.7 \\ -1 \\ 0.7 \end{bmatrix}$$

4) Obtain by the power method, the dominant Eigen value and the corresponding Eigen vector correct to two decimal places for the matrix $\begin{bmatrix} 2 & 2 & 2 \\ 2/3 & 5/3 & 5/3 \\ 1 & 5/2 & 11/2 \end{bmatrix}$ **taking** $[1 \quad 0 \quad 0]^T$ **as the initial approximation to this Eigen vector.**

Solution:

Eigen Value = 7

$$\text{Eigen Vector} = \begin{bmatrix} 0.55 \\ 0.38 \\ 1 \end{bmatrix}$$

UNIT - 4

INTERPOLATION, NUMERICAL DIFFERENTIATION AND NUMERICAL INTEGRATION

Outline:

Topic (1): Interpolation With Unequal Intervals

(i) Lagrange's Interpolation

(ii) Newton's Divided Difference Interpolation

Topic (2): Interpolation with Equal Intervals.

(i) Newton's Forward Interpolation

(ii) Newton's Backward Interpolation

Topic (3): Numerical Differentiation

Topic (4): Numerical Integration

4.1 INTRODUCTION

Consider the function, $y=f(x)$, where x is called independent variable and y is called dependent variable. The Process of finding the value of y at an intermediate value of x is known as ***Interpolation***. If the values of x are equally spaced, this process of estimation is known as ***Interpolation with equal intervals***. But if the values of x are not equally spaced, this process is known as ***Interpolation with unequal intervals***. The process of finding the value of y at a value of x lying out of its given range is known as ***Extrapolation***.

4.2 INTERPOLATION WITH UNEQUAL INTERVALS

Consider, $y=f(x)$ having the following values:

x:	x_0	x_1	x_2	...	x_n
y:	y_0	y_1	y_2	...	y_n

If the values of x are not equally spaced we use the following formulae for interpolation:

(i) Langrange's interpolation formula

(iii) Newton's divided difference interpolation formula

4.2.1 Lagrange's Interpolation Formula

The Lagrange's Interpolation formula is :

$$y = f(x) = \frac{(x-x_1)(x-x_2)...(x-x_n)}{(x_0-x_1)(x_0-x_2)...(x_0-x_n)}y_0 + \frac{(x-x_0)(x-x_2)...(x-x_n)}{(x_1-x_0)(x_1-x_2)...(x_1-x_n)}y_1$$
$$+.....+\frac{(x-x_0)(x-x_1)...(x-x_{n-1})}{(x_n-x_0)(x_n-x_1)...(x_n-x_{n-1})}y_n$$

PROBLEMS

1) Find the polynomial *f(x)* by using Lagrange's formula and hence find *f*(3).

x:	0	1	2	5
f(x)	2	3	12	147

Solution:

Given

x:	(x_0) 0	(x_1) 1	(x_2) 2	(x_3) 5
f(x):	(y_0) 2	(y_1) 3	(y_2) 12	(y_3) 147

By Lagrange's Interpolation Formula is

$$y = f(x) = \frac{(x-x_1)(x-x_2)(x-x_3)}{(x_0-x_1)(x_0-x_2)(x_0-x_3)}y_0 + \frac{(x-x_0)(x-x_2)(x-x_3)}{(x_1-x_0)(x_1-x_2)(x_1-x_3)}y_1$$
$$+\frac{(x-x_0)(x-x_1)(x-x_3)}{(x_2-x_0)(x_2-x_1)(x_2-x_3)}y_2 + \frac{(x-x_0)(x-x_1)(x-x_2)}{(x_3-x_0)(x_3-x_1)(x_3-x_2)}y_3 + ...$$

$$= \frac{(x-1)(x-2)(x-5)}{(0-1)(0-2)(0-5)}(2) + \frac{(x-0)(x-2)(x-5)}{(1-0)(1-2)(1-5)}(3)$$
$$+\frac{(x-0)(x-1)(x-5)}{(2-0)(2-1)(2-5)}(12) + \frac{(x-0)(x-1)(x-2)}{(5-0)(5-1)(5-2)}(147)$$

$$= \frac{(x-1)(x-2)(x-5)}{(-10)}(2) + \frac{x(x-2)(x-5)}{4}(3)$$
$$+ \frac{x(x-1)(x-5)}{(-6)}(12) + \frac{x(x-1)(x-2)}{60}(147)$$

$$y = f(3) = \frac{(3-1)(3-2)(3-5)}{-10}(2) + \frac{3(3-1)(3-2)}{4}(3)$$
$$+ \frac{3(3-1)(3-5)}{(-6)}(12) + \frac{3(3-2)(3-5)}{60}(147)$$

$$= \frac{(2)(1)(-2)}{-10}(2) + \frac{3(1)(-2)}{4}(3) + \frac{3(2)(-2)}{(-6)}(12) + \frac{3(2)(1)}{60}(147)$$

$$= \frac{4}{10}(2) - \frac{6}{4}(3) + 2(12) + \frac{1}{10}(147)$$
$$= \frac{8}{10} - \frac{18}{4} + 24 + \frac{147}{10}$$

$$f(3) = 35$$

2) Using Lagrange's interpolation, calculate the profit in the year 2000 from the following data:

Year:	**1997**	**1999**	**2001**	**2002**
Profit in lakhs of Rs:	**43**	**65**	**159**	**248**

Solution:

Given

Year:	(x_0) 1997	(x_1) 1999	(x_2) 2001	(x_3) 2002
Profit in lakhs Rs:	(y_0) 43	(y_1) 65	(y_2) 159	(y_3) 248

By Lagrange interpolation formula,

$$y = f(x) = \frac{(x-x_1)(x-x_2)(x-x_3)}{(x_0-x_1)(x_0-x_2)(x_0-x_3)}y_0 + \frac{(x-x_0)(x-x_2)(x-x_3)}{(x_1-x_0)(x_1-x_2)(x_1-x_3)}y_1$$
$$+ \frac{(x-x_0)(x-x_1)(x-x_3)}{(x_2-x_0)(x_2-x_1)(x_2-x_3)}y_2 + \frac{(x-x_0)(x-x_1)(x-x_2)}{(x_3-x_0)(x_3-x_1)(x_3-x_2)}y_3 + \ldots$$

$$y = f(2000) = \frac{(2000-1999)(2000-2001)(2000-2002)}{(1997-1999)(1997-2001)(1997-2002)}(43)$$
$$+\frac{(2000-1997)(2000-2001)(2000-2002)}{(1999-1997)(1999-2001)(1999-2002)}(65)$$
$$+\frac{(2000-1997)(2000-1999)(2000-2002)}{(2001-1997)(2001-1999)(2001-2002)}(159)$$
$$+\frac{(2000-1997)(2000-1999)(2000-2001)}{(2002-1997)(2002-1999)(2000-2001)}(248)$$

$$= \frac{(1)(-1)(-2)}{(-2)(-4)(-5)}(43) + \frac{3(-1)(-2)}{2(-2)(-3)}(65) + \frac{3(1)(-2)}{4(2)(-1)}(159)$$
$$+\frac{3(1)(-1)}{5(3)(1)}(248)$$
$$= \frac{-43}{20} + \frac{65}{2} + \frac{477}{4} - \frac{248}{5}$$
$$= 100$$

3) Using Lagrange's formula fit a polynomial to the data.

x	–1	1	2
y	7	5	15

Solution:

Given:

x:	(x_0) –1	(x_1) 1	(x_2) 2
y:	(y_0) 7	(y_1) 5	(y_2) 15

By Lagrange's interpolation formula,

$$y = f(x) = \frac{(x-x_1)(x-x_2)}{(x_0-x_1)(x_0-x_2)}y_0 + \frac{(x-x_0)(x-x_2)}{(x_1-x_0)(x_1-x_2)}y_1 + \frac{(x-x_0)(x-x_1)}{(x_2-x_0)(x_2-x_1)}y_2$$
$$= \frac{(x-1)(x-2)}{(-1-1)(-1-2)}(7) + \frac{(x+1)(x-2)}{(1+1)(1-2)}(5) + \frac{(x+1)(x-1)}{(2+1)(2-1)}(15)$$
$$= \frac{x^2-3x+2}{(-2)(-3)}(7) + \frac{(x+1)(x-2)}{(2)(-1)}(5) + \frac{(x+1)(x-1)}{(3)(1)}(15)$$

$$=\frac{7}{6}(x^2-3x+2)-\frac{5}{2}(x^2-x-2)+5(x^2-1)$$

$$=\frac{7}{6}x^2-\frac{7}{6}(3x)+\frac{7}{6}(2)-\frac{5}{2}x^2+\frac{5}{2}x+\frac{10}{2}+5x^2-5$$

$$=\left(\frac{7}{6}-\frac{5}{2}+5\right)x^2+\left(\frac{-7}{2}+\frac{5}{2}\right)x+\left(\frac{7}{3}+5-5\right)$$

$$=\left(\frac{7-15+30}{6}\right)x^2+\left(\frac{-2}{2}\right)x+\left(\frac{7}{3}\right)$$

$$=\frac{22}{6}x^2-x+\frac{7}{3}$$

$$=\frac{11}{3}x^2-x+\frac{7}{3}$$

$$=\frac{1}{3}(11x^2-3x+7)$$

4) Using Lagrange's interpolation formula find *y*(10) given that *y*(5)=12, *y*(6)=13, *y*(9)=14, y(11)=16

Solution:

Given

x:	(x_0) 5	(x_1) 6	(x_2) 9	(x_3) 11
y:	(y_0) 12	(y_1) 13	(y_2) 14	(y_3) 16

By Lagrange's interpolation formula

$$y=f(x)=\frac{(x-x_1)(x-x_2)(x-x_3)}{(x_0-x_1)(x_0-x_2)(x_0-x_3)}y_0+\frac{(x-x_0)(x-x_2)(x-x_3)}{(x_1-x_0)(x_1-x_2)(x_1-x_3)}y_1$$
$$+\frac{(x-x_0)(x-x_1)(x-x_3)}{(x_2-x_0)(x_2-x_1)(x_2-x_3)}y_2+\frac{(x-x_0)(x-x_1)(x-x_2)}{(x_3-x_0)(x_3-x_1)(x_3-x_2)}y_3$$

$$y=f(x)=\frac{(x-6)(x-9)(x-11)}{(5-6)(5-9)(5-11)}(12)+\frac{(x-5)(x-9)(x-11)}{(6-5)(6-9)(6-11)}(13)$$
$$+\frac{(x-5)(x-6)(x-11)}{(9-5)(9-6)(9-11)}(14)+\frac{(x-5)(x-6)(x-9)}{(11-5)(11-6)(11-9)}(16)$$

Putting $x=10$

$$y=f(10)=\frac{(10-6)(10-9)(10-11)}{(-1)(-4)(-6)}(12)+\frac{(10-5)(10-9)(10-11)}{(1)(-3)(-5)}(13)$$
$$+\frac{(10-5)(10-6)(10-11)}{(4)(3)(-2)}(14)+\frac{(10-5)(10-6)(10-9)}{(6)(5)(2)}(16)$$

$$=\frac{4(1)(-1)}{-24}(12)+\frac{5(1)(-1)}{15}(13)+\frac{5(4)(-1)(4)}{-24}+\frac{5(4)(1)}{60}16$$
$$=2-4.3333+11.6667+5.3332$$
$$y=14.6666$$

5) Find the missing term in the following table using Lagrange' interpolation formula:

x	0	1	2	3	4
y	1	3	9	–	81

Solution:

Given:

x:	(x_0) 0	(x_1) 1	(x_2) 2	(x_3) 4
y:	(y_0) 1	(y_1) 3	(y_2) 9	(y_3) 81

By Lagrange's interpolation formula,

$$y=f(x)=\frac{(x-x_1)(x-x_2)(x-x_3)}{(x_0-x_1)(x_0-x_2)(x_0-x_3)}y_0+\frac{(x-x_0)(x-x_2)(x-x_3)}{(x_1-x_0)(x_1-x_2)(x_1-x_3)}y_1$$
$$+\frac{(x-x_0)(x-x_1)(x-x_3)}{(x_2-x_0)(x_2-x_1)(x_2-x_3)}y_2+\frac{(x-x_0)(x-x_1)(x-x_2)}{(x_3-x_0)(x_3-x_1)(x_3-x_2)}y_3$$

$$f(x)=\frac{(x-1)(x-2)(x-4)}{(0-1)(0-2)(0-4)}(1)+\frac{(x-0)(x-2)(x-4)}{(1-0)(1-2)(1-4)}(3)$$
$$+\frac{(x-0)(x-1)(x-4)}{(2-0)(2-1)(2-4)}(9)+\frac{(x-0)(x-1)(x-2)}{(4-0)(4-1)(4-2)}(81)$$

$$y(3)=\frac{(3-1)(3-2)(3-4)}{(-1)(-2)(-4)}(1)+\frac{(3-0)(3-2)(3-4)}{1(-1)(-3)}(3)$$
$$+\frac{(3-0)(3-1)(3-4)}{2(1)(-2)}(9)+\frac{(3-0)(3-1)(3-2)}{4(3)(2)}(81)$$

$$=\frac{-2}{-8}(1)+\frac{-3}{3}(3)+\frac{-6}{-4}(9)+\frac{6}{24}(81)$$

$$=\frac{1}{4}-3+\frac{27}{2}+\frac{81}{4}$$

$$=\frac{82}{4}+\frac{27}{2}-3$$
$$=\frac{82+54-12}{4}$$

$$y(3)=31$$

6) Using Lagrange Interpolation find y(2) from the following data.

x	0	1	3	4	5
y	0	1	81	256	625

Solution:

Given

x	(x_0) 0	(x_1) 1	(x_2) 3	(x_3) 4	(x_4) 5
y	0 (y_0)	1 (y_1)	81 (y_2)	256 (y_3)	625 (y_4)

By Lagrange's Interpolation formula,

$$y=f(x)=\frac{(x-x_1)(x-x_2)(x-x_3)(x-x_4)}{(x_0-x_1)(x_0-x_2)(x_0-x_3)(x_0-x_4)}y_0+\frac{(x-x_0)(x-x_2)(x-x_3)(x-x_4)}{(x_1-x_0)(x_1-x_2)(x_1-x_3)(x_1-x_4)}y_1$$
$$+\frac{(x-x_0)(x-x_1)(x-x_3)(x-x_4)}{(x_2-x_0)(x_2-x_1)(x_2-x_3)(x_0-x_4)}y_2+\frac{(x-x_0)(x-x_1)(x-x_2)(x-x_4)}{(x_3-x_0)(x_3-x_1)(x_3-x_2)(x_3-x_4)}y_3$$
$$+\frac{(x-x_0)(x-x_1)(x-x_2)(x-x_3)}{(x_4-x_0)(x_4-x_1)(x_4-x_2)(x_4-x_3)}y_4$$

$$y(2)=\frac{(2-1)(2-3)(2-4)(2-5)}{(0-1)(0-3)(0-4)(0-5)}(0)+\frac{(2-0)(2-3)(2-4)(2-5)}{(1-0)(1-3)(1-4)(1-5)}(1)$$
$$+\frac{(2-0)(2-1)(2-4)(2-5)}{(3-0)(3-1)(3-4)(3-5)}(81)+\frac{(2-0)(2-1)(2-3)(2-5)}{(4-0)(4-1)(4-3)(4-5)}(256)$$
$$+\frac{(2-0)(2-1)(2-3)(2-4)}{(5-0)(5-1)(5-3)(5-4)}(625)$$

$$y(2)=\frac{12}{24}+\frac{12}{12}(81)-\frac{6}{12}(256)+\frac{4}{40}(625)$$
$$=\frac{1}{2}+81-128+62.5$$
$$=0.5+81-128+62.5$$
$$y(2)=16$$

7) Use Lagrange's method to find $\log_{10}656$ given that $\log_{10}654=2.8156$, $\log_{10}658=2.8182$, $\log_{10}659=2.8189$ and $\log_{10}661=2.8202$.

Solution:

Given

x	(x_0) 654	(x_1) 658	(x_2) 659	(x_3) 661
$y=\log_{10}x$	2.8156 (y_0)	2.8182 (y_1)	2.8189 (y_2)	2.8202 (y_3)

By Lagrange's Interpolation formula,

$$y=f(x)=\frac{(x-x_1)(x-x_2)(x-x_3)}{(x_0-x_1)(x_0-x_2)(x_0-x_3)}y_0+\frac{(x-x_0)(x-x_2)(x-x_3)}{(x_1-x_0)(x_1-x_2)(x_1-x_3)}y_1$$
$$+\frac{(x-x_0)(x-x_1)(x-x_3)}{(x_2-x_0)(x_2-x_1)(x_2-x_3)}y_2+\frac{(x-x_0)(x-x_1)(x-x_2)}{(x_3-x_0)(x_3-x_1)(x_3-x_2)}y_3$$

Here $x=656$,

$$y=f(656)=\frac{(-2)(-3)(-5)}{(-4)(-5)(-7)}(2.8156)+\frac{(2)(-3)(-5)}{(4)(-1)(-3)}(2.8182)$$
$$+\frac{(2)(-2)(-5)}{(5)(1)(-2)}(2.8189)+\frac{(2)(-2)(-3)}{(7)(3)(2)}(2.8202)$$

$$=0.6033+7.0455-5.6378+0.8058$$

$$y=2.8168$$

8) Given the value

x	14	17	31	35
$f(x)$	68.7	64.0	44.0	39.1

Find $f(27)$ by using lagrange's interpolation formula.

Solution:

Given

x	(x_0) 14	(x_1) 17	(x_2) 31	(x_3) 35
$f(x)$	68.7 (y_0)	64.0 (y_1)	44.0 (y_2)	39.1 (y_3)

By Lagrange's Interpolation formula,

$$y=f(x)=\frac{(x-x_1)(x-x_2)(x-x_3)}{(x_0-x_1)(x_0-x_2)(x_0-x_3)}y_0+\frac{(x-x_0)(x-x_2)(x-x_3)}{(x_1-x_0)(x_1-x_2)(x_1-x_3)}y_1$$
$$+\frac{(x-x_0)(x-x_1)(x-x_3)}{(x_2-x_0)(x_2-x_1)(x_2-x_3)}y_2+\frac{(x-x_0)(x-x_1)(x-x_2)}{(x_3-x_0)(x_3-x_1)(x_3-x_2)}y_3$$

$$y=f(27)=\frac{(27-17)(27-31)(27-35)}{(14-17)(14-31)(14-35)}(68.7)+\frac{(27-14)(27-31)(27-35)}{(17-14)(17-31)(17-35)}(64.0)$$
$$+\frac{(27-14)(27-17)(27-35)}{(31-14)(31-17)(31-35)}(44.0)+\frac{(27-14)(27-17)(27-31)}{(35-14)(35-17)(37-31)}(39.1)$$

$$=-20.52+35.22+48.07-13.45$$

$$f(27)=49.3$$

EXERCISE

1) Find the third degree polynomial $f(x)$ satisfying the following data, hence find $f(4)$

x	1	3	5	7
y	24	120	336	720

[Ans: $x^3+6x^2+11x+6, \quad f(4)=210$]

2) Using Lagrange's interpolation formula, find $f(4)$ given that $f(0)=2,\ f(1)=3,\ f(2)=12,\ f(15)=3587$.

[Ans: $f(4)=78$]

3) Use Lagrange's formula to find the value of y at $x=6$ from the following data.

x	3	7	9	10
y	168	120	72	63

[Ans: $f(6)=147$]

4) Find the expression of *f(x)* using Lagrange's formula for the following data:

x	0	1	4	5
y	4	3	24	39

[Ans: $f(x)=2x^2-3x+4$]

5) Find *f(x)* and also find *f* (2)

x	0	1	3	4
y	–12	0	6	12

[Ans: $f(x) = x^3-7x^2+18x-12, \quad f(2)=4$]

4.2.2 Lagrange's Inverse Interpolation

Lagrange's inverse interpolation formula is

$$x=\frac{(y-y_1)(y-y_2)...(y-y_n)}{(y_0-y_1)(y_0-y_2)...(y_0-y_n)}x_0+\frac{(y-y_0)(y-y_2)...(y-y_n)}{(y_1-y_0)(y_1-y_2)...(y_1-y_n)}x_1+$$

$$+.....+\frac{(y-y_0)(y-y_1)...(y-y_{n-1})}{(y_n-y_0)(y_n-y_1)...(y_n-y_{n-1})}x_n$$

PROBLEMS

1) Find the value of x when y=20 using Lagrange's formula from the following data.

x	1	2	3	4
$y=f(x)$	1	8	27	64

Solution:

Given:

x:	(x_0) 1	(x_1) 2	(x_2) 3	(x_3) 4
y:	(y_0) 1	(y_1) 8	(y_2) 27	(y_3) 64

By Lagrange's inverse formula,

$$x = f(y) = \frac{(y-y_1)(y-y_2)(y-y_3)}{(y_0-y_1)(y_0-y_2)(y_0-y_3)}x_0 + \frac{(y-y_0)(y-y_2)(y-y_3)}{(y_1-y_0)(y_1-y_2)(y_1-y_3)}x_1 + \frac{(y-y_0)(y-y_1)(y-y_3)}{(y_2-y_0)(y_2-y_1)(y_2-y_3)}x_2 + \frac{(y-y_0)(y-y_1)(y-y_2)}{(y_3-y_0)(y_3-y_1)(y_3-y_2)}x_3$$

$$f(20) = \frac{(20-8)(20-27)(20-64)}{(1-8)(1-27)(1-64)}(1) + \frac{(20-1)(20-27)(20-64)}{(8-1)(8-27)(8-64)}(2) + \frac{(20-1)(20-8)(20-64)}{(27-1)(27-8)(27-64)}(3) + \frac{(20-1)(20-8)(20-27)}{(64-1)(64-8)(64-27)}(4)$$

$$= \frac{(12)(-7)(-44)}{(-7)(-26)(-63)} + \frac{(19)(-7)(-44)}{(7)(-19)(-56)}(2) + \frac{(19)(12)(-44)}{(26)(19)(-37)}(3) + \frac{(19)(12)(-7)}{(63)(56)(37)}(4)$$

$$= -0.32234 + 1.57143 + 1.64657 - 0.04891$$

$$f(2) = 2.84675$$

2) Find the age corresponding to the annuity value 13.6 from the table values

Age(*x*)	**30**	**35**	**40**	**45**	**50**
Annuity value(*y*)	**15.9**	**14.9**	**14.1**	**13.3**	**12.5**

Solution:

Given

x:	(x_0) 30	(x_1) 35	(x_2) 40	(x_3) 45	(x_4) 50
y:	(y_0) 15.9	(y_1) 14.9	(y_2) 14.1	(y_3) 13.3	(y_4) 12.5

By Lagrange's inverse interpolation,

$$x = \frac{(y-y_1)(y-y_2)...(y-y_n)}{(y_0-y_1)(y_0-y_2)...(y_0-y_n)}x_0 + \frac{(y-y_0)(y-y_2)...(y-y_n)}{(y_1-y_0)(y_1-y_2)...(y_1-y_n)}x_1 + ... + \frac{(y-y_0)(y-y_1)...(y-y_{n-1})}{(y_n-y_0)(y_n-y_1)...(y_n-y_{n-1})}x_n$$

$$x(13.6)=\frac{(13.6-14.9)(13.6-14.1)(13.6-13.3)(13.6-12.5)}{(15.9-14.9)(15.9-14.1)(15.9-13.3)(15.9-12.5)}(30)$$

$$+\frac{(13.6-15.9)(13.6-14.1)(13.6-13.3)(13.6-12.5)}{(14.9-15.9)(14.9-14.1)(14.9-13.3)(14.9-12.5)}(35)$$

$$+\frac{(13.6-15.9)(13.6-14.9)(13.6-13.3)(13.6-12.5)}{(14.1-15.9)(14.1-14.9)(14.1-13.3)(14.1-12.5)}(40)$$

$$+\frac{(13.6-15.9)(13.6-14.9)(13.6-14.1)(13.6-12.5)}{(13.3-15.9)(13.3-14.9)(13.3-14.1)(13.3-12.5)}(45)$$

$$+\frac{(13.6-15.9)(13.6-14.9)(13.6-14.1)(13.6-13.3)}{(12.5-15.9)(12.5-14.9)(12.5-14.1)(12.5-13.3)}(50)$$

$$=0.0254-4.3237+21.4128+27.7954-2.1470$$

$$x(y=13.6)=43$$

3) Find the value of θ given $f(\theta)=0.3887$ where $f(\theta)=\int_0^\theta \frac{1}{\sqrt{1-\frac{1}{2}\sin^2\theta}}\,d\theta$ using the following table

θ	21°	23°	25°
f(θ)	0.3706	0.4068	0.4433

Solution:

Now Take $f(\theta)$ as independent and θ as dependent

$y=f(\theta)$	(y_0) 0.3706	(y_1) 0.4068	(y_2) 0.4433
θ	21 (x_0)	23 (x_1)	25 (x_2)

By Lagrange's inverse interpolation formula

$$x=\frac{(y-y_1)(y-y_2)}{(y_0-y_1)(y_0-y_2)}(x_0)+\frac{(y-y_0)(y-y_2)}{(y_1-y_0)(y_1-y_2)}(x_1)+\frac{(y-y_0)(y-y_1)}{(y_2-y_0)(y_2-y_1)}(x_2)$$

$$\theta(y=0.3887)=\frac{(0.3887-0.4068)(0.3887-0.4433)}{(0.3706-0.4068)(0.3706-0.4433)}(21)$$

$$+\frac{(0.3887-0.3706)(0.3887-0.4433)}{(0.4068-0.3706)(0.4068-0.4433)}(23)$$

$$+\frac{(0.3887-0.3706)(0.3887-0.4068)}{(0.4433-0.3706)(0.443-0.4068)}(25)$$

$$=7.885832+17.202739-3.086525$$

$$\theta=22.0020$$

4) The following table gives the value of the probability integral $f(x) = \frac{2}{\sqrt{\pi}} \int_0^x e^{-x^2} dx$ corresponding to certain values of x. For what value of x in this integral is equal to 0.5.

x	**0.46**	**0.47**	**0.48**	**0.49**
f(x)	**0.4846555**	**0.4937452**	**0.5027498**	**0.5116683**

Solution:

Given

x	0.46	0.47	0.48	0.49
f(x)	0.4846555	0.4937452	0.5027498	0.5116683

By Lagrange's inverse interpolation formula

$$x = \frac{(y-y_1)(y-y_2)(y-y_3)}{(y_0-y_1)(y_0-y_2)(y_0-y_3)}(x_0) + \frac{(y-y_0)(y-y_2)(y-y_3)}{(y_1-y_0)(y_1-y_2)(y_1-y_3)}(x_1)$$

$$+ \frac{(y-y_0)(y-y_1)(y-y_3)}{(y_2-y_0)(y_2-y_1)(y_2-y_3)}(x_2) + \frac{(y-y_0)(y-y_1)(y-y_2)}{(y_3-y_0)(y_3-y_1)(y_3-y_2)}(x_3)$$

$$x(0.5) = \frac{(0.5-0.4937452)(0.5-0.5027498)(0.5-0.51166831)}{(0.4846555-0.4937452)(0.4846555-0.5027498)(0.4846555-0.5116683)}(0.46)$$

$$+ \frac{(0.5-0.4846555)(0.5-0.5027498)(0.5-0.5116683)}{(0.4937452-0.4846555)(0.4937452-0.5027498)(0.4937452-0.5116683)}(0.47)$$

$$+ \frac{(0.5-0.4846555)(0.5-0.4937452)(0.5-0.5116683)}{(0.5027498-0.4846555)(0.5027498-0.4937452)(0.5027498-0.5116683)}(0.48)$$

$$+ \frac{(0.5-0.4846555)(0.5-0.4937452)(0.5-0.5027498)}{(0.5116683-0.4846555)(0.5116683-0.4937452)(0.5116683-0.5027498)}(0.49)$$

$$x(0.5) = \frac{(0.062548)(-0.0027498)(-0.01166831)}{(-0.0090897)(-0.0180943)(-0.0270128)}(0.46)$$

$$+ \frac{(0.0153445)(-0.0027498)(-0.0116683)}{(0.0090897)(-0.0090046)(-0.0179231)}(0.47)$$

$$+ \frac{(0.0153445)(0.0062548)(-0.0116683)}{(0.0180943)(0.0090046)(-0.0089185)}(0.48)$$

$$+ \frac{(0.0153445)(0.0062548)(-0.0027498)}{(0.0270128)(0.0179231)(-0.0089185)}(0.49)$$

$$= -0.02077873 + 0.157736496 + 0.369927795 - 0.029949447$$

$$x(0.5) = 0.476936113$$

5) Using Lagrange's formula find the polynomial to the given data

x	0	1	3
y	5	6	50

Solution:

Given

	(x_0)	(x_1)	(x_2)
x	0	1	3
y	5	6	50
	(y_0)	(y_1)	(y_2)

By Lagrange's interpolation formula

$$y = f(x) = \frac{(x-x_1)(x-x_2)}{(x_0-x_1)(x_0-x_2)} y_0 + \frac{(x-x_0)(x-x_2)}{(x_1-x_0)(x_1-x_2)} y_1 + \frac{(x-x_0)(x-x_1)}{(x_2-x_0)(x_2-x_1)} y_2$$

$$= \frac{(x-1)(x-3)}{(-1)(-3)}(5) + \frac{(x)(x-3)}{(1)(-2)}(6) + \frac{(x)(x-1)}{(3)(2)}(50)$$

$$= \frac{5}{3}(x-1)(x-3) - 3x(x-3) + \frac{25}{3}x(x-1)$$

$$= \frac{5}{3}(x-1)[x-3+5x] - 3x(x-3)$$

$$= \frac{5}{3}(x-1)[6x-3] - 3(x^2-3x)$$

$$= 5(x-1)(2x-1) - 3(x^2-3x)$$

$$= 5[2x^2 - x - 2x + 1] - 3x^2 + 9x$$

$$y = 7x^2 - 6x + 5$$

EXERCISE

1) Find the value of θ given $f(\theta) = 0.3887$, where $f(\theta) = \int_0^{\infty} \left(\frac{1}{\sqrt{1 - \frac{1}{2}\sin^2\theta}} \right) d\theta$ using the following table

θ	21°	23°	25°
$f(\theta)$	0.3706	0.4068	0.4433

[Ans: θ(y=0.3887)=22.0020]

4.2.3 Newton's Divided Difference formula

Consider $y=f(x)$ such that

x:	x_0	x_1	x_2	...	x_n
$y=f(x)$:	y_0	y_1	y_2	...	y_n

Newton's divided difference interpolation formula is

$$f(x)=f(x_0)+(x-x_0)\Delta f(x_0)+(x-x_0)(x-x_1)\Delta^2 f(x_0)$$
$$+...(x-x_0)(x-x_1)...(x-x_{n-1})\Delta^n f(x_n)$$

PROBLEMS

1) Find f(x) as a polynomial in x for the following data by Newton's divided difference formula.

x:	**–4**	**–1**	**0**	**2**	**5**
f(x):	**1245**	**33**	**5**	**9**	**1335**

Solution:

x	$f(x)$	$\Delta f(x)$	$\Delta^2 f(x)$	$\Delta^3 f(x)$	$\Delta^4 f(x)$
-4	1245				
		$\frac{33-1245}{-1-(-4)}=-404$			
-1	33		$\frac{-28+(404)}{0-(-4)}=94$		
		$\frac{5-33}{0-(-1)}=-28$		$\frac{10-94}{2-(-4)}=-14$	
0	5		$\frac{2-(-28)}{2-(-1)}=10$		$\frac{13-(-14)}{5-(-4)}=3$
		$\frac{9-5}{2-0}=2$		$\frac{88-10}{5-(-1)}=13$	
2	9		$\frac{442-2}{5-0}=88$		
		$\frac{1335-9}{5-2}=442$			
5	1335				

By Newton's divided difference interpolation formula

$$f(x)=f(x_0)+(x-x_0)\Delta f(x_0)+(x-x_0)(x-x_1)\Delta^2 f(x_0)+(x-x_0)(x-x_1)$$
$$(x-x_2)\Delta^3 f(x_0)+(x-x_0)(x-x_1)(x-x_2)(x-x_3)\Delta^4 f(x_0)+...$$

Here $x_0=-4$, $x_1=-1$, $x_2=0$, $x_3=2$, $x_4=5$

$$f(x_0) = 1245$$
$$\Delta f(x_0) = -404$$
$$\Delta^2 f(x_0) = 94$$
$$\Delta^3 f(x_0) = -14$$
$$\Delta^4 f(x_0) = 3$$

$$f(x) = 1245 + (x+4)(-404) + (x+4)(x+1)(94) + (x+4)(x+1)(x)(-14) + (x+4)(x+1)x(x-2)(3)$$

$$= 1245 - 404x - 1616 + (94)[x^2+5x+4] - 14x(x^2+5x+4) + 3x[(x^2+5x+4)(x-2)]$$

$$= 1245 - 404x - 1616 + 94x^2 + 470x + 376 - 14x^3 - 70x^2 - 56x + 3x[x^3 - 2x^2 + 5x^2 - 10x + 4x - 8]$$

$$= -14x^3 + 24x^2 + 10x + 5 + 3x[x^3 + 3x^2 - 6x - 8]$$

$$= -14x^3 + 24x^2 + 10x + 5 + 3x^4 + 9x^3 - 18x^2 - 24x$$

$$f(x) = 3x^4 - 5x^3 + 6x^2 - 14x + 5$$

2) Find $f(8)$ by Newton's divided difference formula for the data:

x:	4	5	7	10	11	13
f(x):	48	100	294	900	1210	2028

Solution:

x	$f(x)$	$\Delta f(x)$	$\Delta^2 f(x)$	$\Delta^3 f(x)$	$\Delta^4 f(x)$
4	48				
		$\frac{100-48}{5-4}=52$			
5	100		$\frac{97-52}{7-4}=15$		
		$\frac{294-100}{7-5}=97$		$\frac{21-15}{10-4}=1$	
7	294		$\frac{202-97}{10-5}=21$		0
		$\frac{900-294}{10-7}=202$		$\frac{27-21}{11-5}=1$	
10	900		$\frac{310-202}{11-7}=27$		0
		$\frac{1210-900}{11-10}=310$		$\frac{33-27}{13-7}=1$	
11	1210		$\frac{409-310}{13-10}=33$		
		$\frac{2028-1210}{13-11}=409$			
13	2028				

By Newton's divided difference interpolation formula,

$$f(x)=f(x_0)+(x-x_0)\Delta f(x_0)+(x-x_0)(x-x_1)\Delta^2 f(x_0)+(x-x_0)(x-x_1)$$
$$(x-x_2)\Delta^3 f(x_0)+(x-x_0)(x-x_1)(x-x_2)(x-x_3)\Delta^4 f(x_0)+\ldots$$

Here $x_0= 4, x_1=5, x_2=7, x_3=10, x_4=11, x_5=13$

$$f(x_0)=48$$
$$\Delta f(x_0)=52$$
$$\Delta^2 f(x_0)=15$$
$$\Delta^3 f(x_0)=1$$

$$f(x)=48+(x-4)(52)+(x-4)(x-5)(15)+(x-4)(x-5)(x-7)(1)$$

$$f(8)=48+(8-4)(52)+(8-4)(8-5)(15)+(8-4)(8-5)(8-7)(1)$$
$$=48+(4)(52)+(4)(3)(15)+4(3)(1)(1)$$
$$=448$$

3) Using Newton's divided difference formula find f(x) and f(6) from the following data:

x:	1	2	7	8
f(x):	1	5	5	4

Solution:

The divided difference table is

x	$f(x)$	$\Delta f(x)$	$\Delta^2 f(x)$	$\Delta^3 f(x)$
1	1			
		$\frac{5-1}{2-1}=4$		
2	5		$\frac{0-4}{7-1}=\frac{-4}{6}$	
		$\frac{5-5}{7-2}=0$		$\frac{-1/6+4/6}{8-1}=\frac{1/2}{7}=\frac{1}{14}$
7	5		$\frac{-1-0}{8-2}=\frac{-1}{6}$	
		$\frac{4-5}{8-7}=-1$		
8	4			

By Newton's divided difference interpolation formula,

$$f(x)=f(x_0)+(x-x_0)\Delta f(x_0)+(x-x_0)(x-x_1)\Delta^2 f(x_0)+(x-x_0)$$
$$(x-x_1)(x-x_2)\Delta^3 f(x_0)$$

$$=1+(x-1)(4)+(x-1)(x-2)\left(\frac{-4}{6}\right)+(x-1)(x-2)(x-7)\left(\frac{1}{14}\right)$$

$$=1+4x-4-\frac{2}{3}(x^2-3x+2)+\frac{1}{14}(x^2-3x+2)(x-7)$$

$$=\frac{42}{42}[4x-3]-\frac{2\times 14}{3\times 14}(x^2-3x+2)+\frac{1\times 3}{14\times 3}[x^3-3x^2+2x-7x^2+21x-14]$$

$$=\frac{1}{42}[168x-126-28x^2+84x-56]+3[x^3-3x^2+2x-7x^2+21x-14]$$

$$=\frac{1}{42}[-28x^2+252x-182+3x^3-9x^2+6x-21x^2+63x-42]$$

$$=\frac{1}{42}[3x^3-58x^2+321x-224]$$

$$f(6)=\frac{1}{42}[3(6)^3-58(6)^2+321(6)-224]$$

$$=\frac{1}{42}[262]$$

$$=6.2381$$

4) **Find *f(1)*, *f(5)* and *f(9)* using Newton's divided difference formula from the following data.**

x:	**0**	**2**	**3**	**4**	**7**	**8**
y=f(x):	**4**	**26**	**58**	**112**	**466**	**668**

Solution:

x	$f(x)$	$\Delta f(x)$	$\Delta^2 f(x)$	$\Delta^3 f(x)$	$\Delta^4 f(x)$
0	4				
		$\frac{26-4}{2-0}=11$			
2	26		$\frac{32-11}{3-0}=7$		
		$\frac{58-26}{3-2}=32$		$\frac{11-7}{4-0}=1$	
3	58		$\frac{54-32}{4-2}=11$		
		$\frac{112-58}{4-3}=54$		$\frac{16-11}{7-2}=1$	0
4	112		$\frac{118-54}{7-3}=16$		
		$\frac{466-112}{7-4}=118$		$\frac{21-16}{8-3}=1$	0
7	466		$\frac{202-118}{8-4}=21$		
		$\frac{668-466}{8-7}=202$			
8	668				

Newton's divided difference formula is

$$y = f(x) = y_0 + (x - x_0)\Delta f(x_0) + (x - x_0)(x - x_1)\Delta^2 f(x_0) + (x - x_0)(x - x_1)(x - x_2)\Delta^3 f(x_0) + \ldots$$

Here $x_0=0$, $y_0=4$, $x_1=2$, $x_2=3$

$\Delta f(x_0)=11$, $\Delta^2 f(x_0)=7$, $\Delta^3 f(x_0)=1$

$$f(x) = 4 + (x-0)11 + x(x-0)(x-2)(7) + x(x-0)(x-2)(x-3)(1)$$
$$= 4 + 11x + (x^2 - 2x)(7) + x(x^2 - 5x + 6)$$
$$= x^3 + 7x^2 - 5x^2 + 11x + 6x - 14x + 4$$
$$f(x) = x^3 + 2x^2 + 3x + 4 \qquad \rightarrow (1)$$

Put $x=1$ in (1), we get

$$f(1) = (1)^3 + 2(1)^2 + 3(1) + 4$$
$$= 1 + 2 + 3 + 4$$
$$f(1) = 10$$

Put $x=5$ in (1), we get

$$f(5) = (5)^3 + 2(5)^2 + 3(5) + 4$$
$$= 194$$

Put $x=9$ in (1) we get

$$f(9) = (9)^3 + 2(9)^2 + 3(9) + 4$$
$$= 922$$

5) Using Newton's divided difference formula, find $u(3)$ given $u(1)=-26$, $u(2)=12$, $u(4)=256$, u(6)=844

Solution:

We form the divided difference table

x	$u(x)=f(x)$	$\Delta f(x)$	$\Delta^2 f(x)$	$\Delta^3 f(x)$
1	–26			
		$\frac{12+26}{2-1}=38$		
2	12		$\frac{122-38}{4-1}=28$	
		$\frac{256-12}{4-2}=122$		$\frac{43-28}{6-1}=3$
4	256		$\frac{294-122}{6-2}=43$	
		$\frac{844-256}{6-4}=294$		
6	844			

By Newton's divided difference interpolation formula is

$$f(x) = f(x_0) + (x - x_0)\Delta f(x_0) + (x - x_0)(x - x_1)\Delta^2 f(x_0) + (x - x_0)(x - x_1)$$
$$(x - x_2)\Delta^3 f(x_0) + \ldots$$

$x_0=1,\ x_1=2,\ x_2=4,\ x_3=6$

$f(x_0)=-26,\ \Delta f(x_0)=38,\ \Delta^2 f(x_0)=28,\ \Delta^3 f(x_0)=3$

$$f(x) = -26 + (x-1)38 + (x-1)(x-2)28 + (x-1)(x-2)(x-4)3$$

$$f(3) = u(3) = -26 + 2(38) + 2(1)(28) + 2(1)(-1)(3)$$

$$= -26+76+56-6$$

$$u(3)=100$$

6) Given the following data find $y'(6)$, $y'(5)$ and the maximum value of y.

x	0	2	3	4	7	9
y	4	26	58	112	466	922

Solution:

The given arguments are not equally spaced, so we will use Newton's divided difference formula.

The divided difference Table is

x	$f(x)$	$\Delta f(x)$	$\Delta^2 f(x)$	$\Delta^3 f(x)$	$\Delta^4 f(x)$
0	4				
		11			
2	26		7		
		32		1	
3	58		11		0
		54		1	
4	112		16		0
		118		1	
7	466		22		
		228			
9	922				

Newton's divided difference formula,

$$y = f(x) = f(x_0) + (x - x_0)f(x_0, x_1) + (x - x_0)(x - x_1)f(x_0, x_1, x_2)$$
$$+ (x - x_0)(x - x_1)(x - x_2)f(x_0, x_1, x_2, x_3) + \ldots$$

$$= 4 + (x-0)11 + (x-0)(x-2)7 + (x-0)(x-2)(x-3)(1)$$

$$y(x) = x^3 + 2x^2 + 3x + 4$$

$$y'(x) = 3x^2 + 4x + 3$$

$$y'(6) = 3(6)^2 + 4(6) + 3 = 135$$

$$y'(5) = 3(5)^2 + 4(5) + 3 = 98$$

$y(x)$ is maximum if $y'(x) = 0$.

$$\therefore 3x^2 + 4x + 3 = 0$$

But the roots are imaginary.

$\therefore$ Therefore, there is no extremum value in the range. In fact, it is an increasing curve.

7) Using Newton's divided difference formula find the missing value from the table.

x	**1**	**2**	**4**	**5**	**6**
y	**14**	**15**	**5**	**–**	**9**

Solution:

The divided difference table is,

x	$f(x)$	$\Delta f(x)$	$\Delta^2 f(x)$	$\Delta^3 f(x)$
1	14			
		$\boxed{1}$		
2	15		$\boxed{-2}$	
		–5		$\boxed{\frac{3}{4}}$
4	5		$\frac{7}{4}$	
		2		
6	9			

By Newton's divided difference interpolation formula

$$f(x) = f(x_0) + (x - x_0) f(x_0, x_1) + (x - x_0)(x - x_1) f(x_0, x_1, x_2)$$
$$+ (x - x_0)(x - x_1)(x - x_2) f(x_0, x_1, x_2, x_3) + \ldots$$

$$= 14 + (x-1) + (x-1)(x-2)(-2) + (x-1)(x-2)(x-4)\left(\frac{3}{4}\right)$$

$$= 14 + x - 1 - 2(x-1)(x-2) + \frac{3}{4}(x-1)(x-2)(x-4)$$

$$f(5) = 13 + 5 - 2(4)(3) + \frac{3}{4}(4)(3)(1)$$

$$=13–24+9$$

$$f(5) = 3$$

8) Find the function *f(x)* from the following table using Newton's divided difference formula

x	0	1	2	4	5	7
y	0	0	–12	0	600	7308

Also find *f(6)*.

Solution:

x	$f(x)$	$\Delta f(x)$	$\Delta^2 f(x)$	$\Delta^3 f(x)$	$\Delta^4 f(x)$	$\Delta^5 f(x)$
0	0					
		$\frac{0-0}{1-0}=\boxed{0}$				
1	0		$\frac{-12-0}{2-0}=\boxed{-6}$			
		$\frac{0-0}{1-0}=0$		$\frac{6+6}{4-0}=\boxed{3}$		
2	–12		$\frac{6+12}{4-1}=6$		$\frac{48-3}{5-0}=\boxed{9}$	
		$\frac{0+12}{4-2}=6$		$\frac{198-6}{5-1}=48$		$\frac{16-9}{7-0}=\boxed{1}$
4	0		$\frac{600-6}{5-2}=198$		$\frac{144-48}{7-1}=16$	
		$\frac{600-0}{5-4}=600$		$\frac{918-198}{7-2}=144$		
5	600		$\frac{3354-600}{7-4}=918$			
		$\frac{7308-600}{7-4}=3354$				
7	7308					

By Newton's divided difference interpolation formula

$$f(x)=f(x_0)+(x-x_0)f(x_0,x_1)+(x-x_0)(x-x_1)f(x_0,x_1,x_2)$$
$$+(x-x_0)(x-x_1)(x-x_2)f(x_0,x_1,x_2,x_3)+\ldots$$

$$=0+(x-0)(0)+(x-0)(x-1)(-6)+(x-0)(x-1)(x-2)(3)$$
$$+(x-0)(x-1)(x-2)(x-4)(9)+(x-0)(x-1)(x-2)(x-4)(x-5)(1)$$

$$=-6x(x-1)+3x(x-1)(x-2)+9x(x-1)(x-2)(x-4)$$
$$+x(x-1)(x-2)(x-4)(x-5)$$

$$=-6x(x-1)+3x(x-1)(x-2)+x(x-1)(x-4)(x-2)(9+x-5)$$

$$=-6x(x-1)+x(x-1)(x-2)(3+x^2-16)$$

$$=-6x(x-1)+x(x-1)(x-2)(x^2-13)$$

$$=x(x-1)(-6+x^3-13x-2x^2+26)$$

$$=x(x-1)(x^3-2x^2-13x+20)$$

$$=x(x^4-2x^3-13x^2+20x-x^3+2x^2+13x-20)$$

$$=x(x^4-3x^3-11x^2+33x-20)$$

$$f(x) = x^5 - 3x^4 - 11x^3 + 33x^2 - 20x$$

$$f(6) = (6)^5 - 3(6)^4 - 11(6)^3 + 33(6)^2 - 20(6)$$

$$f(6) = 2580$$

9) Find the divided difference of $f(x) = x^3 + x + 2$ for the arguments 1, 3, 6,11

Solution:

The divided difference table is,

x	$f(x)$	$\Delta f(x)$	$\Delta^2 f(x)$	$\Delta^3 f(x)$
1	4			
		$\frac{32-4}{3-1} = \boxed{14}$		
3	32		$\frac{64-14}{6-1} = \boxed{10}$	
		$\frac{224-32}{6-3} = 64$		$\frac{20-10}{11-1} = \boxed{1}$
6	224		$\frac{224-64}{11-3} = 20$	
		$\frac{1344-224}{11-6} = 224$		
11	1344			

10) Given the values

x:	**5**	**7**	**11**	**13**	**17**
f(x):	**150**	**392**	**1452**	**2366**	**5202**

Evaluate *f(9)* using Newton's divided difference formula.

Solution:

The divided difference table is,

x	$f(x)$	$\Delta f(x)$	$\Delta^2 f(x)$	$\Delta^3 f(x)$	$\Delta^4 f(x)$
5	150				
		$\frac{392-150}{7-5} = \boxed{121}$			
7	392		$\frac{265-121}{11-5} = \boxed{24}$		
		$\frac{1452-392}{11-7} = 265$		$\frac{32-24}{13-5} = \boxed{1}$	
11	1452		$\frac{457-265}{13-7} = 32$		0
		$\frac{2366-1452}{13-11} = 457$		$\frac{42-32}{17-7} = 1$	
13	2366		$\frac{709-457}{17-11} = 42$		
		$\frac{5202-2366}{17-13} = 709$			
17	5202				

By Newton's divided difference interpolation formula

$$f(x) = f(x_0) + (x - x_0) f(x_0, x_1) + (x - x_0)(x - x_1) f(x_0, x_1, x_2) + (x - x_0)(x - x_1)(x - x_2) f(x_0, x_1, x_2, x_3) + \ldots$$

$$f(x) = 150 + (x-5)(121) + (x-5)(x-7)24 + (x-5)(x-7)(x-13)(1)$$

$$= 150 + 121x - 605 + 24(x^2 - 12x + 35) + (x-13)(x^2 - 12x + 35)$$

$$= -455 + 121x + 24x^2 - 288x + 840 + x^3 - 12x^2 + 35x - 13x^2 + 156x - 455$$
$$= x^3 - x^2 + 24x - 70$$

$$f(9) = (9)^3 - (9)^2 + 24(9) - 70$$
$$f(9) = 794$$

EXERCISE

1) Using Newton's divided difference formula, find the function *f(x)* from the following:

x:	0	1	2	4	5	7
f(x):	0	0	–12	0	600	7308

[Ans:
$$f(x) = x^5 - 3x^4 - 11x^3 + 33x^2 - 20x,$$
$$f(6) = 2580$$
]

2) Using Newton's divided difference formula find $u(5)$ given $u(1)= 14$, $u(2)=15$, $u(4)=5$, $u(6)=9$.

[Ans: $u(5)=3$.]

3) Given the values

x:	5	7	11	13	17
f(x):	150	392	1452	2366	5202

Evaluate *f(9)* using Newton's divided difference formula.

[Ans: *f(9)*=794]

4) Given the data.

x:	0	1	2	5
$f(x)$:	2	3	12	147

Find the cubic function of x

[Ans: $f(x) = x^3 + x^2 - x + 2$]

5) **Use Newton's divided difference formula to find $f(5)$ from the following data.**

x:	0	2	3	4	7
$f(x)$:	4	26	58	112	466

[Ans: $f(5) = 194$]

4.3 INTERPOLATION WITH EQUAL INTERVAL

4.3.1 Newton's Forward Interpolation

Newton's forward interpolation formula for equal intervals: when interpolation is needed near the beginning of the table value.

Let the function $y = f(x)$ take the values $y_0, y_1, \ldots, y_n$ at the points $x_0, x_1, x_2, \ldots, x_n$ where $x_i = x_0 + ih$. Then Newton's forward interpolation polynomial is given by

$$y(x) = P_n(x) = P_n(x_0 + uh)$$

$$= y_0 + \frac{u}{1!}\Delta y_0 + \frac{u(u-1)}{2!}\Delta^2 y_0 + \frac{u(u-1)(u-2)}{3!}\Delta^3 y_0 + \ldots + \frac{u(u-1)(u-2)(u-3)}{4!}\Delta^4 y_0 \quad \rightarrow (1)$$

Where $u = \dfrac{x - x_0}{h}$

This equation (1) is also known as Gregory-Newton forward interpolation formula.

4.3.2 Newton's Backward Interpolation

When interpolation is needed near the end of the table value:

Newton's Backward Interpolation formula is

$$P_n(x) = P(x_0 + vh) = y_n + \frac{v}{1!}\nabla y_n + \frac{v(v+1)}{2!}\nabla^2 y_n + \frac{v(v+1)(v+2)}{3!}\nabla^3 y_n + \ldots \quad \rightarrow (2)$$

Where $v = \frac{x - x_n}{h}$

This equation (2) is also known as Gregory-Newton backward difference interpolation formula.

PROBLEMS

1) Using Newton's forward interpolation formula find the polynomial *f(x)* satisfying the following data. Hence evaluate y at *x*=5.

x:	**4**	**6**	**8**	**10**
y:	**1**	**3**	**8**	**10**

Solution:

We form the difference table

x	y	Δy	$\Delta^2 y$	$\Delta^3 y$
$4(x_0)$	$1(y_0)$			
		$3-1=2(\Delta y_0)$		
$6(x_1)$	$3(y_1)$		$5-2=3(\Delta^2 y_0)$	
		$8-3=5(\Delta y_1)$		$-3-3=-6(\Delta^2 y_0)$
$8(x_2)$	$8(y_2)$		$2-5=-3(\Delta^2 y_0)$	
		$10-8=2(\Delta y_2)$		
$10(x_3)$	$10(y_3)$			

There are only 4 data given:

Hence the polynomial will be degree 3.

$$y(x) = P_3(x) = y_0 + \frac{u}{1!}\Delta y_0 + \frac{u(u-1)}{2!}\Delta^2 y_0 + \frac{u(u-1)(u-2)}{3!}\Delta^3 y_0 + \ldots$$

Where $u = \frac{x - x_0}{h}$

Hence, x_0=4, h=6–4=2

$$y(x) = P_3(x) = 1 + \frac{\left(\frac{x-4}{2}\right)}{1!}(2) + \frac{\left(\frac{x-4}{2}\right)\left(\frac{x-6}{2}\right)}{2!}(3) + \frac{\left(\frac{x-4}{2}\right)\left(\frac{x-6}{2}\right)\left(\frac{x-8}{2}\right)}{3!}(-6)$$

$$= 1 + x - 4 + \frac{(x-4)(x-6)}{8}(3) + \frac{(x-4)(x-6)(x-8)}{8(6)}(-6)$$

$$= x-3+\frac{3}{8}(x-4)(x-6)-\frac{1}{8}(x-4)(x-6)(x-8)$$

$$= x-3+\frac{3}{8}[x^2-10x+24]-\frac{1}{8}[(x^2-10x+24)(x-8)]$$

$$= x-3+\frac{3}{8}[x^2-10x+24]-\frac{1}{8}[x^3-10x^2+24x-8x^2+80x-192]$$

$$= \frac{1}{8}[8x-24+3(x^2-10x+24)-x^3+10x^2-24x+8x^2-80x+192]$$

$$= \frac{1}{8}[8x-24+3x^2-30x+72-x^3+10x^2-24x+8x^2-80x+192]$$

$$= \frac{1}{8}[-x^3+21x^2-126x+240]$$

$$y(5) = \frac{1}{8}[-(-5)^3+21(5)^2-126(5)+240]$$

$$= \frac{1}{8}[-125+21(25)-630+240]$$

$$= \frac{1}{8}[10]$$

$$= 1.25$$

2) Using Newton's forward interpolation formula find the cubic polynomial which taken places the following values.

x:	**0**	**1**	**2**	**3**
f(x):	**1**	**2**	**1**	**10**

Evaluate *f(4)* using Newton's backward formula. Is it the same as obtained from the cubic polynomial found above?

Solution:

We form the difference table

x	y	Δy	$\Delta^2 y$	$\Delta^3 y$
$0(x_0)$	$1(y_0)$			
		$2-1=1(\nabla y_0)$		
$1(x_1)$	$2(y_1)$		$-1-1=-2(\nabla^2 y_0)$	
		$1-2=-1(\nabla y_1)$		$10+2=12(\nabla^3 y_0)$
$2(x_2)$	$1(y_2)$		$9+1=10(\nabla^2 y_1)$	
		$10-1=9(\nabla y_2)$		
$3(x_3)$	$10(y_3)$			

Hence, $x_0=4, y_0=1 \quad u=\frac{x-x_0}{h}$

$h=1-0=1, \quad u=x$

$\Delta y_0=1 \quad \Delta^2 y_0=-2 \quad \Delta^3 y_0=12$

To find y when $x=4$

By Newton's forward interpolation formula

$$y(x)=P_n(x)=y_0+\frac{u}{1!}\Delta y_0+\frac{u(u-1)}{2!}\Delta^2 y_0+\frac{u(u-1)(u-2)}{3!}\Delta^3 y_0+\ldots$$

$$=1+x-x(x-1)+2x(x-1)(x-2)$$
$$=1+x-x^2+x+2x[x^2-3x+2]$$

$$=1+2x-x^2+2x^3-6x^2+4x$$
$$=2x^3-7x^2+6x+1$$

Verification:

$$P_3(2)=16-28+12+1$$
$$=29-28=1$$

$\therefore$ The polynomial is correct.

$$y(4)=2(4)^3-7(4)^2+6(4)+1$$
$$=2(64)-7(16)+24+1$$
$$=41$$

Using Newton's backward Interpolation formula

$$y(x)=y_3+\frac{v}{1!}\nabla y_3+\frac{v(v+1)}{2!}\nabla^2 y_3+\frac{v(v+1)(v+2)}{3!}\nabla^3 y_3+\ldots$$

Here $x_3=3 \qquad h=1-0=1$

$$v=\frac{x-x_3}{h}=\frac{x-3}{1}=x-3$$

$$y(x)=10+\frac{(x-3)}{1!}(9)+\frac{(x-3)(x-2)}{2!}(10)+\frac{(x-3)(x-2)(x-1)}{3!}(12)$$
$$=10+9(x-3)+5(x-3)(x-2)+2(x-3)(x-2)(x-1)$$
$$=10+9x-27+5[x^2-5x+6]+2[x^2-5x+6](x-1)$$

$$= 9x^2 - 17 + 5x^2 - 25x + 30 + 2[x^3 - 5x^2 + 6x - x^2 + 5x - 6]$$

$$= 5x^2 - 16x + 13 + 2[x^3 - 6x^2 + 11x - 6]$$

$$= 5x^2 - 16x + 13 + 2x^3 - 12x^2 + 22x - 12$$

$$= 2x^3 - 7x^2 + 6x + 1$$

$$y(4) = P_3(4) = 2(4)^3 - 7(4)^2 + 6(4) + 1$$
$$= 41$$

∴ The cubic polynomial same for both the cases.

3) From the following table, find the number of student whose weight is between 60 to 70.

Weight:	**0–40**	**40–60**	**60–80**	**80–100**	**100–720**
No. of Students:	**250**	**120**	**100**	**70**	**50**

Solution:

Difference table:

x	y	Δy	$\Delta^2 y$	$\Delta^3 y$	$\Delta^4 y$
Below 40	250				
		120			
Below 60	370		–20		
		100		–10	
Below 80	470		–30		20
		70		10	
Below 100	540		–20		
		50			
Below 120	590				

Here x_0=40 y_0=250

$$\Delta y_0 = 120 \quad \Delta^2 y_0 = -20 \quad \Delta^3 y_0 = -10, \quad \Delta^4 y_0 = 20$$

Let x=70

$$u = \frac{x - x_0}{h} = \frac{70 - 40}{20} = 1.5$$

$$\boxed{u = 1.5}$$

By Newton's forward formula,

$$y(x) = y_0 + u\Delta y_0 + \frac{u(u-1)}{2!}\Delta^2 y_0 + \frac{u(u-1)(u-2)}{3!}\Delta^3 y_0 + \frac{u(u-1)(u-2)(u-3)}{4!}\Delta^4 y_0 + \ldots$$

$$y(70) = 250 + (1.5)(120) + \frac{(1.5)(0.5)}{2}(-20) + \frac{(1.5)(0.5)(-0.5)}{6}(-10)$$
$$+ \frac{(1.5)(0.5)(-0.5)(-1.5)}{24}(20)$$

$$= 250 + 180 - 7.5 + 0.625 + 0.46875$$

$$= 423.59$$

$$y(70) = 424$$

Number of students whose weight is between 60 and 70

$$= y(70) - y(60)$$
$$= 424 - 370$$
$$= 54$$

4) The following data are taken from the steam table:

Temperature's:	**140**	**150**	**160**	**170**	**180**
Pressure:	**3.685**	**4.854**	**6.302**	**8.076**	**10.225**

Find the pressure at temperature t=142° and t=175°

Solution:

We form the difference table:

x	y	Δy	$\Delta^2 y$	$\Delta^3 y$	$\Delta^4 y$
140	3.685				
		1.169			
150	4.854		0.279		
		1.448		0.047	
160	6.302		0.326		0.002
		1.774		0.049	
170	8.076		0.375		
		2.149			
180	10.225				

$$u = \frac{x - x_0}{h} = \frac{142 - 140}{10} = \frac{1}{5} = 0.2$$

$$y(x) = y_0 + u\Delta y_0 + \frac{u(u-1)}{2!}\Delta^2 y_0 + \frac{u(u-1)(u-2)}{3!}\Delta^3 y_0$$
$$+ \frac{u(u-1)(u-2)(u-3)}{4!}\Delta^4 y_0 + \ldots$$

$$y(142°) = 3.685 + (0.2)(1.169) + \frac{(0.2)(-0.8)}{2}(0.279) + \frac{(0.2)(-0.8)(-1.8)}{6}(0.047)$$

$$+ \frac{(0.2)(-0.8)(-1.8)(-2.8)}{24}(0.002)$$

$$= 3.685 + 0.2338 - 0.0223 + 0.0023 - 0.0001$$

$$= 3.8987$$

$$y(142°) = 3.898$$

$$y(175°) = y_n + v\nabla y_n + \frac{v(v+1)}{2!}\nabla^2 y_n + \frac{v(v+1)(v+2)}{3!}\nabla^3 y_n$$

$$+ \frac{v(v+1)(v+2)(v+3)}{4!}\nabla^4 y_n + ...$$

$$v = \frac{175-180}{10} = -0.5$$

$$y(175°) = 10.225 + (-0.5)(2.149) + \frac{(-0.5)(0.5)}{2}(0.375) + \frac{(-0.5)(0.5)(1.5)}{6}(0.049)$$

$$+ \frac{(-0.5)(0.5)(1.5)(2.5)}{24}(0.002)$$

$$= 10.225 - 1.0745 - 0.0469 - 0.0031 - 0.0001$$

$$= 9.1004$$

$$y(175°) = 9.10$$

5) Using Newton's forward interpolation formula, find the value of *sin 52* given that *sin 45°*=0.7071, *sin 50°*=0.7660, *sin 55°*=0.8192, and *sin 60°*=0.8660.

Solution:

x:	45°	50°	55°	60°
y=sinx :	0.7071	0.7660	0.8192	0.8660

The difference table is

x	y	Δy	$\Delta^2 y$	$\Delta^3 y$
45	0.7071			
		0.0589		
50	0.7660		–0.0057	
		0.0532		–0.0007
55	0.8192		–0.0064	
		0.0468		
60	0.8660			

Here x_0=45 y_0=0.7071 Δy_0=0.0589 $\Delta^2 y_0$=–0.0057 $\Delta^3 y_0$=–0.0007

Let x=52

$$u = \frac{52-45}{5} = \frac{7}{5} = 1.4$$

By Newton's forward Interpolation formula is

$$y(x) = y_0 + u\Delta y_0 + \frac{u(u-1)}{2!}\Delta^2 y_0 + \frac{u(u-1)(u-2)}{3!}\Delta^3 y_0$$

$$= 0.7071 + (1.4)(0.0589) + \frac{(1.4)(0.4)}{2}(-0.0057) + \frac{(1.4)(0.4)(-0.6)}{6}(-0.00007)$$

$$y(52) = 0.7071 + 0.0825 - 0.0016 + 0.0000$$

$$y(52) = 0.7880$$

Sin 52°= 0.7880

6) From the following data, using Newton's backward interpolation formula, compute log 58.75

x:	**40**	**45**	**50**	**55**	**60**
log x	**1.6021**	**1.6532**	**1.6990**	**1.7403**	**1.7781**

Solution:

The difference table is:

x	y	∇y	$\nabla^2 y$	$\nabla^3 y$	$\nabla^4 y$
40	1.6021				
		0.0511			
45	1.6532		–0.0053		
				0.0008	
50	1.6990	0.0458			0.0002
			–0.0045		
55	1.7403	0.0413		0.0010	
			–0.0035		
60	1.7781	0.0378			

Here x_n=60, h=5, ∇y_n=0.0378, $\nabla^2 y_n$= –0.035, $\nabla^3 y_n$=0.0010, $\nabla^4 y_n$=0.0002

Let x=58.75 $$v = \frac{x - x_n}{h} = \frac{58.75-60}{5} = -0.25$$

By Newton's Backward Interpolation formula

$$y(x) = y_n + v\nabla y_n + \frac{v(v+1)}{2!}\nabla^2 y_n + \frac{v(v+1)(v+2)}{3!}\nabla^3 y_n + \frac{v(v+1)(v+2)(v+3)}{4!}\nabla^4 y_n + \ldots$$

$$y(58.75)=1.7781-(0.25)(0.0378)+\frac{(-0.25)(0.75)}{2}(-0.0035)$$

$$+\frac{(-0.25)(0.75)(1.75)}{6}(0.0010)+\frac{(-0.25)(0.75)(1.75)(2.75)}{24}(0.0002)$$

$$=1.7781-0.0095+0.0003-0.0001-0$$

$$y(58.75)=1.7689$$

7) Form the following data find θ at *x*=43

x:	40	50	60	70	80	90
θ:	184	204	226	250	276	304

Solution:

The difference table is

x	y	Δy	$\Delta^2 y$	$\Delta^3 y$
40	184			
50	204	20	2	0
60	226	22	2	0
70	250	24	2	0
80	276	26	2	
90	304	28		

Here x_0=40, y_0=184, h=14, Δy_0=20, $\Delta^2 y_0$=2

$$u=\frac{x-x_0}{h}=\frac{43-40}{10}=0.3$$

By Newton's forward interpolation is

$$y(x)=y_0+u\Delta y_0+\frac{u(u-1)}{2!}\Delta^2 y_0+\frac{u(u-1)(u-2)}{3!}\Delta^3 y_0+\ldots$$

$$y(43)=184+(0.3)(20)+\frac{(0.3)(0.3-1)}{2!}(2)$$

$$=184+6-0.21$$

$$y(43)=189.79$$

8) Construct Newton's forward interpolation polynomial for the following data and hence find $f(3.5), f'(3.5)$

x:	1	2	3	4	5
$f(x)$:	1	–1	1	–1	1

Solution:

x	y	Δy	$\Delta^2 y$	$\Delta^3 y$	$\Delta^4 y$
1	1				
		–2			
2	–1		4		
		2		–8	
3	1		–4		16
		–2		8	
4	–1		4		
		2			
5	1				

Here $x_0=1$, $y_0=1$, $h=1$, $\Delta y_0=-2$, $\Delta^2 y_0=4$, $\Delta^3 y_0=-8$, $\Delta^4 y_0=16$

$$u=\frac{x-1}{1}=x-1$$

$$u=x-1$$

By Newton's forward interpolation is

$$f(x)=1+(x-1)(-2)+\frac{(x-1)(x-2)}{2}(4)+\frac{(x-1)(x-2)(x-3)}{6}(-8)$$
$$+\frac{(x-1)(x-2)(x-3)(x-4)}{24}(16)$$

$$=1-2x+2+2\left(x^2-3x+2\right)+\left(x^3-6x^2+11x-6\right)\left(\frac{-4}{3}\right)$$
$$+\frac{2}{3}\left(x^4-10x^3+35x^2-50x+24\right)$$

$$f(x)=\frac{1}{3}\left[2x^4-24x^3+100x^2-168x+93\right] \qquad \rightarrow (1)$$

$$f(3.5)=\frac{1}{3}\left[2(3.5)^4-24(3.5)^3+100(3.5)^2-168(3.5)+93\right]$$

$$=\frac{1.1258}{3}$$

$$f(3.5)=0.375$$

From (1), $f'(x)=\frac{1}{3}\left[8x^3-72x^2+200x-168\right]$

$$f'(3.5)=\frac{1}{3}\left[8(3.5)^3-72(3.5)^2+200(3.5)-168\right]$$
$$f'(3.5)=-2.33$$

9) Given the table

x:	0	0.1	0.2	0.3	0.4
e^x	1	1.1052	1.2214	1.3499	1.4918

Find the value of $y=e^x$ when $x=0.38$.

Solution:

x	y	∇y	$\nabla^2 y$	$\nabla^3 y$	$\nabla^4 y$
0	1.0000				
		0.1052			
0.1	1.1052		0.0110		
		0.1162		0.0013	
0.2	1.2214		0.0123		−0.0002 ($\nabla^4 y_0$)
		0.1285		0.0011($\nabla^3 y_0$)	
0.3	1.3499		0.0134 ($\nabla^2 y_0$)		
		0.1419(∇y_0)			
0.4(x_0)	1.4918(y_0)				

Here $h=0.1$

$$v=\frac{x-x_n}{h}=\frac{0.38-0.4}{0.1}=-0.2$$

By Newton's Backward Interpolation formula

$$y(x)=y_n+v\nabla y_n+\frac{v(v+1)}{2!}\nabla^2 y_n+\frac{v(v+1)(v+2)}{3!}\nabla^3 y_n+...$$

$$y(0.38)=1.4918+(-0.2)(0.1419)+\frac{(-0.2)(-0.2+1)}{2!}(0.0134)$$
$$+\frac{(-0.2)(-0.2+1)(-0.2+2)}{3!}(0.0011)+\frac{(0.2)(-0.2+1)(-0.2+2)(-0.2+3)}{4!}(-0.0002)$$

$$y(0.38)=1.4918-0.0284-0.0011-0.0001+0$$

$$y=e^{0.38}=1.4623$$

10) From the following data find θ at x=43 and x=84

x:	40	50	60	70	80	90
θ:	184	204	226	250	276	304

Solution:

The difference table is

x	y	Δy	$\Delta^2 y$	$\Delta^3 y$	$\Delta^4 y$
40	184				
		20			
50	204		2		
		22		0	
60	226		2		0
		24		0	
70	250		2		0
		26		0	
80	276		2		
		28			
90	304				

h=10 $\quad u=\dfrac{x-x_0}{h}=\dfrac{43-40}{10}=0.3$

By Newton's forward interpolation is

$$y(x)=y_0+u\Delta y_0+\frac{u(u-1)}{2!}\Delta^2 y_0+\ldots$$

$$=184+(0.3)(20)+\frac{(0.3)(-0.7)}{2}(2)$$

$$=184+6.0-0.21$$

$$y(43)=189.79$$

By Newton's Backward Interpolation formula

$$y(x)=y_0+v\nabla y_0+\frac{v(v+1)}{2!}\nabla^2 y_0+\ldots$$

$$v=\frac{x-x_n}{h}=\frac{84-90}{10}=-0.6$$

$$y(x)=304+(-0.6)(28)+\frac{(-0.6)(0.4)}{2}(2)$$

$$y(84)=286.96$$

EXERCISE

1) **Find $y(1.02)$ from the following table**

x:	1.00	1.05	1.10	1.15	1.20
y:	0.3413	0.3531	0.3643	0.3749	0.3849

[Ans: $y(1.02) = 0.34614$]

2) **Find the values of y at x=21 and x=28 from the following data:**

x:	20	23	26	29
y:	0.3420	0.3907	0.4384	0.4848

[Ans: $y(21)$=0.3583 $y(28)$=0.4695]

3) **Find the values of tan(0.12) and tan(0.26) from the following data:**

x:	0.10	0.15	0.20	0.25	0.30
$y=\tan x$:	0.1003	0.1511	0.2027	0.2553	0.3093

[Ans: tan(0.12)=0.1205, tan(0.26)=0.2668]

4) **From the following table estimate the number of students who obtained marks between 40 and 45**

Marks:	30-40	40-50	50-60	60-70	70-80
No.of.students:	31	42	51	35	31

[Ans: 17]

PART -A

QUESTIONS AND ANSWERS

1) State Lagrange's interpolation formula.

Solution:

Let $y=f(x)$ be a function which takes the values $y_0, y_1, ... y_n$ corresponding to $x=x_0, x_1, ... x_n$.

Then Lagrange's interpolation formula is

$$y = f(x) = \frac{(x-x_0)(x-x_2)...(x-x_n)}{(x_0-x_1)(x_0-x_2)...(x_0-x_n)} y_0 + \frac{(x-x_0)(x-x_2)...(x-x_n)}{(x_1-x_0)(x_1-x_2)(x_1-x_n)} y_1 + ...$$
$$+ ..... + \frac{(x-x_0)(x-x_1)...(x-x_{n-1})}{(x_n-x_0)(x_n-x_1)...(x_n-x_{n-1})} y_n$$

2) What is the assumption we make when Lagrange's formula is used?

Solution:

Lagrange's interpolation formula can be used whether the values of x, the independent variable are equally spaced or not whether the difference of y become smaller or not

3) What advantage has Lagrange's formula over Newton?

Lagrange's method	Newton's Method
We can apply both equally and unequally spaced arguments	The arguments are equally spaced
Can be used to interpolate any where in the range	Newton's forward formula suitable to interpolate near the beginning. Newton's backward formula is suitable to interpolate near end of the value

4) Give the inverse of Lagrange's interpolation formula.

Solution:

$$x = \frac{(y-y_1)(y-y_2)...(y-y_n)}{(y_0-y_1)(y_0-y_2)...(y_0-x_n)} x_0 + \frac{(y-y_0)(y-y_2)...(y-y_n)}{(y_1-y_0)(y_1-y_2)...(y_1-y_n)} x_1 + ...$$
$$+ ..... + \frac{(y-y_0)(y-y_1)...(y-y_{n-1})}{(y_n-y_0)(y_n-y_1)...(y_n-y_{n-1})} x_n$$

5) What do you meant by interpolation?

The process of finding the values of a function inside the given range is called interpolation.

6) Given the Newton's divided difference interpolation formula.

Solution:

$$f(x)=f(x_0)+(x-x_0)f(x_0,x_1)+(x-x_0)(x-x_1)f(x_0,x_1,x_2)+ \\ ....+(x-x_0)(x-x_1)...(x-x_{n-1})f(x_0,\, x_1...x_n)$$

7) What is the nature of nth divided difference of a polynomial of nth degree?

The nth divided difference of a polynomial of degree n are constants.

8) State Newton's forward difference formula by using operator method.

Solution:

$$P_n(x)=P_n(x_0+uh)$$

$$y(x)=y_0+\frac{u}{1!}\Delta y_0+\frac{u(u-1)}{2!}\Delta^2 y_0+\frac{u(u-1)(u-2)}{3!}\Delta^3 y_0+...$$

Where $u=\dfrac{x-x_0}{h}$

9) When Newton's backward interpolation formula is used?

The formula is used mainly to interpolate the value of y near the end of a set of tabular values and also for extrapolating the values of y a short distance ahead of y_n.

10) State Newton's Backward difference interpolation formula.

$$P_n(x)=y_n+v\nabla y_n+\frac{v(v+1)}{2!}\nabla^2 y_n+\frac{v(v+1)(v+2)}{3!}\nabla^3 y_n+...$$

Where $v=\dfrac{x-x_n}{h}$

11) Newton's forward interpolation formula used only for ___ intervals

Solution:

Equal intervals (or) Equidistant intervals.

12) When will we use Newton's forward interpolation formula?

The formula is used to interpolate the values of y near the beginning of the table values and also for extrapolating the value of y short distance ahead of y_0

13) What is the error in Newton's forward interpolation formula?

Solution:

$$f(x)-\phi_n x=\frac{r(r-1)(r-2)....(r-n)}{(n+1)!}\Delta^{n+1}f(x)$$

14) What is the error in Newton's backward interpolation formula.

$$f(x)-\phi_n x=\frac{r(r+1)(r+2)....(r+n)}{(n+1)!}h^{n+1}f^{(n+1)}(z)$$

15) Give the relation between the divided differences and forward or backward differences.

Solution:

$$f(x_0,x_1,...x_n)=\frac{1}{n!h^n}\Delta^n f_0=\frac{1}{n!h^n}\nabla^n f_n$$

4.4 NUMERICAL DIFFERENTIATION

Introduction

Numerical differentiation is the process of computing the value of $\frac{dy}{dx},\frac{d^2y}{dx^2}....$ for some particular value of x from the given data (x_i, y_i), i=1,2.......n where $y=f(x)$ is not known explicitly.

The Interpolation formula to be used depends on the particular value of x at which the derivatives are required. If the values of x are not equally spaced, we represent the function by Lagrange's (or) Newton's divided difference formula and the derivatives are obtained. If the values of x are equally spaced, the derivatives are calculated by using Newton's forward or backward Interpolation Formula. If the derivatives are required at a point near the beginning of the table, we use Newton's Forward Interpolation formula and if the derivatives are required at a point near the end of the table, we use Newton's backward Interpolation formula.

Approximation of Derivatives Using Interpolation Polynomials

(a) Newton's Forward Difference Formula

To find the derivative of $y=f(x)$ passing through the $(n+1)$ points, at a point nearer to the starting value $x=x_0$:

Newton's Forward difference Interpolation formula is,

$$y(x_0+uh)=y(x)=y_0+u\Delta y_0+\frac{u(u-1)}{2!}\Delta^2 y_0+\frac{u(u-1)(u-2)}{3!}\Delta^3 y_0+...\rightarrow(1)$$

where $y(x)$ is a polynomial of degree n in x and $u=\frac{x-x_0}{h}$

differentiating (1), w.r. to x, we get

$$\frac{dy}{dx}=\frac{dy}{du}\frac{du}{dx}$$

$$= \frac{du}{dx}\frac{dy}{du}$$

$$= \frac{1}{h}\frac{dy}{du}$$

$$\frac{dy}{dx} = \frac{1}{h}\left[\Delta y_0 + \frac{2u-1}{2}\Delta^2 y_0 + \frac{3u^2-6u+2}{6}\Delta^3 y_0 + \frac{4u^3-18u^2+22u-6}{24}\Delta^4 y_0 + ..\right] \rightarrow (2)$$

Similarly,

$$\frac{d^2y}{dx^2} = \frac{1}{h^2}\left[\Delta^2 y_0 + (u-1)\Delta^3 y_0 + \frac{(6u^2-18u+11)}{12}\Delta^4 y_0 + ...\right] \rightarrow (3)$$

$$\frac{d^3y}{dx^3} = \frac{1}{h^3}\left[\Delta^3 y_0 + \frac{12u-18}{12}\Delta^4 y_0 + ...\right] \rightarrow (4)$$

$$\left(\frac{dy}{dx}\right)_{x=x_0} = \left(\frac{dy}{dx}\right)_{u=0} = \frac{1}{h}\left[\Delta y_0 - \frac{1}{2}\Delta^2 y_0 + \frac{1}{3}\Delta^3 y_0 - \frac{1}{4}\Delta^4 y_0 + ...\right] \rightarrow (5)$$

$$\left(\frac{d^2y}{dx^2}\right)_{x=x_0} = \frac{1}{h^2}\left[\Delta^2 y_0 + \Delta^3 y_0 + \frac{11}{12}\Delta^4 y_0 + ...\right] \rightarrow (6)$$

$$\left(\frac{d^3y}{dx^3}\right)_{x=x_0} = \frac{1}{h^3}\left[\Delta^3 y_0 - \frac{3}{2}\Delta^4 y_0 + ...\right] \rightarrow (7)$$

equations (5) (6) (7) give the values of First, second and third derivatives at the starting value $x = x_0$

(b) Newton's Backward Difference Formula

Newton's Backward difference formula is,

$$y(x) = y(x_n + vh) = y_n + v\nabla y_n + \frac{v(v+1)}{2!}\nabla^2 y_n + \frac{v(v+1)(v+2)}{3!}\nabla^3 yn + ... \rightarrow (1)$$

where $v = \frac{x - x_n}{h}$

Differentiate (1) w. r. to x, we get

$$\frac{dy}{dx} = \frac{dy}{dv}\cdot\frac{dv}{dx} = \frac{dy}{dv}\left(\frac{1}{h}\right) = \frac{1}{h}\frac{dy}{dv}$$

$$=\frac{1}{h}\left[\nabla y_n+\frac{2v+1}{2}\nabla^2 y_n+\frac{(3v^2+6v+2)}{6}\nabla^3 y_n+\frac{4v^3+18v^2+22v+6}{24}\nabla^4 y_n+...\right]\rightarrow(2)$$

Similarly,

$$\frac{d^2y}{dx^2}=\frac{1}{h^2}\left[\nabla^2 y_n+(v+1)\nabla^3 y_n+\frac{6v^2+18v+11}{12}\nabla^4 y_n+...\right]\rightarrow(3)$$

$$\frac{d^3y}{dx^3}=\frac{1}{h^3}\left[\nabla^3 y_n+\frac{12v+18}{12}\nabla^4 y_n+...\right]\rightarrow(4)$$

$$\Rightarrow\quad\left(\frac{dy}{dx}\right)_{x=x_n}=\left(\frac{dy}{dx}\right)_{v=0}=\frac{1}{h}\left[\nabla y_n+\frac{1}{2}\nabla^2 y_n+\frac{1}{3}\nabla^3 y_n+...\right]\rightarrow(5)$$

$$\left(\frac{d^2y}{dx^2}\right)_{x=x_n}=\frac{1}{h^2}\left[\nabla^2 y_n+\nabla^3 y_n+\frac{11}{12}\nabla^4 y_n+...\right]\rightarrow(6)$$

$$\left(\frac{d^3y}{dx^3}\right)_{x=x_n}=\frac{1}{h^3}\left[\nabla^3 y_n+\frac{3}{2}\nabla^4 y_n+...\right]\rightarrow(7)$$

equations (5) (6) (7) gives the values of First, second and third derivatives at $x = x_n$

Problems Based On Forward Difference At $x = x_0$

At the point $x = x_0$ we use the following formulas.

$$\left(\frac{dy}{dx}\right)_{x=x_0}=\left(\frac{dy}{dx}\right)_{u=0}=\frac{1}{h}\left[\Delta y_0-\frac{1}{2}\Delta^2 y_0+\frac{1}{3}\Delta^3 y_0-\frac{1}{4}\Delta^4 y_0+...\right]$$

$$\left(\frac{d^2y}{dx^3}\right)_{x=x_0}=\left(\frac{d^2y}{dx^2}\right)_{u=0}=\frac{1}{h^2}\left[\Delta^2 y_0-\Delta^3 y_0+\frac{11}{12}\Delta^4 y_0+...\right]$$

$$\left(\frac{d^3y}{dx^3}\right)_{x=x_0}=\left(\frac{d^3y}{dx^3}\right)_{u=0}=\frac{1}{h^2}\left[\Delta^3 y_0-\frac{3}{2}\Delta^4 y_0+...\right]$$

1) Find *f′(3)* and *f″(3)* for the following data

x	3.0	3.2	3.4	3.6	3.8	4.0
$f(x)$	–14	–10.032	–5.296	–0.256	6.672	14

Solution :

Since we require *f′(3)* and *f″(3)*, we use Newton's Forward Formula.

Difference Table :

x	y	Δy	$\Delta^2 y$	$\Delta^3 y$	$\Delta^4 y$	$\Delta^5 y$
3.0	−14					
		(−10.032 − (−14)) [3.968]				
3.2	−10.032		(4.736 − 3.968) [0.768]			
		(−5.296 − (−10.032)) 4.736		(0.304 − 0.768) [−0.464]		
3.4	−5.296		(5.04 − 4.736) 0.304		(1.584 − (−0.464)) [2.048]	
		(−0.256 − (−5.296)) 5.04		(1.888 − 0.304) 1.584		(−3.072 − 2.048) [−5.12]
3.6	−0.256		(6.928 − 5.04) 1.888		(−1.488 − 1.584) − 3.072	
		(6.672 − (−0.256)) 6.928		(0.4 − 1.888) − 1.488		
3.8	6.672		(7.328 − 6.928) 0.4			
		(14 − 6.672) 7.328				
4.0	14					

From the table,

$$\Delta y_0 = 3.968,\ \Delta^2 y_0 = 0.768,\ \Delta^3 y_0 = -0.464\ \ \Delta^4 y_0 = 2.048,\ \Delta^5 y_0 = -5.12$$

By Newton's forward formula, we have

$$\frac{dy}{dx} = \frac{1}{h}\left[\Delta y_0 - \frac{1}{2}\Delta^2 y_0 + \frac{1}{3}\Delta^3 y_0 - \frac{1}{4}\Delta^4 y_0 + \ldots\right]$$

Hence $h = 0.2$

$$\frac{dy}{dx} = \frac{1}{0.2}\left[3.968 - \frac{1}{2}(0.768) + \frac{1}{3}(-0.464) - \frac{1}{4}(2.048) + \frac{1}{5}(-5.12)\right]$$

$$= \frac{1}{0.2}[3.968 - 0.384 - 0.1547 - 0.512 - 1.024]$$

$$= \frac{1}{0.2}[1.8933]$$

$$= 9.4665$$

$$f'(3) = 9.4665$$

$$\frac{d^2 y}{dx^2} = \frac{1}{h^2}\left[\Delta^2 y_0 - \Delta^3 y_0 + \frac{11}{12}\Delta^4 y_0 - \frac{5}{6}\Delta^5 y_0 + \ldots\right]$$

$$= \frac{1}{(0.2)^2}\left[0.768-(-0.464)+\frac{11}{12}(2.048)-\frac{5}{6}(-5.12)\right]$$

$$= \frac{1}{0.04}[0.768+0.464+1.8773+4.267]$$

$$= \frac{1}{0.04}[7.3763]$$

$$f''(3) = 184.4075$$

2) Find the first and second derivatives of *y* at *x* = 15 from the table given below:

x	15	17	19	21	23	25
y	3.873	4.123	4.359	4.583	4.796	5.000

Solution:

Since we require $y'(15)$ and $y''(15)$ we use Newton's Forward formula

Difference Table :

x	y	Δy	$\Delta^2 y$	$\Delta^3 y$	$\Delta^4 y$	$\Delta^5 y$
15	3.873					
		0.250				
17	4.123		−0.014			
		0.236		0.002		
19	4.359		−0.012		−0.001	
		0.224		0.001		0.002
21	4.583		−0.011		0.001	
		0.213		0.002		
23	4.796		−0.009			
		0.204				
25	5.000					

From the table,

$$\Delta y_0 = 0.250,\ \Delta^2 y_0 = -0.014,\ \Delta^3 y_0 = 0.002\ \Delta^4 y_0 = -0.001,\ \Delta^5 y_0 = 0.002$$

Here $h = 2$

$$\frac{dy}{dx} = \frac{1}{h}\left[\Delta y_0 - \frac{1}{2}\Delta^2 y_0 + \frac{1}{3}\Delta^3 y_0 - \frac{1}{4}\Delta^4 y_0 + \ldots\right]$$

$$= \frac{1}{2}\left[0.250 + \frac{0.014}{2} + \frac{0.002}{3} + \frac{0.001}{4} + \frac{0.002}{5}\right]$$

$$=\frac{1}{2}[0.250+0.0070+0.00066+0.00025+0.00040]$$

$$=\frac{1}{2}[0.25831]$$

$$=0.1291$$

$$\frac{d^2y}{dx^2}=\frac{1}{h^2}\left[\Delta^2 y_0-\Delta^3 y_0+\frac{11}{12}\Delta^4 y_0-\frac{5}{6}\Delta^5 y_0+...\right]$$

$$=\frac{1}{4}\left[-0.014-0.002+\frac{11}{12}(-0.001)-\frac{5}{6}(0.002)\right]$$

$$=\frac{1}{4}[-0.014-0.002-0.0009-0.0017]$$

$$=\frac{1}{4}[-0.01860]$$

$$=-0.0046$$

3) Find the value of *sec*31° using the following data

x°	**31**	**32**	**33**	**34**
tan x	**0.6008**	**0.6249**	**0.6494**	**0.6745**

Solution :

Since we require Sec 31° we use Newton's Forward Formula

Before that, if $y=\tan x$ then $\frac{dy}{dx}=\sec^2 x$

First we find $sec^2 31°$

Difference Table :

x	y	Δy	$\Delta^2 y$	$\Delta^3 y$
31	0.6008			
		0.0241		
32	0.6249		0.0004	
		0.0245		0.0002
33	0.6494		0.0006	
		0.0251		
34	0.6745			

From the table, $\Delta y_0=0.0241$ $\Delta^2 y_0=0.0004,$ $\Delta^3 y_0=0.0002$

Here, $h = 1°$ i.e., $h = 0.01745$ radians

$$\left(\frac{dy}{dx}\right)_{x=x_0} = \frac{1}{h}\left[\Delta y_0 - \frac{1}{2}\Delta^2 y_0 + \frac{1}{3}\Delta^3 y_0 - \frac{1}{4}\Delta^4 y_0 + \ldots\right]$$

$$= \frac{1}{0.01745}\left[0.0241 - \frac{1}{2}(0.0004) + \frac{1}{3}(0.0002)\right]$$

$$= \frac{1}{0.01745}[0.0241 - 0.00020 + 0.000067]$$

$$= \frac{1}{0.01745}[0.02396]$$

$$= 1.3734$$

$$\sec^2 31° = 1.3734$$

$$\Rightarrow \sec\ 31° = 1.1719$$

PROBLEMS BASED ON FORWARD DIFFERENCE AT $x = x_0 + uh$

At the point $x = x_0 + uh$ we use the following formulas

$$\frac{dy}{dx} = \frac{1}{h}\left[\Delta y_0 + \frac{2u-1}{2}\Delta^2 y_0 + \frac{3u^2 - 6u + 2}{6}\Delta^3 y_0 + \frac{(4u^3 - 18u^2 + 22u - 6)}{24}\Delta^4 y_0 + \ldots\right]$$

$$\frac{d^2y}{dx^2} = \frac{1}{h^2}\left[\Delta^2 y_0 + (u-1)\Delta^3 y_0 + \frac{(16u^2 - 18u + 11)}{12}\Delta^4 y_0 + \ldots\right]$$

$$\frac{d^3y}{dx^3} = \frac{1}{h^3}\left[\Delta^3 y_0 + \frac{12u - 18}{12}\Delta^4 y_0 + \ldots\right]$$

1) Find $\frac{dy}{dx}$ and $\frac{d^2y}{dx^2}$ at $x = 51$, from the following data.

x	50	60	70	80	90
y	19.96	36.65	58.81	77.21	94.61

Solution :

Here h=10, To find the derivatives of y at x=51 we use forward difference formula taking the origin at u=50

we have $u = \frac{x - x_0}{h} = \frac{51 - 50}{10} = 0.1$

at x= 51, u=0.1

Difference Table :

x	u	y	Δy	$\Delta^2 y$	$\Delta^3 y$	$\Delta^4 y$
50	0	19.96				
			16.69			
60	1	36.65		5.47		
			22.16		–9.23	
70	2	58.81		–3.76		11.99
			18.40		2.76	
80	3	77.21		–1.00		
			17.40			
90	4	94.61				

From the table $\Delta y_0 = 16.69 \;\; \Delta^2 y_0 = 5.47, \;\; \Delta^3 y_0 = -9.23 \;\; \Delta^4 y_0 = 11.99$

$$\left(\frac{dy}{dx}\right) = \frac{1}{h}\left[\begin{array}{l}\Delta y_0 + \dfrac{2u-1}{2}\Delta^2 y_0 + \dfrac{3u^2-6u+2}{6}\Delta^3 y_0 \\ \quad + \dfrac{(4u^3-18u^2+22u-6)}{24}\Delta^4 y_0 + \ldots\end{array}\right]$$

$$= \frac{1}{10}\left[\begin{array}{l}16.69 + \dfrac{(0.2-1)}{2}(5.47) + \dfrac{(3(0.1)^2-6(0.1)+2)}{6}(-9.23) \\ + \dfrac{4(0.1)^3-18(0.1)^2+22(0.1)-6}{24}(11.99)\end{array}\right]$$

$$= \frac{1}{10}[16.69 - 2.188 + \frac{1.4300}{6}(-9.23) - \frac{3.9760}{24}(11.99)]$$

$$= \frac{1}{10}[16.69 - 2.188 - 2.1998 - 1.9863]$$

$$= \frac{1}{10}[10.3159]$$

$$= 1.0316$$

$$\frac{d^2 y}{dx^2} = \frac{1}{h^2}\left[\Delta^2 y_0 + (u-1)\Delta^3 y_0 + \frac{(6u^2-18u+11)}{12}\Delta^4 y_0 + \ldots\right]$$

$$= \frac{1}{100}\left[5.47 + (0.1-1)(-9.23) + \frac{6(0.1)^2-18(0.1)+11}{12}(11.99)\right]$$

$$= \frac{1}{100}[5.47 + 8.307 + 9.2523]$$

$$= \frac{1}{100}[23.0293]$$

$$= 0.2303$$

2) Find the first and second derivatives of the function at a point x=1.2 from the following data

x	1	2	3	4	5
y	0	1	5	6	8

Solution :

We use Newton's Forward Formula since x=1.2 is at the beginning

$$u = \frac{x - x_0}{h} = \frac{1.2 - 1}{1} = 0.2$$

Here x= 1.2, x_0 = 1, h= 1

Difference Table :

x	y	Δy	$\Delta^2 y$	$\Delta^3 y$	$\Delta^4 y$
1	0				
		1			
2	1		3		
		4		–6	
3	5		–3		10
		1		4	
4	6		1		
		2			
5	8				

From the table , $\Delta y_0 = 1,\ \Delta^2 y_0 = 3,\ \Delta^3 y_0 = -6,\ \Delta^4 y_0 = 10$

Newton's Forward Formula is

$$\frac{dy}{dx} = \frac{1}{h}\left[\Delta y_0 + \frac{2u-1}{2}\Delta^2 y_0 + \frac{3u^2 - 6u + 2}{6}\Delta^3 y_0 + \frac{(4u^3 - 18u^2 + 22u - 6)}{24}\Delta^4 y_0 + \ldots\right]$$

$$= \frac{1}{1}\left[1 + \frac{2(0.2-1)}{2}(3) + \frac{(3(0.2)^2 - 6(0.2) + 2)}{6}(-6) + \frac{4(0.2)^3 - 18(0.2)^2 + 22(0.2) - 6}{24}(10) \right]$$

$$= \left[1 + \frac{0.400-1}{2}(3) + \frac{0.1200 - 1.2000 + 2}{6}(-6) + \frac{0.0320 - 0.7200 + 4.4000 - 6}{24}(10) \right]$$

$$= [1 - 0.3000(3) + 0.1533(-6) - (0.0953)(10)]$$

$$= [1 - 0.9000 - 0.9198 - 0.9530]$$

$$= -1.773$$

$$\frac{d^2y}{dx^2} = \frac{1}{h^2}\left[\Delta^2 y_0 + (u-1)\Delta^3 y_0 + \frac{(6u^2 - 18u + 11)}{12}\Delta^4 y_0 + \ldots \right]$$

$$= \frac{1}{1}\left[3 + (0.2-1)(-6) + \frac{6(0.2)^2 - 18(0.2) + 11}{12}(10) \right]$$

$$= \left[3 + 4.8000 + \frac{0.2400 - 3.6000 + 11}{12}(10) \right]$$

$$= [3 + 4.8000 + 6.366]$$

$$= 14.17$$

3) Find *y′(x)* at a point *x*=0.5 from the following data.

x	**0**	**1**	**2**	**3**	**4**
y (x)	**1**	**1**	**15**	**40**	**85**

Solution :

We use Newton's Forward Formula since x=0.5 is at the beginning

$$u = \frac{x - x_0}{h} = \frac{0.5 - 0}{1} = 0.5$$

Here $x = 0.5$, $x_0 = 0$, $h = 1$

Difference Table :

x	y	Δy	$\Delta^2 y$	$\Delta^3 y$	$\Delta^4 y$
0	1				
		0			
1	1		14		
		14		–3	
2	15		11		12
		25		9	
3	40		20		
		45			
4	85				

From the table $\Delta y_0 = 0,\ \Delta^2 y_0 = 14,\ \Delta^3 y_0 = -3\ \Delta^4 y_0 = 12$

Newton's Forward Formula is

$$\frac{dy}{dx} = \frac{1}{h}\left[\begin{array}{l}\Delta y_0 + \dfrac{2u-1}{2}\Delta^2 y_0 + \dfrac{3u^2-6u+2}{6}\Delta^3 y_0 \\ \qquad + \dfrac{(4u^3-18u^2+22u-6)}{24}\Delta^4 y_0 + \ldots\end{array}\right]$$

$$= \frac{1}{1}\left[\begin{array}{l}0 + \dfrac{2(0.5)-1}{2}(14) + \dfrac{3(0.5)^2-6(0.5)+2}{6}(-3) \\ \qquad + \dfrac{4(0.5)^3-18(0.5)^2+22(0.5)^{-6}}{24}(12)\end{array}\right]$$

$$= \left[\begin{array}{l}\dfrac{1.00-1}{2}(14) + \dfrac{(3(0.25)-3.00+2)}{6}(-3) + \\ \qquad + \dfrac{4(0.125)-18(0.25)+22(0.5)-6}{24}(12)\end{array}\right]$$

$$= \left[0 + \frac{0.75-3.00+2}{6}(-3) + \frac{(0.500-4.500+11-6)}{24}(12)\right]$$

$$= [0.1250 + 0.5000]$$

$$= 0.625$$

PROBLEMS BASED ON NEWTON'S BACKWARD DIFFERENCE AT $x = x_0$

At the point $x = x_0$ we use the following formulas

$$\left(\frac{dy}{dx}\right)_{x=x_n} = \left(\frac{dy}{dx}\right)_{v=0} = \frac{1}{h}\left[\nabla y_n + \frac{1}{2}\nabla^2 y_n + \frac{1}{3}\nabla^3 y_n + \ldots\right]$$

$$\left(\frac{d^2y}{dx^2}\right)_{x=x_n} = \frac{1}{h^2}\left[\nabla^2 y_n + \nabla^3 y_n + \frac{11}{12}\nabla^4 y_n + \ldots\right]$$

$$\left(\frac{d^3y}{dx^3}\right)_{x=x_n} = \frac{1}{h^3}\left[\nabla^3 y_n + \frac{3}{2}\nabla^4 y_n + \ldots\right]$$

1) Find the first two derivatives of y at x=54 from the following data

x	50	51	52	53	54
y	3.6840	3.7084	3.7325	3.7563	3.7798

Solution :

We use Newton's Backward Formula since x= 54 is at the end

Here, $h = 1$

Difference Table :

x	y	∇y	$\nabla^2 y$	$\nabla^3 y$	$\nabla^4 y$
50	3.6840				
		0.0244			
51	3.7084		–0.0003		
		0.0241		0	
52	3.7325		–0.0003		0
		0.0238		0	
53	3.7563		–0.0003		
		0.0235			
54	3.7798				

From the table $\nabla y_n = 0.0235,\ \nabla^2 y_n = -0.003,\ \nabla^3 y_n = 0,\ \nabla^4 y_n = 0$

Newton's Backward Formula is

$$\frac{dy}{dx} = \frac{1}{h}\left[\nabla y_n + \frac{1}{2}\nabla^2 y_n + \frac{1}{3}\nabla^3 y_n + \ldots\right]$$

$$= \frac{1}{1}\left[0.0235 + \left(\frac{-0.0003}{2}\right) + 0 + 0\right]$$

$$= [0.0235 - 0.00015]$$

$$= 0.02335$$

$$\frac{d^2y}{dx^2} = \frac{1}{h^2}\left[\nabla^2 y_n + \nabla^3 y_n + \ldots\right]$$

$$= \frac{1}{1}[-0.0003]$$

$$= -0.0003$$

2) Find the first two derivatives of the function tabulated below at the point $x = 2.2$

x	1.0	1.2	1.4	1.6	1.8	2.0	2.2
y	2.7183	3.3201	4.0552	4.9530	6.0496	7.3891	9.0250

Solution :

We use Newton's Backward difference Formula since $x = 2.2$ is at the end

Here, $h = 0.2$

Difference Table :

x	y	∇y	$\nabla^2 y$	$\nabla^3 y$	$\nabla^4 y$	$\nabla^5 y$	$\nabla^6 y$
1.0	2.7183						
		0.6010					
1.2	3.3201		0.3141				
		0.7351		0.0288			
1.4	4.0552		0.1629		0.0071		
		0.8978		0.0359		0.0011	
1.6	4.9530		0.1988		0.0082		0.0001
		1.0965		0.0441		0.0012	
1.8	6.0496		0.2429		0.0094		
		1.3395		0.0535			
2.0	7.3891		0.2964				
		1.6359					
2.2	9.0250						

From the table, $\nabla y_n = 1.6359$, $\nabla^2 y_n = 0.2964$, $\nabla^3 y_n = 0.0535$, $\nabla^4 y_n = 0.0094$, $\nabla^5 y_n = 0.0012$, $\nabla^6 y_n = 0.001$,

Newton's Backward Formula is

$$\frac{dy}{dx} = \frac{1}{h}\left[\nabla y_n + \frac{\nabla^2 y_n}{2} + \frac{\nabla^3 y_n}{3} + \frac{\nabla^4 y_n}{4} + \frac{\nabla^5 y_n}{5} + \frac{\nabla^6 y_n}{6}\right]$$

$$= \frac{1}{0.2}\left[1.6359 + \frac{0.2964}{2} + \frac{0.0535}{3} + \frac{0.0094}{4} + \frac{0.0012}{5} + \frac{0.001}{6}\right]$$

$$=\frac{1}{0.2}[1.6359+0.1482+0.0178+0.00235+0.00024+0.000166]$$

$$=\frac{1}{0.2}[1.804656]$$

$$=9.0232$$

$$\frac{d^2y}{dx^2}=\frac{1}{h^2}\left[\nabla^2 y_n+\nabla^3 y_n+\frac{11}{12}\nabla^4 y_n+\frac{5}{6}\nabla^5 y_n\right]$$

$$=\frac{1}{(0.2)^2}\left[0.2964+0.535+\frac{11}{12}(0.0094)+\frac{5}{6}(0.0012)\right]$$

$$=\frac{1}{(0.04)}[0.2964+0.0535+0.008616+0.001]$$

$$=\frac{1}{0.04}[0.35951]$$

$$=8.9879$$

PROBLEMS BASED ON NEWTON'S BACKWARD DIFFERENCE AT $x = x_{n+}vh$

At the point $x=x_n+vh$ we use the following formulas

$$\frac{dy}{dx}=\frac{1}{h}\left[\nabla y_n+\frac{2v+1}{2}\nabla^2 y_n+\frac{3v^2+6v+2}{6}\nabla^3 y_n+\frac{(4v^3+18v^2+22v+6)}{24}\nabla^4 y_n+\ldots\right]$$

$$\frac{d^2y}{dx^2}=\frac{1}{h^2}\left[\nabla^2 y_n+(v+1)\nabla^3 y_n+\frac{(6v^2+18v+11)}{12}\nabla^4 y_n+\ldots\right]$$

$$\frac{d^3y}{dx^3}=\frac{1}{h^3}\left[\nabla^3 y_n+\frac{12v+18}{12}\nabla^4 y_n+\ldots\right]$$

1) Find the $f'(x)$ and $f''(x)$ at I= 2.9 from the following data

x	1	1.5	2	2.5	3
y	27	106.75	324	783.75	1620.5

Solution :

We use Newton's Backward Formula since x=2.9 is at the end

Here, h=0.5

Difference Table :

x	y	∇y	$\nabla^2 y$	$\nabla^3 y$	$\nabla^4 y$
1	27				
		79.75			
1.5	106.75		137.5		
		217.25		105	
2	324		242.5		30
		459.75		135	
2.5	783.25		377.5		
		837.25			
3	1620.5				

From the table , $\nabla y_n = 837.25,\ \nabla^2 y_n = 377.5,\ \nabla^3 y_n = 135,\ \nabla^4 y_n = 30,$

$$v = \frac{x - x_n}{h} \Rightarrow \frac{2.9 - 3}{0.5} = -0.2$$

where $x = 2.9$, $x_n = 3$, $h = 0.5$

$$\frac{dy}{dx} = \frac{1}{h}\left[\nabla y_n + \frac{2v+1}{2}\nabla^2 y_n + \frac{3v^2+6v+2}{6}\nabla^3 y_n + \frac{(4v^3+18v^2+22v+6)}{24}\nabla^4 y_n + \ldots\right]$$

$$= \frac{1}{0.5}\left[837.5 + \frac{2(-0.2)+1}{2}(377.5) + \frac{3(-0.2)^2+6(-0.2)+2}{6}(135) + \frac{4(-0.2)^3+18(-0.2)^2+22(-0.2)+6}{24}(30)\right]$$

$$= \frac{1}{0.5}\left[837.5 + \frac{(-0.40+1)}{2}(377.5) + \frac{3(0.0400)+6(-0.2)+2}{6}(135) + \frac{4(-0.0080)+18(0.0400)+22(-0.2)+6}{24}(30)\right]$$

$$= \frac{1}{0.5}\left[837.5 + 113.25 + \frac{0.1200 - 1.200 + 2}{6}(135) + \frac{-0.03200 + 0.7200 - 4.400 + 6}{24}(30)\right]$$

$$= \frac{1}{0.5}[837.5 + 113.25 + 20.70 + 2.860]$$

$$= 1948.6$$

$$\frac{d^2y}{dx^2} = \frac{1}{h^2}\left[\nabla^2 y_n + (v+1)\nabla^3 y_n + \frac{(6v^2+18v+11)}{12}\nabla^4 y_n + \ldots\right]$$

$$= \frac{1}{(0.5)^2}\left[377.5 + (-0.2+1)135 + \frac{6(-0.2)^2+18(-0.2)+11}{12}(30)\right]$$

$$= \frac{1}{0.25}\left[377.5 + (0.80)135 + \frac{6(0.0400)+18(-0.2)+11}{12}30\right]$$

$$= \frac{1}{0.25}\left[377.5 + 108.00 + \frac{0.2400-3.60+11}{12}30\right]$$

$$= \frac{1}{0.25}[377.5+108.00+19.100]$$

$$= \frac{1}{0.25}[504.6]$$

$$= 2018.4$$

2) Find $\frac{dy}{dx}$ and $\frac{d^2y}{dx^2}$ at x= 0.9 from the following data

x	0	0.2	0.4	0.6	0.8	1.0
$f(x)$	1.00	1.16	3.56	13.96	41.96	101.00

Solution :

We use Newton's Backward Formula since $x = 0.9$ is at the end

Here, $h = 0.2$

Difference Table :

x	y	∇y	$\nabla^2 y$	$\nabla^3 y$	$\nabla^4 y$	$\nabla^5 y$
0	1.00					
		0.116				
0.2	1.16		2.324			
		2.44		5.636		
0.4	3.56		7.96		4.004	
		10.4		9.64		−0.204
0.6	13.96		17.6		3.8	
		28		13.44		
0.8	41.96		31.04			
		59.4				
1.0	101.00					

From the table , $\nabla y_n = 59.4,\ \nabla^2 y_n = 31.04,\ \nabla^3 y_n = 13.44,\ \nabla^4 y_n = 3.8,\ \nabla^5 y_n = -0.204$.

$$v = \frac{x - x_n}{h} \Rightarrow \frac{0.9 - 1.0}{0.2} = -0.5$$

where x= 0.9, x_n = 1.0 , h=0.2

Newton's Backward Formula is

$$\frac{dy}{dx} = \frac{1}{h}\left[\begin{array}{l} \nabla y_n + \frac{2v+1}{2}\nabla^2 y_n + \frac{3v^2+6v+2}{6}\nabla^3 y_n \\ \quad + \frac{(4v^3+18v^2+22v+6)}{24}\nabla^4 y_n + \ldots \end{array}\right]$$

$$= \frac{1}{(0.2)}\left[\begin{array}{l} 59.4 + \frac{2(-0.5)+1}{2}(31.04) + \frac{3(-0.5)^2+6(-0.5)+2}{6}(13.44) \\ \quad + \frac{4(-0.5)^3+8(-0.5)^2+22(-0.5)+6}{24}(3.8) \end{array}\right]$$

$$= \frac{1}{0.2}\left[59.4 + 0 - 0.0416(13.44) + \frac{0.5+2-11+6}{24}(3.8)\right]$$

$$= \frac{1}{0.2}[59.4 - 0.5591 - 0.3958]$$

$$= \frac{1}{0.2}[58.4451]$$

$$= 292.225$$

$$\frac{d^2y}{dx^2} = \frac{1}{h^2}\left[\nabla^2 y_n + (v+1)\nabla^3 y_n + \frac{(6v^2+18v+11)}{12}\nabla^4 y_n + \ldots\right]$$

$$= \frac{1}{(0.2)^2}\left[(31.04) + (-0.5+1)(13.44) + \frac{6(-0.5)^2+18(-0.5)+11}{12}(3.8)\right]$$

$$= \frac{1}{0.04}\left[31.04 + 0.5(13.44) + \frac{6(0.25)+18(-0.5)+11}{12}(3.8)\right]$$

$$= \frac{1}{0.04}[31.04 + 6.72 + 1.10833]$$

$$= \frac{1}{0.04}[38.8683]$$

$$= 971.708$$

PROBLEMS BASED ON BOTH NEWTON'S FORWARD & BACKWARD DIFFERENCE AT $x = x_0$ AND $x = x_0 + uh$.

1) Find the first and second derivatives of the function tabulated below at the point at x=1.5 and x=4

x	1.5	2.0	2.5	3.0	3.5	4.0
y	3.375	7.000	13.625	24.000	38.875	59.00

Solution:

We use Newton's Forward & Backward difference Formula since x= 1.5 at the beginning x=4 at the end.

Difference Table :

x	y	Δy	$\Delta^2 y$	$\Delta^3 y$	$\Delta^4 y$
1.5	3.375				
		3.625			
2.0	7.000		3.000		
		6.625		0.75	
2.5	13.625		3.750		0
		10.375		0.75	
3.0	24.000		4.500		0
		14.875		0.75	
3.5	38.875		5.250		
		20.125			
4.0	59.000				

Newton's Forward difference formula

$$\frac{dy}{dx} = \frac{1}{h}\left[\Delta y_0 - \frac{1}{2}\Delta^2 y_0 + \frac{1}{3}\Delta^3 y_0 - \frac{1}{4}\Delta^4 y_0 + ..\right]$$

Here h= 0.5

From the table, $\Delta y_0 = 3.625,\ \Delta^2 y_0 = 3.000,\ \Delta^3 y_0 = 0.75,\ \Delta^4 y_0 = 0$

$$\frac{dy}{dx} = \frac{1}{0.5}\left[3.625 - \frac{3.000}{2} + \frac{0.75}{3} - 0\right]$$

$$= \frac{1}{0.5}[3.625 - 1.5000 + 0.250]$$

$$= \frac{1}{0.5}[2.3750]$$

$$= 4.75$$

$$\frac{d^2y}{dx^2} = \frac{1}{h^2}\left[\Delta^2 y_0 - \Delta^3 y_0 + \frac{11}{12}\Delta^4 y_0 - ....\right]$$

$$= \frac{1}{(0.5)^2}[3.000 - 0.75]$$

$$= \frac{1}{0.25}[2.2500]$$

$$= 9.000$$

Newton's Backward difference formula

$$\frac{dy}{dx} = \frac{1}{h}\left[\nabla y_n + \frac{\nabla^2 y_n}{2} + \frac{\nabla^3 y_n}{3} + ...\right]$$

$h = 0.5$

From the table $\nabla y_n = 20.125,\ \nabla^2 y_n = 5.250,\ \nabla^3 y_n = 0.75$

$$\frac{dy}{dx} = \frac{1}{0.5}\left[20.125 + \frac{5.250}{2} + \frac{0.75}{3}\right]$$

$$= \frac{1}{0.5}[23.500]$$

$$= 47$$

$$\frac{d^2y}{dx^2} = \frac{1}{h^2}\left[\nabla^2 y_n + \nabla^3 y_n + \frac{11}{12}\nabla^4 y_n + ...\right]$$

$$= \frac{1}{0.25}[5.250 + 0.75]$$

$$= 24$$

2) Compute $y'(0)$ and $y''(4)$ from the data

x	**0**	**1**	**2**	**3**	**4**
y	**1**	**2.718**	**7.381**	**20.086**	**54.598**

Solution :

We use Newton's Forward & Backward difference Formula since $x= 0$ at the beginning $x=4$ at the end.

Difference Table :

x	y	Δy	$\Delta^2 y$	$\Delta^3 y$	$\Delta^4 y$
0	1				
		1.718			
1	2.718		2.945		
		4.663		5.097	
2	7.381		8.042		8.668
		12.705		13.765	
3	20.086		21.807		
		34.512			
4	54.598				

Newton's Forward difference formula

$$\frac{dy}{dx} = \frac{1}{h}\left[\Delta y_0 - \frac{1}{2}\Delta^2 y_0 + \frac{1}{3}\Delta^3 y_0 - \frac{1}{4}\Delta^4 y_0 + ..\right]$$

Here $h= 1$

From the table, $\Delta y_0 = 1.718,\ \Delta^2 y_0 = 2.945,\ \Delta^3 y_0 = 5.097,\ \Delta^4 y_0 = 8.668$

$$\frac{dy}{dx} = \frac{1}{1}\left[1.178 - \frac{1}{2}(2.945) + \frac{1}{3}(5.097) - \frac{1}{4}(8.668)\right]$$

$$= [1.718 - 1.4725 + 1.699 - 2.167]$$
$$= -0.2225$$

Newton's Backward difference formula

$$\frac{dy}{dx} = \frac{1}{h}\left[\nabla y_n + \frac{1}{2}\nabla^2 y_n + \frac{1}{3}\nabla^3 y_n + ...\right]$$

Here $h= 1$

From the table, $\nabla y_n = 34.512\ \nabla^2 y_n = 21.807,\ \nabla^3 y_n = 13.765,\ \nabla^4 y_n = 8.668$

$$\frac{dy}{dx} = \frac{1}{1}\left[34.512 + \frac{1}{2}(21.807) + \frac{1}{3}(13.765) + \frac{1}{4}(8.668)\right]$$

$$= 34.512 + 10.9035 + 4.588 + 2.167$$

$=52.1705$

$$\frac{d^2y}{dx^2}=\frac{1}{h^2}\left[\nabla^2 y_n+\nabla^3 y_n+\frac{11}{12}\nabla^4 y_n+\frac{5}{6}\nabla^5 y_n+....\right]$$

$$=\frac{1}{1}\left[21.807+13.765+\frac{11}{12}(8.668)\right]$$

$$=21.807+13.765+7.9457$$

$$=43.5177$$

3) The population of a certain town is given below find the rate of growth of the population in 1931, 1941, 1961 and 1971

Year (x)	**1931**	**1941**	**1951**	**1961**	**1971**
Population in thousand (y)	**40.62**	**60.80**	**79.95**	**103.56**	**132.65**

Solution :

We use Newton's Forward & Backward difference Formula since x= 1931, x=1941 at the beginning x=1961, x=1971 at the end.

Difference Table :

x	y	Δy	$\Delta^2 y$	$\Delta^3 y$	$\Delta^4 y$
1931	40.62				
		20.18			
1941	60.80		–1.03		
		19.15		5.49	
1951	79.95		4.46		–4.47
		23.61		1.02	
1961	103.56		5.48		
		29.09			
1971	132.65				

From the table $\Delta y_0=20.18,\ \Delta^2 y_0=-1.03,\ \Delta^3 y_0=5.49,\ \Delta^4 y_0=-4.47$

$$\nabla y_n=29.09,\ \nabla^2 y_n=5.48,\ \nabla^3 y_n=1.02\ \nabla^4 y_n=-4.47$$

Here h=1

(i) Newton's Forward difference formula at $x=x_0$

$$\frac{dy}{dx}=\frac{1}{h}\left[\Delta y_0-\frac{1}{2}\Delta^2 y_0+\frac{1}{3}\Delta^3 y_0-\frac{1}{4}\Delta^4 y_0+..\right]$$

$$=\frac{1}{10}\left[20.18+\frac{1.03}{2}+\frac{5.49}{3}+\frac{4.47}{4}\right]$$

$$=\frac{1}{10}[20.18+0.515+1.83+1.1175]$$

$$=2.36425$$

(ii) Newton's backward difference formula at $x=x_n$

$$\frac{dy}{dx}=\frac{1}{h}\left[\nabla y_n+\frac{1}{2}\nabla^2 y_n+\frac{1}{3}\nabla^3 y_n+\frac{1}{4}\nabla^4 y_n\ldots\right]$$

$$=\frac{1}{10}\left[29.09+\frac{1}{2}(5.48)+\frac{1.02}{3}-\frac{4.47}{4}\right]$$

$$=\frac{1}{10}[29.09+2.740+0.3400-1.117]$$

$$=\frac{1}{10}[31.0525]$$

$$=3.10525$$

(iii) Newton's Forward difference formula at $x=x_0+uh$

$x=1941$, $\qquad u=\frac{x-x_0}{h}=\frac{1941-1931}{10}=1$

$u=1$, $x=1941$, $x_0=1931$, $h=10$

$$\frac{dy}{dx}=\frac{1}{h}\left[\Delta y_0+\frac{2u-1}{2}\Delta^2 y_0+\frac{3u^2-6u+2}{6}\Delta^3 y_0+\frac{(4u^3-18u^2+22u-6)}{24}\Delta^4 y_0+\ldots\right]$$

$$=\frac{1}{10}\left[20.18+\frac{1}{2}(-1.03)-\frac{1}{6}(5.49)+\frac{1}{12}(-4.47)\right]$$

$$=\frac{1}{10}[20.18-0.515-0.915-0.3725]$$

$$=1.83775$$

(iv) Newton's backward difference formula at $x=x_0+uh$

$$v=\frac{x-x_n}{h}=\frac{1961-1971}{10}=-1$$

Here h=10, x=1961, x_n=1971, v=–1

$$\frac{dy}{dx}=\frac{1}{h}\left[\nabla y_n+\frac{2v+1}{2}\nabla^2 y_n+\frac{3v^2+6v+2}{6}\nabla^3 y_n+...\right]$$

$$=\frac{1}{10}\left[29.09-\frac{1}{2}(5.48)-\frac{1}{6}(1.02)-\frac{4.47}{12}\right]$$

$$=\frac{1}{10}[29.09-2.74-0.17+0.3725]$$

$$=2.65525$$

4) Find the first two derivatives of x at x=50 and x=56 for the given table.

x:	50	51	52	53	54	55	56
y:	3.6840	3.7084	3.7325	3.7563	3.7798	3.8030	3.8259

Solution:

Now we use Newton's forward & Backward difference formula.

Difference table

x	y	Δy	$\Delta^2 y$	$\Delta^3 y$
50	3.6840			
		0.0244		
51	3.7084		–0.0003	
		0.0241		0
52	3.7325		–0.0003	
		0.0238		0
53	3.7563		–0.0003	
		0.0235		0
54	3.7798		–0.0003	
		0.0232		0
55	3.8030		–0.0003	
		0.0229		
56	3.8259			

By Newton's forward difference formula

$$\frac{dy}{dx}=\frac{1}{h}\left[\Delta y_0-\frac{1}{2}\Delta^2 y_0+\frac{1}{3}\Delta^3 y_0...\right]$$

$$=\frac{1}{1}\left[0.0244-\frac{1}{2}(-0.0003)+\frac{1}{3}(0)\right]$$

$$=0.0246$$

$$\frac{d^2y}{dx^2} = \frac{1}{h^2}\left[\Delta^2 y_0 - \Delta^3 y_0 + \ldots\right]$$

$$= \frac{1}{1^2}[-0.0003]$$

$$= -0.0003$$

Newton's Backward difference formula

$$\frac{dy}{dx} = \frac{1}{h}\left[\nabla y_n + \frac{1}{2}\nabla^2 y_n + \frac{1}{3}\nabla^3 y_n + \ldots\right]$$

$$= \frac{1}{1}\left[0.0229 + \frac{1}{2}(-0.0003) + 0\right]$$

$$= 0.0228$$

$$\frac{d^2y}{dx^2} = \frac{1}{h^2}\left[\nabla^2 y_n + \nabla^3 y_n + \ldots\right]$$

$$= \frac{1}{1}[-0.0003]$$

$$= -0.0003$$

SHORT QUESTIONS AND ANSWERS

1) State Newton's formula to find $f'(x)$ and $f''(x)$ using the forward difference.

Solution:

Let $y = f(x)$ be a function taking the values $y_0, y_1, \ldots y_n$ corresponding to $x_0, x_1 \ldots x_n$ of the independent variable x. let the values of x be at equidistant intervals of size h.

Then $$f'(x) = \frac{dy}{dx} = \frac{1}{h}\left[\Delta y_0 + \frac{2u-1}{1\cdot 2}\Delta^2 y_0 + \frac{3u^2-6u+2}{1\cdot 2\cdot 3}\Delta^3 y_0 + \ldots\right]$$

where $u = \dfrac{x - x_0}{h}$ $\rightarrow (1)$

(1) Gives the values of $\frac{dy}{dx}$ at any x, which is a non-tabular value.

In particular at $x=x_0$, $u=0$. Then putting $u=0$ in (1) we have

$$\left(\frac{dy}{dx}\right)_{x=x_0} = f'(x_0) = \frac{1}{h}\left[\Delta y_0 - \frac{\Delta^2 y_0}{2} + \frac{\Delta^3 y_0}{3} + \ldots\right]$$

$$\left(\frac{d^2y}{dx^2}\right)_{x=x_0} = \frac{1}{h^2}\left[\Delta^2 y_0 - \Delta^3 y_0 + \frac{11}{12}\Delta^4 y_0 - \ldots\right]$$

2) Using Newton's Backward difference formula, write the formula for the first and second order derivatives at the end values $x=x_n$ upto the fourth order difference term.

Solution:

$$\left(\frac{dy}{dx}\right)_{x=x_n} = \frac{1}{h}\left[\nabla y_n + \frac{1}{2}\nabla^2 y_n + \frac{1}{3}\nabla^3 y_n + ..\right]$$

$$\left(\frac{d^2y}{dx^2}\right)_{x=x_n} = \frac{1}{h^2}\left[\nabla^2 y_n + \nabla^3 y_n + \frac{11}{12}\nabla^4 y_n + \ldots\right]$$

$$\left(\frac{d^3y}{dx^3}\right)_{x=x_n} = \frac{1}{h^3}\left[\nabla^3 y_n + \frac{3}{2}\nabla^4 y_n + \ldots\right]$$

EXERCISE

[DERIVATIVE FROM DIFFERENCE]

1) Obtain the second derivative of y at $x=0.96$ from the data

x	0.96	0.98	1.00	1.02	1.04
y	0.7825	0.7739	0.7651	0.7563	0.7473

[Ans: –1.91666]

2) Find the first and second derivatives of the function tabulates below at the point $x=1.1$

x	1	1.2	1.4	1.6	1.8	2.0
$f(x)$	0	0.1280	0.5440	1.2960	2.4320	4.00

3) From the table given below, find $f'(30)$, $f'(31)$ and $f'(35)$

x	30	31	32	33	34	35	36
$f(x)$	85.90	86.85	87.73	88.64	89.52	90.37	91.1

[Ans: $f'(30)$=1.403, $f'(31)$=0.806, $f'(35)$=0.894]

4) Calculate $\frac{dy}{dx}$ and $\frac{d^2y}{dx^2}$ at x=1.35 from the following data:

x	1.1	1.2	1.3	1.4	1.5	1.6
y	−1.62628	0.15584	2.45256	5.39168	9.12500	13.83072

4.5 NUMERICAL INTERGRATION BY TRAPEZOIDAL AND SIMPSON'S 1/3rd RULE.

(a) Trapezoidal rule:

Consider,

x	x_1	x_2	...	x_n
$y=f(x)$	y_1	y_2	...	y_n

By Trapezoidal rule,

$$\int_a^b f(x)dx = \frac{h}{2}\begin{bmatrix}(\text{sum of the first and last ordinates})\\ +2(\text{sum of the remaining ordinates})\end{bmatrix}$$

$$\int_a^b f(x)dx = \frac{h}{2}[(y_1+y_n)+2(y_2+y_3+..+y_{n-1})]$$

(b) Simpson's 1/3rd Rule:

By Simpson's one third rule,

$$\int_a^b f(x)dx = \frac{h}{3}\begin{bmatrix}(\text{sum of the first and last ordinates})\\ +2(\text{sum of the odd ordinates})\\ +4(\text{sum of the even ordinates})\end{bmatrix}$$

$$\int_a^b f(x)dx = \frac{h}{3}[(y_1+y_n)+4(y_2+y_4+...)+2(y_3+y_5+...)]$$

PROBLEMS BASED ON TRAPEZOIDAL RULE

1) Using Trapezoidal rule, evaluate $\int_{-1}^{1}\frac{1}{1+x^2}dx$ taking 8 equal intervals.

Solution:

Given $f(x)=\int_{-1}^{1}\frac{1}{1+x^2}$

$$y = \frac{1}{1+x^2}, \quad a = -1, \quad b = 1$$

$$h = \frac{b-a}{Given\ Intervals} = \frac{2}{8} = 0.25$$

We form a table

x	x_1 –1	x_2 –0.75	x_3 –0.5	x_4 –0.25	x_5 0	x_6 0.25	x_7 0.5	x_8 0.75	x_9 1
y	y_1 0.5	y_2 0.64	y_3 0.8	y_4 0.9412	y_5 1	y_6 0.9412	y_7 0.8	y_8 0.64	y_9 0.5

$$\int_a^b f(x)dx = \frac{h}{2}[(y_1 + y_9) + 2(y_2 + y_3 + y_4 + y_5 + y_6 + y_7 + y_8)]$$

$$= \frac{0.25}{2}[(0.5+0.5) + 2(0.64+0.8+0.9412+1+0.9412+0.8+0.64)]$$

$$= \frac{0.25}{2}[1+2(5.7624)]$$

$$= \frac{0.25}{2}[12.5248]$$

$$= 1.5656$$

2) Evaluate $\int_0^1 \frac{1}{1+x^2}dx$ with $h = \frac{1}{6}$ by trapezoidal rule.

Solution:

Given $f(x) = \frac{1}{1+x^2}$ i.e, $y = \frac{1}{1+x^2}$, a=0, b=1

$$h = \frac{1}{6}$$

x	0	$\frac{1}{6}$	$\frac{2}{6}$	$\frac{3}{6}$	$\frac{4}{6}$	$\frac{5}{6}$	1
$y=f(x)$	1	$\frac{36}{37}$	$\frac{9}{10}$	$\frac{4}{5}$	$\frac{9}{13}$	$\frac{36}{61}$	$\frac{1}{2}$

By Trapezoidal rule,

$$\int_a^b f(x)dx = \frac{h}{2}[(y_1 + y_7) + 2(y_2 + y_3 + y_4 + y_5 + y_6)]$$

$$= \frac{\frac{1}{6}}{2}\left[\left(1+\frac{1}{2}\right)+2\left(\frac{36}{37}+\frac{9}{10}+\frac{4}{5}+\frac{9}{13}+\frac{36}{61}\right)\right]$$

$$= \frac{1}{12}\left[\frac{3}{2}+7.9108\right]$$

$$= 0.7842$$

3) Evaluate $\int_1^2 \frac{1}{1+x^2}dx$ using Trapezoidal rule with two sub intervals

Solution:

Given $f(x) = \frac{1}{1+x^2} \Rightarrow y = \frac{1}{1+x^2}$

$a=1$, $b=2$

$$h = \frac{b-a}{Given\ Intervals} = \frac{1}{2} = 0.5$$

We form a table

x	1	1.5	2
y	0.5	0.3077	0.2

By Trapezoidal rule we get,

$$\int_1^2 \frac{1}{1+x^2}dx = \frac{h}{2}[(y_1 + y_3) + 2(y_2)]$$

$$= \frac{0.5}{2}[0.5 + 0.2 + 2(0.3077)]$$

$$= \frac{0.5}{2}[0.7 + 0.6154]$$

$$= \frac{0.5}{2}[1.3154]$$

$$= 0.3289$$

PROBLEMS BASED ON SIMPSON'S RULE

1) Using Simpson's one third rule evaluate $\int_0^1 xe^x dx$ taking 4 intervals. Compare your results with actual value

Solution:

Given $f(x) = xe^x \Rightarrow y = xe^x$

$$h = \frac{b-a}{4} = \frac{1}{4} = 0.25$$

We form a table,

x	0	0.25	0.5	0.75	1
y	0	0.321	0.824	1.588	2.718

By Simpson's formula,

$$\int_a^b f(x)dx = \frac{h}{3}[(y_1 + y_5) + 2(y_3) + 4(y_2 + y_4)]$$

$$= \frac{0.25}{3}[(0 + 2.718) + 2(0.824) + 4(0.321 + 1.588)]$$

$$= \frac{0.25}{3}[2.718 + 1.648 + 7.636]$$

$$= \frac{0.25}{3}[12.002]$$

$$= \frac{3.0005}{2} = 1 \qquad \rightarrow (1)$$

Actual value

$$\int_0^1 xe^x dx = \int udv = uv - \int vdu$$

$$u = x \quad dv = e^x du$$

$$du = dx \quad \int dv = \int e^x dx$$

$$v = e^x$$

$$= \left[xe^x\right]_0^1 - \int_0^1 e^x dx$$

$$= \left[e^1 - 0\right] - \left(e^x\right)_0^1$$

$$= e - [e - 1] = 1 \qquad \rightarrow (2)$$

Here (1) = (2)

2) Find $\int_0^1 \frac{dx}{1+x^2}$ by using Simpson's 1/3 rule. Hence obtain the approximate value of π in each case.

Solution:

They didn't give the intervals. So we divide the range (0,1) into six equal parts.

Given, $f(x)=\frac{1}{1+x^2} \Rightarrow y=\frac{1}{1+x^2}$, a=0, b=1

$$h=\frac{b-a}{6}=\frac{1-0}{6}=\frac{1}{6}$$

We form the table,

x	0	$\frac{1}{6}$	$\frac{2}{6}$	$\frac{3}{6}$	$\frac{4}{6}$	$\frac{5}{6}$	1
y	1	0.97	0.9	0.8	0.69	0.59	0.5

By Simpson's rule,

$$\int_0^1 \frac{dx}{1+x^2}=\frac{h}{3}[(y_1+y_7)+2(y_3+y_5)+4(y_0+y_4+y_6)]$$

$$=\frac{\frac{1}{6}}{3}[(1+0.5)+2(0.9+0.69)+4(0.97+0.8+0.59)]$$

$$=\frac{1}{18}[1.5+4(2.3632)+2(1.5923)]$$

$$=0.7854$$

Approximate value of π

$$\int_0^1 \frac{dx}{1+x^2}=\left(\tan^{-1}x\right)_0^1$$

$$=\tan^{-1}(1)-\tan^{-1}(0)$$

$$=\frac{\pi}{4}$$

$$\frac{\pi}{4}=0.7854$$

$$\pi=3.1416$$

3) Find the value of $\log_e 2$ form $\int_0^1 \frac{x^2}{1+x^3}dx$ using Simpson's 1/3 rule, by dividing the range into 6 equal points.

Solution:

Given,

$$f(x)=\frac{x^2}{1+x^3} \Rightarrow y=\frac{x^2}{1+x^3} \qquad a=0,\ b=1$$

$$h=\frac{1-0}{6}=\frac{1}{6}$$

We form the table,

x	0	$\frac{1}{6}$	$\frac{2}{6}$	$\frac{3}{6}$	$\frac{4}{6}$	$\frac{5}{6}$	1
y	1	0.0276	0.1071	0.2222	0.3428	0.4399	0.5

By Simpson's 1/3 rule,

$$\int_0^1 \frac{x^3}{1+x^3} = \frac{\frac{1}{6}}{3}[(y_1+y_7)+2(y_3+y_5)+4(y_2+y_4+y_6)]$$

$$=\frac{\frac{1}{6}}{3}[(0.+0.5)+2(0.1671+0.3428)+4(0.0276+0.2222+0.4399)]$$

$$=\frac{1}{18}[0.5+0.8998+2.7588]$$

$$=\frac{1}{18}[4.1586]$$

$$=0.2310$$

By actual integration,

$$\int_0^1 \frac{x^2}{1+x^3}dx=\frac{1}{3}\log_e 2$$

$$\frac{1}{3}\log_{e^2}=0.2310$$

$$\log_{e^2}=0.6930$$

4) The velocity V of a particle at a distance S from a point on its path is given by the table below:

S in metre	0	10	20	30	40	50	60
V (m/sec)	47	58	64	65	61	52	38

Estimate the time taken to travel 60 meters by using Simpson's one-third rule.

Solution:

We know that $v = \frac{ds}{dt}$

$$t = \int_0^{60} \frac{1}{v} ds$$

$$\therefore \ f(x) = y = \frac{1}{v}, \quad h{=}3$$

We form the table,

v	47	58	64	65	61	52	38
y	0.02127	0.101724	0.015625	0.01538	0.01639	0.01923	0.026316

$$t = \int_0^{60} \frac{1}{v} ds = \frac{h}{3}[(y_1 + y_7) + 2(y_3 + y_5) + 4(y_2 + y_4 + y_6)]$$

$$= \frac{10}{3}\begin{bmatrix}(0.02127 + 0.026316) + 2(0.015625 + 0.01639) \\ +4(0.01724 + 0.01538 + 0.01923)\end{bmatrix}$$

$$= \frac{10}{3}[(0.0476) + 0.0640 + 0.2074]$$

$$= \frac{10}{3}[0.3190]$$

$$= 1.0633\,\text{sec}$$

PROBLEMS BASED ON BOTH SIMPSON'S & TRAPEZOIDEL RULES

1) By dividing the range into ten equal ports evaluate $\int_0^{\pi} \sin x dx$ by trapezoidal and Simpson's rule verify your answer with integration

Solution:

Given, $f(x) = \sin x \Rightarrow y = \sin x$

$$h = \frac{b-a}{10} = \frac{\pi}{10}$$

We form a table,

x	0	$\frac{\pi}{10}$	$\frac{2\pi}{10}$	$\frac{3\pi}{10}$	$\frac{4\pi}{10}$	$\frac{5\pi}{10}$	$\frac{6\pi}{10}$	$\frac{7\pi}{10}$	$\frac{8\pi}{10}$	$\frac{9\pi}{10}$	π
y	0	0.3090	0.5878	0.8090	0.9511	1.0	0.9511	0.8090	0.5878	0.390	0

By Trapezoidal rule,

$$\int_0^\pi \sin x dx = \frac{h}{2}[(y_1 + y_{11}) + 2(y_2 + y_3 + y_4 + y_5 + y_6 + y_7 + y_8 + y_9 + y_{10})]$$

$$= \frac{\frac{\pi}{10}}{2}\begin{bmatrix}(0+0) + 2(0.3090 + 0.5878 + 0.8090 + 0.9511 \\ +1.0 + 0.9511 + 0.8090 + 0.5878 + 0.3090)\end{bmatrix}$$

$$= \frac{\pi}{20}[12.6276]$$

$$= 1.9843 \text{(approximately)}$$

By Simpson 1/3rd rule,

$$\int_0^\pi \sin x dx = \frac{h}{3}\begin{bmatrix}(y_1 + y_{11}) + 2(y_3 + y_5 + y_7 + y_9) + \\ 4(y_2 + y_4 + y_6 + y_8 + y_{10})\end{bmatrix}$$

$$= \left(\frac{\frac{\pi}{10}}{3}\right)\begin{bmatrix}(0+0) + 2(0.5878 + 0.9511 + 0.9511 + 0.5878) \\ +4(0.3090 + 0.8090 + 1.0 + 0.8090 + 0.3090)\end{bmatrix}$$

$$= \frac{\pi}{30}[2(3.0778) + 4(3.236)]$$

$$= \frac{\pi}{30}[19.0996]$$

$$= 2.0001$$

By actual Integration,

$$\int_0^\pi \sin x dx = (-\cos x)_0^\pi$$

$$=2$$

Hence Simpson's rule is more accurate then the Trapezoidal rule.

2) Dividing the range into 10equal parts. Find the value of $\int_0^{\pi/2} \sin x dx$ by (i) Trapezoidal rule (ii) Simpson's rule.

Solution:

Given:

$$f(x) = \sin x \Rightarrow y = \sin x \qquad a = 0,\ b = \frac{\pi}{2}$$

$$h = \frac{b-a}{given\ \text{interval}} = \frac{\frac{\pi}{2}-0}{10} = \frac{\pi}{20}$$

We form a table,

x	0	$\frac{\pi}{20}$	$\frac{2\pi}{20}$	$\frac{3\pi}{20}$	$\frac{4\pi}{20}$	$\frac{5\pi}{20}$	$\frac{6\pi}{20}$	$\frac{7\pi}{20}$	$\frac{8\pi}{20}$	$\frac{9\pi}{20}$	$\frac{\pi}{2}$
y	0	0.1564	0.3090	0.4540	0.5878	0.7071	0.8090	0.8910	0.9511	0.9877	1

(i) By Trapezoidal rule,

$$\int_0^{\pi/2} \sin x dx = \frac{h}{2}[(y_1 + y_{11}) + 2(y_2 + y_3 + y_4 + y_5 + y_6 + y_7 + y_8 + y_9 + y_{10})]$$

$$= \frac{\frac{\pi}{20}}{2}\left[\begin{array}{l}(0+1) + 2(0.1564 + 0.3090 + 0.4540 + 0.5878 + \\ \qquad 0.7071 + 0.8090 + 0.8910 + 6.9511 + 0.9877)\end{array}\right]$$

$$= \frac{\pi}{40}[1 + 11.7062]$$

$$= \frac{\pi}{40}[12.7062]$$

$$= 0.9980$$

(ii) By Simpson's 1/3rd rule.

$$\int_0^{\pi/2} \sin x dx = \frac{h}{3}[(y_1 + y_{11}) + 2(y_3 + y_5 + y_7 + y_9) + 4(y_2 + y_4 + y_6 + y_8 + y_{10})]$$

$$= \frac{\frac{\pi}{20}}{3}\left[\begin{array}{l}(0+1) + 2(0.3090 + 0.5878 + 0.8090 + 0.9511) + \\ \qquad 4(0.1564 + 0.4540 + 0.7071 + 0.8910 + 0.9877)\end{array}\right]$$

$$= \frac{\pi}{60}[1 + 5.3138 + 12.7848]$$

$$= \frac{\pi}{60}[19.0986]$$

$$= 1.0000$$

3) Evaluate $\int_0^6 \frac{1}{1+x^2} dx$ by (i).Trapezoidal rule (ii) Simpson rule. Also check the results by actual integration.

Solution:

Given

$$f(x) = \frac{1}{1+x^2} \Rightarrow y = \frac{1}{1+x^2}, \quad a = 0, b = 6$$

$$h = \frac{6-0}{6} = 1$$

We form a table,

x:	0	1	2	3	4	5	6
f(x):	1.00	0.500	0.200	0.100	0.058824	0.038462	0.27027

(i) By Trapezoidal rule,

$$\int_0^6 \frac{1}{1+x^2} dx = \frac{1}{2}[(y_1 + y_7) + 2(y_2 + y_3 + y_4 + y_5 + y_6)]$$

$$= \frac{1}{2}\begin{bmatrix}(1.00 + 0.27027) + 2(0.500 + 0.200 + 0.100 \\ + 0.058824 + 0.038462)\end{bmatrix}$$

$$= \frac{1}{2}[1.027027 + 1.794572]$$

$$= \frac{1}{2}[2.821599]$$

$$= 1.4107995$$

(ii) By Simpson's rule.

$$\int_0^6 \frac{1}{1+x^2} dx = \frac{h}{3}[(y_1 + y_7) + 2(y_3 + y_5) + 4(y_2 + y_4 + y_6)]$$

$$= \frac{1}{3}\begin{bmatrix}(1+0.027027)+2(0.2+0.58824) \\ +4(0.5+0.1+0.038462)\end{bmatrix}$$

$$= \frac{1}{3}[(1.027027+0.517648+2.553848)]$$

$$= 1.36617433$$

By actual Integration

$$\int_0^6 \frac{1}{1+x^2}dx = \left(\tan^{-1}x\right)_0^6$$

$$= \tan^{-1}6$$

$$= 1.40564765$$

Hence Trapezoidal rule is closer to the actual value than the value by Simpson's rule.

4) Evaluate $\int_4^{5.2} \log_e x dx$ by using (i) Trapezoidal rule (ii) Simpson's 1/3 rule.

x	**4**	**4.2**	**4.4**	**4.6**	**4.8**	**5.0**	**5.2**
y	**1.386**	**1.435**	**1.482**	**1.526**	**1.569**	**1.609**	**1.649**

Solution:

Given $f(x) = \log_e x \Rightarrow y = \log_e x, \quad a = 4, b = 5.2$

$$h = \frac{5.2-4}{6} = \frac{1.2}{6} = 0.2$$

(i) Trapezoidal rule,

$$\int_4^{5.2} \log_e x\,dx = \frac{h}{2}[(y_1+y_7)+2(y_2+y_3+y_4+y_5+y_6)]$$

$$= \frac{0.2}{2}[(1.386+1.649)+2(1.435+1.482+1.52+1.569+1.609)]$$

$$= \frac{0.2}{2}[3.035+15.2422]$$

$$= 1.8277$$

(ii) Simpson's 1/3 rule

$$\int_4^{5.2} \log_e x\,dx = \frac{h}{3}[(y_1+y_7)+2(y_3+y_5)+4(y_2+y_4+y_6)]$$

$$= \frac{0.2}{3}[(1.306+1.649)+2(1.482+1.569)+4(1.435+1.526+1.609)]$$

$$= \frac{0.2}{3}[3.035+6.102+18.28]$$

$$= \frac{0.2}{3}[27.417]$$

$$= 1.8278$$

SHORT QUESTIONS AND ANSWERS

1) Evaluate $\int_{1/2}^{1} \frac{1}{x} dx$ by Trapezoidal rule, dividing the range into 4 equal ports.

Solution:

Here $h = \dfrac{1-\frac{1}{2}}{4} = \dfrac{1}{8}$

$y = \dfrac{1}{x}$

x	$\frac{1}{2}=\frac{4}{8}$	$\frac{5}{8}$	$\frac{6}{8}$	$\frac{7}{8}$	$\frac{8}{8}$
$f(x)$	$\frac{8}{4}$	$\frac{8}{5}$	$\frac{8}{6}$	$\frac{8}{7}$	$\frac{8}{8}$

By Trapezoidal rule,

$$\int_{1/2}^{1} \frac{1}{x} dx = \frac{h}{2} \begin{bmatrix} (\text{sum of the first and last ordinates}) \\ +2(\text{sum of the remaining ordinates}) \end{bmatrix}$$

$$= \frac{\frac{1}{8}}{2}\left[\left(\frac{8}{4}+\frac{8}{8}\right)+2\left(\frac{8}{5}+\frac{8}{6}+\frac{8}{7}\right)\right]$$

$$= \frac{1}{16}\left[3+2\left(\frac{856}{210}\right)\right]$$

$$= \frac{1171}{1680}$$

$$= 0.6971$$

2) When does Simpson's rule give exact result?

Solution:

Simpson's rule will give exact result, if the entire curve $y = f(x)$ is itself a parabola.

3) What is the general Newton-Cotes quadrature formula? How is the Trapezoidal rule its special case?

Solution:

The general Newton-Cotes quadrature formula is

$$\int_{a}^{a+nh} f(x)dx = nh\left[y_0 + \frac{n\Delta}{2} + \frac{n(2n-3)}{12}\Delta^2 + \frac{n(n-2)^2}{24}\Delta^3 + ... \right] f(a)$$

This is also known as the general Gauss-Lagenre Integration formula. Putting n=1 and omitting second and higher differences in the above we get

$$\int_{a}^{a+h} f(x)dx = \frac{h}{2}\left[f(a) + f(a+h) \right]$$

$$= \frac{h}{2}(y_1 + y_2)$$

Which is the Trapezoidal rule.

4) What is the order of error in Trapezoidal formula?

Solution:

Error in the Trapezoidal formula is of the order h^2.

5) What is the order of error in Simpson's formula?

Solution:

Error in the Simpson's formula is of the order h^4.

6) State the local error term in Simpson's one-third rule?

Solution:

Principal part of the error in the interval

$$(x_1, x_3) = -\frac{h^5}{90} y_1^{iv}$$

Where y, is the value of first derivation of y and y_1^{iv} is the value of the fourth derivation of y at $x=x_1$

7) What are the errors in Trapezoidal and Simpson's rules of numerical Integration?

Solution:

Error in Trapeozoidal rule $|E| < \frac{(b-a)}{12} h^2$

M in the interval (a,b), $h = \frac{b-a}{n}$

Error in Simpson's rule $|E| < \frac{(b-a)}{180} h^4 M$

8) Using Simpson's rule find $\int_0^4 e^x dx$ given $e^0 = 1$, $e^1 = 2.72$, $e^2 = 7.39$, $e^3 = 20.09$ and $e^4 = 54.6$

Solution:

Let $y = e^x$ and $h = 1$

By Simpson's rule.

$$\int_0^4 e^x dx = \frac{h}{3}\left[(y_0 + y_4) + 2y_2 + 4(y_1 + y_3)\right]$$

$$= \frac{1}{3}\left[(1 + 54.6) + 2(7.39) + 4(2.72 + 20.09)\right]$$

=53.8733

9) What approximation is used in deriving Simpson's rule of integration?

Solution:

Simpson's one third rule approximates the area of two adjacent strips by the area under a quadratic parabola.

10) Compare Trapezoidal rule and Simpson's ⅓ rule for evaluating numerical integration.

Trapezoidal rule	Simpson's ⅓rd rule
1) It has no specific restriction of number of segments	1) It requires even number of segments and odd number of points
2) Degree of y(x) is one	2) Degree of y(x) is two
3) $\lvert E \rvert < \frac{(b-a)h^2}{12} M$	3) $\lvert E \rvert < \frac{(b-a)h^4}{180} M$
4) Order h^2	4) Order h^4
5) It is approximated by trapezoids	5) It is approximated by set of parabolas

EXERCISE

[TRAPEZOIDAL RULE AND SIMPSON'S 1/3 RULE]

1) **Evaluate,** $\int_0^1 \sqrt{\sin x + \cos x}\, dx$ **correct to two decimal places, using seven ordinates.**

   [Ans: 1.3935]

2) **Find the values of** $\log 2^{1/3}$ **from** $\int_0^1 \frac{x^2}{1+x^3} dx$ **using Simpson's one third rule with** $h=0.025$**.**

   [Ans: 0.23108]

3) **Compute the value of** $\int_1^2 \frac{1}{x} dx$ **using Simpson's rule and trapezoidal rule take** $h=0.25$

   [Ans: 0.6931, 0.6971]

4.6 EVALUATION OF DOUBLE INTEGRALS BY TRAPEZOIDAL AND SIMPSON'S 1/3rd RULES

(a) Trapezoidal rule for double integrations

$$\int_a^b \int_a^b f(x,y)\,dx\,dy = \frac{hk}{4}\begin{bmatrix}\text{(sum of the values of f at the four corners)+} \\ \text{2(sum of the values of f at the remaining nodes on boundary)} \\ \text{+4(sum of the values of f at the interior nodes)}\end{bmatrix}$$

EXAMPLES

1) **Evaluate** $\int_0^1 \int_1^2 \frac{2xy}{(1+x^2)(1+y^2)} dx\,dy$ **by trapezoidal rule with** $h=k=0.25$

Solution:

Given

$$\int_0^1 \int_1^2 \frac{2xy}{(1+x^2)(1+y^2)} dx\,dy$$

$h=k=0.25$

y/x	1	1.25	1.5	1.75	2
0	0	0	0	0	0
0.25	0.2353	0.2295	0.2172	0.2027	0.1882
0.5	0.4	0.3902	0.3692	0.3446	0.32
0.75	0.48	0.5854	0.4431	0.4135	0.384
1	0.5	0.4878	0.4615	0.4308	0.4

By Trapezoidal rule,

$$I=\frac{hk}{4}\begin{bmatrix}\text{(sum of the values of f at the four corners)} + \\ 2\text{(sum of the values of f at the remaining nodes on boundary)} \\ +4\text{(sum of the values of f at the interior nodes)}\end{bmatrix}$$

$$I=\frac{(0.25)(0.25)}{4}\left[\begin{matrix}(0+0+0.4+0.5)+2\begin{pmatrix}0.48+0.4+0.2353+0+0+0+0.1882 \\ +0.32+0.384+0.4308+0.4615+0.4878\end{pmatrix} \\ +4\begin{pmatrix}0.2295+0.2172+0.2027+0.3902+0.3692 \\ +0.3446+0.5854+0.4431+0.4135\end{pmatrix}\end{matrix}\right]$$

$$=(0.0156)\left[(0.9)+2(3.3876)+4(3.1954)\right]$$

$$=(0.0156)[0.9+6.7752+12.7816]$$

$$=(0.0156)[20.4568]$$

$$=0.31913$$

2) Evaluate $\int_1^2\int_1^2 \frac{1}{x^2+y^2}dx\,dy$, numerically with h=0.2 along x-direction and k=0.25 along y direction .

Solution:

Given $\int_1^2\int_1^2 \frac{1}{x^2+y^2}dx\,dy$

$h=0.2$ and $k=0.25$

y/x	1	1.2	1.4	1.6	1.8	2
1	0.5	0.4098	0.3378	0.2809	0.2359	0.2
1.25	0.3902	0.3331	0.2839	0.2426	0.2082	0.1798
1.5	0.3077	0.2710	0.2375	0.2079	0.1821	0.16
1.75	0.2462	0.2221	0.1991	0.1779	0.1587	0.1416
2	0.2	0.1838	0.1679	0.1524	0.1381	0.125

By Trapezoidal rule,

$$\int_a^b\int_a^b f(x,y)dx\,dy=\frac{hk}{4}\begin{bmatrix}\text{(sum of the values of f at the four corners)} +\\ \text{2(sum of the values of f at the remaining nodes on boundary)}\\ \text{+4(sum of the values of f at the interior nodes)}\end{bmatrix}$$

$$=\frac{(0.2)(0.5)}{4}\left[\begin{matrix}(0.5+0.2+0.125+0.2)+2\begin{pmatrix}0.2462+0.3077+0.3902+0.4098+0.3378\\+0.2809+0.2359+0.1798+0.16+0.1416\\+0.1381+0.1524+0.1679+0.1838\end{pmatrix}\\ +4\begin{pmatrix}0.3331+0.2839+0.2426+0.2710+0.2082+0.2375\\+0.2079+0.1821+0.1991+0.1779+0.1587\end{pmatrix}\end{matrix}\right]$$

$$=\frac{(0.2)(0.5)}{4}[1.025+6.6642+10.8964]$$

$$=\frac{(0.2)(0.5)}{4}[18.5856]$$

$$=0.2323$$

3) Evaluate, numerically $\int_1^2\int_1^2 \frac{xy}{x+y}dx\,dy$ with $h=k=0.25$

Solution:

y/x	1	1.25	1.5	1.75	2
0	0.5	0.5556	0.6	0.6364	0.6667
1.25	0.5556	0.625	0.6818	0.7292	0.7692
1.5	0.6	0.6818	0.75	0.8077	0.8571
1.75	0.6364	0.7292	0.8077	0.875	0.9333
2	0.6667	0.7692	0.8571	0.9333	1

By using Trapezoidal rule,

$$I=\frac{hk}{4}\begin{bmatrix}\text{(sum of the values of f at the four corners)} +\\ \text{2(sum of the values of f at the remaining nodes on boundary)}\\ \text{+4(sum of the values of f at the interior nodes)}\end{bmatrix}$$

$$I=\frac{(0.25)(0.25)}{4}\left[\begin{pmatrix}0.5+0.6667+1\\+0.6667\end{pmatrix}+2\begin{pmatrix}0.6364+0.6+0.5556+0.5556+0.6\\+0.6364+0.7692+0.8571+0.9333\\+0.9333+0.8571+0.7692\end{pmatrix}\\+4\begin{pmatrix}0.625+0.6818+0.7292+0.6818+0.75\\+0.8077+0.7292+0.8077+0.875\end{pmatrix}\right]$$

$$=(0.0156)[2.8334+2(8.7032)+4(6.6874)]$$

$$=(0.0156)[2.8334+17.4064+26.7496]$$

$$=0.73303$$

SIMPSON'S RULE FOR DOUBLE INTERGRATION.

$$I=\frac{hk}{9}\begin{bmatrix}\text{(sum of the values of f at the four corners) +}\\ \text{4(sum of the values of f at the remaining nodes on boundary)}\\ \text{+16(sum of the values of f at the central point)}\end{bmatrix}$$

EXTENSION TO GENERAL FORM OF SIMPSON'S RULE

$$I=\frac{hk}{9}\left[\begin{array}{l}\text{(sum of the values of f at the four corners)+2}\begin{pmatrix}\text{sum of the values of f at the odd positions}\\ \text{on the boundary except the corners}\end{pmatrix}\\ +4\begin{pmatrix}\text{sum of the values of f at the even}\\ \text{positions on the boundary}\end{pmatrix}+\left\{\begin{array}{l}4(\text{sum of the values of f at odd positions})\\ +8(\text{sum of the values of f at even positions})\\ \text{on the odd rows of the matrix except boundary rows}\end{array}\right\}\\ +\left\{\begin{array}{l}8(\text{sum of the values of f at the odd positions})\\ +16(\text{sum of the values of f at the even positions})\text{ on the even row of the matrix}\end{array}\right\}\end{array}\right]$$

EXAMPLES

1) Using Simpson's 1/3 rules, evaluate $\int_0^1\int_0^1 \frac{1}{1+x+y}\,dx\,dy$ taking $h=k=0.5$

Solution:

Given $\int_0^1\int_0^1 \frac{1}{1+x+y}\,dx\,dy$

$h=k=0.5$ $\qquad f(x,y)=\frac{1}{1+x+y}$

	1	4	1	
x/y	0	0.5	1	
0	1 (1)	0.6667 (4)	0.5 (1)	1
0.5	0.6667 (4)	0.5 (16)	0.4 (4)	4
1	0.5 (1)	0.4 (4)	0.3333 (1)	1

By Simpson's $\frac{1}{3}$ rule,

$$I = \left(\frac{0.5}{3}\right)\left(\frac{0.5}{3}\right)\begin{bmatrix}(1+0.5+0.333+0.5)+4(0.6667+0.6667\\+0.4+0.4)+16(0.5)\end{bmatrix}$$

$$= (0.0278)[18.8669]$$

$$= 0.5245$$

2) Using Simpson's rule, evaluate $\int_1^2\int_1^2 \frac{1}{x+y}\,dx\,dy$ by dividing the interval (1, 2) into two equal sub intervals.

Solution:

Given $\int_1^2\int_1^2 \frac{1}{x+y}\,dx\,dy$

$$f(x,y) = \frac{1}{x+y}$$

	1	4	1	
x/y	1	1.5	2	
1	0.5 (1)	0.4 (4)	0.3333 (1)	1
1.5	0.4 (4)	0.3333 (16)	0.2857 (4)	4
2	0.3333 (1)	0.2857 (4)	0.25 (1)	4

By Simpson's rule,

$$I = \left(\frac{h}{3}\right)\left(\frac{k}{3}\right)\begin{bmatrix}(0.5+0.3333+0.25+0.3333)+4(0.4+0.4+0.2857+0.2857)\\+16(0.3333)\end{bmatrix}$$

$$= \left(\frac{0.5}{3}\right)\left(\frac{0.5}{3}\right)[12.235]$$

$$= (0.0278)[12.235]$$

$$= 0.3401$$

3) Evaluate $\mathbf{I} = \int_0^{1/2}\int_0^{1/2} \frac{\sin(x,y)}{1+xy}\,dx\,dy$ **using Simpson's rule with** $h = k = \frac{1}{4}$

Solution:

Given $f(x,y) = \dfrac{\sin(x,y)}{1+xy}$

	1	4	1	
x/y	0	¼	½	
0	0 (1)	0 (4)	0 (1)	1
¼	0 (4)	0.0588 (16)	0.1108 (4)	4
½	0 (1)	0.1108 (4)	0.1979 (1)	1

By Simpson's rule,

$$I = \left[\frac{\frac{1}{4}}{3}\right]\left[\frac{\frac{1}{4}}{3}\right]\begin{bmatrix}(0+0+0.1979+0)+4(0+0+0.1108+0.1108)\\+16(0.0588)\end{bmatrix}$$

$$= \left(\frac{1}{144}\right)(2.0251)$$

$$= 0.0141$$

PROBLEM BASED ON BOTH SIMPSON'S AND TRAPEZOIDAL RULES

1) Evaluate $\int_1^{1.4}\int_2^{2.4}\frac{1}{xy}dx\,dy$, using trapezoidal and Simpson's and Trapezoidal and Simpson's rule. Verify your result by actual integration.

Solution:

Given $\int_1^{1.4}\int_2^{2.4}\frac{1}{xy}dx\,dy$

Let $f(x,y)=\frac{1}{xy}$

Divide the range of x and y into 4 equal parts

$$h=\frac{2.4-2}{4}=0.1$$

$$k=\frac{1.4-1}{4}=0.1$$

	1	4	2	4	1	
x/y	2	2.1	2.2	2.3	2.4	
1	1 0.5	4 0.4762	2 0.4545	4 0.4348	1 0.4167	1
1.1	4 0.4545	16 0.4329	8 0.4132	16 0.3953	4 0.3788	4
1.2	2 0.4167	8 0.3968	4 0.3788	8 0.3623	2 0.3472	2
1.3	4 0.3846	16 0.3663	8 0.3497	16 0.3344	4 0.3205	4
1.4	1 0.3571	4 0.3401	2 0.3247	4 0.3106	1 0.2976	1

(i) By Trapezoidal rule,

$$\mathrm{I}=\frac{hk}{4}\left[\begin{array}{l}\text{(sum of the values of f at the four corners) +}\\ \text{2(sum of the values of f at the remaining nodes on boundary)}\\ \text{+4(sum of the values of f at the interior nodes)}\end{array}\right]$$

$$= \frac{(0.1)(0.1)}{4}\left[\begin{pmatrix}0.5+0.4167\\+0.3571+0.2976\end{pmatrix}+2\begin{pmatrix}0.3846+0.4167+0.4545+0.4762\\+0.4545+0.4348+0.3788+0.3472\\+0.3205+0.3106+0.3247+0.3401\end{pmatrix} +4\begin{pmatrix}0.4329+0.4132+0.3953+0.3968+0.3788+0.3623\\+0.3663+0.3497+0.3344\end{pmatrix}\right]$$

$$= \frac{0.01}{4}[1.5714+9.2864+13.7188]$$

$$= 0.0614$$

(ii) By Simpson's rule,

$$I = \left(\frac{h}{3}\right)\left(\frac{k}{3}\right)\left[\begin{pmatrix}0.5+0.4167\\+0.3571+0.2976\end{pmatrix}+2\begin{pmatrix}0.4167+0.4545\\+0.3472+0.3247\end{pmatrix} +4\begin{pmatrix}0.3846+0.4545+0.4762+0.4348+0.3788\\+0.3205+0.3106+0.3401+0.3788\end{pmatrix} +8(0.3968+0.3623+0.3497+0.4132) +16(0.3663+0.3344+0.4329+0.3953)\right]$$

$$= \left(\frac{0.01}{3}\right)\left(\frac{0.01}{3}\right)(55.2116)$$

$$= 0.0613$$

(iii) By actual Integration

$$\int_1^{1.4}\int_2^{2.4}\frac{1}{xy}dx\,dy = \left(\int_1^{1.4}\frac{1}{y}dy\right)\left(\int_2^{2.4}\frac{1}{x}dy\right)$$

$$= (\log y)_1^{1.4}(\log x)_2^{2.4}$$

$$= (\log 1.4)(\log 2.4 - \log 2)$$

$$= \log(1.4)\log(1.2)$$

$$= 0.0613$$

2) Evaluate $\int_1^2\int_3^4 \frac{1}{(x+y)^2}dx\,dy$, taking $h=k=0.5$ by both Trapezoidal and Simpson's rule

Solution:

Given $\int_1^2\int_3^4 \frac{1}{(x+y)^2}dx\,dy$

Let $f(x,y)=\dfrac{1}{(x+y)^2}$

	1	4	1	
x/y	3	3.5	4	
1	0.0625 [1]	0.0494 [4]	0.04 [1]	1
1.5	0.0494 [4]	0.04 [16]	0.0331 [4]	4
2	0.04 [1]	0.0331 [4]	0.0278 [1]	1

(i) By trapezoidal rule,

$$\int_1^2\int_3^4 \frac{1}{(x+y)^2}\,dx\,dy=\frac{hk}{4}\begin{bmatrix}(0.0625+0.04+0.04+0.0278)+2(0.0494+0.0494\\+0.0331+0.0331)+4(0.04)\end{bmatrix}$$

$$=\frac{0.25}{4}[0.1703+0.3300+0.16]$$
$$=0.0413$$

(ii) By Simpson's rule,

$$\int_1^2\int_3^4 \frac{1}{(x+y)^2}\,dx\,dy=\frac{0.25}{9}\begin{bmatrix}(0.0625+0.04+0.04+0.0278)+\\4(0.0494+0.0494+0.0331+0.0331)+\\16(0.04)\end{bmatrix}$$

$$=\frac{0.25}{9}[0.1703+0.6600+0.64]$$
$$=0.0408$$

3) Evaluate I=$\int_0^1\int_0^1 e^{x+y}dxdy$ using the trapezoidal and simpson's rules.

Solution:

Given I=$\int_0^1\int_0^1 e^{x+y}dxdy$

$h=k=0.5$

	1	4	1	
x/y	0	0.5	1	
0	$\lfloor 1$ 1	$\lfloor 4$ 1.6487	$\lfloor 1$ 2.7183	1
0.5	$\lfloor 4$ 1.6487	$\lfloor 16$ 2.7183	$\lfloor 4$ 4.4817	4
1	$\lfloor 1$ 2.7183	$\lfloor 4$ 4.4817	$\lfloor 1$ 7.3891	1

(i) By trapezoidal rule,

$$\int_0^1\int_0^1 e^{x+y}dxdy = \frac{hk}{4}\begin{bmatrix}(1+2.7183+2.7183+7.3891) \\ +2(1.6487+4.4817+4.4817+1.6487)+4(2.7183)\end{bmatrix}$$

$$= \frac{(0.5)(0.5)}{4}[13.8257+24.5216+10.8732]$$

$$= \frac{0.25}{4}[49.22050]$$

$$=3.0762$$

(ii) By simpson's rule,

$$\int_0^1\int_0^1 e^{x+y}dxdy = \frac{hk}{4}\begin{bmatrix}(1+2.7183+2.7183+7.3891) \\ +4(1.6487+4.4817+4.4817+1.6487)+16(2.7183)\end{bmatrix}$$

$$= \frac{0.25}{9}[13.827+49.0432+43.49280]$$

$$= \frac{26.59043}{9}$$

$$= 2.95449$$

SHORT QUESTIONS AND ANSWERS

1) Short Trapezoidal rule evaluating

Solution:

$$I = \frac{hk}{4}\begin{bmatrix}\text{(sum of the values of f at the four corners) +} \\ \text{2(sum of the values of f at the remaining nodes on boundary)} \\ \text{+4(sum of the values of f at the interior nodes)}\end{bmatrix}$$

2) State Simpson's rule for evaluating $\int_a^b\int_c^d f(x,y)\,dx\,dy$

Solution:

$$I=\frac{hk}{9}\left[\begin{array}{l}\text{(sum of the values of f at the four corners)} + \\ \text{2(sum of the values of f at the odd positions on the boundary except the corners)} \\ \text{+4(sum of the values of f at the even positions on the boundary)} \\ \text{+\{4(sum of the values of f at odd positions)+8(sum of the values of f at even positions) on the odd} \\ \text{rows of the matrix except boundary rows)\}+\{8(sum of the values of f at the odd positions)} \\ \text{+16(sum of the values of f at the even positions) on the even row of the matrix\}}\end{array}\right]$$

EXERCISE

[DOUBLE INTEGRALS USING TRAPEZOIDAL AND SIMPSON'S RULE]

1) **Evaluate,** $\int_1^2\int_3^4 \frac{1}{(x+y)^2}\,dx\,dy$ **taking *h*=*k*=0.5 by both trapezoidal rule and Simpson's rule**

   [Ans: T.R 0.0413, S.R 0.0408]

2) **Evaluate** $\int_1^2\int_1^2 \frac{1}{x+y}\,dx\,dy$**, Using the Trapezoidal rule with *h*=*k*=0.5 and *k*=*h*= 0.25**

   [Ans: 0.343304, 0.340668]

3) **Evaluate** $\int_1^{1.2}\int_1^{1.4} \frac{1}{x+y}\,dx\,dy$**, Using the Trapezoidal rule and Simpson's rule**

   [Ans: TR: 0.4292, SR: 0.4296]

UNIT - 5

NUMERICAL SOLUTION OF ORDINARY DIFFERENTIAL EQUATIONS

5.1 INTRODUCTION

An ordinary differential equation of order 'n' is a relation of the form

$$F\left[x, y, y', y'', \ldots, y^{(n)}\right]=0$$

Where $y = y(x)$ and $y(r) = \dfrac{d^r y}{dx^r}$

The solution of this differential equation involves 'n' constants and those constants are determined with the help of 'n' conditions.

If $y, y', y'', \ldots, y^{(n-1)}$ are prescribed at $x=x_0$ by $y(x_0) = y_0$, $y'(x_0) = y_0', \ldots y^{(n-1)}(x_0) = y_0^{n-1}$, these conditions are called the initial conditions because they depend only on x_0.

The differential equation together with the initial conditions is called an initial value problem.

In this unit, we are interested to solve numerically the 1st order initial value problem defined by

$$\frac{dy}{dx} = f(x, y), \quad y(x_0) = y_0$$

The solution of such initial value problem can be obtained by two different methods. They are

1) Single – Step methods
2) Multi – Step methods

1) Single-Step Methods

In this methods we use information about the curve at one point and we do not iterate the solution. The method involves more evaluation of the function.

We will discuss the numerical solution by

1) Taylor's series method
2) Euler method
3) Modified Euler method
4) Runge-Kutta method.

All require the information at a single point $x=x_0$

2) Multi-Step Methods

These methods require fewer evaluations of the functions to estimate the solution at a point and iterations are performed till sufficient accuracy is achieved. Estimation of error is possible and the methods are called predictor – corrector method.

In this type, we mainly discuss Milne's Methods and Adam's – Bash forth method.

In multi-step method, to compute y_{n+1}, we need the functional values:

$$y_n, y_{n-1}, y_{n-2} \; \& \; y_{n-3}$$

TYPES OF SINGLE – STEP METHODS

5.2 TAYLOR'S SERIES METHOD

To find the numerical solution of the equation

$$\frac{dy}{dx} = f(x,y)$$

Given the initial condition $y(x_0) = y_0$

Now we expand $y(x)$ about the points $x = x_0, x_1, x_2, \ldots, x_n$ in a Taylor's series, we get

$$y_{n+1} = y_n + \frac{h}{1!}y'_n + \frac{h^2}{2!}y''_n + \frac{h^3}{3!}y'''_n + \frac{h^4}{4!}y^{iv}_n + \ldots \qquad \rightarrow (1)$$

Where $h = x - x_0$

> ***Note:***
>
> If 'h' is small and the terms after 'n' terms are neglected from (1), the error is
>
> $$\frac{h^n}{n!} f^n(\theta)$$
>
> Where $x_0 < \theta < x_1$, if $x_1 - x_0 = h$.

PROBLEMS BASED ON TAYLOR'S SERIES METHOD

1) Solve $y' = x + y,\ y(0) = 1$ by Taylor's series method and find the value of $y(0.1)$.

Solution:

Given, $y' = x + y,\ y(0) = 1$

Here

x:	x_0 0	x_1 0.1
y:	y_0 1	y_1 ?

Then $h = x_1 - x_0 = 0.1 - 0 = 0.1$

and h=0.1

We know that, the Taylor's series formula,

$$y_{n+1} = y_n + \frac{h}{1!}y'_n + \frac{h^2}{2!}y''_n + \frac{h^3}{3!}y'''_n + \frac{h^4}{4!}y^{iv}_n + ..$$

$$\begin{array}{l|l} y' = x + y & y'_0 = x_0 + y_0 = 0 + 1 = 1 \\ y'' = 1 + y' & y''_0 = 1 + y'_0 = 1 + 1 = 2 \\ y''' = y'' & y'''_0 = y''_0 = 2 \\ y^{iv} = y''' & y^{iv}_0 = y'''_0 = 2 \end{array}$$

Taylor's series formula for y_1:

$$y_1 = y_0 + \frac{h}{1!}y'_0 + \frac{h^2}{2!}y''_0 + \frac{h^3}{3!}y'''_0 + \frac{h^4}{4!}y^{iv}_0 + ...$$

$$= 1 + \frac{0.1}{1!}(1) + \frac{(0.1)^2}{2!}(2) + \frac{(0.1)^3}{3!}(2) + \frac{(0.1)^4}{4!}(2)$$

$$= 1 + 0.1 + 0.01 + 0.0003 + 0.000083$$

$$y_1 = 1.110383$$

2) Using Taylor's series method, find correct to four decimal places, the value of y(0.1), given $\frac{dy}{dx} = x^2 + y^2$ and $y(0) = 1$.

Solution:

Given, $y' = \frac{dy}{dx} = x^2 + y^2, \qquad y(0) = 1$

Here

x:	x_0 0	x_1 0.1
y:	y_0 1	y_1 ?

& h=0.1

We know that, the Taylor's series formula,

$$y_{n+1} = y_n + \frac{h}{1!} y'_n + \frac{h^2}{2!} y''_n + \frac{h^3}{3!} y'''_n + \frac{h^4}{4!} y^{iv}_n + ..$$

$$y' = x^2 + y^2$$
$$y'' = 2x + 2yy'$$
$$y''' = 2 + 2yy'' + 2y'.y'$$
$$= 2 + 2yy'' + 2(y')^2$$
$$y^{iv} = 2yy''' + 2y'y'' + 4y'.y''$$
$$= 6y'y'' + 2yy'''$$

$$y'_0 = x_0^2 + y_0^2 = 0 + 1^2 = 1$$
$$y''_0 = 2x_0 + 2y_0 y'_0 = 0 + 2(1)(1) = 2$$
$$y'''_0 = 2 + 2y_0 y''_0 + 2(y'_0)^2$$
$$= 2 + 2(1)(2) + 2(1)^2 = 8$$
$$y^{iv}_0 = 6y'_0 y''_0 + 2y_0 y'''_0$$
$$= 6(2)(1) + 2(1)(8) = 28$$

Taylor's series formula for y_1:

$$y_1 = y_0 + \frac{h}{1!} y'_0 + \frac{h^2}{2!} y''_0 + \frac{h^3}{3!} y'''_0 + \frac{h^4}{4!} y^{iv}_0 + ..$$

$$= 1 + \frac{0.1}{1!}(1) + \frac{(0.1)^2}{2!}(2) + \frac{(0.1)^3}{3!}(8) + \frac{(0.1)^4}{4!}(28)$$

$= 1+0.1+0.01+0.00133+0.000116$

$=1.111446$

$y_1=1.11149$

3) Using Taylor's series method, find y at $x=0.1$ if $\frac{dy}{dx} = x^2 y - 1, \quad y(0) = 1$

Solution:

Given, $y' = \frac{dy}{dx} = x^2 y - 1, \quad y(0) = 1$

Here

x:	x_0 0	x_1 0.1
y:	y_0 1	y_1 ?

& h=0.1

We know that, the Taylor's series formula

$$y_{n+1} = y_n + \frac{h}{1!}y'_n + \frac{h^2}{2!}y''_n + \frac{h^3}{3!}y'''_n + \frac{h^4}{4!}y^{iv}_n + \ldots$$

$y' = x^2y - 1$

$y'' = 2xy + x^2y'$

$y''' = 2(xy' + y) + x^2y'' + 2xy'$

$\quad = 2xy' + 2y + x^2y'' + 2xy'$

$y''' = 2y + 4xy' + x^2y''$

$y^{iv} = 2y' + 4(xy'' + y') + x^2y''' + 2xy''$

$\quad = 2y' + 4xy'' + 4y' + x^2y''' + 2xy''$

$\quad = 6y' + 6xy'' + x^2y'''$

$y_0' = x_0^2y_0 - 1 = 0 - 1 = -1$

$y_0'' = 2x_0y_0 + x_0^2y_0^1 = 2(0)(1) - (0)2(1) = 0$

$y_0''' = 2y_0 + 4x_0y_0' + x_0^2y_0''$

$\quad = 2(1) + 4(0)(-1) + (0)^2(0)$

$y_0''' = 2$

$y_0^{iv} = 6y_0' + 6x_0y_0'' + x_0^2y_0'''$

$\quad = 6(-1) + 6(0)(0) + (0)^2(2)$

$y_0^{iv} = -6$

Taylor's series formula for y_1:

$$y_1 = y_0 + \frac{h}{1!}y'_0 + \frac{h^2}{2!}y''_0 + \frac{h^3}{3!}y'''_0 + \frac{h^4}{4!}y^{iv}_0 + ..$$

$$= 1 + \frac{0.1}{1!}(-1) + \frac{(0.1)^2}{2!}(0) + \frac{(0.1)^3}{3!}(2) + \frac{(0.1)^4}{4!}(-6)$$

$$= 1 - 0.1 + 0.00033 - 0.000025$$

$$y_1 = 0.900305$$

4) Using Taylor's series method, compute $y(0.2)$ and $y(0.4)$. given $y' = \frac{dy}{dx} = 1 - 2xy$, $y(0) = 0$.

Solution:

Given, $y' = \dfrac{dy}{dx} = 1 - 2xy,\ y(0) = 0$

Here

x:	x_0 0	x_1 0.2	x_2 0.4
y:	y_0 0	y_1 ?	y_2 ?

& $h = 0.2$

We know that, the Taylor's series formula

$$y_{n+1} = y_n + \frac{h}{1!} y_n' + \frac{h^2}{2!} y_n'' + \frac{h^3}{3!} y_n''' + \frac{h^4}{4!} y_n^{iv} + \ldots$$

To find y_1 (or) $y(0.2)$:

$y' = 1 - 2xy$	$y_0' = 1 - 2x_0y_0 = 1 - (0)(0) = 1$
$y'' = 0 - 2(xy' + y)$	$y_0'' = -2x_0y_0' - 2y_0 = -2(0)(1) - 2(0) = 0$
$= -2xy' - 2y$	$y_0''' = -2x_0y_0'' - 4y_0' = -2(0)(0) - 4(1) = -4$
$y''' = -2(xy'' + y') - 2y'$	
$= -2xy'' - 2y' - 2y'$	
$= -2xy'' - 4y'$	

Taylor's series formula for y_1:

$$y_1 = y_0 + \frac{h}{1!} y_0' + \frac{h^2}{2!} y_0'' + \frac{h^3}{3!} y_0''' + \frac{h^4}{4!} y_0^{iv} + \ldots$$

$$= 0 + \frac{0.2}{1!}(1) + \frac{(0.2)^2}{2!}(0) + \frac{(0.2)^3}{3!}(-4)$$

$$= 0.2 - 0.00533$$

$$y_1 = 0.19467$$

To find y_2 (or) $y(0.4)$:

Here

x:	x_0 0	x_1 0.2	x_2 0.4
y:	y_0 0	y_1 0.19467	y_2 ?

& *h=0.2*

$y' = 1 - 2xy$	$y' = 1 - 2x_1y_1 = 1 - 2(0.2)(0.19467) = 0.92209$
$y'' = -2xy' - 2y$	$y_1'' = -2x_1y_1' - 2y_1 = -2(0.2)(0.92209) - 2(0.19467)$
	$= -0.75834$
$y''' = -2xy'' - 4y'$	$y_1''' = -2x_1y_1'' - 4y_1 = -2(0.2)(0.75834) - 4(0.9220)$
	$= -3.38505$

The Taylor's series formula for y_2:

$$y_2 = y_1 + \frac{h}{1!}y_1' + \frac{h^2}{2!}y_1'' + \frac{h^3}{3!}y_1''' + ...$$

$$= 0.19467 + \frac{0.2}{1!}(0.92209) + \frac{(0.2)^2}{2!}(-0.75834) + \frac{(0.2)^3}{3!}(-3.38505)$$

$$y_2 = 0.35941$$

5) Using Taylor's series, find $y(0.1)$ and $y(0.2)$ correct to three significant digits, given $\frac{dy}{dx} - 2y = 3e^x,\ y(0) = 0$.

Solution:

Given $\frac{dy}{dx} - 2y = 3e^x,\ y(0) = 0$

$$y' = \frac{dy}{dx} = 3e^x + 2y$$

Here

x:	x_0 0	x_1 0.1	x_2 0.2
y:	y_0 0	y_1 ?	y_2 ?

& *h=0.1*

We know that, the Taylor's series formula

$$y_{n+1} = y_n + \frac{h}{1!}y_n' + \frac{h^2}{2!}y_n'' + \frac{h^3}{3!}y_n''' + ...$$

To find y_1 (or) y (0.1) :

$$y' = 3e^x + 2y \qquad y_0' = 3e^{x_0} + 2y_0 = 3e^0 + 2(0) = 3$$

$$y'' = 3e^x + 2y' \qquad y_0'' = 3e^{x_0} + 2y_0' = 3e^0 + 2(3) = 9$$

$$y''' = 3e^x + 2y'' \qquad y_0''' = 3e^{x_0} + 2y_0'' = 3e^0 + 2(9) = 21$$

Taylor's series formula for y_1 :

$$y_1 = y_0 + \frac{h}{1!}y_0' + \frac{h^2}{2!}y_0'' + \frac{h^3}{3!}y_0''' + ...$$

$$= 0 + \frac{(0.1)}{1!}(3) + \frac{(0.1)^2}{2!}(9) + \frac{(0.1)^3}{3!}(21)$$

$= 0 + 0.3 + 0.045 + 0.0035$

$y_1 = 0.350$

To find y_2 (or) $y(0.2)$:

Here

x:	x_0 0	x_1 0.1	x_2 0.2
y:	y_0 0	y_1 0.35	y_2 ?

& $h=0.1$

$y' = 3e^x + 2y$	$y_1' = 3e^{x_1} + 2y_1 = 3e^{0.1} + 2(0.35) = 4.0128$
$y'' = 3e^x + 2y'$	$y_1'' = 3e^{x_1} + 2y_1' = 3e^{0.1} + 2(4.0128) = 11.0257$
$y''' = 3e^x + 2y''$	$y_1''' = 3e^{x_1} + 2y_1'' = 3e^{0.1} + 2(11.0257) = 25.3670$

Taylor's series formula for y_2:

$$y_2 = y_1 + \frac{h}{1!}y_1' + \frac{h^2}{2!}y_1'' + \frac{h^3}{3!}y_1''' + \ldots$$

$$= 0.35 + \frac{0.1}{1!}(4.0128) + \frac{(0.1)^2}{2!}(11.0257) + \frac{(0.1)^3}{3!}(25.3670)$$

$y_2 = 0.8\ 11$

5.3 EULER METHOD

Introduction:

In Taylor series method, we obtain approximate solutions of the initial value problem,

$$\frac{dy}{dx} = f(x,y), \quad y(x_0) = y_0$$

As a power series in x and the solution can be used to compute 'y' numerically specified value 'x' near x_0.

In Euler method, we compute the values of 'y' for $x_i = x_0+ih$, $i = 1,2,3\ldots$. With a step size $h>0$.

(ie) $y_i = y(x_i)$ where $x_i=x_0+ih$, $i=1,2,3\ldots\ldots$

Euler Method:

Let $y_1=y(x_i)$ where $x_1=x_0+h$

Then $y_1=y(x_0+h)$

By Taylor's series,

$$y_1 = y(x_0) + \frac{h}{1!} y'(x_0) + \frac{h^2}{2!} y''(x_0) + \frac{h^3}{3!} y'''(x_0) + \ldots \quad \rightarrow (1)$$

Neglecting the terms with h^2 and higher powers of h, we get from (1)

$$y_1 = y_0 + h\,f(x_0, y_0) \quad \rightarrow (2)$$

Expression (2) gives an approximate value of 'y' at $x_1 = x_0 + h$

Similarly we get

$$y_2 = y_1 + hf(x_1, y_1) \quad \text{for} \quad x_2 = x_1 + h.$$

For any,

$$y_{n+1} = y_n + h\,f(x_n, y_n) \quad n=0,1,2,\ldots \rightarrow (3)$$

In Euler method we use (3) to compute successively $y_1, y_2 \ldots\ldots$

> ***Note:***
> Error in Euler method is $O(h^2)$.

PROBLEMS BASED ON EULER METHOD

1) Using Euler's method, find the solution of the initial value problem $\frac{dy}{dx} = \log(x+y), \quad y(0) = 2$ at x=0.2 by assuming h=0.2.

Solution:

Given $y' = \frac{dy}{dx} = \log(x+y), \quad y(0) = 2$

$$f(x,y) = \log(x+y)$$

Here

x:	x_0 0	x_1 0.2
y:	y_0 2	y_1 ?

& h=0.2

We know that, the Euler formula

$$y_{n+1} = y_n + h\,f(x_n, y_n)$$

Put n=0,

$$y_1 = y_0 + h f(x_0, y_0)$$

$= 2 + (0.2)\, log(x_0 + y_0)$

$= 2 + (0.2)\, log(0+2)$

$= 2 + (0.2)\,(0.30)$

$= 2 + 0.060$

$y_1 = 2.060$

2) Using Euler method, find *y(0.3)* of *y(x)* satisfies the initial value problem $\frac{dy}{dx} = \frac{1}{2}(x^2+1)y^2,\ y(0.2) = 1.1114$

Solution:

Given $f(x,y) = \frac{dy}{dx} = \frac{1}{2}(x^2+1)y^2 \quad y(0.2) = 1.1114$

Here

x:	x_0 0.2	x_1 0.3
y:	y_0 1.1114	y_1 ?

& h=0.1

We know that, the Euler formula

$$y_{n+1} = y_n + h f(x_n, y_n)$$

Put n=0,

$$y_1 = y_0 + h f(x_0, y_0)$$

$$= 1.1114 + (0.1)\frac{1}{2}\left(x_0^2+1\right)y_0^2$$

$$= 1.1114 + \frac{(0.1)}{2}\left[(0.2)^2+1\right](1.1114)^2$$

$$= 1.1114 + \frac{(0.1)}{2}(1.04)(1.2352)$$

$$= 1.1114 + 0.06423$$

$$y_1 = 1.17563$$

3) Using Euler method, find $y(0.2)$ and $y(0.4)$ from $\frac{dy}{dx} = x + y$, $y(0)=1$ with $h=0.2$

Solution:

Given $f(x, y) = \frac{dy}{dx} = x + y$, $y(0)=1$

Here

x	x_0 0	x_1 0.2	x_2 0.4
y:	y_0 1	y_1 ?	y_2 ?

& $h=0.2$

We know that, the Euler formula

$$y_{n+1} = y_n + h f(x_n, y_n)$$

Put $n=0$

$$y_1 = y_0 + h f(x_0, y_0)$$

$$= 1 + (0.2) f(x_0, y_0)$$

$$= 1 + (0.2)[x_0 + y_0]$$

$$= 1 + (0.2)[0+1]$$

$$= 1 + 0.2$$

$$y_1 = 1.2$$

Put $n=1$

$$y_2 = y_1 + h f(x_1, y_1)$$

$$= 1.2 + (0.2)(x_1 + y_1)$$

$$= 1.2 + (0.2)(0.2 + 1.2)$$

$$= 1.2 + (0.2)(1.4)$$

$$= 1.2 + 0.28$$

$$y_2 = 1.48$$

4) Given $y' = x + y + xy$, $y(0) = 1$, compute 'y' at $x=0.1$ taking $h= 0.05$ by Euler's method

Solution:

Given, $y' = x + y + xy$, $y(0) = 1$

Here

x:	x_0 0	x_1 0.05	x_2 0.1
y:	y_0 1	y_1 ?	y_2 ?

& $h=0.05$

We know that, the Euler formula

$$y_{n+1}=y_n+hf(x_n, y_n)$$

Put $n=0$,

$$y_1=y_0+hf(x_0, y_0)$$

$=1+(0.05)(x_0+y_0+x_0y_0)$

$=1+(0.05)(0+1+(0)(1))$

$=1+0.05$

$y_1=1.05$

Put $n=1$

$$y_2=y_1+hf(x_1, y_1)$$

$=1.05+(0.05)(x_1+y_1+x_1y_1)$

$=1.05+(0.05)(0.05+1.05+(0.05)(1.05))$

$=1.05+(0.05)(1.1525)$

$=1.05+0.057625$

$y_2=1.107625$

5.4 MODIFIED EULER METHOD

The Modified Euler method formula is

$$y_{n+1}=y_n+h\left[f\left(x_n+\frac{h}{2}\right), y_n+\frac{h}{2}f(x_n, y_n)\right]$$

Where $y_{n+1}=f(x_n+h)$

PROBLEMS BASED ON MODIFIED EULER METHOD

1) Compute y at $x=0.25$ by Modified Euler method given $y'=2xy,\ y(0)=1$.

Solution:

Given $f(x,y)=y'=2xy, \quad y(0)=1$

Here

x	x_0 0	x_1 0.25
y:	y_0 1	y_1 ?

& $h = 0.25$

We know that, the Modified Euler formula is,

$$y_{n+1} = y_n + h\left[f\left(x_n + \frac{h}{2}\right), y_n + \frac{h}{2} f(x_n, y_n)\right]$$

Put $n=0$,

$$y_1 = y_0 + h\left[f\left(x_0 + \frac{h}{2}\right), y_0 + \frac{h}{2} f(x_0, y_0)\right]$$

$$= 1 + (0.25)\left[f\left(0 + \frac{0.25}{2},\ 1 + \frac{0.25}{2}(2x_0 y_0)\right)\right]$$

$$= 1 + 0.25\left[f\left(0.125, 1 + \frac{0.25}{2} 2(0)(1)\right)\right]$$

$$= 1 + 0.25\left[f(0.125, 1)\right]$$

$$= 1 + 0.25\left[2(0.125)(1)\right]$$

$$= 1.025(0.25)$$

$$= 1 + 0.0625$$

$$y_1 = 1.0625$$

2) Using modified Euler method to compute $y(0.1)$ with h=0.1 from $y' = y - \frac{2x}{y}$, $y(0) = 1$

Solution:

Given, $y' = f(x, y) = y - \frac{2x}{y}$, $y(0) = 1$

Here

x	x_0 0	x_1 0.1
y:	y_0 1	y_1 ?

& $h = 0.1$

We know that, the Modified Euler formula is,

$$y_{n+1} = y_n + h\left[f\left(x_n + \frac{h}{2}, y_n + \frac{h}{2} f(x_n, y_n) \right) \right]$$

Put n=0,

$$y_1 = y_0 + h\left[f\left(x_0 + \frac{h}{2}, y_0 + \frac{h}{2} f(x_0, y_0) \right) \right]$$

$$= 1 + (0.1)\left[f\left(0 + \frac{0.1}{2},\ 1 + \frac{0.1}{2}\left(y_0 - \frac{2x_0}{y_0} \right) \right) \right]$$

$$= 1 + (0.1)\left[f\left(0.05,\ 1 + \frac{0.05}{2}\left(1 - \frac{2(0)}{1} \right) \right) \right]$$

$$= 1 + (0.1)\left[f(0.05,\ 1 + 0.05(1)) \right]$$

$$= 1 + (0.1)\left[f(0.05,\ 1.05) \right]$$

$$= 1 + (0.1)\left[1.05 - \frac{2(0.05)}{1.05} \right]$$

$$= 1 + (0.1)[1.05 - 0.0952]$$

$$= 1 + 0.09548$$

$$y_1 = 1.09548$$

3) Consider the initial value problem $\frac{dy}{dx} = y - x^2 + 1$, $y(0)$ =0.5 using the modified Euler's method, find $y(0.2)$

Solution:

Given $f(x,y) = \frac{dy}{dx} = y - x^2 + 1, \quad y(0) = 0.5$

Here

x	x_0 0	x_1 0.2
y:	y_0 0.5	y_1 ?

& h=0.2

We know that, the Modified Euler formula is,

$$y_{n+1} = y_n + h\left[f\left(x_n + \frac{h}{2}\right), y_n + \frac{h}{2} f(x_n, y_n)\right]$$

Put n=0,

$$y_1 = y_0 + h\left[f\left(x_0 + \frac{h}{2}\right), y_0 + \frac{h}{2} f(x_0, y_0)\right]$$

$$= 0.5 + (0.2)\left[f\left(0 + \frac{0.2}{2}\right), 0.5 + \frac{0.2}{2} f\left(y_0 - x_0^2 + 1\right)\right]$$

$$= 0.5 + (0.2)\left[f\left(0.1, 0.5 + 0.1(0.5 - 0 + 1)\right)\right]$$

$$= 0.5 + (0.2)[f(0.1, 0.5 + (0.1)(1.5))]$$

$$= 0.5 + (0.2)[f(0.1, (0.5 + 0.15))]$$

$$= 0.5 + (0.2)[f(0.1, 0.65)]$$

$$= 0.5 + (0.2)(0.65 - (0.1)^2 + 1)$$
$$= 0.5 + (0.2)(1.64)$$
$$= 0.5 + 0.328$$

$$y_1 = 0.828$$

4) Using Modified Euler method to find y(0.1), if $\frac{dy}{dx} = x^2 + y^2$, $y(0) = 1$.

Solution:

Given $f(x, y) = \frac{dy}{dx} = x^2 + y^2$, $y(0) = 1$

Here

x:	x_0 0	x_1 0.1
y:	y_0 1	y_1 ?

& h=0.1

We know that, the Modified Euler Method formula,

$$y_{n+1} = y_n + h\left[f\left(x_n + \frac{h}{2}\right), y_n + \frac{h}{2} f(x_n, y_n)\right]$$

Put n=0,

$$y_1 = y_0 + h\left[f\left(x_0 + \frac{h}{2}\right), y_0 + \frac{h}{2} f\left(x_0, y_0\right)\right]$$

$$= 1 + (0.1)\left[f\left(0 + \frac{0.1}{2},\ 1 + \frac{0.1}{2}\left(x_0^2 + y_0^2\right)\right)\right]$$

$$= 1 + (0.1)\left[f(0.5, 1 + 0.05(0 + 1^2))\right]$$

$$= 1 + (0.1)\left[f(0.5, 1 + 0.05(1))\right]$$

$$= 1 + (0.1)\left[f(0.05, 1.05)\right]$$

$$= 1 + (0.1)\left[(0.05)^2 + (1.05)^2\right]$$

$$= 1 + (0.1)\left[0.025 + 1.1025\right]$$

$$= 1 + (0.1)(1.105)$$

$$y_1 = 1 + 0.1105 = 1.1105$$

5) Find y(0.1)) and y(0.2), using modified Euler method given that $\frac{dy}{dx} = 1 - y,\ y(0) = 0$

Solution:

Given $f(x, y) = \frac{dy}{dx} = 1 - y, \quad y(0) = 0$

Here,

x:	x_0 0	x_1 0.1	x_2 0.2
y:	y_0 0	y_1 ?	y_2 ?

& h=0.1

We know that, the Modified Euler formula is,

$$y_{n+1} = y_n + h\left[f\left(x_n + \frac{h}{2}\right), y_n + \frac{h}{2} f\left(x_n, y_n\right)\right] \rightarrow (1)$$

To find y_1 or y(0.1):

Put n=0 in (1)

$$y_1 = y_0 + h\left[f\left(x_0 + \frac{h}{2}\right), y_0 + \frac{h}{2} f\left(x_0, y_0\right)\right]$$

$$= 1 + (0.1)\left[f\left(0 + \frac{0.1}{2},\ 0 + \frac{0.1}{2}\left(1 - y_0\right)\right)\right]$$

$$= (0.1)\left[f(0.05, 0.05(1-0))\right]$$

$$= (0.1)\left[f(0.05, 0.05)\right]$$

$$= (0.1)(1 - 0.05)$$

$$= (0.1)(0.95)$$

$$y_1 = 0.095$$

To find y_2 (or) y(0.2):

Here,

x:	x_0 0	x_1 0.1	x_2 0.2
y:	y_0 0	y_1 0.095	y_2 ?

& h=0.1

Put n=1 in (1)

$$y_2 = y_1 + h\left[f\left(x_1 + \frac{h}{2}\right), y_1 + \frac{h}{2} f\left(x_1, y_1\right)\right]$$

$$= 0.095 + (0.1)\left[f\left(0.1 + \frac{0.1}{2},\ 0.095 + \frac{0.1}{2}\left(1 - y_1\right)\right)\right]$$

$$= 0.095 + (0.1)\left[f(0.1 + 0.05, 0.095 + 0.05(1 - 0.095))\right]$$

$$= 0.095 + (0.1)\left[f(0.15, 0.095 + 0.05(0.91))\right]$$

$$= 0.095 + (0.1)\left[f(0.15, 0.14)\right]$$

$$= 0.095 + (0.1)\left[1 - 0.14\right]$$

$$= 0.095 + (0.1)(0.86)$$

$$= 0.095 + 0.086$$

$$y_2 = 0.181$$

5.5 RUNGE - KUTTA METHOD

The Taylor's series method of solving differential equations numerically is restricted because of the evaluation of the higher order derivatives. Runge-Kutta methods of solving initial value problems do not require the calculations of higher order derivatives and give greater accuracy.

The Runge-Kutta formula possess the advantage of requiring only the function values at some selected points. These methods agree with Taylor series solution upto the terms in h^r where r is called the order of that method.

Fourth Order Runge- Kutta Method

This method is commonly used for solving the initial value problem,

$$\frac{dy}{dx} = f(x,y),\ y(x_0) = y_0$$

In general form of Runge-Kutta method formula can be written as

$$y_{n+1} = y_n + \Delta y$$

$$\Delta y = \frac{1}{6}(k_1 + 2k_2 + 2k_3 + k_4)$$

$$k_1 = hf(x_n, y_n)$$

$$k_2 = hf\left(x_n + \frac{h}{2}, y_n + \frac{k_1}{2}\right)$$

$$k_3 = hf\left(x_n + \frac{h}{2}, y_n + \frac{k_1}{2}\right)$$

$$k_4 = hf(x_n + h, y_n + k_3)$$

> ***Note:***
>
> Error in fourth order Runge-Kuttor method is O(h^5).

PROBLEMS BASED ON RUNGE-KUTTA METHOD

1) Using Runge-Kutta method of fourth order, solve $\frac{dy}{dx} = \frac{y^2 - x^2}{y^2 + x^2}$ with $y(0) = 1$ at x=0.2

Solution:

Given, $f(x,y) = \dfrac{y^2 - x^2}{y^2 + x^2}$ $\quad y(0) = 1$

Here,

x:	x_0 0	x_1 0.2
y:	y_0 1	y_1 ?

& h=0.2

We know that, the Runge-Kutta method formula

$$y_{n+1} = y_n + \Delta y$$

$$\Delta y = \frac{1}{6}(k_1 + 2k_2 + 2k_3 + k_4)$$

$$k_1 = hf(x_n, y_n)$$

$$k_2 = hf\left(x_n + \frac{h}{2}, y_n + \frac{k_1}{2}\right)$$

$$k_3 = hf\left(x_n + \frac{h}{2}, y_n + \frac{k_2}{2}\right)$$

$$k_4 = hf(x_n + h, y_n + k_3)$$

Put n=0, $y_1 = y_0 + \Delta y \quad \rightarrow (1)$

$$\Delta y = \frac{1}{6}(k_1 + 2k_2 + 2k_3 + k_4) \quad \rightarrow (2)$$

$$k_1 = hf(x_0, y_0)$$

$$= (0.2)\left(\frac{y_0^2 - x_0^2}{y_0^2 + x_0^2}\right)$$

$$= (0.2)\left(\frac{1^2 - 0^2}{1^2 + 0^2}\right)$$

$$k_1 = 0.2$$

$$k_2 = hf\left(x_0 + \frac{h}{2}, y_0 + \frac{k_1}{2}\right)$$

$$= (0.2)f\left(0 + \frac{0.2}{2}, 1 + \frac{0.2}{2}\right)$$

$$= (0.2)f(0.1, 1 + 0.1)$$

$$= (0.2)f(0.1, 1.1)$$

$$= (0.2)\left(\frac{(1.1)^2 - (0.1)^2}{(1.1)^2 + (0.1)^2}\right)$$

$$= (0.2)\left(\frac{1.21 - 0.01}{1.21 + 0.01}\right)$$

$$= (0.2)\left(\frac{1.2}{1.22}\right)$$

$$= (0.2)(0.9836)$$

$$k_2 = 0.19672$$

$$k_3 = hf\left(x_0 + \frac{h}{2}, y_0 + \frac{k_2}{2}\right)$$

$$= (0.2)f\left(0 + \frac{0.2}{2}, 1 + \frac{0.19672}{2}\right)$$

$$= (0.2)f(0.1, 1 + 0.09836)$$

$$= (0.2)f(0.1, 1.0983)$$

$$= (0.2)\left(\frac{(1.098)^2 - (0.1)^2}{(1.098)^2 + (0.1)^2}\right)$$

$$= (0.2)\left(\frac{1.2056 - 0.01}{1.2056 + 0.01}\right)$$

$$= (0.2)\left(\frac{1.1956}{1.2156}\right)$$

$$= (0.2)(0.98354)$$

$$k_3 = 0.1967$$

$$k_4 = hf\left(x_0 + h, y_0 + k_3\right)$$

$$= (0.2)f\left(0 + 0.2, 1 + 0.1967\right)$$

$$= (0.2)f(0.2, 1.1967)$$

$$= (0.2)\left(\frac{(1.1967)^2 - (0.2)^2}{(1.1967)^2 + (0.2)^2}\right)$$

$$= (0.2)\left(\frac{1.4320 - 0.04}{1.4320 + 0.04}\right)$$

$$= (0.2)\left(\frac{1.392}{1.472}\right)$$

$$= (0.2)(0.9456)$$

$$k_4 = 0.18913$$

From (2),

$$\Delta y = \frac{1}{6}(k_1 + 2k_2 + 2k_3 + k_4)$$

$$= \frac{1}{6}(0.2 + 2(0.1967) + 2(0.1967) + 0.1891)$$

$$= \frac{1}{6}(1.1759)$$

$$\Delta y = 0.19598$$

From (1)

$$y_1 = y_0 + \Delta y$$

$$= 1 + 0.19598$$

$$y_1 = 1.19598$$

2) Find $y(0.1)$ and $y(0.2)$ correct to 5 decimal places by Runge-Kutta method given by $\frac{dy}{dx} = y - x, \quad y(0) = 2$

Solution:

Given $f(x, y) = y' = y - x, \quad y(0) = 2$

Here,

x:	x_0 0	x_1 0.1	x_2 0.2
y:	y_0 2	y_1 ?	y_2 ?

& $h = 0.1$

We know that, the Runge-Kutta method formula,

$$y_{n+1} = y_n + \Delta y$$

$$\Delta y = \frac{1}{6}(k_1 + 2k_2 + 2k_3 + k_4)$$

$$k_1 = hf(x_n, y_n)$$

$$k_2 = hf\left(x_n + \frac{h}{2}, y_n + \frac{k_1}{2}\right)$$

$$k_3 = hf\left(x_n + \frac{h}{2}, y_n + \frac{k_2}{2}\right)$$

$$k_4 = hf(x_n + h, y_n + k_3)$$

To find y_1 (or) $y(0.1)$:

Put n=0,

$$y_1 = y_0 + \Delta y \qquad \to (1)$$

$$\Delta y = \frac{1}{6}(k_1 + 2k_2 + 2k_3 + k_4) \qquad \to (2)$$

$$k_1 = hf(x_0, y_0)$$

$$= (0.1)(y_0 - x_0)$$
$$= (0.1)(2-0)$$
$$= (0.1)(2)$$

$$k_1 = 0.2$$

$$k_2 = hf\left(x_0 + \frac{h}{2}, y_0 + \frac{k_1}{2}\right)$$

$$= (0.1)f\left(0 + \frac{0.1}{2}, 2 + \frac{0.2}{2}\right)$$

$$= (0.1)f(0.05,\ 2+0.1)$$

$$= (0.1)f(0.05,\ 2.1)$$

$$= (0.1)(2.1-0.05)$$
$$= (0.1)(2.05)$$

$$k_2 = 0.205$$

$$k_3 = hf\left(x_0 + \frac{h}{2}, y_0 + \frac{k_2}{2}\right)$$

$$= (0.1)f\left(0 + \frac{0.1}{2}, 2 + \frac{0.205}{2}\right)$$

$$= (0.1)f(0.05,\ 2+0.1025)$$

$$= (0.1)f(0.05,\ 2.1025)$$
$$= (0.1)(2.1025-0.05)$$
$$= (0.1)(2.0525)$$

$$k_3 = 0.20525$$

$$k_4 = hf(x_0 + h, y_0 + k_3)$$
$$= (0.1) f(0 + 0.1,\ 2 + 0.20525)$$
$$= (0.1) f(0.1,\ 2.20525)$$
$$= (0.1)(2.20525 - 0.1)$$
$$= (0.1)(2.10525)$$
$$k_4 = 0.21052$$

From (2) $\Delta y = \frac{1}{6}(k_1 + 2k_2 + 2k_3 + k_4)$

$$= \frac{1}{6}(0.2 + 2(0.205) + 2(0.2052) + 0.21052)$$
$$= \frac{1}{6}(1.23102)$$
$$\Delta y = 0.20517$$

From (1) $y_1 = y_0 + \Delta y$

$$=2+0.20517$$
$$y_1 = 2.20517$$

To find y_2 (or) $y(0.2)$

Here,

x:	x_0 0	x_1 0.1	x_2 0.2
y:	y_0 2	y_1 2.20517	y_2 ?

Put n=1,

$$y_2 = y_1 + \Delta y \qquad \rightarrow (3)$$
$$\Delta y = \frac{1}{6}(k_1 + 2k_2 + 2k_3 + k_4) \qquad \rightarrow (4)$$
$$k_1 = hf(x_1, y_1)$$
$$= (0.1)(y_1 - x_1)$$
$$= (0.1)(2.20517 - 0.1)$$
$$= (0.1)(2.10517)$$
$$k_1 = 0.21051$$

$$k_2 = hf\left(x_1+\frac{h}{2},\ y_1+\frac{k_1}{2}\right)$$

$$=(0.1)f\left(0.1+\frac{0.1}{2},\ 2.20517+\frac{0.21051}{2}\right)$$

$$=(0.1)f(0.1+0.05,\ 2.20517+0.10525)$$

$$=(0.1)f(0.15,\ 2.31042)$$

$$=(0.1)(2.31042-0.15)$$

$$=(0.1)(2.16042)$$

$$k_2 = 0.21604$$

$$k_3 = hf\left(x_1+\frac{h}{2}, y_1+\frac{k_2}{2}\right)$$

$$=(0.1)f\left(0.1+\frac{0.1}{2},\ 2.20517+\frac{0.21604}{2}\right)$$

$$=(0.1)f(0.1+0.05,\ 2.20517+0.10802)$$

$$=(0.1)f(1.05,\ 2.31319)$$

$$=(0.1)(2.31319-0.15)$$

$$=(0.1)(2.16319)$$

$$k_3 = 0.21631$$

$$k_4 = hf(x_1+h, y_1+k_3)$$

$$=(0.1)f(0.1+0.1,\ 2.20517+0.21631)$$

$$=(0.1)f(0.2,\ 2.42148)$$

$$=(0.1)(2.42148-0.2)$$

$$=(0.1)(2.22148)$$

$$k_4 = 0.22214$$

From (4) $\Delta y = \frac{1}{6}(k_1+2k_2+2k_3+k_4)$

$$=\frac{1}{6}(0.21051+2(0.21604)+2(0.21631)+0.22214)$$

$$=\frac{1}{6}(1.29738)$$

$$\Delta y = 0.21623$$

From (3) $y_2 = y_1 + \Delta y$

$$=2.20517 + 0.21623$$

$$y_2 = 2.42140$$

3) Given $\dfrac{dy}{dx} = x^3 + y,\ y(0) = 2$ compute $y(0.2)$, $y(0.4)$ and $y(0.6)$ by Runge-Kutta method of fourth order.

Solution:

Given , $f(x,y) = \dfrac{dy}{dx} = x^3 + y,\ y(0) = 2$

Here,

x:	x_0 0	x_1 0.2	x_2 0.4	x_3 0.6
y:	y_0 2	y_1 ?	y_2 ?	y_3 ?

& h=0.2

We know that the Runge-Kutta method formula,

$$y_{n+1} = y_n + \Delta y$$

$$\Delta y = \frac{1}{6}(k_1 + 2k_2 + 2k_3 + k_4)$$

$$k_1 = hf(x_n, y_n)$$

$$k_2 = hf\left(x_n + \frac{h}{2}, y_n + \frac{k_1}{2}\right)$$

$$k_3 = hf\left(x_n + \frac{h}{2}, y_n + \frac{k_2}{2}\right)$$

$$k_4 = hf\left(x_n + h, y_n + k_3\right)$$

To find y_1 (or) $y(0.2)$:

Put n=0, $y_1 = y_0 + \Delta y$ $\rightarrow (1)$

$$\Delta y = \frac{1}{6}(k_1 + 2k_2 + 2k_3 + k_4) \qquad \rightarrow (2)$$

$$k_1 = hf(x_0, y_0)$$

$$= (0.2)(x_0^3 + y_0)$$
$$= (0.2)(0+2)$$
$$k_1 = 0.4$$

$$k_2 = hf\left(x_0 + \frac{h}{2}, y_0 + \frac{k_1}{2}\right)$$
$$= (0.2)f\left(0+\frac{0.2}{2}, 2+\frac{0.4}{2}\right)$$
$$= (0.2)f(0.1, 2+0.2)$$
$$= (0.2)f(0.1, 2.2)$$
$$= (0.2)\left((0.1)^3 + 2.2\right)$$
$$= (0.2)(0.001+2.2)$$
$$= (0.2)(2.201)$$
$$k_2 = 0.4402$$

$$k_3 = hf\left(x_0 + \frac{h}{2}, y_0 + \frac{k_2}{2}\right)$$
$$= (0.2)f\left(0+\frac{0.2}{2}, 2+\frac{0.4402}{2}\right)$$
$$= (0.1)f(0.1, 2+0.2201)$$
$$= (0.2)f(0.1, 2.2201)$$
$$= (0.2)\left((0.1)^3 + 2.2201\right)$$
$$= (0.2)(0.001+2.2201)$$
$$= (0.2)(2.2211)$$
$$k_3 = 0.44422$$

$$k_4 = hf(x_0 + h, y_0 + k_3)$$
$$= (0.2)f(0+0.2, 2+0.44422)$$
$$= (0.2)f(0.2, 2.44422)$$
$$= (0.2)\left((0.2)^3 + 2.44422\right)$$
$$= (0.2)(0.008+2.44422)$$
$$= (0.2)(2.45222)$$
$$k_4 = 0.49044$$

From (2) $\Delta y = \frac{1}{6}(k_1 + 2k_2 + 2k_3 + k_4)$

$$= \frac{1}{6}(0.4 + 2(0.4402) + 2(0.4442) + 0.49044)$$

$$= \frac{1}{6}(2.6592)$$

$$\Delta y = 0.44321$$

From (1), $y_1 = y_0 + \Delta y$

$$=2+0.44321$$

$$y_1 = 2.44321$$

To find y_2 (or) $y(0.4)$:

Here,

x:	x_0 0	x_1 0.2	x_2 0.4	x_3 0.6
y:	y_0 2	y_1 2.4432	y_2 ?	y_3 ?

& $h=0.2$

put $n=1$, $\qquad y_2 = y_1 + \Delta y \qquad \rightarrow (3)$

$$\Delta y = \frac{1}{6}(k_1 + 2k_2 + 2k_3 + k_4) \qquad \rightarrow (4)$$

$$k_1 = hf(x_1, y_1)$$

$$= (0.2) f(0.2,\ 2.44321)$$

$$= (0.2)\left((0.2)^3 + 2.44321\right)$$

$$= (0.2)(0.008 + 2.44321)$$

$$= (0.2)(2.45121)$$

$$k_1 = 0.49024$$

$$k_2 = hf\left(x_1 + \frac{h}{2},\ y_1 + \frac{k_1}{2}\right)$$

$$= (0.2) f\left(0.2 + \frac{0.2}{2},\ 2.44321 + \frac{0.49024}{2}\right)$$

$$= (0.2) f\left(0.2 + 0.1, 2.44321 + 0.24512\right)$$

$$= (0.2) f(0.3, 2.6883)$$

$$= (0.2)\left((0.3)^2 + 2.6883\right)$$

$$= (0.2)(0.027 + 2.6883)$$

$$= (0.2)(2.7153)$$

$$k_2 = 0.5430$$

$$k_3 = hf\left(x_1 + \frac{h}{2}, y_1 + \frac{k_2}{2}\right)$$

$$= (0.2) f\left(0.2 + \frac{0.2}{2}, 2.44321 + \frac{0.5430}{2}\right)$$

$$= (0.2) f(0.2 + 0.1, 2.44321 + 0.2715)$$

$$= (0.2) f(0.3, 2.7145)$$

$$= (0.2)\left((0.3)^3 + 2.7145\right)$$

$$= (0.2)(0.027 + 2.7145)$$

$$= (0.2)(2.7415)$$

$$k_3 = 0.5483$$

$$k_4 = hf\left(x_1 + h, y_1 + k_3\right)$$

$$= (0.2) f(0.2 + 0.2, 2.44321 + 0.5483)$$

$$= (0.2) f(0.4, 2.9913)$$

$$= (0.2)\left((0.4)^3 + 2.9913\right)$$

$$= (0.2)(0.064 + 2.9913)$$

$$= (0.2)(3.0553)$$

$$k_4 = 0.6111$$

From (4) $\Delta y = \frac{1}{6}\left(k_1 + 2k_2 + 2k_3 + k_4\right)$

$$= \frac{1}{6}\left(0.4902 + 2(0.5430) + 2(0.5483) + 0.6111\right)$$

$$= \frac{1}{6}(3.2839)$$

$$\Delta y = 0.5473$$

From (3) $y_2 = y_1 + \Delta y$

$$=2.4432 + 0.5493$$

$$y_2 = 2.9925$$

To find y_3 (or) $y(0.6)$:

Here

x:	x_0 0	x_1 0.2	x_2 0.4	x_3 0.6
y:	y_0 2	y_1 2.4432	y_2 2.9925	y_3 ?

& h=0.2

Put n=2, $y_3 = y_2 + \Delta y$

$$\Delta y = \frac{1}{6}\left(k_1 + 2k_2 + 2k_3 + k_4\right)$$

$$k_1 = hf(x_2, y_2)$$
$$= (0.2)(0.4,\ 2.9925)$$
$$= (0.2)\left((0.4)^3 + 2.9925\right)$$
$$= (0.2)(0.064 + 2.9925)$$
$$= (0.2)(3.0565)$$
$$k_1 = 0.6113$$

$$k_2 = hf\left(x_2 + \frac{h}{2},\ y_2 + \frac{k_1}{2}\right)$$

$$= (0.2)f\left(0.4 + \frac{0.2}{2},\ 2.9925 + \frac{0.6113}{2}\right)$$

$$= (0.2)f\left(0.4 + 0.1, 2.9925 + 0.30565\right)$$
$$= (0.2)f\left(0.5,\ 3.29815\right)$$

$$= (0.2)\left((0.5)^3 + 3.29815\right)$$
$$= (0.2)(0.125 + 3.29815)$$
$$= (0.2)(3.42315)$$

$$k_2 = 0.6846$$

$$k_3 = hf\left(x_2 + \frac{h}{2}, y_2 + \frac{k_2}{2}\right)$$

$$= (0.2)f\left(0.4+\frac{0.2}{2}, 2.9925+\frac{0.6846}{2}\right)$$

$$= (0.2)f(0.4+0.1, 2.9925+0.34231)$$

$$= (0.2)f(0.5, 3.33481)$$

$$= (0.2)\left((0.5)^3+3.33481\right)$$

$$= (0.2)(0.125+3.33481)$$

$$= (0.2)(3.45981)$$

$$k_3 = 0.6919$$

$$k_4 = hf\left(x_2+h, y_2+k_3\right)$$

$$= (0.2)f(0.4+0.2, 2.9925+0.6919)$$

$$= (0.2)f(0.6, 3.6844)$$

$$= (0.2)\left((0.6)^3+3.6844\right)$$

$$= (0.2)(0.216+3.6844)$$

$$= (0.2)(3.9004)$$

$$k_4 = 0.7801$$

From (6) $\Delta y = \frac{1}{6}\left(k_1+2k_2+2k_3+k_4\right)$

$$= \frac{1}{6}\left(0.6113+2(0.6846)+2(0.6919)+0.78008\right)$$

$$= \frac{1}{6}(4.14438)$$

$$\Delta y = 0.69073$$

From (5) $y_3 = y_2 + \Delta y$

$$=2.9925 + 0.69073$$

$$y_3 = 3.6832$$

4) Apply fourth order Runge-Kutta method to determine $y(0.2)$ with h=0.1 from $\frac{dy}{dx} = x^2 + y^2,\ y(0) = 1$

Solution:

Given, $f(x,y) = \frac{dy}{dx} = x^2 + y^2,\ y(0) = 1$

Here,

x:	x_0 0	x_1 0.1	x_2 0.2
y:	y_0 1	y_1 ?	y_2 ?

& h=0.1

We know that, the R-K method formula,

$$y_{n+1} = y_n + \Delta y$$

$$\Delta y = \frac{1}{6}(k_1 + 2k_2 + 2k_3 + k_4)$$

$$k_1 = hf(x_n, y_n)$$
$$k_2 = hf\left(x_n + \frac{h}{2}, y_n + \frac{k_1}{2}\right)$$
$$k_3 = hf\left(x_n + \frac{h}{2}, y_n + \frac{k_2}{2}\right)$$
$$k_4 = hf(x_n + h, y_n + k_3)$$

To find y_1(or) $y(0.1)$:

Put n=0, $y_1 = y_0 + \Delta y \quad \rightarrow (1)$

$$\Delta y = \frac{1}{6}(k_1 + 2k_2 + 2k_3 + k_4) \quad \rightarrow (2)$$

$$k_1 = hf(x_0, y_0)$$
$$= (0.2)(x_0^2 + y_0^2)$$
$$= (0.1)(0+1)$$
$$k_1 = 0.1$$

$$k_2 = hf\left(x_0 + \frac{h}{2}, y_0 + \frac{k_1}{2}\right)$$

$$= (0.1) f\left(0 + \frac{0.1}{2}, 1 + \frac{0.1}{2}\right)$$

$$= (0.1) f(0.0.5, 1 + 0.0.5)$$

$$= (0.1) f(0.05,\ 1.05)$$

$$= (0.1)\left((0.05)^2 + (1.05)^2\right)$$

$$= (0.1)(0.0025 + 1.1025)$$

$$= (0.1)(1.1050)$$

$$k_2 = 0.1105$$

$$k_3 = hf\left(x_0 + \frac{h}{2}, y_0 + \frac{k_2}{2}\right)$$

$$= (0.1) f\left(0 + \frac{0.1}{2},\ 1 + \frac{0.1105}{2}\right)$$

$$= (0.1) f(0.05, 1 + 0.0552)$$

$$= (0.1) f(0.05, 1.0552)$$

$$= (0.1)\left((0.05)^2 + (1.0552)^2\right)$$

$$= (0.1)(0.0025 + 1.11355)$$

$$= (0.1)(1.11605)$$

$$k_3 = 0.111605$$

$$k_4 = hf\left(x_0 + h, y_0 + k_3\right)$$

$$= (0.1) f(0 + 0.1, 1 + 0.111605)$$

$$= (0.1) f(0.1, 1.111605)$$

$$= (0.1)\left((0.1)^2 + (1.111605)^2\right)$$

$$= (0.1)(0.01 + 1.2356)$$

$$= (0.1)(1.24565)$$

$$k_4 = 0.12456$$

From (2) $\Delta y = \frac{1}{6}(k_1 + 2k_2 + 2k_3 + k_4)$

$$= \frac{1}{6}(0.1 + 2(0.1105) + 2(0.11160) + 0.12456)$$

$$= \frac{1}{6}(0.6687)$$

$$\Delta y = 0.11145$$

From (1), $y_1 = y_0 + \Delta y$

$$= 1 + 0.11145$$

$$y_1 = 1.11145$$

To find y_2 (or) $y(0.2)$:

Here,

x:	x_0 0	x_1 0.1	x_2 0.2
y:	y_0 1	y_1 1.11145	y_2 ?

& h=0.1

put n=1, $\quad y_2 = y_1 + \Delta y \quad \rightarrow (3)$

$$\Delta y = \frac{1}{6}(k_1 + 2k_2 + 2k_3 + k_4) \quad \rightarrow (4)$$

$$k_1 = hf(x_1, y_1)$$

$$= (0.1) f(0.1,\ 1.11145)$$

$$= (0.1)\left((0.1)^2 + (1.11145)^2\right)$$

$$= (0.1)(0.01 + 1.2353)$$

$$= (0.1)(1.2453)$$

$$k_1 = 0.12453$$

$$k_2 = hf\left(x_1 + \frac{h}{2},\ y_1 + \frac{k_1}{2}\right)$$

$$= (0.1) f\left(0.1 + \frac{0.1}{2},\ 1.11145 + \frac{0.1245}{2}\right)$$

$$= (0.1) f(0.1 + 0.05,\ 1.11145 + 0.0622)$$

$$= (0.1) f(0.15,\ 1.1737)$$

$$= (0.1)\left((0.15)^2 + (1.1737)^2\right)$$
$$= (0.1)(0.0225 + 1.3776)$$
$$= (0.1)(1.4001)$$
$$k_2 = 0.14001$$

$$k_3 = hf\left(x_1 + \frac{h}{2}, y_1 + \frac{k_2}{2}\right)$$
$$= (0.1)f\left(0.1 + \frac{0.1}{2}, 1.11145 + \frac{0.14001}{2}\right)$$
$$= (0.1)f(0.1 + 0.05, 1.11145 + 0.0700)$$
$$= (0.1)f(0.15, 1.18145)$$
$$= (0.1)\left((0.15)^2 + (1.18145)^2\right)$$
$$= (0.1)(0.0225 + 1.3958)$$
$$= (0.1)(1.4183)$$
$$k_3 = 0.14183$$

$$k_4 = hf\left(x_1 + h, y_1 + k_3\right)$$
$$= (0.1)f(0.1 + 0.1, 1.11145 + 0.14183)$$
$$= (0.1)f(0.2, 1.2532)$$
$$= (0.1)\left((0.2)^2 + (1.2532)^2\right)$$
$$= (0.1)(0.04 + 1.5707)$$
$$= (0.1)(1.6107)$$
$$k_4 = 0.16107$$

From (4) $\Delta y = \frac{1}{6}\left(k_1 + 2k_2 + 2k_3 + k_4\right)$

$$= \frac{1}{6}\left(0.1245 + 2(0.14001) + 2(0.1418) + 0.16107\right)$$
$$= \frac{1}{6}(0.84919)$$
$$\Delta y = 0.1415$$

From (3) $y_2 = y_1 + \Delta y$

$$=1.11145 + 0.145$$

$$y_2 = 1.2529$$

5) Find $y(0.7)$ & $y(0.8)$ given that $y' = y - x^2$, $y(0.6) = 1.7379$ by using Runge-kutta method of fourth order. Take h=0.1.

Solution:

Given $f(x,y) = \frac{dy}{dx} = y - x^2, \quad y(0.6) = 1.7379$

	x_0	x_1	x_2
x:	0.6	0.7	0.8
	y_0	y_1	y_2
y:	1.7370	?	?

To find y_1 or $y(0.7)$:

Put n =0, $y_1 = y_0 + \Delta y$

$$k_1 = hf(x_0, y_0) = (0.1)[y_0 - x_0^2]$$
$$= (0.1)[1.7379 - (0.6)^2]$$
$$= 0.13779$$

$$k_2 = hf\left(x_0 + \frac{h}{2}, y_0 + \frac{k_1}{2}\right)$$
$$= (0.1)f\left[0.6 + \frac{0.1}{2}, 1.7379 + \frac{0.13779}{2}\right]$$
$$= (0.1)\left[1.806795 - (0.65)^2\right]$$
$$= 0.13843$$

$$k_3 = hf\left(x_0 + \frac{h}{2}, y_0 + \frac{k_2}{2}\right)$$
$$= (0.1)f\left[0.6 + \frac{0.1}{2},\ 1.7379 + \frac{0.13843}{2}\right]$$
$$= (0.1)f\left[0.65, 1.807115\right]$$
$$= (0.1)\left[1.807115 - (0.65)^2\right]$$

$$= 0.13846$$

$$k_4 = hf(x_0 + h, y_0 + k_3)$$
$$= (0.1)f[0.6 + 0.1, 1.7379 + 0.13846]$$
$$= (0.1)f[0.7, 1.87636]$$
$$= (0.1)\left[1.87636 - (0.7)^2\right]$$
$$= 0.13864$$

$$\Delta y = \frac{1}{6}[k_1 + 2k_2 + 2k_3 + k_4]$$
$$= \frac{1}{6}[0.13779 + 2(0.13843) + 2(0.13846) + 0.13864]$$
$$= 0.13837$$

$$y_1 = y(0.7) = y_0 + \Delta y$$
$$= 1.7379 + 0.13837 = 1.87627$$
$$y_1 = 1.87627$$

To find y(0.8)

	x_0	x_1	x_2
x:	0.6	0.7	0.8
	y_0	y_1	y_2
y:	1.7379	1.876	?

$$\therefore x_1 = 0.7, \quad y_1 = 1.876, \Rightarrow \boxed{y(0.7) = 1.876}$$

$$k_1 = hf(x_1, y_1) = (0.1)f[0.7, \ 1.876]$$
$$= (0.1)[1.876 - (0.7)^2]$$
$$= 0.1386$$

$$k_2 = hf\left[x_1 + \frac{h}{2}, y_1 + \frac{k_1}{2}\right]$$
$$= (0.1)f\left[0.7 + \frac{0.1}{2}, 1.876 + \frac{0.1386}{2}\right]$$
$$= (0.1)f[0.75, 1.9453]$$
$$= (0.1)\left[1.9453 - (0.75)^2\right] = 0.13828$$

$$k_3 = hf\left[x_1 + \frac{h}{2}, y_1 + \frac{k_2}{2}\right]$$

$$= (0.1)f\left[0.75+, 1.876 + \frac{0.1328}{2}\right]$$

$$= (0.1)f[0.75, 1.94514]$$

$$= (0.1)\left[1.94514 - (0.75)^2\right] = 0.138264$$

$$k_4 = hf\left[x_1 + h, y_1 + k_3\right]$$

$$= (0.1)f[0.7 + 0.1, 1.876 + 0.138264]$$

$$= (0.1)f[0.8, 2.014264]$$

$$= (0.1)\left[2.014264 - (0.8)^2\right] = 0.1374264$$

$$\Delta y = \frac{1}{6}\left[k_1 + 2k_2 + 2k_3 + k_4\right]$$

$$= \frac{1}{6}\left[0.136 + 2(0.13828) + 2(0.138264) + 0.1374264\right]$$

$$= 0.138186$$

$$y_2 = y(0.8) = y_1 + \Delta y = 1.876 + 0.138186 = 2.014186$$

$$y_2 = 2.0142$$

TYPES OF MULTI-STEP METHOD

Predictor- Corrector Method

Introduction:

Predictor-corrector methods are methods which require four function values at x_n, x_{n-1}, x_{n-2} and x_{n-3} for the computation of the function value at x_{n+1}. A predictor is used to find the value of y at x_{n+1} and then a corrector formula is used to improve the value of y_{n+1}.

The following two methods are discussed in this chapter,

1) Milne's method
2) Adam's method

5.6 MILNE'S PREDICTOR-CORRECTOR METHOD

In general, Milne's predictor formula is

$$y_{n+1}, P = y_{n-3} + \frac{4h}{3}\left(2y'_{n-2} - y'_{n-1} + 2y'_n\right)$$

and Milne's corrector formula is

$$y_{n+1}, C = y_{n-1} + \frac{h}{3}\left(y'_{n-1} + 4y'_n + y'_{n+1}\right)$$

> *Note:*
>
> 1) Error in the Milne's Predictor formula is $\frac{14h^5}{45}\Delta^4 y'_0$
>
> 2) Error in the Milne's corrector formula is $-\frac{h^5}{90}\Delta^4 y'_0$

PROBLEMS BASED ON MILNE'S METHOD

1) Given $\frac{dy}{dx} = x^3 + y$, $y(0) = 2$. The values of $y(0.2) = 2.073$, $y(0.4) = 2.452$ and $y(0.6) = 3.023$ are got by R-K method of fourth order. Find $y(0.8)$ by Milne's Predictor-corrector method taking h=0.2

Solution:

Given $y' = \frac{dy}{dx} = x^3 + y$

Here,

x:	x_0 0	x_1 0.2	x_2 0.4	x_3 0.6	x_4 0.8
y:	y_0 2	y_1 2.073	y_2 2.452	y_3 3.023	y_4 ?

& h=0.2

We know that, the Milne's Predictor-corrector formula

$$y_{n+1,\,P} = y_{n-3} + \frac{4h}{3}\left(2y'_{n-2} - y'_{n-1} + 2y'_n\right)$$

$$y_{n+1,\,C} = y_{n-1} + \frac{h}{3}\left(y'_{n-1} + 4y'_n + y'_{n+1}\right)$$

Milne's Predictor formula for y_4:

$$y_{4,\,P} = y_0 + \frac{4h}{3}\left(2y'_1 - y'_2 + 2y'_3\right) \qquad \rightarrow (1)$$

$$y' = x^3 + y$$

$$y'_1 = x_1^3 + y_1 = (0.2)^3 + 2.073 = 0.008 + 2.073 = 2.081$$

$$y'_2 = x_2^3 + y_2 = (0.4)^3 + 2.452 = 0.064 + 2.452 = 2.516$$

$$y_3' = x_3^3 + y_3 = (0.6)^3 + 3.023 = 0.216 + 3.023 = 3.239$$

From (1), $y_{4,P} = 2 + \frac{4(0.2)}{3}[2(2.081) - 2.516 + 2(3.239)]$

$$= 2 + \frac{0.8}{3}(8.124)$$

$$= 2 + (0.2666)(8.124)$$

$$= 2 + 2.1664$$

$$y_{4,P} = 4.1664$$

Milne's Corrector formula for y_4:

$$y_{4,C} = y_2 + \frac{h}{3}(y_2' + 4y_3' + y_4') \quad \rightarrow (2)$$

$$y' = x^3 + y$$

$$y_4' = x_4^3 + y_4 = (0.8)^3 + 4.1664 = 0.512 + 4.1664 = 4.6784$$

From (2), $y_{4,C} = 2.452 + \frac{0.2}{3}[2.5164 + 4(3.239) + 4.6784]$

$$= 2.452 + \frac{0.2}{3}(20.1504)$$

$$= 2.452 + \frac{4.03008}{3}$$

$$= 2.452 + 1.34336$$

$$y_{4,C} = 3.7954$$

2) Using Milne's method, find $y(4,4)$ given $5xy' + y^2 - 2 = 0$, $y(4) = 1$, $y(4.1) = 1.0049$, $y(4.2) = 1.0097$ and $y(4.3)=1.0143$.

Solution:

Given

$$5xy' + y^2 - 2 = 0$$

$$5xy' = -y^2 + 2$$

$$5xy' = 2 - y^2$$

$$y' = \frac{2 - y^2}{5x}$$

Here,

x:	x_0 4	x_1 4.1	x_2 4.2	x_3 4.3	x_4 4.4
y:	y_0 1	y_1 1.0049	y_2 1.0097	y_3 1.0143	y_4 ?

& $h=0.1$

We know that, the Milne's method formula,

$$y_{n+1,\,P} = y_{n-3} + \frac{4h}{3}\left(2y'_{n-2} - y'_{n-1} + 2y'_n\right)$$

$$y_{n+1,\,C} = y_{n-1} + \frac{h}{3}\left(y'_{n-1} + 4y'_n + y'_{n+1}\right)$$

Milne's Predictor formula for y_4:

$$y_{4,\,P} = y_0 + \frac{4h}{3}\left(2y'_1 - y'_2 + 2y'_3\right) \qquad \rightarrow (1)$$

$$y' = \frac{2-y^2}{5x}$$

$$y'_1 = \frac{2-y_1^2}{5x_1} = \frac{2-(1.0049)^2}{5(4.1)} = \frac{2-1.0098}{20.5} = 0.0483$$

$$y'_2 = \frac{2-y_2^2}{5x_2} = \frac{2-(1.0097)^2}{5(4.2)} = \frac{2-1.0194}{21} = 0.0466$$

$$y'_3 = \frac{2-y_3^2}{5x_3} = \frac{2-(1.0143)^2}{5(4.3)} = \frac{2-1.0288}{21.5} = 0.0451$$

From (1) $y_{4,\,P} = 1 + \frac{4(0.1)}{3}\left[2(0.0483) - 0.0466 + 2(0.0451)\right]$

$$= 1 + \frac{0.4}{3}(0.1402)$$

$$= 1 + \frac{0.0560}{3}$$

$$= 1 + 0.01869$$

$$y_{4,\,P} = 1.01869$$

Milne's Corrector formula for y_4:

$$y_{4,\,C} = y_2 + \frac{h}{3}\left(y'_2 + 4y'_3 + y'_4\right) \qquad \rightarrow (2)$$

$$y' = \frac{2-y^2}{5x}$$

$$y_4' = \frac{2-y_4^2}{5x_4} = \frac{2-(1.0186)^2}{5(4.4)} = \frac{2-1.0375}{22} = 0.0437$$

From (2) $y_{4,C} = 1.0097 + \frac{0.1}{3}[0.0466 + 4(0.0451) + 0.0437]$

$$= 1.0097 + \frac{0.1}{3}(0.2707)$$

$$= 1.0097 + \frac{0.02707}{3}$$

$$= 1.0097 + 0.00902$$

$$y_{4,C} = 1.01872$$

3) Using Milne's Predictor-corrector method, find *y*(2), if *y(x)* is the solution of $\frac{dy}{dx} = \frac{1}{2}(x+y)$ given *y*(0)=2, *y*(0.5)=2.636, *y*(1)=3.595 and *y*(1.5)=4.968.

Solution:

Given $y' = \frac{1}{2}(x+y)$

Here,

x:	x_0 0	x_1 0.5	x_2 1	x_3 1.5	x_4 2
y:	y_0 2	y_1 2.636	y_2 3.595	y_3 4.968	y_4 ?

& h=0.5

We know that, the Milne's Predictor-corrector formula

$$y_{n+1,P} = y_{n-3} + \frac{4h}{3}(2y'_{n-2} - y'_{n-1} + 2y'_n)$$

$$y_{n+1,C} = y_{n-1} + \frac{h}{3}(y'_{n-1} + 4y'_n + y'_{n+1})$$

Milne's Predictor formula for y_4:

$$y_{4,P} = y_0 + \frac{4h}{3}(2y'_1 - y'_2 + 2y'_3) \qquad \rightarrow (1)$$

$$y' = \frac{1}{2}(x+y)$$

$$y_1' = \frac{1}{2}(x_1+y_1) = \frac{1}{2}(0.5+2.636) = \frac{1}{2}(3.136) = 1.568$$

$$y_2' = \frac{1}{2}(x_2+y_2) = \frac{1}{2}(1+3.595) = \frac{1}{2}(4.595) = 2.2975$$

$$y_3' = \frac{1}{2}(x_3+y_3) = \frac{1}{2}(1.5+4.968) = \frac{1}{2}(6.468) = 3.234$$

From (1)

$$y_{4,P} = 2 + \frac{4(0.5)}{3}\left(2(1.568) - 2.2975 + 2(3.234)\right)$$

$$= 2 + \frac{2}{3}(7.3065)$$

$$= 2 + \frac{14.613}{3}$$

$$= 2 + 4.871$$

$$y_{4,P} = 6.871$$

Milne's Corrector formula for y_4:

$$y_{4,C} = y_2 + \frac{h}{3}\left(y_2' + 4y_3' + y_4'\right) \qquad \rightarrow (2)$$

$$y' = \frac{1}{2}(x+y)$$

$$y_4' = \frac{1}{2}(x_4+y_4) = \frac{1}{2}(2+6.871) = \frac{1}{2}(8.871) = 4.435$$

From (2)

$$y_4 = 3.595 + \frac{0.5}{3}(2.2975 + 4(3.234) + 4.435)$$

$$= 3.595 + \frac{0.5}{3}(19.669)$$

$$= 3.595 + \frac{9.8345}{3}$$

$$= 3.595 + 3.2781$$

$$y_{4,C} = 6.8732$$

4) Given $y' = \frac{1}{x+y}$, $y(0) = 2$, $y(0.2) = 2.0933$, $y(0.4) = 2.1755$, and $y(0.6) = 2.2493$.

Find $y(0.8)$ by Milne's Predictor-corrector method.

Solution:

Given, $y' = \frac{1}{x+y}$,

Here,

x:	x_0 0	x_1 0.2	x_2 0.4	x_3 0.6	x_4 0.8
y:	y_0 2	y_1 2.0933	y_2 2.1755	y_3 2.2493	y_4 ?

& h=0.2

We know that, the Milne's method formula

$$y_{n+1,\,P} = y_{n-3} + \frac{4h}{3}\left(2y'_{n-2} - y'_{n-1} + 2y'_n\right)$$

$$y_{n+1,\,C} = y_{n-1} + \frac{h}{3}\left(y'_{n-1} + 4y'_n + y'_{n+1}\right)$$

Milne's Predictor formula for y_4:

$$y_{4,\,P} = y_0 + \frac{4h}{3}\left(2y'_1 - y'_2 + 2y'_3\right) \qquad \rightarrow (1)$$

$$y' = \frac{1}{x+y}$$

$$y'_1 = \frac{1}{x_1 + y_1} = \frac{1}{0.2 + 2.0933} = \frac{1}{2.2933} = 0.4361$$

$$y'_2 = \frac{1}{x_2 + y_2} = \frac{1}{0.4 + 2.1755} = \frac{1}{2.5755} = 0.3882$$

$$y'_3 = \frac{1}{x_3 + y_3} = \frac{1}{0.6 + 2.2493} = \frac{1}{2.8493} = 0.3509$$

From (1)

$$y_{4,\,P} = 2 + \frac{4(0.2)}{3}\left(2(0.4361) - 0.3882 + 2(0.3509)\right)$$

$$= 2 + \frac{0.8}{3}(1.1859)$$

$$= 2 + \frac{0.9487}{3}$$

$$= 2 + 0.3162$$

$$y_{4,\,P} = 2.3162$$

Milne's Corrector formula for y_4:

$$y_4, C = y_2 + \frac{h}{3}(y_2' + 4y_3' + y_4') \quad \rightarrow (2)$$

$$y' = \frac{1}{x+y},$$

$$y_4' = \frac{1}{x_4 + y_4} = \frac{1}{0.8 + 2.3162} = \frac{1}{3.1162} = 0.3209$$

From (2)

$$y_4 = 2.1755 + \frac{0.2}{3}(0.3882 + 4(0.3509) + 0.3209)$$

$$= 2.1755 + \frac{0.2}{3}(2.1127)$$

$$= 2.1755 + 0.1408$$

$$y_{4}, _C = 2.31634$$

5) Determine the value of $y(0,4)$ using Milne's method given $y' = xy + y^2$, $y(0)$=1. Use Taylor's series to get the values of $y(0.1)$, $y(0.2)$ and $y(0.3)$.

Solution:

Given $y' = xy + y^2$

Here,

x:	x_0 0	x_1 0.1	x_2 0.2	x_3 0.3	x_4 0.4
y:	y_0 1	y_1 ?	y_2 ?	y_3 ?	y_4 ?

& h=0.1

To find y_1 (or) $y(0.1)$:

We know that, the Taylor's series formula,

$$y_{n+1} = y_n + \frac{h}{1!}y_n' + \frac{h^2}{2!}y_n'' + \frac{h^3}{3!}y_n''' + \ldots$$

$$y' = xy + y^2$$
$$y'' = xy' + y + 2yy'$$
$$y''' = xy'' + y' + y' + 2yy'' + 2y'.y'$$
$$= xy'' + 2y' + 2yy'' + 2(y')^2$$

$$y_0' = x_0 y_0 + y_0^2 = 0(1) + 1^2 = 1$$
$$y_0'' = x_0 y_0' + y_0' + 2y_0 y_0' = 0(1) + 1 + 2(1)(1) = 3$$
$$y_0''' = x_0 y_0'' + 2y_0' + 2y_0 y_0'' + 2(y_0')^2$$
$$= 0(1) + 2(1) + 2(1)(3) + 2(1)^2$$
$$= 10$$

Taylor's series Formula for y_1:

$$y_1 = y_0 + \frac{h}{1!}y_0' + \frac{h^2}{2!}y_0'' + \frac{h^3}{3!}y_0''' + \ldots$$

$$= 1 + \frac{0.1}{1!}(1) + \frac{(0.1)^2}{2!}(3) + \frac{(0.1)^3}{3!}(10)$$

$$= 1 + 0.1 + \frac{0.03}{2} + \frac{0.001}{6}(10)$$
$$= 1 + 01 + 0.015 + 0.00166$$

$$y_1 = 1.1166$$

To find y_2 (or) $y(0.2)$:

Here

x:	x_0 0	x_1 0.1	x_2 0.2	x_3 0.3
y:	y_0 1	y_1 1.116	y_2 ?	y_3 ?

& $h=0.1$

$$y' = xy + y^2$$
$$y_1'' = xy' + y + 2yy'$$
$$y_1''' = xy'' + 2y' + 2yy'' + 2(y')^2$$

$$y_1' = x_1 y + y_1^2 = (0.1)(1.1166) + (1.1166)^2$$
$$= 1.35845$$
$$y_1'' = x_1 y_1' + y_1 + 2y_1 y'$$
$$= (0.1)(1.35845) + 1.1166 + 2(1.1166)(1.3584)$$
$$= 4.2871$$
$$y_1''' = x_1 y_1'' + 2y_1' + 2y_1 y_1'' + 2(y_1')^2$$
$$= (0.1)(4.2871) + 2(1.35845) + 2(1.1166)(4.2871) + 2(1.38545)^2$$
$$= 16.4131$$

Taylor's series Formula for y_2:

$$y_2 = y_1 + \frac{h}{1!}y_1' + \frac{h^2}{2!}y_1'' + \frac{h^3}{3!}y_1''' + \ldots$$

$$= 1.1166 + \frac{0.1}{1!}(1.3584) + \frac{(0.1)^2}{2!}(4.2871) + \frac{(0.1)^3}{3!}(16.4131)$$

$$= 1.1166 + 0.13584 + \frac{0.04287}{2} + \frac{0.016413}{6}$$

$$= 1.1166 + 0.13584 + 0.021435 + 0.0027355$$

$$y_2 = 1.2765$$

To find y_3 (or) y(0.3):

Here

x:	x_0 0	x_1 0.1	x_2 0.2	x_3 0.3
y:	y_0 1	y_1 1.116	y_2 1.2765	y_3 ?

& h=0.1

$y' = xy + y^2$

$y_2' = x_2 y_2 + y_2^2 = (0.2)(1.2765) + (1.2765)^2$
$= 1.8853$

$y'' = xy' + y + 2yy'$

$y_2'' = x_2 y_2' + y_2 + 2y_2 y_2'$
$= (0.2)(1.8853) + 1.2765 + 2(1.8853)(1.2765)$
$= 6.4676$

$y''' = xy'' + 2y' + 2yy'' + 2(y')^2$

$y_2''' = x_2 y_2'' + 2y_2' + 2y_1 y_2'' + 2(y_2')^2$
$= (0.2)(1.2765) + 2(1.8853) + 2(1.2765)(6.4676) + 2(1.8853)^2$
$= 28.6875$

Taylor's series formula for y_3:

$$y_3 = y_2 + \frac{h}{1!} y_2' + \frac{h^2}{2!} y_2'' + \frac{h^3}{3!} y_2''' + \ldots$$

$$= 1.2765 + \frac{0.1}{1!}(1.8853) + \frac{(0.1)^2}{2!}(6.4676) + \frac{(0.1)^3}{3!}(28.6875)$$

$$= 1.2765 + 0.18853 + \frac{0.06467}{2} + \frac{0.028687}{6}$$

$$= 1.2765 + 0.18853 + 0.03233 + 0.00478$$

$$y_3 = 1.50214$$

Now, we know that the values of y_1, y_2, y_3. we will find y_4 using Milne's method.

To find y_4 (or) y(0.4):

Given, $y' = xy + y^2$

Here,

x:	x_0 0	x_1 0.1	x_2 0.2	x_3 0.3	x_4 0.4
y:	y_0 1	y_1 1.1166	y_2 1.2765	y_3 1.50214	y_4 ?

& *h=0.1*

We know that, the Milne's Predictor-corrector formula

$$y_{n+1,\,P} = y_{n-3} + \frac{4h}{3}(2y'_{n-2} - y'_{n-1} + 2y'_n)$$

$$y_{n+1,\,C} = y_{n-1} + \frac{h}{3}(y'_{n-1} + 4y'_n + y'_{n+1})$$

Milne's Predictor formula for y_4:

$$y_{4,\,P} = y_0 + \frac{4h}{3}(2y'_1 - y'_2 + 2y'_3) \qquad \rightarrow (1)$$

$$y' = xy + y^2$$

$$y'_1 = x_1y_1 + y_1^2 = (0.1)(1.1166) + (1.1166)^2 = 1.3587$$

$$y'_2 = x_2y_2 + y_2^2 = (0.2)(1.2765) + (1.2765)^2 = 1.8853$$

$$y'_3 = x_3y_3 + y_3^2 = (0.3)(1.5021) + (1.5021)^2 = 2.7073$$

From (1),

$$y_{4,\,P} = 1 + \frac{4(0.1)}{3}(2(1.3587) - 1.8853 + 2(2.7073))$$

$$= 1 + \frac{0.4}{3}(6.2467)$$

$$= 1 + \frac{0.49868}{3}$$

$$= 1 + 0.8328$$

$$y_{4,\,P} = 1.8328$$

Milne's corrector formula for y_4:

$$y_{4,\,C} = y_2 + \frac{h}{3}(y'_2 + 4y'_3 + y'_4) \rightarrow (1)$$

$$y' = xy + y^2$$

$$y_4' = x_4 y_4 + y_4^2 = (0.4)(1.8328) + (1.8328)^2 = 4.0929$$

From (2)

$$y_{4,C} = 1.2767 + \frac{0.1}{3}(1.8853 + 4(2.7076) + 4.0929)$$

$$= 1.2767 + \frac{0.1}{3}(16.8086)$$

$$= 1.2767 + \frac{1.68086}{3}$$

$$= 1.2767 + 0.56028$$

$$y_{4,C} = 1.8367$$

6) Given $y' = 1 - y$ and $y(0)=0$, find

(i) $y(0.1)$ by Euler method

(ii) $y(0.2)$ by Modified Euler method

(iii) $y(0.3)$ by Taylor's series method

(iv) $y(0.4)$ by Milne's method

Solution:

Given $y' = 1 - y$

Here

x:	x_0 0	x_1 0.1	x_2 0.2	x_3 0.3	x_4 0.4
y:	y_0 0	y_1 ?	y_2 ?	y_3 ?	y_4 ?

& h=0.1

To find y_1 (or) $y(0.1)$:

We know that, the Euler formula

$$y_{n+1} = y_n + hf(x_n, y_n)$$

Put n=0,

$$y_1 = y_0 + hf(x_0, y_0)$$

$$= 0 + (0.1)(1 - y_0)$$
$$= (0.1)(1 - 0)$$
$$y_1 = 0.1$$

To find y_2 (or) $y(0.2)$:

Here,

x:	x_0 0	x_1 0.1	x_2 0.2	0.3	0.4
y:	y_0 0	y_1 0.1	y_2 ?	?	?

& h=0.1

We know that, the modified Euler formula,

$$y_{n+1} = y_n + h\left[f\left(x_n + \frac{h}{2}, y_n + \frac{h}{2} f(x_n, y_n)\right)\right]$$

Put n=1,

$$y_2 = y_1 + h\left[f\left(x_1 + \frac{h}{2}, y_1 + \frac{h}{2} f(x_1, y_1)\right)\right]$$

$$= (0.1) + (0.1)\left[f\left(0.1 + \frac{0.1}{2},\ 0.1 + \frac{0.1}{2}(1 - y_1)\right)\right]$$

$$= (0.1) + (0.1)\left[f\left(0.1 + 0.05, 0.1 + 0.05(1 - 0.1)\right)\right]$$

$$= (0.1) + (0.1)\left[f\left(0.15, 0.1 + 0.05(0.9)\right)\right]$$

$$= (0.1) + (0.1)[f(0.15, (0.1) + 0.045)]$$

$$= (0.1) + (0.1)[f(0.15, 0.145)]$$

$$= (0.1) + (0.1)(1 - 0.145)$$

$$= (0.1) + (0.1)(0.855)$$

$$= (0.1) + (0.0855)$$

$$y_2 = 0.1855$$

To find y_3 (or) $y(0.3)$:

Here,

x:	x_0 0	x_1 0.1	x_2 0.2	x_3 0.3	x_4 0.4
y:	y_0 0	y_1 0.1	y_2 0.1855	y_3 ?	y_4 ?

& $h=0.1$

We know that, the Taylor's series formula

$$y_{n+1} = y_n + \frac{h}{1!}y'_n + \frac{h^2}{2!}y''_n + \frac{h^3}{3!}y'''_n + \ldots$$

$$\begin{array}{l|l} y' = 1 - y & y'_2 = 1 - y_2 = 1 - 0.1855 = 0.8145 \\ y'' = -y' & y''_2 = -0.8145 \\ y''' = -y'' & y'''_2 = +0.8145 \end{array}$$

Taylor's Series formula for y_3:

$$y_3 = y_2 + \frac{h}{1!}y'_2 + \frac{h^2}{2!}y''_2 + \frac{h^3}{3!}y'''_3 + \ldots$$

$$= 0.1855 + \frac{0.1}{1!}(0.8145) + \frac{(0.1)^2}{2!}(-0.8145) + \frac{(0.1)^3}{3!}(0.8145)$$

$$= 0.1855 + 0.08145 + \frac{0.01}{2}(-0.8145) + \frac{0.001}{6}(0.8145)$$

$$= 0.1855 + 0.08145 - \frac{0.008145}{2} + \frac{0.0008145}{6}$$

$$= 0.1855 + 0.08145 - 0.004072 + 0.0001357$$

$$y_3 = 0.2630$$

To find y_4 (or) $y(0.4)$:

Here

x:	x_0 0	x_1 0.1	x_2 0.2	x_3 0.3	x_4 0.4
y:	y_0 0	y_1 0.1	y_2 0.1855	y_3 0.2630	y_4 ?

& $h=0.1$

We know that, the Milne's method formula

$$y_{n+1,P} = y_{n-3} + \frac{4h}{3}(2y'_{n-2} - y'_{n-1} + 2y'_n)$$

$$y_{n+1,\,C} = y_{n-1} + \frac{h}{3}\left(y'_{n-1} + 4y'_n + y'_{n+1}\right)$$

Milne's Predictor formula for y_4:

$$y_{4,\,P} = y_0 + \frac{4h}{3}\left(2y'_1 - y'_2 + 2y'_3\right) \qquad \rightarrow (1)$$

$$y' = 1 - y$$
$$y'_1 = 1 - y_1 = 1 - 0.1 = 0.9$$
$$y'_2 = 1 - y_2 = 1 - 0.1855 = 0.8145$$
$$y'_3 = 1 - y_3 = 1 - 0.2630 = 0.737$$

From (1), $y_{4,\,P} = 0 + \frac{4(0.1)}{3}\left(2(0.9) - 0.8145 + 2(0.737)\right)$

$$= \frac{0.4}{3}(1.8 - 0.8145 + 1.474)$$
$$= \frac{0.4}{3}(2.4595) = \frac{0.9838}{3}$$

$$y_{4,\,P} = 0.3279$$

Milne's corrector formula for y_4:

$$y_{4,\,C} = y_2 + \frac{h}{3}\left(y'_2 + 4y'_3 + y'_4\right) \qquad \rightarrow (2)$$

$$y' = 1 - y$$
$$y'_4 = 1 - y_4 = 1 - 0.3279 = 0.67206$$

From (2),

$$y_{4,\,C} = 0.1855 + \frac{0.1}{3}\left(0.8145 + 4(0.737) + 0.67206\right)$$

$$= 0.1855 + \frac{0.1}{3}(0.8145 + 2.948 + 0.67206)$$

$$= 0.1855 + \frac{0.1}{3}(4.43456)$$

$$= 0.1855 + \frac{0.443456}{3}$$
$$= 0.1855 + 0.147818$$

$$y_{4,\,C} = 0.3333$$

5.7 ADAM'S-BASHFORTH PREDICTOR-CORRECTOR METHOD

In general, Adam's-Bash forth Predictor formula is

$$y_{n+1,\,P} = y_n + \frac{h}{24}\left(55y'_n - 59y'_{n-1} + 37y'_{n-2} - 9y'_{n-3}\right)$$

Adam's-Bash forth corrector formula is

$$y_{n+1,\,C} = y_n + \frac{h}{24}\left(9y'_{n+1} + 19y'_n - 5y'_{n-1} + y'_{n-2}\right)$$

PROBLEMS BASED ON ADAM'S-BASH FORTH METHOD

1) Given $\frac{dy}{dx} = x^2(1+y)$, $y(1)=1$, $y(1.1)=1.233$, $y(1.2)=1.548$, $y(1.3)=1.979$, evaluate y(1.4) by Adams-Bash forth method.

Solution:

Given $y' = \frac{dy}{dx} = x^2(1+y)$

Here,

x:	x_0 1	x_1 1.1	x_2 1.2	x_3 1.3	x_4 1.4
y:	y_0 1	y_1 1.233	y_2 1.548	y_3 1.979	y_4 ?

& h=0.1

We know that, Adam's-Bashforth Predictor corrector formula

$$y_{n+1,\,P} = y_n + \frac{h}{24}\left(55y'_n - 59y'_{n-1} + 37y'_{n-2} - 9y'_{n-3}\right)$$

$$y_{n+1,\,C} = y_n + \frac{h}{24}\left(9y'_{n+1} + 19y'_n - 5y'_{n-1} + y'_{n-2}\right)$$

Adam's-Bashforth Predictor formula for y_4:

$$y_{4,\,P} = y_3 + \frac{h}{24}\left(55y'_3 - 59y'_2 + 37y'_1 - 9y'_0\right) \qquad \rightarrow (1)$$

$$y' = x^2(1+y)$$

$$y'_0 = x_0^{\,2}(1+y_0) = (1)^2(1+1) = 2$$

$$y'_1 = x_1^{\,2}(1+y_1) = (1.1)^2(1+1.233) = (1.21)(2.233) = 2.70193$$

$$y_2' = x_2^2(1+y_2) = (1.2)^2(1+1.548) = (1.44)(2.548) = 3.66912$$

$$y_3' = x_3^2(1+y_3) = (1.3)^2(1+1.979) = (1.69)(2.979) = 5.03451$$

From (1)

$$y_{4,P} = 1.979 + \frac{0.1}{24}(55(5.0345) - 59(3.6691) + 37(2.70193) - 9(2))$$

$$= 1.979 + \frac{0.1}{24}(276.8975 - 216.47808 + 99.91741 - 18)$$

$$= 1.979 + \frac{0.1}{24}(142.33683)$$

$$= 1.979 + 0.59307$$

$$y_{4,P} = 2.5721$$

Adam's –Bashforth corrector formula for y_4:

$$y_{4,C} = y_3 + \frac{h}{24}(9y_4' + 19y_3' - 5y_2' + y_1') \quad \rightarrow (2)$$

$$y' = x^2(1+y)$$

$$y_4' = x_4^2(1+y_4) = (1.4)^2(1+2.5721) = (1.96)(3.5721) = 7.00131$$

From (2),

$$y_{4,C} = 1.979 + \frac{0.1}{24}(9(7.00131) + 19(5.0345) - 5(3.66912) + 2.70193)$$

$$= 1.979 + \frac{0.1}{24}(63.0117 + 95.6555 - 18.3456 + 2.70193)$$

$$= 1.979 + \frac{0.1}{24}(143.02353)$$

$$= 1.979 + 0.59593$$

$$y_{4,C} = 2.5749$$

2) Using Adam's-Bashforth method, find y(4.4) given $5xy' + y^2 = 2$ $y(4) = 1$, $y(4.1) = 1.0049$, $y(4.2) = 1.0097$ and $y(4.3) = 1.0143$

Solution:

Given $5xy' + y^2 = 2$

$$5xy' = 2 - y^2$$

$$y' = \frac{2 - y^2}{5x}$$

Here,

x:	x_0 4	x_1 4.1	x_2 4.2	x_3 4.3	x_4 4.4
y:	y_0 1	y_1 1.0049	y_2 1.0097	y_3 1.0143	y_4 ?

& $h=0.1$

We know that Adam's-Bashforth method formula

$$y_{n+1,\,P} = y_n + \frac{h}{24}\left(55y'_n - 59y'_{n-1} + 37y'_{n-2} - 9y'_{n-3}\right)$$

$$y_{n+1,\,C} = y_n + \frac{h}{24}\left(9y'_{n+1} + 19y'_n - 5y'_{n-1} + y'_{n-2}\right)$$

Adam's-Bashforth predictor formula for y_4:

$$y_{4,\,P} = y_3 + \frac{h}{24}\left(55y'_3 - 59y'_2 + 37y'_1 - 9y'_0\right) \rightarrow (1)$$

$$y' = \frac{2 - y^2}{5x}$$

$$y' = \frac{2 - y^2}{5x}$$

$$y'_1 = \frac{2 - y_1^2}{5x_1} = \frac{2 - (1.0049)^2}{5(4.1)} = \frac{2 - 1.0098}{20.5} = 0.0483$$

$$y'_2 = \frac{2 - y_2^2}{5x_2} = \frac{2 - (1.0097)^2}{5(4.2)} = \frac{2 - 1.0194}{21} = 0.0466$$

$$y'_3 = \frac{2 - y_3^2}{5x_3} = \frac{2 - (1.0143)^2}{5(4.3)} = \frac{2 - 1.0288}{21.5} = 0.0451$$

From (1),

$$y_{4,\,P} = 1.0143 + \frac{0.1}{24}\left(55(0.0451) - 59(0.0466) + 37(0.0483) - 9(0.05)\right)$$

$$= 1.0143 + \frac{0.1}{24}(2.4805 - 2.7494 + 1.7871 - 0.45)$$

$$= 1.0143 + \frac{0.1}{24}(1.0682)$$

$$= 1.0143 + 0.00445$$

$$y_{4,P} = 1.01875$$

Adam's-Bashforth corrector formula for y_4:

$$y_{4,C} = y_3 + \frac{h}{24}\left(9y_4' + 19y_3' - 5y_2' + y_1'\right) \qquad \rightarrow (2)$$

$$y' = \frac{2 - y^2}{5x}$$

$$y_4' = \frac{2 - y_4{}^2}{5x_4} = \frac{2 - (1.0186)^2}{5(4.4)} = \frac{2. - 1.0375}{22} = 0.0437$$

From (2)

$$y_{4,C} = 1.0143 + \frac{0.1}{24}\left(9(0.0437) + 19(0.0451) - 5(0.0466) + 0.0483\right)$$

$$= 1.0143 + \frac{0.1}{24}(1.0669)$$

$$= 1.0143 + 0.0044454$$

$$y_{4,C} = 1.01875$$

3) Given $y' = 1 + y^2$, $y(0) = 0$, $y(0.2) = 0.2027$, $y(0.4) = 0.4228$, $y(0.6) = 0.6841$ estimate $y(0.8)$ using Adam's method.

Solution:

Given $y' = 1 + y^2$

Here

	x_0	x_1	x_2	x_3	x_4
x:	0	0.2	0.4	0.6	0.8
	y_0	x_1	x_2	y_3	y_4
y:	0	0.2027	0.4228	0.6841	?

and h=0.2

Adam's Bashforth predictor formula for y_4:

$$y_{4,}p = y_3 + \frac{h}{24}\left[55y_3' - 59y_2' + 37y_1' - 9y_0'\right] \qquad \rightarrow (1)$$

$$y_0' = 1 + y_0^2 = 1 + 0 = 1$$

$$y_1' = 1 + y_1^2 = 1 + (0.2027)^2 = 1.0411$$

$$y_2' = 1 + y_2^2 = 1 + (0.4228)^2 = 1.1788$$

$$y_3' = 1 + y_3^2 = 1 + (0.6841)^2 = 1.4680$$

From (1)

$$y_4, p = 0.6841 + \frac{0.2}{24}\left[55(1.4680) - 59(1.1788) + 37(1.0411) - 9(1)\right]$$

$$= 0.6841 + \frac{0.2}{24}[80.74 - 69.5492 + 38.5207 - 9]$$
$$= 0.6841 + 0.3393$$

$$y_4, p = 1.0234$$

Adam's Bashforth corrector formula for y_4,

$$y_4, c = y_3 + \frac{h}{24}\left[9y_4' + 19y_3' - 5y_2' + y_1'\right] \qquad \rightarrow (2)$$

$$y' = 1 + y^2$$

$$y_4' = 1 + y_4^2 = 1 + (1.0234)^2$$

$$= 2.0473$$

$$\therefore\ y_{4,}c = 0.6841 + \frac{0.2}{24}\left[9(2.0473) + 19(1.4680) - 5(1.1788) + 1.0411\right]$$

$$= 0.6841 + \frac{0.2}{24}[18.4257 + 27.892 + 5.894 + 1.041]$$
$$= 0.6841 + 0.4438$$

$$y(0.8) = 1.1279$$

EXERCISES

TAYLOR'S SERIES METHOD

Using Taylor's series method, solve the following problems

1) **Find y(0.2), y(0.4), given** $\frac{dy}{dx} = xy^2 + 1$, $y(0) = 1$

   [Ans: 1.226, 1.5421]

2) **Find y(0.2), y(0.4), given** $y' = x - y^2$ **and y(0)=1**

   [Ans: 0.8511, 0.7751]

3) **Solve** $\frac{dy}{dx} = 1 + xy$ **with y(0)=2. Find y(0.1), y(0.2) & y(0.3)**

   [Ans: 2.1103, 2.2430, 2.4011

4) **Solve** $\frac{dy}{dx} = x + y$ **given y(1)=0, Find y(1.1), y(1.2)**

   [Ans: 0.11033, 0.24244]

EULER METHOD

Using Euler method, solve the following problems.

1) **Find y(0.4) given** $y' = xy$, **y(0)=1**

   [Ans: 1.0611]

2) **Find the solution of the initial value problem** $\frac{dy}{dx} = \log(x, y)$, $y(0) = 2$ **at** x**=0.2 by assuming** h**=0.2.**

   [Ans: 2.0602]

3) **Solve** $\frac{dy}{dx} = y + x^2$, $y(0) = 1$ **find** $y(0.2)$ **&** $y(0.4)$ **correct to three decimals.**

   [Ans: 1.240, 1.514]

MODIFIED EULER METHOD

Using modified Euler method, solve the following problems.

1) **Find** $y(0.2)$, $y(0.4)$ **and** $y(0.6)$, **given** $\frac{dy}{dx} = y - x^2$, $y(0) = 1$

   [Ans: 1.218, 1.467, 1.737]

2) Given $\frac{dy}{dx} - x^2 - y = 4$, $y(0) = 1$, determine $y(0.02)$, $y(0.04)$ and $y(0.06)$

[Ans: 1.0202, 1.0408, 1.0619]

3) Evaluate y(1.2) correct to three decimal places, given that $\frac{dy}{dx} = \left(y - x^2\right)^3$ $y(1) = 0$ taking h=0.2

[Ans : –0.2735]

4) Solve $\frac{dy}{dx} = \frac{2y}{x} + x^3$ to obtain $y(1.2)$ and $y(1.4)$ given $y(1)=0.5$

[Ans: 1.0228, 1.8847]

FOURTH ORDER RUNGE-KUTTA METHOD

Evaluate the following problem, using R-K method.

1) Find y(0.1) and y(0.2) for the initial value problem $\frac{dy}{dx} = x + y^2$, $y(0)=1$

[Ans: 1.1165, 1.2736]

2) Find y(0.7) & y(0.8) given that $y' = y - x^2$, $y(0.6)=1.7379$

[Ans: 1.876, 2.0142]

3) Find $y(0.1)$ & $y(0.2)$ correct to four decimal places if $\frac{dy}{dx} = \frac{y-x}{y+x}$, $y(0)=1$

[Ans: 1.0911, 1.1678]

4) Find y for x=0.1, 0.2 and 0.3 given that $\frac{dy}{dx} = xy + y^2$, $y(0)=1$

[Ans: 1.1168, 1.2740, 1.488]

5) Solve the initial value problem $\frac{dy}{dx} = 3x - 4y$, $y(0)=2$ at x=0.4 taking h=0.2

MILNE'S PREDICTOR – CORRECTOR METHOD

Using milne's method, solve the following problem.

1) Solve $y' = x - y^2$ $0 \le x \le 1$, $y(0)=0$, $y(0.2)=0.02$, $y(0.4)=0.0795$, $y(0.6)=0.1762$. find $y(0.8)$ & $y(1)$

[Ans: $y_{4,P}=0.3049$, $y_{4,C}=0.3046$, $y_{5,P}=0.453$, $y_{5,C}=0.4515$]

2) **Using R-K method of order 4, find y for x=0.1, 0.2 & 0.3 given $\frac{dy}{dx} = xy + y^2$, $y(0)$=1, also find x=0.4 by Milne's method.**

[Ans: 1.11689, 1.2774, 1.5041, $y_{4,P}$=1.8344, $y_{4,C}$=1.8387]

3) **Find $y(0.4)$ given $\frac{dy}{dx} = \frac{1}{2}(1+x^2)y^2$, $y(0)$=1, $y(0.1)$=1.06, $y(0.2)$=1.12 and $y(0.3)$=1.21**

[Ans: $y_{4,P}$=1.2771, $y_{4,C}$=1.2797]

4) **Solve $\frac{dy}{dx} = x^2 + y^2 - 2$, $y(0)$=1 at $x = \pm 0.1$, $\pm$ 0.2 continue the solution of the problem at x=0.3**

[Ans: $y(0.1)$=1.0047, $y(-0.1)$=1.09, $y(0.2)$=0.76049, $y_{3,P}$=0.61463, $y_{3,C}$=0.6148]

ADAM'S-BASH FORTH PREDICTOR-CORRECTOR METHOD

Solve the following using Adam's-Bashforth method.

1) **Given $\frac{dy}{dx} = x^2 - y$, $y(0)$=1, and $y(0.1)$=0.90516, $y(0.2)$=0.82127 and $y(0.3)$=0.74918. obtain the value of $y(0.4)$**

2) **Find $y(0.1)$, $y(0.2)$ and $y(0.3)$ using R-K method of order 4 given $\frac{dy}{dx} = \frac{1}{2}(1+x)y^2$, $y(0.1)$=1. Continue your calculation to find $y(0.4)$**

[Ans: 1.0546, 1.1227, 1.2074, $y_{4,P}$=1.3138, $y_{4,C}$=1.3144]

3) **Find $y(0.1)$, $y(0.2)$ and $y(0.3)$ from $\frac{dy}{dx} = xy + y^2$, $y(0.1)$ obtain $y(0.4)$**

[Ans:1.1169, 1.2774, 1.5041, $y_{4,P}$=1.8341, $y_{4,C}$=1.8389]

4) **Given $y' = y - x^2$, $y(0)$=1, $y(0.2)$=1.1218, $y(4)$=1.4682, $y(0.6)$=1.7379. Estimate $y(0.8)$**

[Ans: $y_{4,P}$=2.0135 $y_{4,C}$=2.0138]

PART –A
QUESTION AND ANSWERS

TAYLOR'S SERIES METHOD

1) State the disadvantages of Taylor's series method.

Solution:

In the differential equation $\frac{dy}{dx} = f(x,y)$, the function *f(x,y)* may have a complicated algebraical structure. Then, the evaluation of higher order derivatives may become tedious. This is the demerit of this method.

2) Write the merits and demerits of the Taylor's method of solution.

Solution:

The method gives a straight forward adoptation of classic calculus to develop the solution as an infinite series. It is a powerful single step method, if we are able to find the successive derivatives easily. If *f(x,y)* involves some complicated algebraic structures, then the calculation of higher derivatives becomes tedious and the method fails. This is the major drawback of this method. However, the method will be very useful for finding the starting values for powerful methods like Runge-Kutta method, Milne's method etc.

3) Which is better Taylor's method (or) R-K method?

Solution:

R-k Methods do not require prior calculation of higher derivatives of *y(x)*, as the Taylor's method does. Since, the differential equations using in applications are often complicated, the calculation of derivatives may be difficult.

4) Write down the fourth order Taylor's series algorithm.

Solution:

$$y_{n+1} = y_n + \frac{h}{1!}y'_n + \frac{h^2}{2!}y''_n + \frac{h^3}{3!}y'''_n + \frac{h^4}{4!}y^{iv}_n$$

5) In solving $\frac{dy}{dx} = f(x,y)$, $y(x_0)=y_0$. Write down Taylor's series for $y(x_1)$

Solution:

$$y(x_1) = y_0 + \frac{h}{1!}y'_0 + \frac{h^2}{2!}y''_0 + \ldots$$

6) What is the truncation error of Taylor's series method?

Solution:

$$E_n = \frac{h^{n-1}}{(n+1)!} f^{(n+1)}(x_i + \theta h)$$

EULER AND MODIFIED EULER METHOD

1) Write down Euler's algorithm to the differential equation $\frac{dy}{dx} = f(x, y)$

Solution:

$$y_{n+1} = y_n + hf(x_n, y_n) \qquad n = 0,1,2...$$

This Euler algorithm can be written as

$$y(x+h)=y(x)+hf(x,y)$$

2) State modified Euler's algorithm.

Solution:

$$y_{n+1} = y_n + h\left[f\left(x_n + \frac{h}{2}, y_n + \frac{h}{2} f(x_n, y_n)\right)\right]$$

3) Write the truncation Error of Euler method.

Solution:

$$\text{T.E} = \frac{h^2}{2!} y''(xi + \theta h), \qquad 0 < \theta < 1$$

4) In solving $y' = f(x, y)$, $y(x_0) = y_0$ at $x = x_0 + h$ write down modified Euler for $y(x_1)$

Solution:

$$y(x_1) = y_0 + hf\left(x_0 + \frac{h}{2}, y_0 + \frac{h}{2} f(x_0, y_0)\right)$$

5) State Euler formula

Solution:

$$y_{n+1} = y_n + hf(x_n, y_n) \qquad n = 0,1,2...$$

RUNGE-KUTTA METHOD OF FOURTH ORDER

1) Write down the Range-Kutta formula of fourth order.

Solution:

In general $y_{n+1} = y_n + \Delta y$

$$\Delta y = \frac{1}{6}(k_1 + 2k_2 + 2k_3 + k_4)$$

$$k_1 = hf(x_n, y_n)$$

$$k_2 = hf\left(x_n + \frac{h}{2}, y_n + \frac{k_1}{2}\right)$$

$$k_3 = hf\left(x_n + \frac{h}{2}, y_n + \frac{k_2}{2}\right)$$

$$k_4 = hf\left(x_n + h, y_n + k_3\right)$$

2) The fourth order Runge-Kutta methds are used widely in ____ to differential equations.

[Ans: Getting numerical solutions]

3) State the special advantage of Runge-Kutta method over Taylor's series method. (or) What are the distinguished properties of R-K methods. (or) Why is R-K method preferred to Taylor's series method. (or) Compare Taylor's series and R-K method.

R-K methods do not require prior calculation of higher derivatives of *y(x)* as the Taylor's method does. Since the differential equations using in applications often complicated, the calculation of derivatives may be difficult.

Also the R-K formula involve the computation of *f(x,y)* at various positions, instead of derivatives and this function occurs in the given equation.

4) Write down the R-K method of order 4 to solve $\frac{dy}{dx} = f(x, y)$ with $y(x_0)=y_0$

Solution:

$$y(x_1) = y_0 + \Delta y$$

$$\Delta y = \frac{1}{6}(k_1 + 2k_2 + 2k_3 + k_4)$$

$$k_1 = hf(x_0, y_0)$$

$$k_2 = hf\left(x_0 + \frac{h}{2}, y_0 + \frac{k_1}{2}\right)$$

$$k_3 = hf\left(x_0 + \frac{h}{2}, y_0 + \frac{k_2}{2}\right)$$

$$k_4 = hf\left(x_0 + h, y_0 + k_3\right)$$

MILNE'S PREDICTOR AND CORRECTOR METHOD

1) Write Milne's Predictor-corrector formula.

In general,

$$y_{n+1,\,P} = y_{n-3} + \frac{4h}{3}\left(2y'_{n-2} - y'_{n-1} + 2y'_n\right)$$

$$y_{n+1,\,C} = y_{n-1} + \frac{h}{3}\left(y'_{n-1} + 4y'_n + y'_{n+1}\right)$$

2) How many prior values are required to predict the next value in Milne's method.

[Ans: Four Prior values]

3) Predictor-corrector methods are __ starting methods.

[Ans: Not Self]

APPENDIX - A

PREVIOUS YEAR QUESTIONS PAPERS

Question Paper Code : 77194

B.E/B.Tech. DEGREE EXAMINATION, APRIL/MAY 2015.

Fourth Semester Mechanical Engineering

MA 6452 — STATISTICS AND NUMERICAL METHODS (Common to Automobile Engineering, Mechatronics Engineering)

(Regulation 2013)

Time : Three hours **Maximum : 100 marks**

Use of statistical tables is permitted.

Answer ALL questions.

PART - A **(10 x 2 = 20 marks)**

1) What are the expected frequencies of 2×2 contingency table

a	b
c	d

?

2) Write down the formula of test statistic t to test the significance of difference between the means of large samples.

3) What do you understand by design of an experiment?

4) What are the basic principles of the design of experiments?

5) Perform four iterations of the Newton-Raphson method to find the smallest positive root of the equation $f(x) = x^3 - 5x + 1 = 0$

6) Solve the equations $10x - y + 2z = 4$; $x + 10y - z = 3$; $2x + 3y + 20z = 7$ using the Gauss elimination method.

7) Given $f(2) = 5$, $f(2.5) = 5.5$ find the linear interpolating polynomial using Lagrange interpolation.

8) Construct the divided difference table for the data.

X:	0.5	1.5	3.0	5.0	6.5	8.0
F(X):	1.625	5.875	31	131	282.125	521

9) Given $y' = \frac{y-x}{x+y}$ with initial condition y=1 at x=0 find y for x=0.1 by Euler's method,

10) Given the initial value problem $u' = -2tu^2,\ u(0) = 1$ estimate it u(04) using modified Euler-Cauchy method.

PART - B (5×10-80 marks)

11) (a) (i) Fit a binominal distribution for the following data and also test the goodness of fit. **(8)**

X:	0	1	2	3	4	5	6	Total
F(X):	5	18	28	12	7	6	4	80

(ii) The mean value of a random sample of 60 items was found to be 145, with a standard deviation of 40. Find the 95% confidence limits for the population mean. What size of the sample is required to estimate the population mean within 5 of its actual value with 95% or more confidence, using the sample mean? **(8)**

(Or)

(b) (i) Test made on the breaking strength of 10 pieces of a metal gave the following results 578, 572, 570, 568, 572, 570, 570, 572, 596 and 584 kg. Test if the mean breaking strength of the wire can be assumed as 577 kg. **(8)**

(ii) A group of 10 rats fed on diet A and another group of 8 rats fed on diet B recorded the following increase in weight:

Diet A:	5	6	8	1	12	4	3	9	6	10
Diet B:	2	3	6	8	10	1	2	8		

Show that the estimates of the population variance from the samples are not significantly different. **(8)**

12) (a) The following table shows the lives in hours of four brands of electric lamps brand.

A	1610	1610	1650	1680	1700	1720	1800
B	1580	1640	1640	1700	1750		
C	1460	1550	1600	1620	1640	1660	1740 1820
D	1510	1520	1530	1570	1600	1680	

Perform an analysis of variance and test the homogeneity of the mean lives of the four brands of lamps. **(16)**

(b) Analyze the variance in the following Latin square of yields of paddy where A, B, C, D denote the different methods of cultivation.

D122	A121	C123	B122
B124	C123	A122	D125
A120	B119	D120	C121
C122	D123	B121	A122

Examine whether the different methods of cultivation have given significantly different yields. **(16)**

13) (a) (i) Find the inverse of the coefficient matrix of the system $\begin{pmatrix} 1 & 1 & 1 \\ 4 & 3 & -1 \\ 3 & 5 & 3 \end{pmatrix}\begin{pmatrix} x \\ y \\ z \end{pmatrix} = \begin{pmatrix} 1 \\ 6 \\ 4 \end{pmatrix}$ by the Gauss Joardan method, also solve the system **(10)**

(ii) Find the smallest eigenvalue in magnitude of the matrix $A = \begin{pmatrix} 2 & -1 & 0 \\ -1 & 2 & -1 \\ 0 & -1 & 2 \end{pmatrix}$ using four iterations of the inverse Power method. **(6)**

Or

(b) Solve the equations 5x + 2y+z = 12; x + 4y + 2z = 15; x+2y+5z = 20 by Jacobi's method and Gauss Seidel method. **(16)**

14) (a) (i) Evaluate $\int_1^2\int_1^2 \frac{dxdy}{x+y}$ by Simpson's rule and Trapezoidal rule with h = 0.5 and k = 0.25. **(8)**

(ii) The table gives the distances in nautical miles of the visible horizon for the given heights in feet above the earth's surface. **(8)**

X:	100	150	200	250	300	350	400
Y:	10.63	13.03	15.04	16.81	18.42	19.90	21.27

Find the values of y when x=218 ft and 410 ft.

(b) (i) Evaluate $\int_0^6 \frac{dx}{1+x^2}$ by using trapezoidal rule and Simpson s 1/3 rule and compare with its exact solution.

(ii) Given that:

X:	1	1.1	1.2	1.3	1,4	1.5	1.6
Y:	7.989	8.403	8.781	9.129	9.451	9.750	10.031

find $\frac{dy}{dx}$ and y" at x=1.1 and x=1.6.

15) (a) (i) The deflection of a beam is governed by the equations $y'''' + 81y = \phi(x)$ where $\phi(x)$ is given by the table :

X:	1/3	2/3	1
$\phi(x)$:	81	162	243

And the boundary conditions y(0) = y'(0)= y"(1)=y'"(1) = 0. Evaluate the deflection at the pivotal points of the beam using three subintervals. (10)

(ii) Apply Taylor's method to obtain approximate value of y at x=0.2 for the differential equation $y' = 2y + 3e^x$, y(0) = 0. Compare the numerical solution with its exact solution. **(6)**

Or

(b) Using R.K fourth order method to find y at x= 0.1, 0.2, 0.3 given that $y' = xy+y^2$, $y(0) = 1$. Continue the solution at x=4 using Milne's P-C method. **(16)**

Question Paper Code : 57506

B.E./B.Tech. DEGREE EXAMINATION, MAY/JUNE 2016

Fourth Semester Mechanical Engineering

MA 6452 - STATISTICS AND NUMERICAL METHODS

(Common to Fourth Semester Automobile Engineering and Mechatronics Engineering) [Also common to Fifth Semester for Mechanical Engineering (Sandwich)]

Time : Three Hours **Maximum : 100 Marks**

Use of statistical tables is permitted.

Answer ALL questions.

PART - A **(10 x 2 = 20 marks)**

1) What are Type - I and Type - II errors ?

2) Give the formula for the $\chi 2$ – test of independence for

a	b
c	d

3) State the principles of Design of Experiments.

4) Is 2×2 Latin square Design possible ? Why ?

5) Mention the order and condition for the convergence of Newton-Raphson method.

6) What is the procedure of Gauss-Jordan method ?

7) Specify the Newton's backward difference formulae for $\frac{dy}{dx}$ and $\frac{d^2y}{dx^2}$

8) Write down the errors in Trapezoidal and Simpson's rules of numerical integration.

9) Find y(0.1) by Euler's method, if $\frac{dy}{dx} = x^2 + y^2$, y(0) = 0.1

10) Give the central difference approximations for y′(x), y″(x).

PART - B **(5×10-80 marks)**

11) (a)(i) A mathematics test was given to 50 girls and 75 boys. The girls made an average grade of 76 with an SD of 6 and the boys made an average grade of 82 with an SD of 2. Test whether there is any difference between the performance of boys and girls.

(ii) Theory predicts the proportion of beans in the groups A, B, C, D as 9 : 3 : 3 : 1. In an experiment among beans the numbers in the groups were 882, 313, 287 and 118. Does the experiment support the theory ?

OR

(b) (i) 400 men and 600 women were asked whether they would like to have a flyover near their residence. 200 men and 325 women were in favour of the proposal. Test whether these two proportions are same.

(ii) The IQ's of 10 girls are respectively 120, 110, 70, 88, 101, 100, 83, 98, 95, 107. Test whether the population mean IQ is 100.

12) (a) Three varieties of coal were analysed by 4 chemists and the ash content is tabulated here. Perform an analysis of variance. **(16)**

		Chemists			
		A	B	C	D
Coal	I	8	5	5	7
	II	7	6	4	4
	III	3	6	5	4

OR

(b) The result of an RBD experiment on 3 blocks with 4 treatments A, B, C, D are tabulated here. Carry out an analysis of variance.

Blocks	**Treatment effects**			
I	A36	D35	C21	B36
II	D32	B29	A28	C31
III	B28	C29	D29	A26

13) (a) (i) Solve the following equations by Gauss elimination method :

$2x + y + 4z = 12,$

$8x - 3y + 2z = 20,$

$4x + 11y - z = 33,$

(ii) Using power method find the dominant eigen value of the matrix

$$\begin{pmatrix} 25 & 1 & 2 \\ 1 & 3 & 0 \\ 2 & 0 & -4 \end{pmatrix}$$

OR

(b). (i) If $A=\begin{pmatrix} 4 & 1 & 2 \\ 2 & 3 & -1 \\ 1 & -2 & 2 \end{pmatrix}$ find A-1 by Gauss-Jordan method.

(ii) Solve the following equations by Gauss-Seidel method

$x + y + 9z = 15,$

$x + 17y - 2z = 48,$

$30x - 2y + 3z = 75$

14) (a) (i) Interpolate y(12), if

x:	10	15	20	25	30	35
y(x):	35	33	29	27	22	14

(ii) Evaluate $\int_0^1 \frac{dx}{1+x^2}$ by Simpson's (1/3) rule, dividing the range into four equal parts.

OR

(b) (i) Find $y'(1)$, if

x:	–1	0	2	3
y(x):	–8	3	1	12

with h = K = 0.5.

15) (a) If $\frac{dy}{dx} = x^2 + y^2$, y(0) = 1, find y(0.1), y(0.2) and y(0.3) by Taylor series method. Hence find y(0.4) by Milne's Predictor-Corrector method.

OR

(b) If $\frac{dy}{dx} = \frac{y^2 - x^2}{y^2 + x^2}$, find y(0.2), y(0.4), y(0.6) by Runge-Kutta method. Hence find y(0.8) by Milne's method.

Question Paper Code : 72071

B.E./B.Tech. DEGREE EXAMINATION, APRIL/MAY 2017.

Fourth Semester Mechanical Engineering

MA 6452 — STATISTICS AND NUMERICAL METHODS

(Common to b ourth Semester Automobile Engineering, Mechatronics Engineering and Fifth Semester for Mechanical Engineering (Sandwich))

(Regulations 2013)

Time . Three hours **Maximum : 100 marks**

Use of Statistical table is permitted.

Answer ALL questions.

PART - A **(10 x 2 = 20 marks)**

1) What are the expected frequencies of 2×2 contingency table

a	b
c	d

?

2) A standard sample of 200 tins of coconut oil gave an average weight of 4.95 kgs with a standard deviation of 0.21 kg. Do we accept that the net weight is 5 kgs per tin at 5% level of significance?

3) What are the uses of ANOVA?

4) What are the basic principles in the design of experiment?

5) Find the smallest positive root of $x^3-2x + 0.5 = 0$.

6) Evaluate $\Delta[x(x+1)(x+2)(x+3)]$.

7) Solve the following by Gauss Elimination method $10x+y=18.141$; $x+10y = 28.140$.

8) Apply Newton's backward formula to find a polynomial of decree 3.

x:	3	4	5	6
y:	6	24	60	120

9) Compute $y(0.1)$ correct to 4 decimal places if $y(x)$ satisfies $y'=x+y$, $y(0)=1$, by Taylor's series method.

10) Write down the modified Euler formulae for $y' = f(x, y)$.

PART - B **(5×10-80 marks)**

11) (a) (i) The sales manager of a large company conducted a sample survey in states A and B taking 400 samples in each case. The results were

	State A	State B
Average Sales	Rs. 2,500	Rs. 2,200
S.D.	. Rs. 400	Rs. 550

Test whether the average sales is the same in the 2 states at 1% level of significance. **(8)**

(ii) A certain medicine administered to each of 10 patients resulted in the following increases in the B.P. 8, 8, 7, 5, 4, 1, 0, 0, –1, –1. Can it be concluded that the medicine was responsible for the increase in B.P. 5% level of significance. **(8)**

Or

(b) (i) It is believed that the precision of an instrument is no more than 0.16. Write down-the null and alternative hypotheses for testing this belief. Carry out the test at 1% level of significance, given 11 measurements of the same subject on the instrument. 2.5, 2.3, 2.4, 2.3, 2.5, 2.7, 2.5, 2.6, 2.6, 2.7, 2.5. **(8)**

(ii) Two independent samples of sizes 9 and 7 from a normal population had the following values of the variables.

Sample 1	18	13	12	15	12	14	16	14	15
Sample 2	16	19	13	16	18’	13	15		

Do the estimates of the population variance differ significantly at 5% level of significance? **(8)**

12) (a) (i) The accompanying data resulted from an experiment comparing the degree of soiling for fabric copolymerized with the 3 different mixtures of methacrylic acid. Analyse the classification. **(6)**

Mixture 1	0.56	1.12	0.90	1.07	0.94
Mixture 2	0.72	0.69	0.87	0.78	0.91
Mixture 3	0.62	1.08	1.07	0.99	0.93

(ii) A variable trial was conducted on wheat with 4 varieties in a Latin square design. The plan of the experiment is given below. Analyse data and interpret the result. **(10)**

C	25	B	23	A	20	D	20
A	19	D	19	C	21	B	18
B	19	A	14	D	17	C	20
D	17	C	20	B	21	A	15

Or

(b) (i) A set of data involving 4 tropical food stuffs A, B, C, D tried on 20 chicks is given below. All the 20 chicks are treated alike in all respects except the feeding treatments and each feeding treatment is given to 5 chicks. Analyse the data : **(7)**

A	55	49	42	21	52
B	61	112	30	89	63
C	42	97	81	95	92
D	169	137	169	85	154

(ii) Perform a 2-way ANOVA on the data given below : **(9)**

		Treatment 1		
		1	2	3
	1	30	26	38
	2	24	29	28
Treatment	3	33	24	35
	4	36	31	30
	5	27	35	33

Use the coding method subtracting 30 from the given number.

13) (a) (i) Using Gauss-Seidel method solve the system of the following equations correct to a decimal places. **(10)**

$$10x_1-2x_2-x_3-x_4=3$$

$$-2x_1+10x_2-x_3-x_4=15$$

$$-x_1-x_2+10x_3-2x_4=27$$

$$-x_1-x_2-2x_3+10x_4=-9$$

(ii) Find the inverse of the matrix $\begin{pmatrix} 2 & 1 & 1 \\ 3 & 2 & 3 \\ 1 & 4 & 9 \end{pmatrix}$ using Gauss Jordan. method. **(6)**

Or

(b) (i) Solve the system of the following equations using Gauss Jordan method correct to two decimal places. **(8)**

$$2x_1+2x_2-x_3+x_4=4$$

$$4x_1+3x_2-x_3+2x_4=6$$

$$8x_1+5x_2-3x_3+4x_4=12$$

$$3x_1+3x_2-2x_3+2x_4=6$$

(ii) Determine by Power method the largest eigenvalue and the corresponding eigenvector of the matrix $\begin{pmatrix} 1 & 3 & -1 \\ 3 & 2 & 4 \\ -1 & 4 & 10 \end{pmatrix}$. **(8)**

14) (a) (i) Given $log_{10}654 = 2.8156$, $log_{10}658 = 2.8182$, $log_{10}659 = 2.8189$ and $log_{10}661 = 2.8202$. Find the value of $log_{10}656$ using Newton's divided difference formula. **(8)**

(ii) Find the first, second and third derivatives of the function *f(x)* at *x*= 1-5. **(8)**

x:	1.5	2.0	2.5	3.0	3.5	4.0
f(x):	3.375	7.0	13.625	24.0	38.875	59.0

Or

(b) (i) The velocity IF of a particle at distances from a point on it's path is given by the table

T feet:	0	10	20	30	40	50	60
V feet/s:	47	58	64	65	61	52	38

Estimate the time taken to travel 60 feet by using Trapezoidal and Simpson's 1/3 rule. Compare the result with Simpson's 3/8 rule. **(9)**

(ii) A rod is rotating a plane. The following table gives the angle θ with respect to time 't' seconds.

t:	0	0.2	0.4	0.6	0.8	1.0
θ:	0	0.12	0.49	1.12	2.02	3.20

Calculate the angular velocity and angular acceleration of the rod when *t*= 0.6 seconds. **(7)**

15) (a) (i) By fourth order Runge-Kutta method find y(0.2) from $\frac{dy}{dx} = y - x$, $y(0) = 2$ taking $h= 0.1$. **(8)**

(ii) Solve the differential equation $\frac{d^2y}{dx^2} = y - x$ with $y(0) = 0$, $y(1) = 0$ and $h = \frac{1}{4}$ by finite difference method. **(8)**

Or

(b) Using Taylor's series method; solve $\frac{dy}{dx} = xy + y^2$, $y(0) = 1$ at $x= 0.1, 0.2, 0.3$. Continue the solution at $x= 0.4$ by Milne's Predictor-Corrector method. **(16)**

Question Paper Code : 50782

B.E./B.Tech. DEGREE EXAMINATION, NOVEMBER/DECEMBER 2017

Fourth/Fifth Semester Mechanical Engineering

MA 6452 - STATISTICS AND NUMERICAL METHODS (Regulations 2013)

(Common to Mechanical Engineering (Sandwich), Automobile Engineering, Mechatronics Engineering)

Time : Three Hours **Maximum : 100 Marks**

Answer ALL questions.

PART-A **(10 x 2 = 20 marks)**

1) What is meant by level of significance and critical region ?

2) State any two applications of Chi-square test.

3) What is the aim of the design of experiment ?

4) What is a completely randomized design ?

5) What are the merits of Newton-Raphson method ?

6) Distinguish between Gauss elimination and Gauss-seidel methods.

7) What is meant by interpolation ?

8) What is the order of error in Trapezoidal and Simpson s one-third rules ?

9) What is main difference between single and multistep methods m solving first order ordinary differential equation ?

10) State the modified Euler's formula for first order ordinary differential equation.

PART - B **(5×10-80 marks)**

11) a) i) A random sample of 100 bulbs from a company P shows a mean life 1300 hours and standard deviation of 82 hours. Another random sample of 100 bulbs from company Q showed a mean life 1248 hours and standard deviation of 93 hours. Are the bulbs of company P superior to bulbs of company Q at 5% level of significance ?

ii) A random sample of 10 boys has the following IQ's 70, 83, 88, 95, 98, 100, 101,107,110 and 120. Do these data support the assumption of a population mean IQ of 100 at 5% level of significance ?

(OR)

b) i) Time taken by workers in performing a job is given below :

Method 1	20	16	26	27	23	22
Method 2	27	33	42	35	34	38

Test whether there is any significant difference between the variances of the time distribution at 5% level of significance. **(8)**

ii) Using the data given in the following table to test at 1% level of significance whether a person's ability in Mathematics is independent of his/her interest in Statistics.

		Ability in Mathematics		
		Low	Average	High
Interest in Statistics	Low	63	42	15
	Average	58	61	31
	High	14	47	29

12) a) The following data represent a certain person to work from Monday to Friday by four different routes.

		Days				
		Mon	The	Wed	Thu	Fri
	1	22	26	25	25	31
	2	25	27	28	26	29
Routes	3	26	29	33	30	33
	4	26	28	27	30	30

Test at 5% levelof significance wheteher the differences among the means obtained for the differences routes are significant and also whether the differences among the means obtained for the different days of the week are significant (16)

(OR)

b) Four air-conditioning compressor designs were tested in four different regions of India. The test was repeated by installing additional air conditioners in a second cooling season. The following are the times to failure (to the nearest month) of each compressor tested.

		Replicate 1				Replicate 2			
		A	B	C	D	A	B	C	D
Design	Northeast	58	35	72	61	49	24	60	64
	Southeast	40	18	54	38	38	22	64	50
	Northwest	63	44	81	52	59	16	60	48
	Southwest	36	09	47	30	29	13	52	41

Test at the 0.05 level of significance whether the differences among the means determined for designs, for regions, and for replicates are significant and for significance of the interaction between compressor designs and regions. **(16)**

13) a) i) Find, by Newton-Raphson method, a positive root of the equation $3x - \cos x - 1 = 0$, correct to 4 decimal places. **(8)**

ii) Using Gauss-Jordan method, find the inverse of $A = \begin{pmatrix} 4 & 1 & 2 \\ 2 & 3 & -1 \\ 1 & -2 & 2 \end{pmatrix}$ **(8)**

(OR)

b) i) Solve, by Gauss-Seidel method, the system of following equations, correct to three decimal places.

$$27x + 6y - z = 85,\ x+y+54z=110,\ 6x+15y+2z=72.$$ **(8)**

ii) Find the numerically largest Eigenvalue and the corresponding eigenvector of a matrix $A = \begin{pmatrix} 25 & 1 & 2 \\ 1 & 3 & 0 \\ 2 & 0 & -4 \end{pmatrix}$

14) a) i) Using Lagrange's interpolation formula, find the polynomial $f(x)$ form the following data: **(8)**

x :	0	1	4	5
$f(x)$:	4	8	24	39

ii) Find the value of cos(1.74), using suitable formula from the following data. **(8)**

x :	1.7	1.74	1.78	1.82	1.86
$sin(x)$:	0.9916	0.9857	0.9781	0.9691	0.9584

(OR)

b) i) From the following values, find f(x) and hence find f(6) by Newton's divided difference formula. **(8)**

x :	1	2	7	8
$f(x)$:	1	5	5	4

ii) Evaluate $\int_1^{1.2}\int_1^{1.4} \frac{1}{1+x} dxdy$ by Trapezoidal rule with $h=k=0.1$. **(8)**

15) a) i) Using Taylor series method, find the value of y at x = 0.1,if y satisfies the equation $\frac{dy}{dx} = x^2 - y$ given that y = 1 when x = 0, correct to 3 decimal places. **(8)**

ii) Solve the equation $\frac{d^2y}{dx^2} = x + y^2$ with boundary conditions $y(0)=1=y(1)$ by finite difference method, by taking 4 subintervals. **(8)**

(OR)

b) i) Using R-K method of fourth order, find the value of y at x = 0.1, if y satisfies the equation $\frac{dy}{dx} = x + y^2$ given that y = 1 when x = 0, correct to 3 decimal places. **(8)**

ii) Given $\frac{dy}{dx} = x^3 + y$, $y(0)=2$, $y(0.2)=2.073$, $y(0.4)=2.452$, $y(0.6)=3.023$, compute $y\ (0.8)$ by Milne's method. **(8)**

Question paper code: 20753

B.E./B.Tech. DEGREE EXAMINATION, NOVEMBER/DECEMBER 2018

Fourth Semester

MA 6452 - STATISTICS AND NUMERICAL METHODS

(Regulations 2013)

Time : Three Hours **Maximum : 100 Marks**

Use of statistical tables is permitted.

Answer all question

Part A – (10×2= 20 marks)

1) State the procedure followed in testing of hypothesis.
2) Define type I error and type ii error in the sampling distribution
3) What are basic principle of design of experiment?
4) What is a 22 factorial design?
5) Find the iterative formula by newton's method for 1/N, when N is a positive integer.
6) What kind of an eigenvalue and eigenvector of a matrix would be obtained by power method?
7) Find the third divided differences of $f(x) = x^2 + x + 2$ for the arguments 1, 3,6,11
8) Write newton's backward difference formula to find the derivation $\frac{dy}{dx}$ and $\frac{d^2y}{dx^2}$ at $x = x_n$
9) Find y(0.01) by using Euler's method, given that $\frac{dy}{dx} = -y,\ y(0) = -1$
10) Write the finite difference approximation for the equation $\frac{d^2y}{dx^2} = x + y$.

Part B – (5×16 = 80 marks)

11) a) i) The mean height of two samples of 1000 and 2000 members are respectively 67.5 and 68.0 inches. Can they be regarded as drawn from the same population with standard deviation 2.5 inches at 5% level of significance?

(ii) A random sample of 10 boys has the following IQ's 0,83,88,95,98,100,101,107,110 and 120. Do these data support the assumption of a population mean IQ of 100 at 5% level of significance?

Or

b) i) Pumpkins were grown under two experimental conditions. Two random samples of 11 and 9 pumpkins show the sample standard deviations of their weights as 0.8 and 0.5 respectively. Assuming that the weight distributions are normal, test the hypothesis that the true variances are equal, against the alternative hypothesis that they are not at the 10% level of significance.

ii) Using the data given in the following table to test at the 0.01 level of significance whether a person's ability in mathematics is independent of his/ her interest is statistics.

		Ability in Mathematics		
		Low	Average	High
Interest in statistics	Low	63	42	18
	Average	58	61	31
	High	14	47	29

12) a) The following data represent a certain person to work from Monday to Friday by four different routes.

		Days				
		Mon	Tue	Wed	Thu	Fri
Routes	1	22	26	25	25	31
	2	25	27	28	26	29
	3	26	29	33	30	33
	4	26	28	27	30	30

Test at the 0.05 level of significances whether the difference among the means obtained for the different routes are significant and also whether the differences among the means obtained for the different days of the week are significant.

Or

b) The following is the Latin square layout of a design when 4 varieties of seeds are tested. Set up the ANOVA table and state your conclusions.

A18	C21	D25	B11
D22	B12	A15	C19
B15	A20	C23	D24
C22	D21	B10	A17

13) a) i) Using Gauss-Jordan method, find the inverse of $A = \begin{bmatrix} 3 & -1 & 1 \\ -15 & 6 & -5 \\ 5 & -2 & 2 \end{bmatrix}$

ii) Solve, by Gauss Seidel method, the system of following equation correct to three decimal places $x+3y+10z=24,\ 28x+4y-z=32,\ 2x+17y+4z=35.$

Or

b) (i) Solve, by Gauss-Elimination with partial pivoting method, the system of following equations correct to three decimal places.

$2x+y+z=10,\ 3x+2y+3z=18,\ x+4y+9z=16.$

(ii) Solve, by Gauss-Jacobi method, the system of following equations correct to three decimal places.

$x+y+54z=110,\ 27x+6y-z=85,\ 6x+15y+2z=72.$

14) a) i) Use Lagrange's interpolation formula to find f(10) from the following data:

x:	5	6	9	11
f(x):	12	13	14	16

(ii) Find the value of $\cos(1.74)$ using suitable formula from the following data.

x:	1.7	1.74	1.78	1.82	1.86
sinx:	0.9916	0.9857	0.9781	0.9691	0.9584

b) i) Use newton's backward difference formula to fit a third degree polynomial for the following data.

x:	–0.75	–0.5	–0.25	0
f(x):	0.9916	0.9857	0.9781	0.9691

(ii) Evaluate $\int_0^1 \frac{1}{1+x} dx$, using

(1) Trapezoidal rule and

(2) Simpson's $\frac{1}{3}$ rule with $h = 0.125$ and compare the values with exact value.

15. (a) Given $\frac{dy}{dx} = xy + y^2$, $y(0) = 1$, $y(0.1) = 1.1169$, $y(0.2) = 1.2773$, find

(i) $y(0.3)$ by Runge-Kutta method of fourth order and

(ii) $y(0.4)$ by Milne's method.

Or

(b) (i) Using Taylor series method find the value of y at $x = 0.1$, if y satisfies the equation $\frac{dy}{dx} = x^2 - y$ given that $y = 1$ when $x = 0$, correct to 3 decimal places.

(ii) Solve $\frac{dy}{dx} = x + y$, $y(0) = 1$ by modified Euler's method to find $y(0.2)$ with $h = 0.1$

Question paper code: 41313

B.E./B.Tech. DEGREE EXAMINATION, APRIL/MAY 2018

Fourth Semester

MA 6452 - STATISTICS AND NUMERICAL METHODS

(Regulations 2013)

Time : Three Hours **Maximum : 100 Marks**

Answer ALL questions.

PART-A (10 x 2 = 20 marks)

1) Define the following terms: statistic, parameter, standard error and random sampling.

2) For the following cases, specify which probability distribution to use in a hypothesis test.

(a) $H_0 : \mu = 27, H_1: \mu \neq 27, \overline{X} = 20.1, \sigma = 5, n = 12$

(b) $H_0 : \mu=98.6, H_1:\mu>98.6, \overline{X} = 65, s=12, n=42$

3) What are the basic element of an ANOVA table for one way classification?

4) What are the basic designs of experiment?

5) State the Newton-Raphson method formula and the criteria for convergences.

6) Write a sufficient condition for Gauss-Seidel method to converge

7) Find the divided difference table for the following data.

x	2	5	10
y	5	29	109

8) Obtain Lagrangian interpolation polynomial form the data.

x	0	1	3
$f(x)$	5	6	14

9) Using Euler's method. Find y of x=0.1 if $\frac{dy}{dx} = 1 + xy,\ y(0) = 2$.

10) Write down the finite difference schemes for solving $y'' + x + y = 0,\ y(0) = y(1) = 0$.

PART-B

11) a) i) The nicotine content in milligram of 2 samples of tobacco were found to be as follows:

Sample A	24	27	26	21	25	
Sample B	27	30	28	31	22	36

Can it be said that these samples were from normal population with the same mean.

ii) Five coins are tossed 320 times. The number of heads observed is given below.

Number of Heads	0	1	2	3	4	5
Frequency	15	45	85	95	60	20

Examine whether the coin is unbiased. Use 5% level of significances.

Or

b) i) Mechanical engineers testing a new are welding technique, classified welds both with respect to appearance and an x-ray inspection.

		Appearance		
X-ray		Bad	Normal	Good
	Bad	20	7	3
	Normal	13	51	16
	Good	7	12	21

Test for independence using 0.05 level of significance.

ii) Given a sample mean of 3, a sample standard deviation of 12.5 and a sample size of 22, test the hypothesis that the value of the population mean is 70 against the alternative that it is more than, 70. Use the 0.025 significance level.

12). a) A chemist wishes to test the effect of four chemical agents on the strength of a particular type of cloth. Because there might by variability from one bolt to another, the chemist decides to use a randomised block design, with the bolts of cloth consider as blocks, she selects five bolts and applies all four chemicals in random order to each bolt. The resulting tensile strengths follows.

	Bolt				
Chemical	1	2	3	4	5
1	73	68	74	71	67
2	73	67	75	72	70
3	75	68	78	73	68
4	73	71	75	75	69

Or

b) A Latin square design was used to compare the bond strength of gold semi conductor lead wires bounded to the lead terminal by 5 different methods. A, B, C, D and E the bonds were made by 5 different operators and the devices were encapsulated using 5 different plastics. With the following results, expressed as pounds of force required to break the bond.

	Operator				
Plastics	1	2	3	4	5
1	A 3	B 2.4	C 1.9	D 2.2	E 1.7
2	B 2.1	C 2.7	D 2.3	E 2.5	A 3.1
3	C 2.1	D 2.6	E 2.5	A 2.9	B 2.1
4	D 2.0	E 2.5	B 3.2	B 2.5	C 2.2
5	E 2.1	A 3.6	B 2.4	C 2.4	D 2.1

Analyse these results and test with 0.01 level of significance.

13) a) i) Solve the following system of equations by Gauss-Seidel method correct to three decimal places.

$$x + y + 54z = 110$$

$$27x + 6y - z = 85$$

$$6x + 15y + 2z = 72$$

ii) Solve the following system of equations by Gauss Jordan method.

$$2x + y + 4z = 12$$

$$8x - 3y + 2z = 85$$

$$4x + 11y - z = 33$$

Or

b) i) solve the following system of equations by Gauss Elimination method

$$2y - 3z = -5$$

$$x + 4y - 7z + t = -8$$

$$2x - y - t = -4$$

$$x + y + z = 6$$

ii) Using the power method, find the largest eigenvalue and the corresponding eigenvector for the matrix.

$$A = \begin{bmatrix} 1 & 4 \\ 3 & 2 \end{bmatrix} \text{ Let } X_0 = \begin{bmatrix} 1 \\ 0 \end{bmatrix}$$